EMPIRE

EMPIRE

Michael Hardt | Antonio Negri

HARVARD UNIVERSITY PRESS

Cambridge, Massachusetts

London, England **2000**

Printed in the United States of America

Library of Congress Cataloging-in-Publication Data

Hardt, Michael.
Empire / Michael Hardt and Antonio Negri.
p. cm.
Includes bibliographical references and index.
ISBN 0-674-25121-0 (alk. paper)
1. Imperialism. I. Negri, Antonio, 1933– . II. Title.
JC359.H279 2000
325′.32′09045—dc21 99-39619

Every tool is a weapon if you hold it right.

Ani DiFranco

Men fight and lose the battle, and the thing that they fought for comes about in spite of their defeat, and then it turns out not to be what they meant, and other men have to fight for what they meant under another name.

William Morris

ACKNOWLEDGMENTS

We would like to thank the friends and colleagues who read parts of this manuscript and from whose comments we benefited: Robert Adelman, Étienne Balibar, Denis Berger, Yann Moulier Boutang, Tom Conley, Arif Dirlik, Luciano Ferrari-Bravo, David Harvey, Fred Jameson, Rebecca Karl, Wahneema Lubiano, Saree Makdisi, Christian Marazzi, Valentin Mudimbe, Judith Revel, Ken Surin, Christine Thorsteinsson, Jean-Marie Vincent, Paolo Virno, Lindsay Waters, and Kathi Weeks.

CONTENTS

PREFACE

Empire is materializing before our very eyes. Over the past several decades, as colonial regimes were overthrown and then precipitously after the Soviet barriers to the capitalist world market finally collapsed, we have witnessed an irresistible and irreversible globalization of economic and cultural exchanges. Along with the global market and global circuits of production has emerged a global order, a new logic and structure of rule—in short, a new form of sovereignty. Empire is the political subject that effectively regulates these global exchanges, the sovereign power that governs the world.

Many argue that the globalization of capitalist production and exchange means that economic relations have become more autonomous from political controls, and consequently that political sovereignty has declined. Some celebrate this new era as the liberation of the capitalist economy from the restrictions and distortions that political forces have imposed on it; others lament it as the closing of the institutional channels through which workers and citizens can influence or contest the cold logic of capitalist profit. It is certainly true that, in step with the processes of globalization, the sovereignty of nation-states, while still effective, has progressively declined. The primary factors of production and exchange—money, technology, people, and goods—move with increasing ease across national boundaries; hence the nation-state has less and less power to regulate these flows and impose its authority over the economy. Even the most dominant nation-states should no longer be thought of as supreme and sovereign authorities, either outside or even within their own borders. *The decline in sovereignty of nation-states, however, does not mean that sovereignty as such has declined.*[1]

Throughout the contemporary transformations, political controls, state functions, and regulatory mechanisms have continued to rule the realm of economic and social production and exchange. Our basic hypothesis is that sovereignty has taken a new form, composed of a series of national and supranational organisms united under a single logic of rule. This new global form of sovereignty is what we call Empire.

The declining sovereignty of nation-states and their increasing inability to regulate economic and cultural exchanges is in fact one of the primary symptoms of the coming of Empire. The sovereignty of the nation-state was the cornerstone of the imperialisms that European powers constructed throughout the modern era. By "Empire," however, we understand something altogether different from "imperialism." The boundaries defined by the modern system of nation-states were fundamental to European colonialism and economic expansion: the territorial boundaries of the nation delimited the center of power from which rule was exerted over external foreign territories through a system of channels and barriers that alternately facilitated and obstructed the flows of production and circulation. Imperialism was really an extension of the sovereignty of the European nation-states beyond their own boundaries. Eventually nearly all the world's territories could be parceled out and the entire world map could be coded in European colors: red for British territory, blue for French, green for Portuguese, and so forth. Wherever modern sovereignty took root, it constructed a Leviathan that overarched its social domain and imposed hierarchical territorial boundaries, both to police the purity of its own identity and to exclude all that was other.

The passage to Empire emerges from the twilight of modern sovereignty. In contrast to imperialism, Empire establishes no territorial center of power and does not rely on fixed boundaries or barriers. It is a *decentered* and *deterritorializing* apparatus of rule that progressively incorporates the entire global realm within its open, expanding frontiers. Empire manages hybrid identities, flexible hierarchies, and plural exchanges through modulating networks of command. The distinct national colors of the imperialist map of the world have merged and blended in the imperial global rainbow.

The transformation of the modern imperialist geography of the globe and the realization of the world market signal a passage within the capitalist mode of production. Most significant, the spatial divisions of the three Worlds (First, Second, and Third) have been scrambled so that we continually find the First World in the Third, the Third in the First, and the Second almost nowhere at all. Capital seems to be faced with a smooth world—or really, a world defined by new and complex regimes of differentiation and homogenization, deterritorialization and reterritorialization. The construction of the paths and limits of these new global flows has been accompanied by a transformation of the dominant productive processes themselves, with the result that the role of industrial factory labor has been reduced and priority given instead to communicative, cooperative, and affective labor. In the postmodernization of the global economy, the creation of wealth tends ever more toward what we will call biopolitical production, the production of social life itself, in which the economic, the political, and the cultural increasingly overlap and invest one another.

Many locate the ultimate authority that rules over the processes of globalization and the new world order in the United States. Proponents praise the United States as the world leader and sole superpower, and detractors denounce it as an imperialist oppressor. Both these views rest on the assumption that the United States has simply donned the mantle of global power that the European nations have now let fall. If the nineteenth century was a British century, then the twentieth century has been an American century; or really, if modernity was European, then postmodernity is American. The most damning charge critics can level, then, is that the United States is repeating the practices of old European imperialists, while proponents celebrate the United States as a more efficient and more benevolent world leader, getting right what the Europeans got wrong. Our basic hypothesis, however, that a new imperial form of sovereignty has emerged, contradicts both these views. *The United*

States does not, and indeed no nation-state can today, form the center of an imperialist project. Imperialism is over. No nation will be world leader in the way modern European nations were.

The United States does indeed occupy a privileged position in Empire, but this privilege derives not from its similarities to the old European imperialist powers, but from its differences. These differences can be recognized most clearly by focusing on the properly imperial (not imperialist) foundations of the United States constitution, where by "constitution" we mean both the *formal constitution,* the written document along with its various amendments and legal apparatuses, and the *material constitution,* that is, the continuous formation and re-formation of the composition of social forces. Thomas Jefferson, the authors of the *Federalist,* and the other ideological founders of the United States were all inspired by the ancient imperial model; they believed they were creating on the other side of the Atlantic a new Empire with open, expanding frontiers, where power would be effectively distributed in networks. This imperial idea has survived and matured throughout the history of the United States constitution and has emerged now on a global scale in its fully realized form.

We should emphasize that we use "Empire" here not as a *metaphor,* which would require demonstration of the resemblances between today's world order and the Empires of Rome, China, the Americas, and so forth, but rather as a *concept,* which calls primarily for a theoretical approach.[2] The concept of Empire is characterized fundamentally by a lack of boundaries: Empire's rule has no limits. First and foremost, then, the concept of Empire posits a regime that effectively encompasses the spatial totality, or really that rules over the entire "civilized" world. No territorial boundaries limit its reign. Second, the concept of Empire presents itself not as a historical regime originating in conquest, but rather as an order that effectively suspends history and thereby fixes the existing state of affairs for eternity. From the perspective of Empire, this is the way things will always be and the way they were always meant to be. In other words, Empire presents its rule not as a transitory moment in the movement of history, but as a regime with no temporal boundaries and in this sense outside of history or at the end of history. Third, the rule of Empire operates on all registers of the social order extending down to the depths of the social world. Empire not only manages a territory and a population but also creates the very world it inhabits. It not only regulates human interactions but also seeks directly to rule over human nature. The object of its rule is social life in its entirety, and thus Empire presents the paradigmatic form of biopower. Finally, although the practice of Empire is continually bathed in blood, the concept of Empire is always dedicated to peace—a perpetual and universal peace outside of history.

The Empire we are faced with wields enormous powers of oppression and destruction, but that fact should not make us nostalgic in any way for the old forms of domination. The passage to Empire and its processes of globalization offer new possibilities to the forces of liberation. Globalization, of course, is not one thing, and the multiple processes that we recognize as globalization are not unified or univocal. Our political task, we will argue, is not simply to resist these processes but to reorganize them and redirect them toward new ends. The creative forces of the multitude that sustain Empire are also capable of autonomously constructing a counter-Empire, an alternative political organization of global flows and exchanges. The struggles to contest and subvert Empire, as well as those to construct a real alternative, will thus take place on the imperial terrain itself—indeed, such new struggles have already begun to emerge. Through these struggles and many more like them, the multitude will have to invent new democratic forms and a new constituent power that will one day take us through and beyond Empire.

The genealogy we follow in our analysis of the passage from imperialism to Empire will be first European and then Euro-American, not because we believe that these regions are the exclusive or privileged source of new ideas and historical innovation, but simply because this was the dominant geographical path along which the concepts and practices that animate today's Empire developed—in step, as we will argue, with the development of the capitalist mode of production.[3] Whereas the genealogy of Empire is in this sense Eurocentric, however, its present powers are not limited to any region. Logics of rule that in some sense originated in Europe and the United States now invest practices of domination throughout the globe. More important, the forces that contest Empire and effectively prefigure an alternative global society are themselves not limited to any geographical region. The geography of these alternative powers, the new cartography, is still waiting to be written—or really, it is being written today through the resistances, struggles, and desires of the multitude.

In writing this book we have tried to the best of our abilities to employ a broadly interdisciplinary approach.[4] Our argument aims to be equally philosophical and historical, cultural and economic, political and anthropological. In part, our object of study demands this broad interdisciplinarity, since in Empire the boundaries that might previously have justified narrow disciplinary approaches are increasingly breaking down. In the imperial world the economist, for example, needs a basic knowledge of cultural production to understand the economy, and likewise the cultural critic needs a basic knowledge of economic processes to understand culture. That is a requirement that our project demands. What we hope to have contributed in this book is a general theoretical framework and a toolbox of concepts for theorizing and acting in and against Empire.[5]

Like most large books, this one can be read in many different ways: front to back, back to front, in pieces, in a hopscotch pattern, or through correspondences. The sections of Part 1 introduce the general problematic of Empire. In the central portion of the book, Parts 2 and 3, we tell the story of the passage from modernity to postmodernity, or really from imperialism to Empire. Part 2 narrates the passage primarily from the standpoint of the history of ideas and culture from the early modern period to the present. The red thread that runs throughout this part is the genealogy of the concept of sovereignty. Part 3 narrates the same passage from the standpoint of production, whereby production is understood in a very broad sense, ranging from economic production to the production of subjectivity. This narrative spans a shorter period and focuses primarily on the transformations of capitalist production from the late nineteenth century to the present. The internal structures of Parts 2 and 3 thus correspond: the first sections of each treat the modern, imperialist phase; the middle sections deal with the mechanisms of passage; and the final sections analyze our postmodern, imperial world.

We structured the book this way in order to emphasize the importance of the shift from the realm of ideas to that of production. The Intermezzo between Parts 2 and 3 functions as a hinge that articulates the movement from one standpoint to the other. We intend this shift of standpoint to function something like the moment in *Capital* when Marx invites us to leave the noisy sphere of exchange and descend into the hidden abode of production. The realm of production is where social inequalities are clearly revealed and, moreover, where the most effective resistances and alternatives to the power of Empire arise. In Part 4 we thus try to identify these alternatives that today are tracing the lines of a movement beyond Empire.

This book was begun well after the end of the Persian Gulf War and completed well before the beginning of the war in Kosovo. The reader should thus situate the argument at the midpoint between those two signal events in the construction of Empire.

PART 1

THE POLITICAL CONSTITUTION OF THE PRESENT

1.1

WORLD ORDER

> Capitalism only triumphs when it becomes identified with the state, when it is the state.
>
> Fernand Braudel

> They make slaughter and they call it peace.
>
> Tacitus

The problematic of Empire is determined in the first place by one simple fact: that there is world order. This order is expressed as a juridical formation. Our initial task, then, is to grasp the *constitution* of the order being formed today. We should rule out from the outset, however, two common conceptions of this order that reside on opposing limits of the spectrum: first, the notion that the present order somehow rises up *spontaneously* out of the interactions of radically heterogeneous global forces, as if this order were a harmonious concert orchestrated by the natural and neutral hidden hand of the world market; and second, the idea that order is dictated by a single power and a single center of rationality *transcendent* to global forces, guiding the various phases of historical development according to its conscious and all-seeing plan, something like a conspiracy theory of globalization.[1]

United Nations

Before investigating the constitution of Empire in juridical terms, we must analyze in some detail the constitutional processes that have come to define the central juridical categories, and in particular give careful attention to the process of the long transition from the sovereign right of nation-states (and the international right that followed from it) to the first postmodern global figures of imperial right. As a first approximation one can think of this as the genealogy of juridical forms that led to, and now leads beyond, the supranational role of the United Nations and its various affiliated institutions.

It is widely recognized that the notion of international order that European modernity continually proposed and reproposed, at least since the Peace of Westphalia, is now in crisis.[2] It has in fact always been in crisis, and this crisis has been one of the motors that has continuously pushed toward Empire. Perhaps this notion of international order and its crisis should be dated from the time of the Napoleonic Wars, as some scholars claim, or perhaps the origin should be located in the Congress of Vienna and the establishment of the Holy Alliance.[3] In any case, there can be no doubt that by the time of the First World War and the birth of the League of Nations, a notion of international order along with its crisis had been definitively established. The birth of the United Nations at the end of the Second World War merely reinitiated, consolidated, and extended this developing international juridical order that was first European but progressively became completely global. The United Nations, in effect, can be regarded as the culmination of this entire constitutive process, a culmination that both reveals the limitations of the notion of *international* order and points beyond it toward a new notion of *global* order. One could certainly analyze the U.N. juridical structure in purely negative terms and dwell on the declining power of nation-states in the international context, but one should also recognize that the notion of right defined by the U.N. Charter also points toward a new positive source of juridical production, effective on a global scale—a new center of normative production that can play a sovereign juridical role. The U.N. functions as a hinge in the genealogy from international to global juridical structures. On the one hand, the entire U.N. conceptual structure is predicated on the recognition and legitimation of the sovereignty of individual states, and it is thus planted squarely within the old framework of international right defined by pacts and treaties. On the other hand, however, this process of legitimation is effective only insofar as it transfers sovereign right to a real *supranational* center. It is not our intention here to criticize or lament the serious (and at times tragic) inadequacies of this process; indeed, we are interested in the United Nations and the project of international order not as an end in itself, but rather as a real historical lever that pushed forward the transition toward a properly global system. It is precisely the inadequacies of the process, then, that make it effective.

To look more closely at this transition in juridical terms, it is useful to read the work of Hans Kelsen, one of the central intellectual figures behind the formation of the United Nations. As early as the 1910s and 1920s, Kelsen proposed that the international juridical system be conceived as the supreme source of every national juridical formation and constitution. Kelsen arrived at this proposal through his analyses of the formal dynamics of the particular orderings of states. The limits of the nation-state, he claimed, posed an insurmountable obstacle to the realization of the idea of right. For Kelsen, the partial ordering of the domestic law of nation-states led back necessarily to the universality and objectivity of the international ordering. The latter is not only logical but also ethical, for it would put an end to conflicts between states of unequal power and affirm instead an equality that is the principle of real international community. Behind the formal sequence that Kelsen described, then, there was a real and substantial drive of Enlightenment modernization. Kelsen sought, in Kantian fashion, a notion of right that could become an "organization of humanity and [would] therefore be one with the supreme ethical idea."[4] He wanted to get beyond the logic of power in international relations so that "the particular states could be regarded juridically as entities of equal rank" and thus a "world and universal state" could be formed, organized as a "universal community superior to the particular states, enveloping them all within itself."[5]

It was only fitting, then, that Kelsen would later have the privilege of attending the meetings in San Francisco that founded the United Nations and seeing his theoretical hypothesis realized. For him the United Nations organized a rational idea.[6] It gave legs to an idea of the spirit; it proposed a real base of effectiveness for a transcendental schema of the validity of right situated above the nation-state. The validity and efficacy of right could now be united in the supreme juridical source, and under these conditions Kelsen's notion of a fundamental norm could finally be realized.

Kelsen conceived the formal construction and validity of the system as independent from the material structure that organizes it, but in reality the structure must somehow exist and be organized materially. How can the system actually be constructed? This is the point at which Kelsen's thought ceases to be of any use to us: it remains merely a fantastic utopia. The transition we wish to study consists precisely in this gap between the formal conception that grounds the validity of the juridical process in a supranational source and the material realization of this conception. The life of the United Nations, from its foundation to the end of the cold war, has been a long history of ideas, compromises, and limited experiences oriented more or less toward the construction of such a supranational ordering. The aporias of this process are obvious, and there is no need for us to describe them in detail here. Certainly the United Nations' domination of the general framework of the supranational project between 1945 and 1989 led to some of the most perverse theoretical and practical consequences. And yet, all this was not enough to block the constitutionalization of a supranational power.[7] In the ambiguous experiences of the United Nations, the juridical concept of Empire began to take shape.

The theoretical responses to this constitutionalization of a supranational world power, however, have been entirely inadequate. Instead of recognizing what was really new about these supranational processes, the vast majority of juridical theorists merely tried to resurrect anachronistic models to apply to the new problems. To a large extent, in fact, the models that had presided over the birth of the nation-state were simply dusted off and reproposed as interpretive schema for reading the construction of a supranational power. The "domestic analogy" thus became the fundamental methodological tool in the analysis of international and supranational forms of order.[8] Two lines of thought have been particularly active during this transition, and as a kind of shorthand we can conceive of them as resurrections of the Hobbesian and the Lockean ideologies that in another era dominated the European conceptions of the sovereign state.

The Hobbesian variant focuses primarily on the transfer of the title of sovereignty and conceives the constitution of the supranational sovereign entity as a contractual agreement grounded on the convergence of preexisting state subjects.[9] A new transcendent power, "tertium super partes," primarily concentrated in the hands of the military (the one that rules over life and death, the Hobbesian "God on earth"), is, according to this school, the only means capable of constituting a secure international system and thus of overcoming the anarchy that sovereign states necessarily produce.[10] By contrast, according to the Lockean variant, the same process is projected in more decentralized, pluralistic terms. In this framework, just when the transfer toward a supranational center is accomplished, networks of local and constitutionally effective counterpowers rise up to contest and/or support the new figure of power. Rather than global security, then, what is proposed here is a global constitutionalism, or really this amounts to a project of overcoming state imperatives by constituting a *global civil society*. These slogans are meant to evoke the values of globalism that would infuse the new international order, or really the new transnational democracy.[11] Whereas the Hobbesian hypothesis emphasizes the contractual process that gives rise to a new unitary and transcendental supranational power, the Lockean hypothesis focuses on the counterpowers that animate the constitutive process and support the supranational power. In both cases, however, the new global power is presented merely in analogy with the classical conception of the national sovereign power of states. Rather than recognizing the new nature of imperial power, the two hypotheses simply insist on the old inherited forms of state constitution: a monarchic form in the Hobbesian case, a liberal form in the Lockean.

Although, given the conditions in which these theories were formulated (during the cold war, when the United Nations only limped forward in the best of times), we must recognize the great foresight of these theorists, we also have to point out that they cannot account for the real novelty of the historical processes we are witnessing today.[12] In this regard these theories can and do become harmful, because they do not recognize the accelerated rhythm, the violence, and the necessity with which the new imperial paradigm operates. *What they do not understand is that imperial sovereignty marks a paradigm shift.* Paradoxically (but it is really not that paradoxical), only Kelsen's conception poses the real problem, even if his conception is limited to a strictly formalist point of view. What political power already exists or can be created, he asks, that is adequate to a globalization of economic and social relations? What juridical source, what fundamental norm, and what command can support a new order and avoid the impending descent into global disorder?

The Constitution of Empire

Many contemporary theorists are reluctant to recognize the globalization of capitalist production and its world market as a fundamentally new situation and a significant historical shift. The theorists associated with the world-systems perspective, for example, argue that from its inception, capitalism has always functioned as a world economy, and therefore those who clamor about the novelty of its globalization today have only misunderstood its history.[13] Certainly, it is important to emphasize both capitalism's continuous foundational relationship to (or at least a tendency toward) the world market and capitalism's expanding cycles of development; but proper attention to the *ab origine* universal or universalizing dimensions of capitalist development should not blind us to the rupture or shift in contemporary capitalist production and global relations of power. We believe that this shift makes perfectly clear and possible today the capitalist project to bring together economic power and political power, to realize, in other words, a properly capitalist order. In constitutional terms, the processes of globalization are no longer merely a fact but also a source of juridical definitions that tends to project a single supranational figure of political power.

Other theorists are reluctant to recognize a major shift in global power relations because they see that the dominant capitalist nation-states have continued to exercise imperialist domination over the other nations and regions of the globe. From this perspective, the contemporary tendencies toward Empire would represent not a fundamentally new phenomenon but simply a perfecting of imperialism.[14] Without underestimating these real and important lines of continuity, however, we think it is important to note that what used to be conflict or competition among several imperialist powers has in important respects been replaced by the idea of a single power that overdetermines them all, structures them in a unitary way, and treats them under one common notion of right that is decidedly postcolonial and postimperialist. This is really the point of departure for our study of Empire: a new notion of right, or rather, a new inscription of authority and a new design of the production of norms and legal instruments of coercion that guarantee contracts and resolve conflicts.

We should point out here that we accord special attention to the juridical figures of the constitution of Empire at the beginning of our study not out of any specialized disciplinary interest—as if right or law in itself, as an agent of regulation, were capable of representing the social world in its totality—but rather because they provide a good index of the processes of imperial constitution. New juridical figures reveal a first view of the tendency toward the centralized and unitary regulation of both the world market and global power relations, with all the difficulties presented by such a project. Juridical transformations effectively point toward changes in the material constitution of world power and order. The transition we are witnessing today from traditional international law, which was defined by contracts and treaties, to the definition and constitution of a new sovereign, supranational world power (and thus to an imperial notion of right), however incomplete, gives us a framework in which to read the totalizing social processes of Empire. In effect, the juridical transformation functions as a symptom of the modifications of the material biopolitical constitution of our societies. These changes regard not only international law and international relations but also the internal power relations of each country. While studying and critiquing the new forms of international and supranational law, then, we will at the same time be pushed to the heart of the political theory of Empire, where the problem of supranational sovereignty, its source of legitimacy, and its exercise bring into focus political, cultural, and finally ontological problems.

To approach the juridical concept of Empire, we might look first at the genealogy of the concept, which will give us some preliminary terms for our investigation. The concept comes down to us through a long, primarily European tradition, which goes back at least to ancient Rome, whereby the juridico-political figure of Empire was closely linked to the Christian origins of European civilizations. There the concept of Empire united juridical categories and universal ethical values, making them work together as an organic whole. This union has continuously functioned within the concept, whatever the vicissitudes of the history of Empire. Every juridical system is in some way a crystallization of a specific set of values, because ethics is part of the materiality of every juridical foundation, but Empire—and in particular the Roman tradition of imperial right—is peculiar in that it pushes the coincidence and universality of the ethical and the juridical to the extreme: in Empire there is peace, in Empire there is the guarantee of justice for all peoples. The concept of Empire is presented as a global concert under the direction of a single conductor, a unitary power that maintains the social peace and produces its ethical truths. And in order to achieve these ends, the single power is given the necessary force to conduct, when necessary, "just wars" at the borders against the barbarians and internally against the rebellious.[15]

From the beginning, then, Empire sets in motion an ethico-political dynamic that lies at the heart of its juridical concept. This juridical concept involves two fundamental tendencies: first, the notion of a right that is affirmed in the construction of a new order that envelops the entire space of what it considers civilization, a boundless, universal space; and second, a notion of right that encompasses all time within its ethical foundation. Empire exhausts historical time, suspends history, and summons the past and future within its own ethical order. In other words, Empire presents its order as permanent, eternal, and necessary.

In the Germanic-Roman tradition that thrived throughout the Middle Ages, these two notions of right went hand in hand.[16] Beginning in the Renaissance, however, with the triumph of secularism, these two notions were separated and each developed independently. On the one hand, there emerged in modern European political thought a conception of international right, and on the other, there developed utopias of "perpetual peace." In the first case, the order that the Roman Empire had promised was sought, long after its fall, through a treaty mechanism that would construct an international order among sovereign states by operating analogously to the contractual mechanisms that guaranteed order within the nation-state and its civil society. Thinkers from Grotius to Puffendorf theorized this process in formal terms. In the second case, the idea of "perpetual peace" continually reappeared throughout modern Europe, from Bernadin de Saint Pierre to Immanuel Kant. This idea was presented as an ideal of reason, a "light" that had to criticize and also unite right and ethicality, a presupposed transcendental of the juridical system and ideal schema of reason and ethics. The fundamental alternative between these two notions ran throughout all of European modernity, including the two great ideologies that defined its mature phase: the liberal ideology that rests on the peaceful concert of juridical forces and its supersession in the market; and the socialist ideology that focuses on international unity through the organization of struggles and the supersession of right.

Would it be correct to claim, then, that these two different developments of the notion of right that persisted side by side through the centuries of modernity tend today toward being united and presented as a single category? We suspect that this is indeed the case, and that in postmodernity the notion of right should be understood again in terms of the concept of Empire. And yet, since a large part of our investigation will turn around this question, leading us toward doubts and perplexities, it does not seem a good idea to jump so quickly to a definitive conclusion, even if here we are limiting ourselves only to the analysis of the notion of right. We can already recognize, however, some important symptoms of the rebirth of the concept of Empire—symptoms that function like logical provocations arising on the terrain of history that theory cannot ignore.

One symptom, for example, is the renewed interest in and effectiveness of the concept of *bellum justum,* or "just war." This concept, which was organically linked to the ancient imperial orders and whose rich and complex genealogy goes back to the biblical tradition, has begun to reappear recently as a central narrative of political discussions, particularly in the wake of the Gulf War.[17] Traditionally the concept rests primarily on the idea that when a state finds itself confronted with a threat of aggression that can endanger its territorial integrity or political independence, it has a *jus ad bellum* (right to make war).[18] There is certainly something troubling in this renewed focus on the concept of *bellum justum,* which modernity, or rather modern secularism, had worked so hard to expunge from the medieval tradition. The traditional concept of just war involves the banalization of war and the celebration of it as an ethical instrument, both of which were ideas that modern political thought and the international community of nation-states had resolutely refused. These two traditional characteristics have reappeared in our postmodern world: on the one hand, war is reduced to the status of police action, and on the other, the new power that can legitimately exercise ethical functions through war is sacralized.

Far from merely repeating ancient or medieval notions, however, today's concept presents some truly fundamental innovations.

Just war is no longer in any sense an activity of defense or resistance, as it was, for example, in the Christian tradition from Saint Augustine to the scholastics of the Counter-Reformation, as a necessity of the "worldly city" to guarantee its own survival. It has become rather an activity that is justified in itself. Two distinct elements are combined in this concept of just war: first, the legitimacy of the military apparatus insofar as it is ethically grounded, and second, the effectiveness of military action to achieve the desired order and peace. The synthesis of these two elements may indeed be a key factor determining the foundation and the new tradition of Empire. Today the enemy, just like the war itself, comes to be at once banalized (reduced to an object of routine police repression) and absolutized (as the Enemy, an absolute threat to the ethical order). The Gulf War gave us perhaps the first fully articulated example of this new epistemology of the concept.[19] The resurrection of the concept of just war may be only a symptom of the emergence of Empire, but what a suggestive and powerful one!

The Model of Imperial Authority

We must avoid defining the passage to Empire in purely negative terms, in terms of what it is not, as for example is done when one says: the new paradigm is defined by the definitive decline of the sovereign nation-states, by the deregulation of international markets, by the end of antagonistic conflict among state subjects, and so forth. If the new paradigm were to consist simply in this, then its consequences would be truly anarchic. Power, however—and Michel Foucault was not the only one to teach us this—fears and despises a vacuum. The new paradigm functions already in completely positive terms—and it could not be otherwise.

The new paradigm is both system and hierarchy, centralized construction of norms and far-reaching production of legitimacy, spread out over world space. It is configured *ab initio* as a dynamic and flexible systemic structure that is articulated horizontally. We conceive the structure in a kind of intellectual shorthand as a hybrid of Niklas Luhmann's systems theory and John Rawls's theory of justice.[20] Some call this situation "governance without government" to indicate the structural logic, at times imperceptible but always and increasingly effective, that sweeps all actors within the order of the whole.[21] The systemic totality has a dominant position in the global order, breaking resolutely with every previous dialectic and developing an integration of actors that seems linear and spontaneous. At the same time, however, the effectiveness of the consensus under a supreme authority of the ordering appears ever more clearly. All conflicts, all crises, and all dissensions effectively push forward the process of integration and by the same measure call for more central authority. Peace, equilibrium, and the cessation of conflict are the values toward which everything is directed. The development of the global system (and of imperial right in the first place) seems to be the development of a machine that imposes procedures of continual contractualization that lead to systemic equilibria—a machine that creates a continuous call for authority. The machine seems to predetermine the exercise of authority and action across the entire social space. Every movement is fixed and can seek its own designated place only within the system itself, in the hierarchical relationship accorded to it. This preconstituted movement defines the reality of the process of the imperial constitutionalization of world order—the new paradigm.

This imperial paradigm is qualitatively different from the various attempts in the period of transition to define a project of international order.[22] Whereas the previous, transitional perspectives focused attention on the legitimating dynamics that would lead toward the new order, in the new paradigm it is as if the new order were already constituted. The conceptual inseparability of the title and exercise of power is affirmed from the outset, as the effective a priori of the system. The imperfect coincidence, or better the ever-present temporal and spatial disjunctions between the new central power and the field of application of its regulation, do not lead to crises or paralysis but merely force the system to minimize and overcome them. In short, the paradigm shift is defined, at least initially, by the recognition that only an established power, overdetermined with respect to and relatively autonomous from the sovereign nation-states, is capable of functioning as the center of the new world order, exercising over it an effective regulation and, when necessary, coercion.

It follows that, as Kelsen wanted, but only as a paradoxical effect of his utopia, a sort of juridical positivism also dominates the formation of a new juridical ordering.[23] The capacity to form a system is, in effect, presupposed by the real process of its formation. Moreover, the process of formation, and the subjects that act in it, are attracted in advance toward the positively defined vortex of the center, and this attraction becomes irresistible, not only in the name of the capacity of the center to exercise force, but also in the name of the formal power, which resides in the center, to frame and systematize the totality. Once again we find a hybrid of Luhmann and Rawls, but even before them we have Kelsen, that utopian and thus involuntary and contradictory discoverer of the soul of imperial right!

Once again, the ancient notions of Empire help us articulate better the nature of this world order in formation. As Thucydides, Livy, and Tacitus all teach us (along with Machiavelli commenting on their work), Empire is formed not on the basis of force itself but on the basis of the capacity to present force as being in the service of right and peace. All interventions of the imperial armies are solicited by one or more of the parties involved in an already existing conflict. Empire is not born of its own will but rather it is *called* into being and constituted on the basis of its capacity to resolve conflicts. Empire is formed and its intervention becomes juridically legitimate only when it is already inserted into the chain of international consensuses aimed at resolving existing conflicts. To return to Machiavelli, the expansion of Empire is rooted in the internal trajectory of the conflicts it is meant to resolve.[24] The first task of Empire, then, is to enlarge the realm of the consensuses that support its own power.

The ancient model gives us a first approximation, but we need to go well beyond it to articulate the terms of the global model of authority operating today. Juridical positivism and natural right theories, contractualism and institutional realism, formalism and systematism can each describe some aspect of it. Juridical positivism can emphasize the necessity for a strong power to exist at the center of the normative process; natural right theories can highlight the values of peace and equilibrium that the imperial process offers; contractualism can foreground the formation of consensus; realism can bring to light the formative processes of the institutions adequate to the new dimensions of consensus and authority; and formalism can give logical support to what systematism justifies and organizes functionally, emphasizing the totalizing character of the process. What juridical model, however, grasps all these characteristics of the new supranational order?

In first attempting a definition, we would do well to recognize that the dynamics and articulations of the new supranational juridical order correspond strongly to the new characteristics that have come to define internal orderings in the passage from modernity to postmodernity.[25] We should recognize this correspondence (perhaps in Kelsen's manner, and certainly in a realistic mode) not so much as a "domestic analogy" for the international system, but rather as a "supranational analogy" for the domestic legal system. The primary characteristics of both systems involve hegemony over juridical practices, such as procedure, prevention, and address. Normativity, sanction, and repression follow from these and are formed within the procedural developments. The reason for the relative (but effective) coincidence of the new functioning of domestic law and supranational law derives first of all from the fact that they operate on the same terrain, namely, the terrain of crisis. As Carl Schmitt has taught us, however, crisis on the terrain of the application of law should focus our attention on the "exception" operative in the moment of its production.[26] Domestic and supranational law are both defined by their exceptionality.

The function of exception here is very important. In order to take control of and dominate such a completely fluid situation, it is necessary to grant the intervening authority (1) the capacity to define, every time in an exceptional way, the demands of intervention; and (2) the capacity to set in motion the forces and instruments that in various ways can be applied to the diversity and the plurality of the arrangements in crisis. Here, therefore, is born, in the name of the exceptionality of the intervention, a form of right that is really a *right of the police*. The formation of a new right is inscribed in the deployment of prevention, repression, and rhetorical force aimed at the reconstruction of social equilibrium: all this is proper to the activity of the police. We can thus recognize the initial and implicit source of imperial right in terms of police action and the capacity of the police to create and maintain order. The legitimacy of the imperial ordering supports the exercise of police power, while at the same time the activity of global police force demonstrates the real effectiveness of the imperial ordering. The juridical power to rule over the exception and the capacity to deploy police force are thus two initial coordinates that define the imperial model of authority.

Universal Values

We might well ask at this point, however, should we still use the juridical term "right" in this context? How can we call right (and specifically imperial right) a series of techniques that, founded on a state of permanent exception and the power of the police, reduces right and law to a question of pure effectiveness? In order to address these questions, we should first look more closely at the process of imperial constitution that we are witnessing today. We should emphasize from the start that its reality is demonstrated not only by the transformations of international law it brings about, but also by the changes it effects in the administrative law of individual societies and nation-states, or really in the administrative law of cosmopolitical society.[27] Through its contemporary transformation of supranational law, the imperial process of constitution tends either directly or indirectly to penetrate and reconfigure the domestic law of the nation-states, and thus supranational law powerfully overdetermines domestic law.

Perhaps the most significant symptom of this transformation is the development of the so-called *right of intervention*.[28] This is commonly conceived as the right or duty of the dominant subjects of the world order to intervene in the territories of other subjects in the interest of preventing or resolving humanitarian problems, guaranteeing accords, and imposing peace. The right of intervention figured prominently among the panoply of instruments accorded the United Nations by its Charter for maintaining international order, but the contemporary reconfiguration of this right represents a qualitative leap. No longer, as under the old international ordering, do individual sovereign states or the supranational (U.N.) power intervene only to ensure or impose the application of voluntarily engaged international accords. Now supranational subjects that are legitimated not by right but by consensus intervene in the name of any type of emergency and superior ethical principles. What stands behind this intervention is not just a permanent state of emergency and exception, but a permanent state of emergency and exception justified by *the appeal to essential values of justice*. In other words, the right of the police is legitimated by universal values.[29]

Should we assume that since this new right of intervention functions primarily toward the goal of resolving urgent human problems, its legitimacy is therefore founded on universal values? Should we read this movement as a process that, on the basis of the fluctuating elements of the historical framework, sets in motion a constitutive machine driven by universal forces of justice and peace? Are we thus in a situation very close to the traditional definition of Empire, the one promulgated in the ancient Roman-Christian imaginary?

It would be going too far to respond affirmatively to these questions at this early stage in our investigation. The definition of the developing imperial power as a science of the police that is founded on a practice of just war to address continually arising emergencies is probably correct but still completely insufficient. As we have seen, the phenomenological determinations of the new global order exist in a profoundly fluctuating situation that could also be characterized correctly in terms of crisis and war. How can we reconcile the legitimation of this order through prevention and policing with the fact that crisis and war themselves demonstrate the very questionable genesis and legitimacy of this concept of justice? As we have already noted, these techniques and others like them indicate that what we are witnessing is a process of the material constitution of the new planetary order, the consolidation of its administrative machine, and the production of new hierarchies of command over global space. Who will decide on the definitions of justice and order across the expanse of this totality in the course of its process of constitution? Who will be able to define the concept of peace? Who will be able to unify the process of suspending history and call this suspension just? Around these questions the problematic of Empire is completely open, not closed.

At this point, the problem of the new juridical apparatus is presented to us in its most immediate figure: a global order, a justice, and a right that are still virtual but nonetheless apply actually to us. We are forced increasingly to feel that we are participants in this development, and we are called upon to be responsible for what it becomes in this framework. Our citizenship, just like our ethical responsibility, is situated within these new dimensions—our power and our impotence are measured here. We could say, in Kantian fashion, that our internal moral disposition, when it is confronted with and tested in the social order, tends to be determined by the ethical, political, and juridical categories of Empire. Or we could say that the external morality of every human being and citizen is by now commensurable only in the framework of Empire. This new framework forces us to confront a series of explosive aporias, because in this new juridical and institutional world being formed our ideas and practices of justice and our means of hope are thrown into question. The means of the private and individual apprehension of values are dissolved: with the appearance of Empire, we are confronted no longer with the local mediations of the universal but with a concrete universal itself. The domesticity of values, the shelters behind which they presented their moral substance, the limits that protect against the invading exteriority—all that disappears. We are all forced to confront absolute questions and radical alternatives. In Empire, ethics, morality, and justice are cast into new dimensions.

Throughout the course of our research we have found ourselves confronted with a classic problematic of political philosophy: the decline and fall of Empire.[30] It may seem paradoxical that we address this topos at the beginning, at the same time that we treat the initial construction of Empire; but the becoming of Empire is actually realized on the basis of the same conditions that characterize its decadence and decline. Empire is emerging today as the center that supports the globalization of productive networks and casts its widely inclusive net to try to envelop all power relations within its world order—and yet at the same time it deploys a powerful police function against the new barbarians and the rebellious slaves who threaten its order. The power of Empire appears to be subordinated to the fluctuations of local power dynamics and to the shifting, partial juridical orderings that attempt, but never fully succeed, to lead back to a state of normalcy in the name of the "exceptionality" of the administrative procedures. These characteristics, however, were precisely those that defined ancient Rome in its decadence and that tormented so many of its Enlightenment admirers. We should not expect that the complexity of the processes that construct the new imperial relationship of right be resolved. On the contrary, the processes are and will remain contradictory. The question of the definition of justice and peace will find no real resolution; the force of the new imperial constitution will not be embodied in a consensus that is articulated in the multitude. The terms of the juridical proposal of Empire are completely indeterminate, even though they are nonetheless concrete. Empire is born and shows itself as crisis. Should we conceive this as an Empire of decadence, then, in the terms Montesquieu and Gibbon described? Or is it more properly understood in classical terms as an Empire of corruption?

Here we should understand corruption first of all not only in moral terms but also in juridical and political terms, because according to Montesquieu and Gibbon, when the different forms of government are not firmly established in the republic, the cycle of corruption is ineluctably set in motion and the community is torn apart.[31] Second, we should understand corruption also in metaphysical terms: where the entity and essence, effectiveness and value, do not find common satisfaction, there develops not generation but corruption.[32] These are some of the fundamental axes of Empire that we will return to later at length.

Allow us, in conclusion, one final analogy that refers to the birth of Christianity in Europe and its expansion during the decline of the Roman Empire. In this process an enormous potential of subjectivity was constructed and consolidated in terms of the prophecy of a world to come, a chiliastic project. This new subjectivity offered an absolute alternative to the spirit of imperial right—a new ontological basis. From this perspective, Empire was accepted as the "maturity of the times" and the unity of the entire known civilization, but it was challenged in its totality by a completely different ethical and ontological axis. In the same way today, given that the limits and unresolvable problems of the new imperial right are fixed, theory and practice can go beyond them, finding once again an ontological basis of antagonism—within Empire, but also against and beyond Empire, at the same level of totality.

1.2

BIOPOLITICAL PRODUCTION

> The "police" appears as an administration heading the state, together with the judiciary, the army, and the exchequer. True. Yet in fact, it embraces everything else. Turquet says so: "It branches out into all of the people's conditions, everything they do or undertake. Its field comprises the judiciary, finance, and the army." The *police* includes everything.
>
> Michel Foucault

From the juridical perspective we have been able to glimpse some of the elements of the ideal genesis of Empire, but from that perspective alone it would be difficult if not impossible to understand how the imperial machine is actually set in motion. Juridical concepts and juridical systems always refer to something other than themselves. Through the evolution and exercise of right, they point toward the material condition that defines their purchase on social reality. Our analysis must now descend to the level of that materiality and investigate there the material transformation of the paradigm of rule. We need to discover the means and forces of the production of social reality along with the subjectivities that animate it.

Biopower in the Society of Control

In many respects, the work of Michel Foucault has prepared the terrain for such an investigation of the material functioning of imperial rule. First of all, Foucault's work allows us to recognize a historical, epochal passage in social forms from *disciplinary society* to the *society of control*.[1] Disciplinary society is that society in which social command is constructed through a diffuse network of *dispositifs* or apparatuses that produce and regulate customs, habits, and productive practices. Putting this society to work and ensuring obedience to its rule and its mechanisms of inclusion and/or exclusion are accomplished through disciplinary institutions (the prison, the factory, the asylum, the hospital, the university, the school, and so forth) that structure the social terrain and present logics adequate to the "reason" of discipline. Disciplinary power rules in effect by structuring the parameters and limits of thought and practice, sanctioning and prescribing normal and/or deviant behaviors. Foucault generally refers to the ancien régime and the classical age of French civilization to illustrate the emergence of disciplinarity, but more generally we could say that the entire first phase of capitalist accumulation (in Europe and elsewhere) was conducted under this paradigm of power. We should understand the society of control, in contrast, as that society (which develops at the far edge of modernity and opens toward the postmodern) in which mechanisms of command become ever more "democratic," ever more immanent to the social field, distributed throughout the brains and bodies of the citizens. The behaviors of social integration and exclusion proper to rule are thus increasingly interiorized within the subjects themselves. Power is now exercised through machines that directly organize the brains (in communication systems, information networks, etc.) and bodies (in welfare systems, monitored activities, etc.) toward a state of autonomous alienation from the sense of life and the desire for creativity. The society of control might thus be characterized by an intensification and generalization of the normalizing apparatuses of disciplinarity that internally animate our common and daily practices, but in contrast to discipline, this control extends well outside the structured sites of social institutions through flexible and fluctuating networks.

Second, Foucault's work allows us to recognize the *biopolitical* nature of the new paradigm of power.[2] Biopower is a form of power that regulates social life from its interior, following it, interpreting it, absorbing it, and rearticulating it. Power can achieve an effective command over the entire life of the population only when it becomes an integral, vital function that every individual embraces and reactivates of his or her own accord. As Foucault says, "Life has now become . . . an object of power."[3] The highest function of this power is to invest life through and through, and its primary task is to administer life. Biopower thus refers to a situation in which what is directly at stake in power is the production and reproduction of life itself.

These two lines of Foucault's work dovetail with each other in the sense that only the society of control is able to adopt the biopolitical context as its *exclusive* terrain of reference. In the passage from disciplinary society to the society of control, a new paradigm of power is realized which is defined by the technologies that recognize society as the realm of biopower. In disciplinary society the effects of biopolitical technologies were still partial in the sense that disciplining developed according to relatively closed, geometrical, and quantitative logics. Disciplinarity fixed individuals within institutions but did not succeed in consuming them completely in the rhythm of productive practices and productive socialization; it did not reach the point of permeating entirely the consciousnesses and bodies of individuals, the point of treating and organizing them in the totality of their activities. In disciplinary society, then, the relationship between power and the individual remained a static one: the disciplinary invasion of power corresponded to the resistance of the individual. By contrast, when power becomes entirely biopolitical, the whole social body is comprised by power's machine and developed in its virtuality. This relationship is open, qualitative, and affective. Society, subsumed within a power that reaches down to the ganglia of the social structure and its processes of development, reacts like a single body. Power is thus expressed as a control that extends throughout the depths of the consciousnesses and bodies of the population—and at the same time across the entirety of social relations.[4]

In this passage from disciplinary society to the society of control, then, one could say that the increasingly intense relationship of mutual implication of all social forces that capitalism has pursued throughout its development has now been fully realized. Marx recognized something similar in what he called the passage from the formal subsumption to the real subsumption of labor under capital,[5] and later the Frankfurt School philosophers analyzed a closely related passage of the subsumption of culture (and social relations) under the totalitarian figure of the state, or really within the perverse dialectic of Enlightenment.[6] The passage we are referring to, however, is fundamentally different in that instead of focusing on the unidimensionality of the process described by Marx and reformulated and extended by the Frankfurt School, the Foucauldian passage deals fundamentally with the paradox of plurality and multiplicity—and Deleuze and Guattari develop this perspective even more clearly.[7] The analysis of the real subsumption, when this is understood as investing not only the economic or only the cultural dimension of society but rather the social *bios* itself, and when it is attentive to the modalities of disciplinarity and/or control, disrupts the linear and totalitarian figure of capitalist development. Civil society is absorbed in the state, but the consequence of this is an explosion of the elements that were previously coordinated and mediated in civil society. Resistances are no longer marginal but active in the center of a society that opens up in networks; the individual points are singularized in a thousand plateaus. What Foucault constructed implicitly (and Deleuze and Guattari made explicit) is therefore the paradox of a power that, while it unifies and envelops within itself every element of social life (thus losing its capacity effectively to mediate different social forces), at that very moment reveals a new context, a new milieu of maximum plurality and uncontainable singularization—a milieu of the event.[8]

These conceptions of the society of control and biopower both describe central aspects of the concept of Empire. The concept of Empire is the framework in which the new omniversality of subjects has to be understood, and it is the end to which the new paradigm of power is leading. Here a veritable chasm opens up between the various old theoretical frameworks of international law (in either its contractual and/or U.N. form) and the new reality of imperial law. All the intermediary elements of the process have in fact fallen aside, so that the legitimacy of the international order can no longer be constructed through mediations but must rather be grasped immediately in all its diversity. We have already acknowledged this fact from the juridical perspective. We saw, in effect, that when the new notion of right emerges in the context of globalization and presents itself as capable of treating the universal, planetary sphere as a single, systemic set, it must assume an immediate prerequisite (acting in a state of exception) and an adequate, plastic, and constitutive technology (the techniques of the police).

Even though the state of exception and police technologies constitute the solid nucleus and the central element of the new imperial right, however, this new regime has nothing to do with the juridical arts of dictatorship or totalitarianism that in other times and with such great fanfare were so thoroughly described by many (in fact too many!) authors.[9] On the contrary, the rule of law continues to play a central role in the context of the contemporary passage: right remains effective and (precisely by means of the state of exception and police techniques) becomes procedure. This is a radical transformation that reveals the unmediated relationship between power and subjectivities, and hence demonstrates both the impossibility of "prior" mediations and the uncontainable temporal variability of the event.[10] Throughout the unbounded global spaces, to the depths of the biopolitical world, and confronting an unforeseeable temporality—these are the determinations on which the new supranational right must be defined. Here is where the concept of Empire must struggle to establish itself, where it must prove its effectiveness, and hence where the machine must be set in motion.

From this point of view, the biopolitical context of the new paradigm is completely central to our analysis. This is what presents power with an alternative, not only between obedience and disobedience, or between formal political participation and refusal, but also along the entire range of life and death, wealth and poverty, production and social reproduction, and so forth. Given the great difficulties the new notion of right has in representing this dimension of the power of Empire, and given its inability to touch biopower concretely in all its material aspects, imperial right can at best only partially represent the underlying design of the new constitution of world order, and cannot really grasp the motor that sets it in motion. Our analysis must focus its attention rather on the *productive* dimension of biopower.[11]

The Production of Life

The question of production in relation to biopower and the society of control, however, reveals a real weakness of the work of the authors from whom we have borrowed these notions. We should clarify, then, the "vital" or biopolitical dimensions of Foucault's work in relation to the dynamics of production. Foucault argued in several works in the mid-1970s that one cannot understand the passage from the "sovereign" state of the ancien régime to the modern "disciplinary" state without taking into account how the biopolitical context was progressively put at the service of capitalist accumulation: "The control of society over individuals is not conducted only through consciousness or ideology, but also in the body and with the body. For capitalist society biopolitics is what is most important, the biological, the somatic, the corporeal."[12]

One of the central objectives of his research strategy in this period was to go beyond the versions of historical materialism, including several variants of Marxist theory, that considered the problem of power and social reproduction on a superstructural level separate from the real, base level of production. Foucault thus attempted to bring the problem of social reproduction and all the elements of the so-called superstructure back to within the material, fundamental structure and define this terrain not only in economic terms but also in cultural, corporeal, and subjective ones. We can thus understand how Foucault's conception of the social whole was perfected and realized when in a subsequent phase of his work he uncovered the emerging outlines of the society of control as a figure of power active throughout the entire biopolitics of society. It does not seem, however, that Foucault—even when he powerfully grasped the biopolitical horizon of society and defined it as a field of immanence—ever succeeded in pulling his thought away from that structuralist epistemology that guided his research from the beginning. By structuralist epistemology here we mean the reinvention of a functionalist analysis in the realm of the human sciences, a method that effectively sacrifices the dynamic of the system, the creative temporality of its movements, and the ontological substance of cultural and social reproduction.[13] In fact, if at this point we were to ask Foucault who or what drives the system, or rather, who is the "bios," his response would be ineffable, or nothing at all. What Foucault fails to grasp finally are the real dynamics of production in biopolitical society.[14]

By contrast, Deleuze and Guattari present us with a properly poststructuralist understanding of biopower that renews materialist thought and grounds itself solidly in the question of the production of social being. Their work demystifies structuralism and all the philosophical, sociological, and political conceptions that make the fixity of the epistemological frame an ineluctable point of reference. They focus our attention clearly on the ontological substance of social production. Machines produce. The constant functioning of social machines in their various apparatuses and assemblages produces the world along with the subjects and objects that constitute it. Deleuze and Guattari, however, seem to be able to conceive positively only the tendencies toward continuous movement and absolute flows, and thus in their thought, too, the creative elements and the radical ontology of the production of the social remain insubstantial and impotent. Deleuze and Guattari discover the productivity of social reproduction (creative production, production of values, social relations, affects, becomings), but manage to articulate it only superficially and ephemerally, as a chaotic, indeterminate horizon marked by the ungraspable event.[15]

We can better grasp the relationship between social production and biopower in the work of a group of contemporary Italian Marxist authors who recognize the biopolitical dimension in terms of the new nature of productive labor and its living development in society, using terms such as "mass intellectuality," "immaterial labor," and the Marxian concept of "general intellect."[16] These analyses set off from two coordinated research projects. The first consists in the analysis of the recent transformations of productive labor and its tendency to become increasingly immaterial. The central role previously occupied by the labor power of mass factory workers in the production of surplus value is today increasingly filled by intellectual, immaterial, and communicative labor power. It is thus necessary to develop a new political theory of value that can pose the problem of this new capitalist accumulation of value at the center of the mechanism of exploitation (and thus, perhaps, at the center of potential revolt). The second, and consequent, research project developed by this school consists in the analysis of the immediately social and communicative dimension of living labor in contemporary capitalist society, and thus poses insistently the problem of the new figures of subjectivity, in both their exploitation and their revolutionary potential. The immediately social dimension of the exploitation of living immaterial labor immerses labor in all the relational elements that define the social but also at the same time activate the critical elements that develop the potential of insubordination and revolt through the entire set of laboring practices. After a new theory of value, then, a new theory of subjectivity must be formulated that operates primarily through knowledge, communication, and language.

These analyses have thus reestablished the importance of production within the biopolitical process of the social constitution, but they have also in certain respects isolated it—by grasping it in a pure form, refining it on the ideal plane. They have acted as if discovering the new forms of productive forces—immaterial labor, massified intellectual labor, the labor of "general intellect"—were enough to grasp concretely the dynamic and creative relationship between material production and social reproduction. When they reinsert production into the biopolitical context, they present it almost exclusively on the horizon of language and communication. One of the most serious shortcomings has thus been the tendency among these authors to treat the new laboring practices in biopolitical society *only* in their intellectual and incorporeal aspects. The productivity of bodies and the value of affect, however, are absolutely central in this context. We will elaborate the three primary aspects of immaterial labor in the contemporary economy: the communicative labor of industrial production that has newly become linked in informational networks, the interactive labor of symbolic analysis and problem solving, and the labor of the production and manipulation of affects (see Section 3.4). This third aspect, with its focus on the productivity of the corporeal, the somatic, is an extremely important element in the contemporary networks of biopolitical production. The work of this school and its analysis of general intellect, then, certainly marks a step forward, but its conceptual framework remains too pure, almost angelic. In the final analysis, these new conceptions too only scratch the surface of the productive dynamic of the new theoretical framework of biopower.[17]

Our task, then, is to build on these partially successful attempts to recognize the potential of biopolitical production. Precisely by bringing together coherently the different defining characteristics of the biopolitical context that we have described up to this point, and leading them back to the ontology of production, we will be able to identify the new figure of the collective biopolitical body, which may nonetheless remain as contradictory as it is paradoxical. This body becomes structure not by negating the originary productive force that animates it but by recognizing it; it becomes language (both scientific language and social language) because it is a multitude of singular and determinate bodies that seek relation. It is thus both production and reproduction, structure and superstructure, because it is life in the fullest sense and politics in the proper sense. Our analysis has to descend into the jungle of productive and conflictual determinations that the collective biopolitical body offers us.[18] The context of our analysis thus has to be the very unfolding of life itself, the process of the constitution of the world, of history. The analysis must be proposed not through ideal forms but within the dense complex of experience.

Corporations and Communication

In asking ourselves how the political and sovereign elements of the imperial machine come to be constituted, we find that there is no need to limit our analysis to or even focus it on the established supranational regulatory institutions. The U.N. organizations, along with the great multi- and transnational finance and trade agencies (the IMF, the World Bank, the GATT, and so forth), all become relevant in the perspective of the supranational juridical constitution only when they are considered within the dynamic of the biopolitical production of world order. The function they had in the old international order, we should emphasize, is not what now gives legitimacy to these organizations. What legitimates them now is rather their newly possible function in the symbology of the imperial order. Outside of the new framework, these institutions are ineffectual. At best, the old institutional framework contributes to the formation and education of the administrative personnel of the imperial machine, the "dressage" of a new imperial élite.

The huge transnational corporations construct the fundamental connective fabric of the biopolitical world in certain important respects. Capital has indeed always been organized with a view toward the entire global sphere, but only in the second half of the twentieth century did multinational and transnational industrial and financial corporations really begin to structure global territories biopolitically. Some claim that these corporations have merely come to occupy the place that was held by the various national colonialist and imperialist systems in earlier phases of capitalist development, from nineteenth-century European imperialism to the Fordist phase of development in the twentieth century.[19] This is in part true, but that place itself has been substantially transformed by the new reality of capitalism. The activities of corporations are no longer defined by the imposition of abstract command and the organization of simple theft and unequal exchange. Rather, they directly structure and articulate territories and populations. They tend to make nation-states merely instruments to record the flows of the commodities, monies, and populations that they set in motion. The transnational corporations directly distribute labor power over various markets, functionally allocate resources, and organize hierarchically the various sectors of world production. The complex apparatus that selects investments and directs financial and monetary maneuvers determines the new geography of the world market, or really the new biopolitical structuring of the world.[20]

The most complete figure of this world is presented from the monetary perspective. From here we can see a horizon of values and a machine of distribution, a mechanism of accumulation and a means of circulation, a power and a language. There is nothing, no "naked life," no external standpoint, that can be posed outside this field permeated by money; nothing escapes money. Production and reproduction are dressed in monetary clothing. In fact, on the global stage, every biopolitical figure appears dressed in monetary garb. "Accumulate, accumulate! This is Moses and the Prophets!"[21]

The great industrial and financial powers thus produce not only commodities but also subjectivities. They produce agentic subjectivities within the biopolitical context: they produce needs, social relations, bodies, and minds—which is to say, they produce producers.[22] In the biopolitical sphere, life is made to work for production and production is made to work for life. It is a great hive in which the queen bee continuously oversees production and reproduction. The deeper the analysis goes, the more it finds at increasing levels of intensity the interlinking assemblages of interactive relationships.[23]

One site where we should locate the biopolitical production of order is in the immaterial nexuses of the production of language, communication, and the symbolic that are developed by the communications industries.[24] The development of communications networks has an organic relationship to the emergence of the new world order—it is, in other words, effect and cause, product and producer. Communication not only expresses but also organizes the movement of globalization. It organizes the movement by multiplying and structuring interconnections through networks. It expresses the movement and controls the sense and direction of the imaginary that runs throughout these communicative connections;

in other words, the imaginary is guided and channeled within the communicative machine. What the theories of power of modernity were forced to consider transcendent, that is, external to productive and social relations, is here formed inside, immanent to the productive and social relations. Mediation is absorbed within the productive machine. The political synthesis of social space is fixed in the space of communication. This is why communications industries have assumed such a central position. They not only organize production on a new scale and impose a new structure adequate to global space, but also make its justification immanent. Power, as it produces, organizes; as it organizes, it speaks and expresses itself as authority. Language, as it communicates, produces commodities but moreover creates subjectivities, puts them in relation, and orders them. The communications industries integrate the imaginary and the symbolic within the biopolitical fabric, not merely putting them at the service of power but actually integrating them into its very functioning.[25]

At this point we can begin to address the question of the *legitimation* of the new world order. Its legitimation is not born of the previously existing international accords nor of the functioning of the first, embryonic supranational organizations, which were themselves created through treaties based on international law. The legitimation of the imperial machine is born at least in part of the communications industries, that is, of the transformation of the new mode of production into a machine. It is a subject that produces its own image of authority. This is a form of legitimation that rests on nothing outside itself and is reproposed ceaselessly by developing its own languages of self-validation.

One further consequence should be treated on the basis of these premises. If communication is one of the hegemonic sectors of production and acts over the entire biopolitical field, then we must consider communication and the biopolitical context coexistent. This takes us well beyond the old terrain as Jürgen Habermas described it, for example. In fact, when Habermas developed the concept of communicative action, demonstrating so powerfully its productive form and the ontological consequences deriving from that, he still relied on a standpoint outside these effects of globalization, a standpoint of life and truth that could oppose the informational colonization of being.[26] The imperial machine, however, demonstrates that this external standpoint no longer exists. On the contrary, communicative production and the construction of imperial legitimation march hand in hand and can no longer be separated. The machine is self-validating, autopoietic—that is, systemic. It constructs social fabrics that evacuate or render ineffective any contradiction; it creates situations in which, before coercively neutralizing difference, seem to absorb it in an insignificant play of self-generating and self-regulating equilibria. As we have argued elsewhere, any juridical theory that addresses the conditions of postmodernity has to take into account this specifically communicative definition of social production.[27] The imperial machine lives by producing a context of equilibria and/or reducing complexities, pretending to put forward a project of universal citizenship and toward this end intensifying the effectiveness of its intervention over every element of the communicative relationship, all the while dissolving identity and history in a completely postmodernist fashion.[28] Contrary to the way many postmodernist accounts would have it, however, the imperial machine, far from eliminating master narratives, actually produces and reproduces them (ideological master narratives in particular) in order to validate and celebrate its own power.[29] In this coincidence of production through language, the linguistic production of reality, and the language of self-validation resides a fundamental key to understanding the effectiveness, validity, and legitimation of imperial right.

Intervention

This new framework of legitimacy includes new forms and new articulations of *the exercise of legitimate force.* During its formation, the new power must demonstrate the effectiveness of its force at the same time that the bases of its legitimation are being constructed. In fact, the legitimacy of the new power is in part based directly on the effectiveness of its use of force.

The way the effectiveness of the new power is demonstrated has nothing to do with the old international order that is slowly dying away; nor has it much use for the instruments the old order left behind. The deployments of the imperial machine are defined by a whole series of new characteristics, such as the unbounded terrain of its activities, the singularization and symbolic localization of its actions, and the connection of repressive action to all the aspects of the biopolitical structure of society. For lack of a better term we continue to call these "interventions." This is merely a terminological and not a conceptual deficiency, for these are not really interventions into independent juridical territories but rather actions within a unified world by the ruling structure of production and communication. In effect, intervention has been internalized and universalized. In the previous section we referred to both the structural means of intervention that involve the deployments of monetary mechanisms and financial maneuvers over the transnational field of interdependent productive regimes and interventions in the field of communication and their effects on the legitimation of the system. Here we want to investigate the new forms of intervention that involve the exercise of physical force on the part of the imperial machine over its global territories. The enemies that Empire opposes today may present more of an ideological threat than a military challenge, but nonetheless the power of Empire exercised through force and all the deployments that guarantee its effectiveness are already very advanced technologically and solidly consolidated politically.[30]

The arsenal of legitimate force for imperial intervention is indeed already vast, and should include not only military intervention but also other forms such as moral intervention and juridical intervention. In fact, the Empire's powers of intervention might be best understood as beginning not directly with its weapons of lethal force but rather with its moral instruments. What we are calling moral intervention is practiced today by a variety of bodies, including the news media and religious organizations, but the most important may be some of the so-called non-governmental organizations (NGOs), which, precisely because they are not run directly by governments, are assumed to act on the basis of ethical or moral imperatives. The term refers to a wide variety of groups, but we are referring here principally to the global, regional, and local organizations that are dedicated to relief work and the protection of human rights, such as Amnesty International, Oxfam, and Médecins sans Frontières. Such humanitarian NGOs are in effect (even if this runs counter to the intentions of the participants) some of the most powerful pacific weapons of the new world order—the charitable campaigns and the mendicant orders of Empire. These NGOs conduct "just wars" without arms, without violence, without borders. Like the Dominicans in the late medieval period and the Jesuits at the dawn of modernity, these groups strive to identify universal needs and defend human rights. Through their language and their action they first define the enemy as privation (in the hope of preventing serious damage) and then recognize the enemy as sin.

It is hard not to be reminded here of how in Christian moral theology evil is first posed as privation of the good and then sin is defined as culpable negation of the good. Within this logical framework it is not strange but rather all too natural that in their attempts to respond to privation, these NGOs are led to denounce publicly the sinners (or rather the Enemy in properly inquisitional terms); nor is it strange that they leave to the "secular wing" the task of actually addressing the problems. In this way, moral intervention has become a frontline force of imperial intervention. In effect, this intervention prefigures the state of exception from below, and does so without borders, armed with some of the most effective means of communication and oriented toward the symbolic production of the Enemy. These NGOs are completely immersed in the biopolitical context of the constitution of Empire; they anticipate the power of its pacifying and productive intervention of justice. It should thus come as no surprise that honest juridical theorists of the old international school (such as Richard Falk) should be drawn in by the fascination of these NGOs.[31] The NGOs' demonstration of the new order as a peaceful biopolitical context seems to have blinded these theorists to the brutal effects that moral intervention produces as a prefiguration of world order.[32]

Moral intervention often serves as the first act that prepares the stage for military intervention. In such cases, military deployment is presented as an internationally sanctioned police action. Today military intervention is progressively less a product of decisions that arise out of the old international order or even U.N. structures. More often it is dictated unilaterally by the United States, which charges itself with the primary task and then subsequently asks its allies to set in motion a process of armed containment and/or repression of the current enemy of Empire. These enemies are most often called terrorist, a crude conceptual and terminological reduction that is rooted in a police mentality.

The relationship between prevention and repression is particularly clear in the case of intervention in ethnic conflicts. The conflicts among ethnic groups and the consequent reenforcement of new and/or resurrected ethnic identities effectively disrupt the old aggregations based on national political lines. These conflicts make the fabric of global relations more fluid and, by affirming new identities and new localities, present a more malleable material for control. In such cases repression can be articulated through preventive action that constructs new relationships (which will eventually be consolidated in peace but only after new wars) and new territorial and political formations that are functional (or rather more functional, better adaptable) to the constitution of Empire.[33] A second example of repression prepared through preventive action is the campaigns against corporative business groups or "mafias," particularly those involved in the drug trade. The actual repression of these groups may not be as important as criminalizing their activities and managing social alarm at their very existence in order to facilitate their control. Even though controlling "ethnic terrorists" and "drug mafias" may represent the center of the wide spectrum of police control on the part of the imperial power, this activity is nonetheless normal, that is, systemic. The "just war" is effectively supported by the "moral police," just as the validity of imperial right and its legitimate functioning is supported by the necessary and continuous exercise of police power.

It is clear that international or supranational courts are constrained to follow this lead. Armies and police anticipate the courts and preconstitute the rules of justice that the courts must then apply. The intensity of the moral principles to which the construction of the new world order is entrusted cannot change the fact that this is really an inversion of the conventional order of constitutional logic. The active parties supporting the imperial constitution are confident that when the construction of Empire is sufficiently advanced, the courts will be able to assume their leading role in the definition of justice. For now, however, although international courts do not have much power, public displays of their activities are still very important. Eventually a new judicial function must be formed that is adequate to the constitution of Empire. Courts will have to be transformed gradually from an organ that simply decrees sentences against the vanquished to a judicial body or system of bodies that dictate and sanction the interrelation among the moral order, the exercise of police action, and the mechanism legitimating imperial sovereignty.[34]

This kind of continual intervention, then, which is both moral and military, is really the logical form of the exercise of force that follows from a paradigm of legitimation based on a state of permanent exception and police action. Interventions are always exceptional even though they arise continually; they take the form of police actions because they are aimed at maintaining an internal order. In this way intervention is an effective mechanism that through police deployments contributes directly to the construction of the moral, normative, and institutional order of Empire.

Royal Prerogatives

What were traditionally called the royal prerogatives of sovereignty seem in effect to be repeated and even substantially renewed in the construction of Empire. If we were to remain within the conceptual framework of classic domestic and international law, we might be tempted to say that a supranational quasi-state is being formed. That does not seem to us, however, an accurate characterization of the situation. When the royal prerogatives of modern sovereignty reappear in Empire, they take on a completely different form. For example, the sovereign function of deploying military forces was carried out by the modern nation-states and is now conducted by Empire, but, as we have seen, the justification for such deployments now rests on a state of permanent exception, and the deployments themselves take the form of police actions. Other royal prerogatives such as carrying out justice and imposing taxes also have the same kind of liminal existence. We have already discussed the marginal position of judicial authority in the constitutive process of Empire, and one could also argue that imposing taxes occupies a marginal position in that it is increasingly linked to specific and local urgencies. In effect, one might say that the sovereignty of Empire itself is realized at the margins, where borders are flexible and identities are hybrid and fluid. It would be difficult to say which is more important to Empire, the center or the margins. In fact, center and margin seem continually to be shifting positions, fleeing any determinate locations. We could even say that the process itself is virtual and that its power resides in the power of the virtual.

One could nonetheless object at this point that even while being virtual and acting at the margins, the process of constructing imperial sovereignty is in many respects very real! We certainly do not mean to deny that fact. Our claim, rather, is that we are dealing here with a special kind of sovereignty—a discontinuous form of sovereignty that should be considered liminal or marginal insofar as it acts "in the final instance," a sovereignty that locates its only point of reference in the definitive absoluteness of the power that it can exercise. Empire thus appears in the form of a very high tech machine: it is virtual, built to control the marginal event, and organized to dominate and when necessary intervene in the breakdowns of the system (in line with the most advanced technologies of robotic production). The virtuality and discontinuity of imperial sovereignty, however, do not minimize the effectiveness of its force;

on the contrary, those very characteristics serve to reinforce its apparatus, demonstrating its effectiveness in the contemporary historical context and its legitimate force to resolve world problems in the final instance.

We are now in the position to address the question whether, on the basis of these new biopolitical premises, the figure and the life of Empire can today be grasped in terms of a juridical model. We have already seen that this juridical model cannot be constituted by the existing structures of international law, even when understood in terms of the most advanced developments of the United Nations and the other great international organizations. Their elaborations of an international order could at the most be recognized as a process of transition toward the new imperial power. The constitution of Empire is being formed neither on the basis of any contractual or treaty-based mechanism nor through any federative source. The source of imperial normativity is born of a new machine, a new economic-industrial-communicative machine—in short, a globalized biopolitical machine. It thus seems clear that we must look at something other than what has up until now constituted the bases of international order, something that does not rely on the form of right that, in the most diverse traditions, was grounded in the modern system of sovereign nation-states. The impossibility, however, of grasping the genesis of Empire and its virtual figure with any of the old instruments of juridical theory, which were deployed in the realist, institutionalist, positivist, or natural right frameworks, should not force us to accept a cynical framework of pure force or some such Machiavellian position. In the genesis of Empire there is indeed a rationality at work that can be recognized not so much in terms of the juridical tradition but more clearly in the often hidden history of industrial management and the political uses of technology. (We should not forget here too that proceeding along these lines will reveal the fabric of class struggle and its institutional effects, but we will treat that issue in the next section.) This is a rationality that situates us at the heart of biopolitics and biopolitical technologies.

If we wanted to take up again Max Weber's famous three-part formula of the forms of legitimation of power, the qualitative leap that Empire introduces into the definition would consist in the unforeseeable mixture of (1) elements typical of traditional power, (2) an extension of bureaucratic power that is adapted physiologically to the biopolitical context, and (3) a rationality defined by the "event" and by "charisma" that rises up as a power of the singularization of the whole and of the effectiveness of imperial interventions.[35] The logic that characterizes this neo-Weberian perspective would be functional rather than mathematical, and rhizomatic and undulatory rather than inductive or deductive. It would deal with the management of linguistic sequences as sets of machinic sequences of denotation and at the same time of creative, colloquial, and irreducible innovation.

The fundamental object that the imperial relations of power interpret is the productive force of the system, the new biopolitical economic and institutional system. The imperial order is formed not only on the basis of its powers of accumulation and global extension, but also on the basis of its capacity to develop itself more deeply, to be reborn, and to extend itself throughout the biopolitical latticework of world society. The absoluteness of imperial power is the complementary term to its complete immanence to the ontological machine of production and reproduction, and thus to the biopolitical context. Perhaps, finally, this cannot be represented by a juridical order, but it nonetheless is an order, an order defined by its virtuality, its dynamism, and its functional inconclusiveness. The fundamental norm of legitimation will thus be established in the depths of the machine, at the heart of social production. Social production and juridical legitimation should not be conceived as primary and secondary forces nor as elements of the base and superstructure, but should be understood rather in a state of absolute parallelism and intermixture, coextensive throughout biopolitical society. In Empire and its regime of biopower, economic production and political constitution tend increasingly to coincide.

1.3

ALTERNATIVES WITHIN EMPIRE

> Once embodied in the power of the workers' councils, which must internationally supplant all other power, the proletarian movement becomes its own product, and this product is the producer itself. The producer is its own end. Only then is the spectacular negation of life negated in turn.
>
> Guy Debord

> Now is the time of furnaces, and only light should be seen.
>
> José Martí

Flirting with Hegel, one could say that the construction of Empire is good *in itself* but not *for itself*.[1] One of the most powerful operations of the modern imperialist power structures was to drive wedges among the masses of the globe, dividing them into opposing camps, or really a myriad of conflicting parties. Segments of the proletariat in the dominant countries were even led to believe that their interests were tied exclusively to their national identity and imperial destiny. The most significant instances of revolt and revolution against these modern power structures therefore were those that posed the struggle against exploitation together with the struggle against nationalism, colonialism, and imperialism. In these events humanity appeared for a magical moment to be united by a common desire for liberation, and we seemed to catch a glimpse of a future when the modern mechanisms of domination would once and for all be destroyed. The revolting masses, their desire for liberation, their experiments to construct alternatives, and their instances of constituent power have all at their best moments pointed toward the internationalization and globalization of relationships, beyond the divisions of national, colonial, and imperialist rule. In our time this desire that was set in motion by the multitude has been addressed (in a strange and perverted but nonetheless real way) by the construction of Empire. One might even say that the construction of Empire and its global networks is a *response* to the various struggles against the modern machines of power, and specifically to class struggle driven by the multitude's desire for liberation. The multitude called Empire into being.

Saying that Empire is good *in itself,* however, does not mean that it is good *for itself.* Although Empire may have played a role in putting an end to colonialism and imperialism, it nonetheless constructs its own relationships of power based on exploitation that are in many respects more brutal than those it destroyed. The end of the dialectic of modernity has not resulted in the end of the dialectic of exploitation. Today nearly all of humanity is to some degree absorbed within or subordinated to the networks of capitalist exploitation. We see now an ever more extreme separation of a small minority that controls enormous wealth from multitudes that live in poverty at the limit of powerlessness. The geographical and racial lines of oppression and exploitation that were established during the era of colonialism and imperialism have in many respects not declined but instead increased exponentially.

Despite recognizing all this, we insist on asserting that the construction of Empire is a step forward in order to do away with any nostalgia for the power structures that preceded it and refuse any political strategy that involves returning to that old arrangement, such as trying to resurrect the nation-state to protect against global capital. We claim that Empire is better in the same way that Marx insists that capitalism is better than the forms of society and modes of production that came before it. Marx's view is grounded on a healthy and lucid disgust for the parochial and rigid hierarchies that preceded capitalist society as well as on a recognition that the potential for liberation is increased in the new situation. In the same way today we can see that Empire does away with the cruel regimes of modern power and also increases the potential for liberation.

We are well aware that in affirming this thesis we are swimming against the current of our friends and comrades on the Left. In the long decades of the current crisis of the communist, socialist, and liberal Left that has followed the 1960s, a large portion of critical thought, both in the dominant countries of capitalist development and in the subordinated ones, has sought to recompose sites of resistance that are founded on the identities of social subjects or national and regional groups, often grounding political analysis on the *localization of struggles*. Such arguments are sometimes constructed in terms of "place-based" movements or politics, in which the boundaries of place (conceived either as identity or as territory) are posed against the undifferentiated and homogeneous space of global networks.[2] At other times such political arguments draw on the long tradition of Leftist nationalism in which (in the best cases) the nation is conceived as the primary mechanism of defense against the domination of foreign and/or global capital.[3] Today the operative syllogism at the heart of the various forms of "local" Leftist strategy seems to be entirely reactive: If capitalist domination is becoming ever more global, then our resistances to it must defend the local and construct barriers to capital's accelerating flows. From this perspective, the real globalization of capital and the constitution of Empire must be considered signs of dispossession and defeat.

We maintain, however, that today this localist position, although we admire and respect the spirit of some of its proponents, is both false and damaging. It is false first of all because the problem is poorly posed. In many characterizations the problem rests on a false dichotomy between the global and the local, assuming that the global entails homogenization and undifferentiated identity whereas the local preserves heterogeneity and difference. Often implicit in such arguments is the assumption that the differences of the local are in some sense natural, or at least that their origin remains beyond question. Local differences preexist the present scene and must be defended or protected against the intrusion of globalization. It should come as no surprise, given such assumptions, that many defenses of the local adopt the terminology of traditional ecology or even identify this "local" political project with the defense of nature and biodiversity. This view can easily devolve into a kind of primordialism that fixes and romanticizes social relations and identities. What needs to be addressed, instead, is precisely the *production of locality,* that is, the social machines that create and recreate the identities and differences that are understood as the local.[4] The differences of locality are neither preexisting nor natural but rather effects of a regime of production. Globality similarly should not be understood in terms of cultural, political, or economic *homogenization.* Globalization, like localization, should be understood instead as a *regime* of the production of identity and difference, or really of homogenization and heterogenization. The better framework, then, to designate the distinction between the global and the local might refer to different networks of flows and obstacles in which the local moment or perspective gives priority to the reterritorializing barriers or boundaries and the global moment privileges the mobility of deterritorializing flows. It is false, in any case, to claim that we can (re)establish local identities that are in some sense *outside* and protected against the global flows of capital and Empire.

This Leftist strategy of resistance to globalization and defense of locality is also damaging because in many cases what appear as local identities are not autonomous or self-determining but actually feed into and support the development of the capitalist imperial machine. The globalization or deterritorialization operated by the imperial machine is not in fact opposed to localization or reterritorialization, but rather sets in play mobile and modulating circuits of differentiation and identification. The strategy of local resistance misidentifies and thus masks the enemy. We are by no means opposed to the globalization of relationships as such—in fact, as we said, the strongest forces of Leftist internationalism have effectively led this process. The enemy, rather, is a specific regime of global relations that we call Empire. More important, this strategy of defending the local is damaging because it obscures and even negates the real alternatives and the potentials for liberation that exist *within* Empire. We should be done once and for all with the search for an outside, a standpoint that imagines a purity for our politics. It is better both theoretically and practically to enter the terrain of Empire and confront its homogenizing and heterogenizing flows in all their complexity, grounding our analysis in the power of the global multitude.

The Ontological Drama of the *Res Gestae*

The legacy of modernity is a legacy of fratricidal wars, devastating "development," cruel "civilization," and previously unimagined violence. Erich Auerbach once wrote that tragedy is the only genre that can properly claim realism in Western literature, and perhaps this is true precisely because of the tragedy Western modernity has imposed on the world.[5] Concentration camps, nuclear weapons, genocidal wars, slavery, apartheid: it is not difficult to enumerate the various scenes of the tragedy. By insisting on the tragic character of modernity, however, we certainly do not mean to follow the "tragic" philosophers of Europe, from Schopenhauer to Heidegger, who turn these real destructions into metaphysical narratives about the negativity of being, as if these actual tragedies were merely an illusion, or rather as if they were our ultimate destiny! Modern negativity is located not in any transcendent realm but in the hard reality before us: the fields of patriotic battles in the First and Second World Wars, from the killing fields at Verdun to the Nazi furnaces and the swift annihilation of thousands in Hiroshima and Nagasaki, the carpet bombing of Vietnam and Cambodia, the massacres from Sétif and Soweto to Sabra and Shatila, and the list goes on and on. There is no Job who can sustain such suffering! (And anyone who starts compiling such a list quickly realizes how inadequate it is to the quantity and quality of the tragedies.) Well, if *that* modernity has come to an end, and if the modern nation-state that served as the ineluctable condition for imperialist domination and innumerable wars is disappearing from the world scene, then good riddance!

We must cleanse ourselves of any misplaced nostalgia for the belle époque of that modernity.

We cannot be satisfied, however, with that political condemnation of modern power that relies on the *historia rerum gestarum,* the objective history we have inherited. We need to consider also the power of the *res gestae,* the power of the multitude to make history that continues and is reconfigured today *within* Empire. It is a question of transforming a necessity imposed on the multitude—a necessity that was to a certain extent solicited by the multitude itself throughout modernity as a line of flight from localized misery and exploitation—into a condition of possibility of liberation, a new possibility on this new terrain of humanity.

This is when the ontological drama begins, when the curtain goes up on a scene in which the development of Empire becomes its own critique and its process of construction becomes the process of its overturning. This drama is ontological in the sense that here, in these processes, being is produced and reproduced. This drama will have to be clarified and articulated much further as our study proceeds, but we should insist right from the outset that this is not simply another variant of dialectical enlightenment. We are not proposing the umpteenth version of the inevitable passage through purgatory (here in the guise of the new imperial machine) in order to offer a glimmer of hope for radiant futures. We are not repeating the schema of an ideal teleology that justifies any passage in the name of a promised end. On the contrary, our reasoning here is based on two methodological approaches that are intended to be nondialectical and absolutely immanent: the first is *critical and deconstructive,* aiming to subvert the hegemonic languages and social structures and thereby reveal an alternative ontological basis that resides in the creative and productive practices of the multitude; the second is *constructive and ethico-political,* seeking to lead the processes of the production of subjectivity toward the constitution of an effective social, political alternative, a new constituent power.[6]

Our critical approach addresses the need for a real ideological and material deconstruction of the imperial order. In the postmodern world, the ruling spectacle of Empire is constructed through a variety of self-legitimating discourses and structures. Long ago authors as diverse as Lenin, Horkheimer and Adorno, and Debord recognized this spectacle as the destiny of triumphant capitalism. Despite their important differences, such authors offer us real anticipations of the path of capitalist development.[7] Our deconstruction of this spectacle cannot be textual alone, but must seek continually to focus its powers on the nature of events and the real determinations of the imperial processes in motion today. The critical approach is thus intended to bring to light the contradictions, cycles, and crises of the process because in each of these moments the imagined necessity of the historical development can open toward alternative possibilities. In other words, the deconstruction of the *historia rerum gestarum,* of the spectral reign of globalized capitalism, reveals the possibility of alternative social organizations. This is perhaps as far as we can go with the methodological scaffolding of a critical and materialist deconstructionism—but this is already an enormous contribution![8]

This is where the first methodological approach has to pass the baton to the second, the constructive and ethico-political approach. Here we must delve into the ontological substrate of the concrete alternatives continually pushed forward by the *res gestae,* the subjective forces acting in the historical context. What appears here is not a new rationality but a new scenario of different rational acts—a horizon of activities, resistances, wills, and desires that refuse the hegemonic order, propose lines of flight, and forge alternative constitutive itineraries. This real substrate, open to critique, revised by the ethico-political approach, represents the real ontological referent of philosophy, or really the field proper to a philosophy of liberation. This approach breaks methodologically with every philosophy of history insofar as it refuses any deterministic conception of historical development and any "rational" celebration of the result. It demonstrates, on the contrary, how the historical event resides in potentiality. "It is not the two that recompose in one, but the one that opens into two," according to the beautiful anti-Confucian (and anti-Platonic) formula of the Chinese revolutionaries.[9] Philosophy is not the owl of Minerva that takes flight after history has been realized in order to celebrate its happy ending; rather, philosophy is subjective proposition, desire, and praxis that are applied to the event.

Refrains of the "Internationale"

There was a time, not so long ago, when internationalism was a key component of proletarian struggles and progressive politics in general. "The proletariat has no country," or better, "the country of the proletariat is the entire world." The "Internationale" was the hymn of revolutionaries, the song of utopian futures. We should note that the utopia expressed in these slogans is in fact not really internationalist, if by internationalist we understand a kind of consensus among the various national identities that preserves their differences but negotiates some limited agreement. Rather, proletarian internationalism was antinationalist, and hence supranational and global. Workers of the world unite!—not on the basis of national identities but directly through common needs and desires, without regard to borders and boundaries.

Internationalism was the will of an active mass subject that recognized that the nation-states were key agents of capitalist exploitation and that the multitude was continually drafted to fight their senseless wars—in short, that the nation-state was a political form whose contradictions could not be subsumed and sublimated but only destroyed. International solidarity was really a project for the destruction of the nation-state and the construction of a new global community. This proletarian program stood behind the often ambiguous tactical definitions that socialist and communist parties produced during the century of their hegemony over the proletariat.[10] If the nation-state was a central link in the chain of domination and thus had to be destroyed, then the *national* proletariat had as a primary task destroying itself insofar as it was defined by the nation and thus bringing international solidarity out of the prison in which it had been trapped. International solidarity had to be recognized not as an act of charity or altruism for the good of others, a noble sacrifice for another national working class, but rather as proper to and inseparable from each national proletariat's own desire and struggle for liberation. Proletarian internationalism constructed a paradoxical and powerful political machine that pushed continually beyond the boundaries and hierarchies of the nation-states and posed utopian futures only on the global terrain.

Today we should all clearly recognize that the time of such proletarian internationalism is over. That does not negate the fact, however, that the concept of internationalism really lived among the masses and deposited a kind of geological stratum of suffering and desire, a memory of victories and defeats, a residue of ideological tensions and needs. Furthermore, the proletariat does in fact find itself today not just international but (at least tendentially) global. One might be tempted to say that proletarian internationalism actually "won" in light of the fact that the powers of nation-states have declined in the recent passage toward globalization and Empire, but that would be a strange and ironic notion of victory. It is more accurate to say, following the William Morris quotation that serves as one of the epigraphs for this book, that what they fought for came about despite their defeat.

The practice of proletarian internationalism was expressed most clearly in the international cycles of struggles. In this framework the (national) general strike and insurrection against the (nation-) state were only really conceivable as elements of communication among struggles and processes of liberation on the internationalist terrain. From Berlin to Moscow, from Paris to New Delhi, from Algiers to Hanoi, from Shanghai to Jakarta, from Havana to New York, struggles resonated with one another throughout the nineteenth and twentieth centuries. A cycle was constructed as news of a revolt was communicated and applied in each new context, just as in an earlier era merchant ships carried the news of slave revolt from island to island around the Caribbean, igniting a stubborn string of fires that could not be quenched. For a cycle to form, the recipients of the news must be able to "translate" the events into their own language, recognize the struggles as their own, and thus add a link to the chain. In some cases this "translation" is rather elaborate: how Chinese intellectuals at the turn of the twentieth century, for example, could hear of the anticolonial struggles in the Philippines and Cuba and translate them into the terms of their own revolutionary projects. In other cases it is much more direct: how the factory council movement in Turin, Italy, was immediately inspired by the news of the Bolshevik victory in Russia. Rather than thinking of the struggles as relating to one another like links in a chain, it might be better to conceive of them as communicating like a virus that modulates its form to find in each context an adequate host.

It would not be hard to map the periods of extreme intensity of these cycles. A first wave might be seen as beginning after 1848 with the political agitation of the First International, continuing in the 1880s and 1890s with the formation of socialist political and trade union organizations, and then rising to a peak after the Russian revolution of 1905 and the first international cycle of anti-imperialist struggles.[11] A second wave arose after the Soviet revolution of 1917, which was followed by an international progression of struggles that could only be contained by fascisms on one side and reabsorbed by the New Deal and antifascist fronts on the other. And finally there was the wave of struggles that began with the Chinese revolution and proceeded through the African and Latin American liberation struggles to the explosions of the 1960s throughout the world.

These international cycles of struggles were the real motor that drove the development of the institutions of capital and that drove it in a process of reform and restructuring.[12] Proletarian, anticolonial, and anti-imperialist internationalism, the struggle for communism, which lived in all the most powerful insurrectional events of the nineteenth and twentieth centuries, anticipated and prefigured the processes of the globalization of capital and the formation of Empire. In this way the formation of Empire is a *response* to proletarian internationalism. There is nothing dialectical or teleological about this anticipation and prefiguration of capitalist development by the mass struggles. On the contrary, the struggles themselves are demonstrations of the creativity of desire, utopias of lived experience, the workings of historicity as potentiality—in short, the struggles are the naked reality of the *res gestae*. A teleology of sorts is constructed only after the fact, *post festum*.

The struggles that preceded and prefigured globalization were expressions of the force of living labor, which sought to liberate itself from the rigid territorializing regimes imposed on it. As it contests the dead labor accumulated against it, living labor always seeks to break the fixed territorializing structures, the national organizations, and the political figures that keep it prisoner. With the force of living labor, its restless activity, and its deterritorializing desire, this process of rupture throws open all the windows of history. When one adopts the perspective of the activity of the multitude, its production of subjectivity and desire, one can recognize how globalization, insofar as it operates a real deterritorialization of the previous structures of exploitation and control, is really a condition of the liberation of the multitude. But how can this potential for liberation be realized today? Does that same uncontainable desire for freedom that broke and buried the nation-state and that determined the transition toward Empire still live beneath the ashes of the present, the ashes of the fire that consumed the internationalist proletarian subject that was centered on the industrial working class? What has come to stand in the place of that subject? In what sense can we say that the ontological rooting of a new multitude has come to be a positive or alternative actor in the articulation of globalization?

The Mole and the Snake

We need to recognize that the very subject of labor and revolt has changed profoundly. The composition of the proletariat has transformed and thus our understanding of it must too. In conceptual terms we understand *proletariat* as a broad category that includes all those whose labor is directly or indirectly exploited by and subjected to capitalist norms of production and reproduction.[13] In a previous era the category of the proletariat centered on and was at times effectively subsumed under the *industrial working class,* whose paradigmatic figure was the male mass factory worker. That industrial working class was often accorded the leading role over other figures of labor (such as peasant labor and reproductive labor) in both economic analyses and political movements. Today that working class has all but disappeared from view. It has not ceased to exist, but it has been displaced from its privileged position in the capitalist economy and its hegemonic position in the class composition of the proletariat. The proletariat is not what it used to be, but that does not mean it has vanished. It means, rather, that we are faced once again with the analytical task of understanding the new composition of the proletariat as a class.

The fact that under the category of proletariat we understand *all* those exploited by and subject to capitalist domination should not indicate that the proletariat is a homogeneous or undifferentiated unit. It is indeed cut through in various directions by differences and stratifications. Some labor is waged, some is not; some labor is restricted to within the factory walls, some is dispersed across the unbounded social terrain; some labor is limited to eight hours a day and forty hours a week, some expands to fill the entire time of life; some labor is accorded a minimal value, some is exalted to the pinnacle of the capitalist economy. We will argue (in Section 3.4) that among the various figures of production active today, the figure of immaterial labor power (involved in communication, cooperation, and the production and reproduction of affects) occupies an increasingly central position in both the schema of capitalist production and the composition of the proletariat. Our point here is that all of these diverse forms of labor are in some way subject to capitalist discipline and capitalist relations of production. This fact of being within capital and sustaining capital is what defines the proletariat as a class.

We need to look more concretely at the form of the struggles in which this new proletariat expresses its desires and needs. In the last half-century, and in particular in the two decades that stretched from 1968 to the fall of the Berlin Wall, the restructuring and global expansion of capitalist production have been accompanied by a transformation of proletarian struggles. As we said, the figure of an international cycle of struggles based on the communication and translation of the common desires of labor in revolt seems no longer to exist. The fact that the cycle as the specific form of the assemblage of struggles has vanished, however, does not simply open up to an abyss. On the contrary, we can recognize powerful events on the world scene that reveal the trace of the multitude's refusal of exploitation and that signal a new kind of proletarian solidarity and militancy.

Consider the most radical and powerful struggles of the final years of the twentieth century: the Tiananmen Square events in 1989, the Intifada against Israeli state authority, the May 1992 revolt in Los Angeles, the uprising in Chiapas that began in 1994, and the series of strikes that paralyzed France in December 1995, and those that crippled South Korea in 1996. Each of these struggles was specific and based on immediate regional concerns in such a way that they could in no respect be linked together as a globally expanding chain of revolt. None of these events inspired a cycle of struggles, because the desires and needs they expressed could not be translated into different contexts. In other words, (potential) revolutionaries in other parts of the world did not hear of the events in Beijing, Nablus, Los Angeles, Chiapas, Paris, or Seoul and immediately recognize them as their own struggles. Furthermore, these struggles not only fail to communicate to other contexts but also lack even a local communication, and thus often have a very brief duration where they are born, burning out in a flash. This is certainly one of the central and most urgent political paradoxes of our time: in our much celebrated age of communication, *struggles have become all but incommunicable.*

This paradox of incommunicability makes it extremely difficult to grasp and express the new power posed by the struggles that have emerged. We ought to be able to recognize that what the struggles have lost in extension, duration, and communicability they have gained in intensity. We ought to be able to recognize that although all of these struggles focused on their own local and immediate circumstances, they all nonetheless posed problems of supranational relevance, problems that are proper to the new figure of imperial capitalist regulation. In Los Angeles, for example, the riots were fueled by local racial antagonisms and patterns of social and economic exclusion that are in many respects particular to that (post-)urban territory, but the events were also immediately catapulted to a general level insofar as they expressed a refusal of the post-Fordist regime of social control. Like the Intifada in certain respects, the Los Angeles riots demonstrated how the decline of Fordist bargaining regimes and mechanisms of social mediation has made the management of racially and socially diverse metropolitan territories and populations so precarious. The looting of commodities and burning of property were not just metaphors but the real global condition of the mobility and volatility of post-Fordist social mediations.[14] In Chiapas, too, the insurrection focused primarily on local concerns: problems of exclusion and lack of representation specific to Mexican society and the Mexican state, which have also to a limited degree long been common to the racial hierarchies throughout much of Latin American. The Zapatista rebellion, however, was also immediately a struggle against the social regime imposed by NAFTA and more generally the systematic exclusion and subordination in the regional construction of the world market.[15] Finally, like those in Seoul, the massive strikes in Paris and throughout France in late 1995 were aimed at specific local and national labor issues (such as pensions, wages, and unemployment), but the struggle was also immediately recognized as a clear contestation of the new social and economic construction of Europe. The French strikes called above all for a new notion of the public, a new construction of public space against the neoliberal mechanisms of privatization that accompany more or less everywhere the project of capitalist globalization.[16] Perhaps precisely because all these struggles are incommunicable and thus blocked from traveling horizontally in the form of a cycle, they are forced instead to leap vertically and touch immediately on the global level.

We ought to be able to recognize that this is not the appearance of a new cycle of internationalist struggles, but rather the emergence of a new quality of social movements. We ought to be able to recognize, in other words, the fundamentally new characteristics these struggles all present, despite their radical diversity. First, each struggle, though firmly rooted in local conditions, leaps immediately to the global level and attacks the imperial constitution in its generality. Second, all the struggles destroy the traditional distinction between economic and political struggles. The struggles are at once economic, political, and cultural—and hence they are biopolitical struggles, struggles over the form of life. They are constituent struggles, creating new public spaces and new forms of community.

We ought to be able to recognize all this, but it is not that easy. We must admit, in fact, that even when trying to individuate the real novelty of these situations, we are hampered by the nagging impression that these struggles are always already old, outdated, and anachronistic. The struggles at Tiananmen Square spoke a language of democracy that seemed long out of fashion; the guitars, headbands, tents, and slogans all looked like a weak echo of Berkeley in the 1960s. The Los Angeles riots, too, seemed like an aftershock of the earthquake of racial conflicts that shook the United States in the 1960s. The strikes in Paris and Seoul seemed to take us back to the era of the mass factory worker, as if they were the last gasp of a dying working class. All these struggles, which pose really new elements, appear from the beginning to be already old and outdated—precisely because they cannot communicate, because their languages cannot be translated. The struggles do not communicate despite their being hypermediatized, on television, the Internet, and every other imaginable medium. Once again we are confronted by the paradox of incommunicability.

We can certainly recognize real obstacles that block the communication of struggles. One such obstacle is the absence of a recognition of a common enemy against which the struggles are directed. Beijing, Los Angeles, Nablus, Chiapas, Paris, Seoul: the situations all seem utterly particular, but in fact they all directly attack the global order of Empire and seek a real alternative. Clarifying the nature of the common enemy is thus an essential political task. A second obstacle, which is really corollary to the first, is that there is no common language of struggles that could "translate" the particular language of each into a cosmopolitan language. Struggles in other parts of the world and even our own struggles seem to be written in an incomprehensible foreign language. This too points toward an important political task: to construct a new common language that facilitates communication, as the languages of anti-imperialism and proletarian internationalism did for the struggles of a previous era. Perhaps this needs to be a new type of communication that functions not on the basis of resemblances but on the basis of differences: a communication of singularities.

Recognizing a common enemy and inventing a common language of struggles are certainly important political tasks, and we will advance them as far as we can in this book, but our intuition tells us that this line of analysis finally fails to grasp the real potential presented by the new struggles. Our intuition tells us, in other words, that the model of the horizontal articulation of struggles in a cycle is no longer adequate for recognizing the way in which contemporary struggles achieve global significance. Such a model in fact blinds us to their real new potential.

Marx tried to understand the continuity of the cycle of proletarian struggles that were emerging in nineteenth-century Europe in terms of a mole and its subterranean tunnels. Marx's mole would surface in times of open class conflict and then retreat underground again—not to hibernate passively but to burrow its tunnels, moving along with the times, pushing forward with history so that when the time was right (1830, 1848, 1870), it would spring to the surface again. "Well grubbed old mole!"[17] Well, we suspect that Marx's old mole has finally died. It seems to us, in fact, that in the contemporary passage to Empire, the structured tunnels of the mole have been replaced by the infinite undulations of the snake.[18] The depths of the modern world and its subterranean passageways have in postmodernity all become superficial. Today's struggles slither silently across these superficial, imperial landscapes. Perhaps the incommunicability of struggles, the lack of well-structured, communicating tunnels, is in fact a strength rather than a weakness—a strength because all of the movements are immediately subversive in themselves and do not wait on any sort of external aid or extension to guarantee their effectiveness. Perhaps the more capital extends its global networks of production and control, the more powerful any singular point of revolt can be. Simply by focusing their own powers, concentrating their energies in a tense and compact coil, these serpentine struggles strike directly at the highest articulations of imperial order. Empire presents a superficial world, the virtual center of which can be accessed immediately from any point across the surface. If these points were to constitute something like a new cycle of struggles, it would be a cycle defined not by the communicative extension of the struggles but rather by their singular emergence, by the intensity that characterizes them one by one. In short, this new phase is defined by the fact that these struggles do not link horizontally, but each one leaps vertically, directly to the virtual center of Empire.

From the point of view of the revolutionary tradition, one might object that the tactical successes of revolutionary actions in the nineteenth and twentieth centuries were all characterized precisely by the capacity to blast open the *weakest link* of the imperialist chain, that this is the ABC of revolutionary dialectics, and thus it would seem today that the situation is not very promising. It is certainly true that the serpentine struggles we are witnessing today do not provide any clear revolutionary tactics, or maybe they are completely incomprehensible from the point of view of tactics. Faced as we are with a series of intense subversive social movements that attack the highest levels of imperial organization, however, it may be no longer useful to insist on the old distinction between strategy and tactics. In the constitution of Empire there is no longer an "outside" to power and thus no longer weak links—if by weak link we mean an external point where the articulations of global power are vulnerable.[19] To achieve significance, every struggle must attack at the heart of Empire, at its strength. That fact, however, does not give priority to any geographical regions, as if only social movements in Washington, Geneva, or Tokyo could attack the heart of Empire. On the contrary, the construction of Empire, and the globalization of economic and cultural relationships, means that the virtual center of Empire can be attacked from any point. The tactical preoccupations of the old revolutionary school are thus completely irretrievable; the only strategy available to the struggles is that of a constituent counterpower that emerges from within Empire.

Those who have difficulty accepting the novelty and revolutionary potential of this situation from the perspective of the struggles themselves might recognize it more easily from the perspective of imperial power, which is constrained to react to the struggles. Even when these struggles become sites effectively closed to communication, they are at the same time the maniacal focus of the critical attention of Empire.[20] They are educational lessons in the classroom of administration and the chambers of government—lessons that demand repressive instruments. The primary lesson is that such events cannot be repeated if the processes of capitalist globalization are to continue. These struggles, however, have their own weight, their own specific intensity, and moreover they are immanent to the procedures and developments of imperial power. They invest and sustain the processes of globalization themselves. Imperial power whispers the names of the struggles in order to charm them into passivity, to construct a mystified image of them, but most important to discover which processes of globalization are possible and which are not. In this contradictory and paradoxical way the imperial processes of globalization assume these events, recognizing them as both limits and opportunities to recalibrate Empire's own instruments. The processes of globalization would not exist or would come to a halt if they were not continually both frustrated and driven by these explosions of the multitude that touch immediately on the highest levels of imperial power.

Two-Headed Eagle

The emblem of the Austro-Hungarian Empire, an eagle with two heads, might give an adequate initial representation of the contemporary form of Empire. But whereas in the earlier emblem the two heads looked outward to designate the relative autonomy and peaceful coexistence of the respective territories, in our case the two heads would have to be turned inward, each attacking the other.

The first head of the imperial eagle is a juridical structure and a constituted power, constructed by the machine of biopolitical command. The juridical process and the imperial machine are always subject to contradictions and crises. Order and peace—the eminent values that Empire proposes—can never be achieved but are nonetheless continually reproposed. The juridical process of the constitution of Empire lives this constant crisis that is considered (at least by the most attentive theoreticians) the price of its own development. There is, however, always a surplus. Empire's continual extension and constant pressure to adhere ever more closely to the complexity and depth of the biopolitical realm force the imperial machine when it seems to resolve one conflict continually to open others. It tries to make them commensurate with its project, but they emerge once again as incommensurable, with all the elements of the new terrain mobile in space and flexible in time.

The other head of the imperial eagle is the plural multitude of productive, creative subjectivities of globalization that have learned to sail on this enormous sea. They are in perpetual motion and they form constellations of singularities and events that impose continual global reconfigurations on the system. This perpetual motion can be geographical, but it can refer also to modulations of form and processes of mixture and hybridization. The relationship between "system" and "asystemic movements" cannot be flattened onto any logic of correspondence in this perpetually modulating atopia.[21] Even the asystemic elements produced by the new multitude are in fact global forces that cannot have a commensurate relationship, even an inverted one, with the system. Every insurrectional event that erupts within the order of the imperial system provokes a shock to the system in its entirety. From this perspective, the institutional frame in which we live is characterized by its radical contingency and precariousness, or really by the unforeseeability of the *sequences of events*—sequences that are always more brief or more compact temporally and thus ever less controllable.[22] It becomes ever more difficult for Empire to intervene in the unforeseeable temporal sequences of events when they accelerate their temporality. The most relevant aspect that the struggles have demonstrated may be sudden accelerations, often cumulative, that can become virtually simultaneous, explosions that reveal a properly ontological power and unforeseeable attack on the most central equilibria of Empire.

Just as Empire in the spectacle of its force continually determines systemic recompositions, so too new figures of resistance are composed through the sequences of the events of struggle. This is another fundamental characteristic of the existence of the multitude today, *within* Empire and *against* Empire. New figures of struggle and new subjectivities are produced in the conjuncture of events, in the universal nomadism, in the general mixture and miscegenation of individuals and populations, and in the technological metamorphoses of the imperial biopolitical machine. These new figures and subjectivities are produced because, although the struggles are indeed antisystemic, they are not posed *merely against* the imperial system—they are not simply negative forces. They also express, nourish, and develop positively their own constituent projects; they work toward the liberation of living labor, creating constellations of powerful singularities. This constituent aspect of the movement of the multitude, in its myriad faces, is really the positive terrain of the historical construction of Empire. This is not a historicist positivity but, on the contrary, a positivity of the *res gestae* of the multitude, an antagonistic and creative positivity. The deterritorializing power of the multitude is the productive force that sustains Empire and at the same time the force that calls for and makes necessary its destruction.

At this point, however, we should recognize that our metaphor breaks down and that the two-headed eagle is not really an adequate representation of the relationship between Empire and the multitude, because it poses the two on the same level and thus does not recognize the real hierarchies and discontinuities that define their relationship. From one perspective Empire stands clearly over the multitude and subjects it to the rule of its overarching machine, as a new Leviathan. At the same time, however, from the perspective of social productivity and creativity, from what we have been calling the ontological perspective, the hierarchy is reversed. The multitude is the real productive force of our social world, whereas Empire is a mere apparatus of capture that lives only off the vitality of the multitude—as Marx would say, a vampire regime of accumulated dead labor that survives only by sucking off the blood of the living.

Once we adopt this ontological standpoint, we can return to the juridical framework we investigated earlier and recognize the reasons for the real deficit that plagues the transition from international public law to the new public law of Empire, that is, the new conception of right that defines Empire. In other words, the frustration and the continual instability suffered by imperial right as it attempts to destroy the old values that served as reference points for international public law (the nation-states, the international order of Westphalia, the United Nations, and so forth) along with the so-called turbulence that accompanies this process are all symptoms of a properly *ontological* lack. As it constructs its supranational figure, power seems to be deprived of any real ground beneath it, or rather, it is lacking the motor that propels its movement. The rule of the biopolitical imperial context should thus be seen in the first instance as an empty machine, a spectacular machine, a parasitical machine.

A new sense of being is imposed on the constitution of Empire by the creative movement of the multitude, or really it is continually present in this process as an alternative paradigm. It is internal to Empire and pushes forward its constitution, not as a negative that constructs a positive or any such dialectical resolution. Rather it acts as an absolutely positive force that pushes the dominating power toward an abstract and empty unification, to which it appears as the distinct alternative. From this perspective, when the constituted power of Empire appears merely as privation of being and production, as a simple abstract and empty trace of the constituent power of the multitude, then we will be able to recognize the real standpoint of our analysis. It is a standpoint that is both strategic and tactical, when the two are no longer different.

Political Manifesto

In an extraordinary text written during his period of seclusion, Louis Althusser reads Machiavelli and poses the quite reasonable question whether The Prince *should be considered a revolutionary political manifesto.*[1] *In order to address this question Althusser first tries to define the "manifesto form" as a specific genre of text by comparing the characteristics of* The Prince *with those of the paradigmatic political manifesto, Marx and Engels's* Manifesto of the Communist Party. *He finds between these two documents an undeniable structural resemblance. In both texts the form of the argument consists of "a completely specific apparatus [dispositif] that establishes particular relationships between the discourse and its 'object' and between the discourse and its 'subject'" (p. 55). In each case the political discourse is born from the productive relationship between the subject and the object, from the fact that this relationship is itself the very point of view of the* res gestae, *a self-constituting collective action aimed at its objective. In short, clearly outside of the tradition of political science (either in its classical form, which was really the analysis of the forms of government, or in its contemporary form, which amounts to a science of management), the manifestos of Machiavelli and Marx-Engels define the political as the movement of the multitude and they define the goal as the self-production of the subject. Here we have a materialist teleology.*

Despite that important similarity, Althusser continues, the differences between the two manifestos are significant. The primary difference consists in the fact that, whereas in the Marx-Engels text the subject that defines the standpoint of the text (the modern proletariat) and the object (the communist party and communism) are conceived as co-present in such a way that the growing organization of the former directly entails the creation of the latter, in the Machiavellian project there is an ineluctable distance between the subject (the multitude) and the object (the Prince and the free state). This distance leads Machiavelli in The Prince *to search for a democratic apparatus capable of linking subject to object. In other words, whereas the Marx-Engels manifesto traces a linear and necessary causality, the Machiavellian text poses rather a project and a utopia. Althusser recognizes finally that both texts effectively bring the theoretical proposal to the level of praxis; both assume the present as empty for the future, "vide pour le futur" (p. 62), and in this open space they establish an immanent act of the subject that constitutes a new position of being.*

Is this choice of the field of immanence, however, enough to define a manifesto form that would be a mode of political discourse adequate to the insurgent subject of postmodernity? The postmodern situation is eminently paradoxical when it is considered from the biopolitical point of view—understood, that is, as an uninterrupted circuit of life, production, and politics, globally dominated by the capitalist mode of production. On the one hand, in this situation all the forces of society tend to be activated as productive forces; but on the other hand, these same forces are submitted to a global domination that is continually more abstract and thus blind to the sense of the apparatuses of the reproduction of life. In postmodernity, the "end of history" is effectively imposed, but in such a way that at the same time paradoxically all the powers of humanity are called on to contribute to the global reproduction of labor, society, and life. In this framework, politics (when this is understood as administration and management) loses all its transparency. Through its institutional processes of normalization, power hides rather than reveals and interprets the relationships that characterize its control over society and life.

How can a revolutionary political discourse be reactivated in this situation? How can it gain a new consistency and fill some eventual manifesto with a new materialist teleology? How can we construct an apparatus for bringing together the subject (the multitude) and the object (cosmopolitical liberation) within postmodernity? Clearly one cannot achieve this, even when assuming entirely the argument of the field of immanence, simply by following the indications offered by the Marx-Engels manifesto. In the cold placidness of postmodernity, what Marx and Engels saw as the co-presence of the productive subject and the process of liberation is utterly inconceivable. And yet, from our postmodern perspective the terms of the Machiavellian manifesto seem to acquire a new contemporaneity. Straining the analogy with Machiavelli a little, we could pose the problem in this way: How can productive labor dispersed in various networks find a center? How can the material and immaterial production of the brains and bodies of the many construct a common sense and direction, or rather, how can the endeavor to bridge the distance between the formation of the multitude as subject and the constitution of a democratic political apparatus find its prince?

This analogy, however, is finally insufficient. There remains in Machiavelli's prince a utopian condition that distances the project from the subject and that, despite the radical immanence of the method, confides the political function to a higher plane. In contrast, any postmodern liberation must be achieved within this world, on the plane of immanence, with no possibility of any even utopian outside. The form in which the political should be expressed as subjectivity today is not at all clear. A solution to this problem would have to weave closer together the subject and the object of the project, pose them in a relationship of immanence still more profound than that achieved by Machiavelli or Marx-Engels, in other words, pose them in a process of self-production.

Perhaps we need to reinvent the notion of the materialist teleology that Spinoza proclaimed at the dawn of modernity when he claimed that the prophet produces its own people.[2] *Perhaps along with Spinoza we should recognize prophetic desire as irresistible, and all the more powerful the more it becomes identified with the multitude. It is not at all clear that this prophetic function can effectively address our political needs and sustain a potential manifesto of the postmodern revolution against Empire, but certain analogies and paradoxical coincidences do seem striking. For example, whereas Machiavelli proposes that the project of constructing a new society from below requires "arms" and "money" and insists that we must look for them outside, Spinoza responds: Don't we already posses them? Don't the necessary weapons reside precisely within the creative and prophetic power of the multitude? Perhaps we, too, locating ourselves within the revolutionary desire of postmodernity, can in turn respond: Don't we already possess "arms" and "money"? The kind of money that Machiavelli insists is necessary may in fact reside in the productivity of the multitude, the immediate actor of biopolitical production and reproduction. The kind of arms in question may be contained in the potential of the multitude to sabotage and destroy with its own productive force the parasitical order of postmodern command.*

Today a manifesto, a political discourse, should aspire to fulfill a Spinozist prophetic function, the function of an immanent desire that organizes the multitude. There is not finally here any determinism or utopia: this is rather a radical counterpower, ontologically grounded not on any "vide pour le futur" but on the actual activity of the multitude, its creation, production, and power—a materialist teleology.

PART 2

PASSAGES OF SOVEREIGNTY

2.1

TWO EUROPES, TWO MODERNITIES

> Whether you affirm infallibility and deduce sovereignty from it or pose sovereignty first and derive infallibility from that, you are forced either way to recognize and sanction an absolute power. And the same result is imposed whether it be through oppression of governments or the reason of philosophers, whether you make the people or the king sovereign.
>
> François Guizot

In the early twentieth-century Vienna of Robert Musil's novel *The Man without Qualities,* an enlightened aristocrat, Count Leinsdorf, puzzles out the complexities of modernity but gets stuck on a central paradox. "What I still don't understand," he says, "is this: That people should love each other, and that it takes a firm hand in government to make them do it, is nothing new. So why should it suddenly be a case of either/or?"[1] For the philanthropists of Musil's world there is a conflict at the center of modernity between, on the one hand, the immanent forces of desire and association, the love of the community, and on the other, the strong hand of an overarching authority that imposes and enforces an order on the social field. This tension was to be resolved, or at least mediated, by the sovereignty of the state, and yet it continually resurfaces as a question of either/or: freedom or servitude, the liberation of desire or its subjugation. Count Leinsdorf lucidly identifies a contradiction that runs throughout European modernity and resides at the heart of the modern concept of sovereignty.

Tracing the emerging figure of the concept of sovereignty through various developments in modern European philosophy should allow us to recognize that Europe and modernity are neither unitary nor pacific constructions, but rather from the beginning were characterized by struggle, conflict, and crisis. We identify three moments in the constitution of European modernity that articulate the initial figure of the modern concept of sovereignty: first, the revolutionary discovery of the plane of immanence; second, the reaction against these immanent forces and the crisis in the form of authority; and third, the partial and temporary resolution of this crisis in the formation of the modern state as a locus of sovereignty that transcends and mediates the plane of immanent forces. In this progression European modernity itself becomes increasingly inseparable from the principle of sovereignty. And yet, as Count Leinsdorf laments, even at the height of modernity the original tension continually breaks through in all its violence.

Modern sovereignty is a European concept in the sense that it developed primarily in Europe in coordination with the evolution of modernity itself. The concept functioned as the cornerstone of the construction of Eurocentrism. Although modern sovereignty emanated from Europe, however, it was born and developed in large part through Europe's relationship with its outside, and particularly through its colonial project and the resistance of the colonized. Modern sovereignty emerged, then, as the concept of European reaction and European domination both within and outside its borders. They are two coextensive and complementary faces of one development: rule within Europe and European rule over the world.

The Revolutionary Plane of Immanence

It all began with a revolution. In Europe, between 1200 and 1600, across distances that only merchants and armies could travel and only the invention of the printing press would later bring together, something extraordinary happened. Humans declared themselves masters of their own lives, producers of cities and history, and inventors of heavens. They inherited a dualistic consciousness, a hierarchical vision of society, and a metaphysical idea of science; but they handed down to future generations an experimental idea of science, a constituent conception of history and cities, and they posed being as an immanent terrain of knowledge and action. The thought of this initial period, born simultaneously in politics, science, art, philosophy, and theology, demonstrates the radicality of the forces at work in modernity.

The origins of European modernity are often characterized as springing from a secularizing process that denied divine and transcendent authority over worldly affairs. That process was certainly important, but in our view it was really only a symptom of the primary event of modernity: the affirmation of the powers of *this* world, the discovery of the plane of immanence. "Omne ens habet aliquod esse proprium"—every entity has a singular essence.[2] Duns Scotus' affirmation subverts the medieval conception of being as an object of analogical, and thus dualistic, predication—a being with one foot in this world and one in a transcendent realm. We are at the beginning of the fourteenth century, in the midst of the convulsions of the late Middle Ages. Duns Scotus tells his contemporaries that the confusion and decadence of the times can be remedied only by recentering thought on the singularity of being. This singularity is not ephemeral nor accidental but ontological. The strength of this affirmation and the effect it had on the thought of the period were demonstrated by Dante Alighieri's response to it, thousands of miles away from Duns Scotus' Britannic north. This singular being is powerful, Dante wrote, in that it is the drive to actualize "totam potentiam intellectus possibilis"—all the power of the possible intellect.[3] At the scene of the birth of European modernity, humanity discovered its power in the world and integrated this dignity into a new consciousness of reason and potentiality.

In the fifteenth century, numerous authors demonstrated the coherence and revolutionary originality of this new immanent ontological knowledge. Let us simply cite three representative voices. First, Nicholas of Cusa: "Speculation is a movement of the intellect from *quia est* to *quid est;* and since *quid est* is infinitely distant from *quia est,* such a movement will never come to an end. And it is a very pleasurable movement, since it is the life itself of the intellect; from this fact such movement finds its satisfaction, since its motion does not generate fatigue but rather light and heat."[4] Second, Pico della Mirandola: "When you conceive of God as a living and knowing being, make sure before all else that this knowledge and this life are understood as free from every imperfection. Conceive of a knowledge that knows all and everything in a most perfect manner; and add still that the knower knows all by itself, so there is no need to search outside itself, which would make it imperfect."[5] In this way Pico della Mirandola, rather than conceiving a distant, transcendent God, makes the human mind into a divine machine of knowledge. Finally, Bovillus: "The one who was by nature merely human [*homo*] becomes, through the rich contribution of art, doubly human, that is, *homohomo*."[6] Through its own powerful arts and practices, humanity enriches and doubles itself, or really raises itself to a higher power: *homohomo,* humanity squared.

In those origins of modernity, then, knowledge shifted from the transcendent plane to the immanent, and consequently, that human knowledge became a doing, a practice of transforming nature. Sir Francis Bacon constructed a world in which "what has been discovered in the arts and the sciences can now be reorganized through usage, meditation, observation, argumentation . . . because it is good to treat the most distant realities and the occult secrets of nature through the introduction of a better use and a more perfect technique of the mind and the intellect."[7] In this process, Galileo Galilei maintains (and this will conclude our circle *de dignitate hominis*), we have the possibility of equaling divine knowledge:

> Taking the understanding to be *intensive,* insofar as that term carries with it intensively, that is perfectly, several propositions, I say that the human intellect understands some things so perfectly and it has such absolute certainty of them that it equals nature's own understanding of them; those things include the pure mathematical sciences, that is, geometry and arithmetic,

> about which the divine intellect knows infinitely more propositions since it knows them all, but of those few understood by the human intellect I believe that its knowledge equals divine knowledge in its objective certainty.[8]

What is revolutionary in this whole series of philosophical developments stretching from the thirteenth to the sixteenth centuries is that the powers of creation that had previously been consigned exclusively to the heavens are now brought down to earth. This is the discovery of the fullness of the plane of immanence.

Just as in philosophy and science, in politics, too, humanity reappropriated in this early period of modernity what medieval transcendence had taken away from it. In the span of three or four centuries, the process of the refoundation of authority on the basis of a human universal and through the action of a multitude of singularities was accomplished with great force, amid dreadful tragedies and heroic conquests. William of Occam, for example, claimed that the church is the multitude of the faithful—"Ecclesia est multitudo fidelium"[9]—meaning that it is not superior to and distinct from the community of Christians but immanent to that community. Marsilius of Padua posed the same definition for the Republic: the power of the Republic and the power of its laws derive not from superior principles but from the assembly of citizens.[10] A new understanding of power and a new conception of liberation were set in motion: from Dante and the late medieval apologia of the "possible intellect" to Thomas More and the celebration of the "immense and inexplicable power" of natural life and labor as foundation for the political arrangement; from the democracy of the Protestant sects to Spinoza and his notion of the absoluteness of the democracy. By the time we arrive at Spinoza, in fact, the horizon of immanence and the horizon of the democratic political order coincide completely. The plane of immanence is the one on which the powers of singularity are realized and the one on which the truth of the new humanity is determined historically, technically, and politically. For this very fact, because there cannot be any external mediation, the singular is presented as the multitude.[11]

Modernity's beginnings were revolutionary, and the old order was toppled by them. The constitution of modernity was not about theory in isolation but about theoretical acts indissolubly tied to mutations of practice and reality. Bodies and brains were fundamentally transformed. This historical process of subjectivization was revolutionary in the sense that it determined a paradigmatic and irreversible change in the mode of life of the multitude.

Modernity as Crisis

Modernity is not a unitary concept but rather appears in at least two modes. The first mode is the one we have already defined, a radical revolutionary process. This modernity destroys its relations with the past and declares the immanence of the new paradigm of the world and life. It develops knowledge and action as scientific experimentation and defines a tendency toward a democratic politics, posing humanity and desire at the center of history. From the artisan to the astronomer, from the merchant to the politician, in art as in religion, the material of existence is reformed by a new life.

This new emergence, however, created a war. How could such a radical overturning not incite strong antagonism? How could this revolution not determine a counterrevolution? There was indeed a counterrevolution in the proper sense of the term: a cultural, philosophical, social, and political initiative that, since it could neither return to the past nor destroy the new forces, sought to dominate and expropriate the force of the emerging movements and dynamics. This is the second mode of modernity, constructed to wage war against the new forces and establish an overarching power to dominate them. It arose within the Renaissance revolution to divert its direction, transplant the new image of humanity to a transcendent plane, relativize the capacities of science to transform the world, and above all oppose the reappropriation of power on the part of the multitude. The second mode of modernity poses a transcendent constituted power against an immanent constituent power, order against desire. The Renaissance thus ended in war—religious, social, and civil war.

The European Renaissance, but above all the Italian Renaissance, with the splendid and perverse works that characterize it, was the site of the civil war over the realization of modernity. When the Reformation spread throughout Europe, it was like a second cyclone added to the first, repeating in the religious consciousness of the masses the alternatives of humanist culture. The civil war thus invested popular life and mingled with the most intimate recesses of human history. Class struggle moved across this terrain, marshaling up in the genesis of capitalism the creativity of the new mode of laboring and the new order of exploitation within a logic that carries together signs of both progress and reaction. It was a clash of titans, like the one Michelangelo depicted on the ceiling of the Sistine Chapel: the tragic conflict of the genesis of modernity.

The revolution of European modernity ran into its Thermidor. In the struggle for hegemony over the paradigm of modernity, victory went to the second mode and the forces of order that sought to neutralize the power of the revolution. Although it was not possible to go back to the way things were, it was nonetheless possible to reestablish ideologies of command and authority, and thus deploy a new transcendent power by playing on the anxiety and fear of the masses, their desire to reduce the uncertainty of life and increase security. The revolution had to be stopped. Throughout the sixteenth century, whenever the fruits of the revolution appeared in all their splendor, the scene had to be painted in twilight colors. The demand for peace became paramount—but which peace? While the Thirty Years' War in the heart of Europe exemplified in the most terrible forms the outlines of this irreversible crisis, the consciousnesses, even the strongest and wisest, yielded to the necessity of the Thermidor and the conditions of the miserable and humiliating peace. Peace was a value that in a short stretch of time had lost the humanist, Erasmian connotations that had previously made it the path of transformation. Peace had become the miserable condition of survival, the extreme urgency of escaping death. Peace was marked simply by the fatigue of the struggle and the usury of the passions. The Thermidor had won, the revolution was over.

The Thermidor of the revolution, however, did not close but only perpetuated the crisis. Civil war did not come to an end but was absorbed within the concept of modernity. *Modernity itself is defined by crisis,* a crisis that is born of the uninterrupted conflict between the immanent, constructive, creative forces and the transcendent power aimed at restoring order.[12] This conflict is the key to the concept of modernity, but it was effectively dominated and held in check. The cultural and religious revolutions were forced toward rigid and sometimes ferocious structures of containment. In the seventeenth century, Europe became feudal again. The counterreformist Catholic Church was the first and most effective example of this reaction, because that church itself earlier had been rocked by an earthquake of reform and revolutionary desire. The Protestant churches and political orders were not far behind in producing the order of the counterrevolution. Throughout Europe the fires of superstition were lit. And yet the movements of renewal continued their work of liberation at the base. Whereever spaces were closed, movements turned to nomadism and exodus, carrying with them the desire and hope of an irrepressible experience.[13]

The internal conflict of European modernity was also reflected simultaneously on a global scale as an external conflict. The development of Renaissance thought coincided both with the European discovery of the Americas and with the beginnings of European dominance over the rest of the world. Europe had discovered its outside. "If the period of the Renaissance marks a qualitative break in the history of humanity," writes Samir Amin, "it is precisely because, from that time on, Europeans become conscious of the idea that the conquest of the world by their civilization is henceforth a possible objective . . . From this moment on, and not before, Eurocentrism crystallizes."[14] On the one hand, Renaissance humanism initiated a revolutionary notion of human equality, of singularity and community, cooperation and multitude, that resonated with forces and desires extending horizontally across the globe, redoubled by the discovery of other populations and territories. On the other hand, however, the same counterrevolutionary power that sought to control the constituent and subversive forces within Europe also began to realize the possibility and necessity of subordinating other populations to European domination. Eurocentrism was born as a reaction to the potentiality of a newfound human equality; it was the counterrevolution on a global scale. Here too the second mode of modernity gained the upper hand, but again not in a definitive way. European modernity is from its beginnings a war on two fronts. European mastery is always in crisis—and this is the very same crisis that defines European modernity.

In the seventeenth century the concept of modernity as crisis was definitively consolidated. The century began with the burning of Giordano Bruno at the stake, and it went on to see monstrous civil wars break out in France and England, and above all it witnessed the horrible spectacle of thirty years of German civil war. At the same time, the European conquest of the Americas and the slaughter and enslavement of its native populations proceeded with ever-increasing intensity. In the second half of the century, monarchic absolutism seemed definitively to block the course of freedom in the countries of continental Europe. Absolutism sought to fix the concept of modernity and strip it of the crisis that defines it through the deployment of a new armory of transcendentals. At the same time, outside of Europe conquest slowly gave way to colonialism, and the precarious search for gold, riches, and plunder was progressively displaced by trade exclusives, stable forms of production, and the African slave trade. The seventeenth century, however—and this is what makes it so ambiguous—was a fragile, baroque century. From the abysses of the social world always arose the memory of what it tried to bury.

We can find testimony to this fact with one single but enormous reference: Spinoza's philosophy of immanence, which dominated the latter half of the century of European thought. It is a philosophy that renewed the splendors of revolutionary humanism, putting humanity and nature in the position of God, transforming the world into a territory of practice, and affirming the democracy of the multitude as the absolute form of politics. Spinoza considered the idea of death—that death that states and powers carried like a weapon against the desire and hope of liberation—merely a hostage used to blackmail the freedom of thought, and thus banned it from his philosophy: "A free man thinks about nothing less than of death, and his knowledge is a meditation on life, not on death."[15] That love that the humanists considered the supreme form of the expression of intelligence was posed by Spinoza as the only possible foundation of the liberation of singularities and as the ethical cement of collective life. "There is nothing in nature which is contrary to this intellectual Love, or which can take it away."[16] In this crescendo of thought, Spinoza testified to the uninterrupted continuity of the revolutionary program of humanism in the course of the seventeenth century.

The Transcendental Apparatus

The counterrevolutionary project to resolve the crisis of modernity unfolded in the centuries of the Enlightenment.[17] The primary task of this Enlightenment was to dominate the idea of immanence without reproducing the absolute dualism of medieval culture by constructing a transcendental apparatus capable of disciplining a multitude of formally free subjects. The ontological dualism of the culture of the ancien régime had to be replaced by a functional dualism, and the crisis of modernity had to be resolved by means of adequate mechanisms of mediation. It was paramount to avoid the multitude's being understood, à la Spinoza, in a direct, immediate relation with divinity and nature, as the ethical producer of life and the world. On the contrary, in every case mediation had to be imposed on the complexity of human relations. Philosophers disputed where this mediation was situated and what metaphysical level it occupied, but it was fundamental that in some way it be defined as an ineluctable condition of all human action, art, and association. Hence the triad *vis-cupiditas-amor* (strength-desire-love) which constituted the productive matrix of the revolutionary thought of humanism was opposed by a triad of specific mediations. Nature and experience are unrecognizable except through *the filter of phenomena;* human knowledge cannot be achieved except through *the reflection of the intellect;* and the ethical world is incommunicable except through the *schematism of reason.* What is at play is a form of mediation, or really a reflexive folding back and a sort of weak transcendence, which relativizes experience and abolishes every instance of the immediate and absolute in human life and history. Why, however, is this relativity necessary? Why cannot knowledge and will be allowed to claim themselves to be absolute? Because every movement of self-constitution of the multitude must yield to a preconstituted order, and because claiming that humans could immediately establish their freedom in being would be a subversive delirium. This is the essential core of the ideological passage in which the hegemonic concept of European modernity was constructed.

The first strategic masterpiece in this construction was accomplished by René Descartes. Although Descartes pretended to pursue a new humanistic project of knowledge, he really reestablished transcendent order. When he posed reason as the exclusive terrain of mediation between God and the world, he effectively reaffirmed dualism as the defining feature of experience and thought. We should be careful here. Mediation in Descartes is never well defined, or really, if we stay close to the text, we find that mediation resides mysteriously only in the will of God. Descartes's cunning stratagem consists primarily in this: When he addresses the centrality of thought in the transcendental function of mediation, he defines a sort of residual of divine transcendence. Descartes claims that the logics of mediation reside in thought and that God is very far from the scene, but a new man such as Blaise Pascal is perfectly right to object that this is just an example of Descartes's trickery.[18] In fact, Descartes's God is very close: God is the guarantee that transcendental rule is inscribed in consciousness and thought as necessary, universal, and thus preconstituted:

> Please do not hesitate to assert and proclaim everywhere that it is God who has laid down these laws in nature just as a king lays down laws in his kingdom. There is no single one that we cannot understand if our mind turns to consider it. They are all inborn in our minds just as a king would imprint

> his laws on the hearts of all his subjects if he had enough power to do so. The greatness of God, on the other hand, is something which we cannot comprehend even though we know it. But the very fact that we judge it incomprehensible makes us esteem it the more greatly; just as a king has more majesty when he is less familiarly known by his subjects, provided of course that they do not get the idea that they have no king—they must know him enough to be in no doubt about that.[19]

The realm of potentiality, which had been opened by the humanist principle of subjectivity, is limited a priori by the imposition of transcendent rule and order. Descartes surreptitiously reproposes theology on the terrain that humanism had cleared, and its apparatus is resolutely transcendental.

With Descartes we are at the beginning of the history of the Enlightenment, or rather bourgeois ideology.[20] The transcendental apparatus he proposes is the distinctive trademark of European Enlightenment thought. In both the empiricist and the idealist currents, transcendentalism was the exclusive horizon of ideology, and in the successive centuries nearly all the major currents of philosophy would be drawn into this project. The symbiosis between intellectual labor and institutional, political, and scientific rhetorics became absolute on this terrain, and every conceptual formation came to be marked by it: the formalization of politics, the instrumentalization of science and technique for profit, the pacification of social antagonisms. Certainly, in each of these fields we find historically specific developments, but everything was always tied up with the line of a grand narrative that European modernity told about itself, a tale told in a transcendental dialect.[21]

In many respects the work of Immanuel Kant stands at the center of this development. Kant's thought is enormously rich and leads in numerous directions, but we are interested here primarily in the line that crowns the transcendental principle as the apex of European modernity. Kant manages to pose the subject at the center of the metaphysical horizon but at the same time control it by means of the three operations we cited earlier: the emptying of experience in phenomena, the reduction of knowledge to intellectual mediation, and the neutralization of ethical action in the schematism of reason. The mediation that Descartes invoked in his reaffirmation of dualism is hypostatized by Kant, not in the divinity but nonetheless in a pseudo-ontological critique—in an ordering function of consciousness and an indistinct appetite of the will. Humanity is the center of the universe, but this is not the humanity that through art and action made itself *homohomo*. It is a humanity lost in experience, deluded in the pursuit of the ethical ideal. Kant throws us back into the crisis of modernity with full awareness when he poses the discovery of the subject itself as crisis, but this crisis is made into an apology of the transcendental as the unique and exclusive horizon of knowledge and action. The world becomes an architecture of ideal forms, the only reality conceded to us.

Romanticism was never expressed so strongly as it is in Kant. This is the leitmotif of Kantian philosophy: the necessity of the transcendental, the impossibility of every form of immediacy, the exorcism of every vital figure in the apprehension and action of being. From this perspective one should perhaps consider Arthur Schopenhauer the most lucid reader of Kantianism and its Romantic gesture. The fact that it is difficult if not impossible to reunite the appearance of the thing with the thing itself is precisely the curse of this world of pain and need. And this is therefore not a world constructed in a way so that noble and high forces, forces that tend to truth and light, can prosper.[22] In other words, Schopenhauer recognizes Kantianism as the definitive liquidation of the humanist revolution.

For this same reason Schopenhauer reacted even more violently against Hegel, calling him an "intellectual Caliban" to indicate the barbarity of his thought.[23] He found it intolerable that Hegel would transform the pallid constitutive function of Kant's transcendental critique into a solid ontological figure with such violence. This was indeed the destiny of the transcendental in the European ideology of modernity. Hegel revealed what was implicit from the beginning of the counterrevolutionary development: that the liberation of modern humanity could only be a function of its domination, that the immanent goal of the multitude is transformed into the necessary and transcendent power of the state. It is true that Hegel restores the horizon of immanence and takes away the uncertainty of knowledge, the irresolution of action, and the fideist opening of Kantianism. The immanence Hegel restores, however, is really a blind immanence in which the potentiality of the multitude is denied and subsumed in the allegory of the divine order. The crisis of humanism is transformed into a dialectical dramaturgy, and in every scene the end is everything and the means are merely ornamentation.

There is no longer anything that strives, desires, or loves; the content of potentiality is blocked, controlled, hegemonized by finality. Paradoxically, the analogical being of the medieval Christian tradition is resurrected as a dialectical being. It is ironic that Schopenhauer would call Hegel a Caliban, the figure that was later held up as a symbol of the resistance to European domination and the affirmation of non-European desire. Hegel's drama of the Other and the conflict between master and slave, however, could not but take place against the historical backdrop of European expansion and the enslavement of African, American, and Asian peoples. It is impossible, in other words, not to link both Hegel's philosophical recuperation of the Other within absolute Spirit and his universal history leading from lesser peoples to its summit in Europe together with the very real violence of European conquest and colonialism. In short, Hegel's history is not only a powerful attack on the revolutionary plane of immanence but also a negation of non-European desire.

Finally, with another act of force, that "intellectual Caliban" inserted into the development of modernity the experience of a new conception of temporality, and he showed this temporality to be a dialectical teleology that is accomplished and arrives at its end. The entire genetic design of the concept found an adequate representation in the conclusion of the process. Modernity was complete, and there was no possibility of going beyond it. It was not by chance, then, that a further and definitive act of violence defined the scene: the dialectic of crisis was pacified under the domination of the state. Peace and justice reign once again: "The state in and for itself is the ethical whole . . . It is essential to God's march through the world that the state exist."[24]

Modern Sovereignty

The political solution offered by Hegel to the metaphysical drama of modernity demonstrates the profound and intimate relationship between modern European politics and metaphysics. Politics resides at the center of metaphysics because modern European metaphysics arose in response to the challenge of the liberated singularities and the revolutionary constitution of the multitude. It functioned as an essential weapon of the second mode of modernity insofar as it provided a transcendent apparatus that could impose order on the multitude and prevent it from organizing itself spontaneously and expressing its creativity autonomously. The second mode of modernity needed above all to guarantee its control over the new figures of social production both in Europe and in the colonial spaces in order to rule and profit from the new forces that were transforming nature. In politics, as in metaphysics, the dominant theme was thus to eliminate the medieval form of transcendence, which only inhibits production and consumption, while maintaining transcendence's effects of domination in a form adequate to the modes of association and production of the new humanity. The center of the problem of modernity was thus demonstrated in political philosophy, and here was where the new form of mediation found its most adequate response to the revolutionary forms of immanence: a transcendent political apparatus.

Thomas Hobbes's proposition of an ultimate and absolute sovereign ruler, a "God on earth," plays a foundational role in the modern construction of a transcendent political apparatus. The first moment of Hobbes's logic is the assumption of civil war as the originary state of human society, a generalized conflict among individual actors. In a second moment, then, in order to guarantee survival against the mortal dangers of war, humans must agree to a pact that assigns to a leader the absolute right to act, or really the absolute power to do all except take away the means of human survival and reproduction. "Seeing right reason is not existent, the reason of some man, or men, must supply the place thereof; and that man, or men, is he or they, that have the sovereign power."[25] The fundamental passage is accomplished by a contract—a completely implicit contract, prior to all social action or choice—that transfers every autonomous power of the multitude to a sovereign power that stands above and rules it.

This transcendent political apparatus corresponds to the necessary and ineluctable transcendent conditions that modern philosophy posed at the pinnacle of its development, in Kantian schematism and Hegelian dialectics. According to Hobbes, the single wills of the various individuals converge and are represented in the will of the transcendent sovereign. Sovereignty is thus defined both by *transcendence* and by *representation,* two concepts that the humanist tradition has posed as contradictory. On the one hand, the transcendence of the sovereign is founded not on an external theological support but only on the immanent logic of human relations. On the other hand, the representation that functions to legitimate this sovereign power also alienates it completely from the multitude of subjects. Like Jean Bodin before him, Hobbes recognized that "the main point of sovereign majesty and absolute power consists of giving the law to subjects in general without their consent,"[26] but Hobbes manages to combine this notion with a contractual schema of representation that legitimates the sovereign power a priori. Here the concept of modern sovereignty is born in its state of transcendental purity. The contract of association is intrinsic to and inseparable from the contract of subjugation. This theory of sovereignty presents the first political solution to the crisis of modernity.

In his own historical period, Hobbes's theory of sovereignty was functional to the development of monarchic absolutism, but in fact its transcendental schema could be applied equally to various forms of government: monarchy, oligarchy, and democracy. As the bourgeoisie rose to prominence, it seemed there was really no alternative to this schema of power. It was not by chance, then, that Rousseau's democratic republicanism turned out to resemble the Hobbesian model. Rousseau's social contract guarantees that the agreement among individual wills is developed and sublimated in the construction of a general will, and that the general will proceeds from the alienation of the single wills toward the sovereignty of the state. As a model of sovereignty, Rousseau's "republican absolute" is really no different from Hobbes's "God on earth," the monarchic absolute. "Properly understood, all of these clauses [of the contract] come down to a single one, namely the total alienation of each associate, with all his rights, to the whole community."[27] The other conditions that Rousseau prescribes for the definition of sovereign power in the popular and democratic sense are completely irrelevant in the face of the absolutism of the transcendent foundation. Specifically, Rousseau's notion of direct representation is distorted and ultimately overwhelmed by the representation of the totality that is necessarily linked to it—and this is perfectly compatible with the Hobbesian notion of representation. Hobbes and Rousseau really only repeat the paradox that Jean Bodin had already defined conceptually in the second half of the sixteenth century. Sovereignty can properly be said to exist only in monarchy, because only one can be sovereign. If two or three or many were to rule, there would be no sovereignty, because the sovereign cannot be subject to the rule of others.[28] Democratic, plural, or popular political forms might be declared, but modern sovereignty really has only one political figure: a single transcendent power.

There is at the base of the modern theory of sovereignty, however, a further very important element—a content that fills and sustains the form of sovereign authority. This content is represented by capitalist development and the affirmation of the market as the foundation of the values of social reproduction.[29] Without this content, which is always implicit, always working inside the transcendental apparatus, the form of sovereignty would not have been able to survive in modernity, and European modernity would not have been able to achieve a hegemonic position on a world scale. As Arif Dirlik has noted, Eurocentrism distinguished itself from other ethnocentrisms (such as Sinocentrism) and rose to global prominence principally because it was supported by the powers of capital.[30]

European modernity is inseparable from capitalism. This central relationship between the form and the content of modern sovereignty is fully articulated in the work of Adam Smith. Smith begins with a theory of industry that poses the contradiction between private enrichment and public interest. A first synthesis of these two levels is confided to the "invisible hand" of the market: the capitalist "intends only his own gain," but he is "led by an invisible hand to promote an end which was no part of his intention."[31] This first synthesis, however, is precarious and fleeting. Political economy, considered a branch of the science of the administrator and legislator, must go much further in conceiving the synthesis. It must understand the "invisible hand" of the market as a product of political economy itself, which is thus directed toward constructing the conditions of the autonomy of the market: "All systems either of preference or of restraint, therefore, being thus completely taken away, the obvious and simple system of natural liberty establishes itself of its own accord."[32] In this case, too, however, the synthesis is not at all guaranteed. In effect, a third passage is necessary. What is needed is for the state, which is minimal but effective, to make the well-being of private individuals coincide with the public interest, reducing all social functions and laboring activities to one measure of value. That this state intervenes or not is secondary; what matters is that it give content to the mediation of interests and represent the axis of rationality of that mediation. The political transcendental of the modern state is defined as an economic transcendental. Smith's theory of value was the soul and substance of the concept of the modern sovereign state.

In Hegel, the synthesis of the theory of modern sovereignty and the theory of value produced by capitalist political economy is finally realized, just as in his work there is a perfect realization of the consciousness of the union of the absolutist and republican aspects—that is, the Hobbesian and Rousseauian aspects—of the theory of modern sovereignty.

> In relation to the spheres of civil law [*Privatrecht*] and private welfare, the spheres of the family and civil society, the state is on the one hand an *external* necessity and the higher power to whose nature their laws and interests are subordinate and on which they depend. But on the other hand, it is their *immanent* end, and its strength consists in the unity of its universal and ultimate end with the particular interest of individuals, in the fact that they have *duties* towards the state to the same extent as they also have rights.[33]

The Hegelian relationship between particular and universal brings together in adequate and functional terms the Hobbes-Rousseau theory of sovereignty and Smith's theory of value. Modern European sovereignty is capitalist sovereignty, a form of command that overdetermines the relationship between individuality and universality as a function of the development of capital.

The Sovereignty Machine

When the synthesis of sovereignty and capital is fully accomplished, and the transcendence of power is completely transformed into a transcendental exercise of authority, then sovereignty becomes a political machine that rules across the entire society. Through the workings of the sovereignty machine the multitude is in every moment transformed into an ordered totality. We should play close attention to this passage because here we can see clearly how the transcendental schema is an ideology that functions concretely and how different modern sovereignty is from that of the ancien régime. In addition to being a political power against all external political powers, a state against all other states, sovereignty is also a police power. It must continually and extensively accomplish the miracle of the subsumption of singularities in the totality, of the will of all into the general will. Modern bureaucracy is the essential organ of the transcendental—Hegel *dixit.* And even if Hegel exaggerates a bit in his quasi-theological consecration of the body of state employees, at least he makes clear their central role in the effective functioning of the modern state. Bureaucracy operates the apparatus that combines legality and organizational efficiency, title and the exercise of power, politics and police. The transcendental theory of modern sovereignty, thus reaching maturity, realizes a new "individual" by absorbing society into power. Little by little, as the administration develops, the relationship between society and power, between the multitude and the sovereign state, is inverted so that now power and the state produce society.

This passage in the history of ideas does indeed parallel the development of social history. It corresponds to the dislocation of the organizational dynamic of the state from the terrain of medieval hierarchy to that of modern discipline, from command to function. Max Weber and Michel Foucault, to mention only the most illustrious, have insisted at length on these metamorphoses in the sociological figures of power. In the long transition from medieval to modern society, the first form of the political regime was, as we have seen, rooted in transcendence. Medieval society was organized according to a hierarchical schema of degrees of power. This is what modernity blew apart in the course of its development. Foucault refers to this transition as the passage from the paradigm of sovereignty to that of governmentality, where by sovereignty he means the transcendence of the single point of command above the social field, and by governmentality he means the general economy of discipline that runs throughout society.[34] We prefer to conceive of this as a passage *within* the notion of sovereignty, as a transition to a new form of transcendence. Modernity replaced the traditional transcendence of command with the transcendence of the ordering function. Arrangements of discipline had begun to be formed already in the classical age, but only in modernity did the disciplinary diagram become the diagram of administration itself. Throughout this passage administration exerts a continuous, extensive, and tireless effort to make the state always more intimate to social reality, and thus produce and order social labor. The old theses, à la Tocqueville, of the continuity of administrative bodies across different social eras are thus profoundly revised when not completely discarded. Foucault, however, goes still further to claim that the disciplinary processes, which are put into practice by the administration, delve so deeply into society that they manage to configure themselves as apparatuses that take into account the collective biological dimension of the reproduction of the population. The realization of modern sovereignty is the birth of biopower.[35]

Before Foucault, Max Weber also described the administrative mechanisms involved in the formation of modern sovereignty.[36] Whereas Foucault's analysis is vast in its diachronic breadth, Weber's is powerful in its synchronic depth. With respect to our discussion of modern sovereignty, Weber's contribution is first of all his claim that the opening of modernity is defined as a scission—a creative condition of individuals and the multitude against the process of state reappropriation. State sovereignty is then defined as a regulation of this relationship of force. Modernity is above all marked by the tension of the opposing forces. Every process of legitimation is regulated by this tension, and operates to block its capacity for rupture and recuperate its creative initiative. The closure of the crisis of modernity in a new sovereign power can be given in old and quasi-naturalist forms, as is the case with traditional legitimation; or rather, it can be given in sacred and innovative, irrationally innovative, forms, as in charismatic legitimation; or finally, and this is to a large extent the most effective form of late modernity, it can be given in the form of administrative rationalization. The analysis of these forms of legitimation is Weber's second relevant contribution, which builds on the first, the recognition of the dualism of the paradigm. The third relevant point is Weber's treatment of the procedural character of the transformation, the always present and possible interweaving of the various forms of legitimation, and their continuous capacity to be extended and deepened in the control of social reality. From this follows a final paradox:

if on the one hand this process closes the crisis of modernity, on the other hand it reopens it. The form of the process of closure is as critical and conflictual as the genesis of modernity. In this respect Weber's work has the great merit to have completely destroyed the self-satisfied and triumphant conception of the sovereignty of the modern state that Hegel had produced.

Weber's analysis was quickly taken up by the writers engaged in the critique of modernity, from Heidegger and Lukács to Horkheimer and Adorno. They all recognized that Weber had revealed the illusion of modernity, the illusion that the antagonistic dualism that resides at the base of modernity could be subsumed in a unitary synthesis investing all of society and politics, including the productive forces and the relations of production. They recognized, finally, that modern sovereignty had passed its peak and begun to wane.

As modernity declines, a new season is opened, and here we find again that dramatic antithesis that was at the origins and basis of modernity. Has anything really changed? The civil war has erupted again in full force. The synthesis between the development of productive forces and relations of domination seems once again precarious and improbable. The desires of the multitude and its antagonism to every form of domination drive it to divest itself once again of the processes of legitimation that support the sovereign power. Certainly, no one would imagine this as a return of that old world of desires that animated the first humanist revolution. New subjectivities inhabit the new terrain; modernity and its capitalist relations have completely changed the scene in the course of its development. And yet something remains: there is a sense of déjà vu when we see the reappearance of the struggles that have continually been passed down from those origins. The experience of the revolution will be reborn after modernity, but within the new conditions that modernity constructed in such a contradictory way. Machiavelli's return to origins seems to be combined with Nietzsche's heroic eternal return. Everything is different and nothing seems to have changed. Is this the coming of a new human power? "For this is the secret of the soul: when the hero hath abandoned it, then only approacheth it in dreams—the super-hero."[37]

HUMANISM AFTER THE DEATH OF MAN

Michel Foucault's final works on the history of sexuality bring to life once again that same revolutionary impulse that animated Renaissance humanism. The ethical care of the self reemerges as a constituent power of self-creation. How is it possible that the author who worked so hard to convince us of the death of Man, the thinker who carried the banner of antihumanism throughout his career, would in the end champion these central tenets of the humanist tradition? We do not mean to suggest that Foucault contradicts himself or that he reversed his earlier position; he was always so insistent about the continuity of his discourse. Rather, Foucault asks in his final work a paradoxical and urgent question: What is humanism after the death of Man? Or rather, what is an antihumanist (or posthuman) humanism?

This question, however, is only a seeming paradox that derives at least in part from a terminological confusion between two distinct notions of humanism. The antihumanism that was such an important project for Foucault and Althusser in the 1960s can be linked effectively to a battle that Spinoza fought three hundred years earlier. Spinoza denounced any understanding of humanity as an imperium in imperio. *In other words, he refused to accord any laws to human nature that were different from the laws of nature as a whole. Donna Haraway carries on Spinoza's project in our day as she insists on breaking down the barriers we pose among the human, the animal, and the machine. If we are to conceive Man as separate from nature, then Man does not exist. This recognition is precisely the death of Man.*

This antihumanism, however, need not conflict with the revolutionary spirit of Renaissance humanism we outlined earlier from Cusano to Marsilius. In fact, this antihumanism follows directly on Renaissance humanism's secularizing project, or more precisely, its discovery of the plane of immanence. Both projects are founded on an attack on transcendence. There is a strict continuity between the religious thought that accords a power above nature to God and the modern "secular" thought that accords that same power above nature to Man. The transcendence of God is simply transferred to Man. Like God before it, this Man that stands separate from and above nature has no place in a philosophy of immanence. Like God, too, this transcendent figure of Man leads quickly to the imposition of social hierarchy and domination. Antihumanism, then, conceived as a refusal of any transcen-

dence, should in no way be confused with a negation of the vis viva, *the creative life force that animates the revolutionary stream of the modern tradition. On the contrary, the refusal of transcendence is the condition of possibility of thinking this immanent power, an anarchic basis of philosophy: "Ni Dieu, ni maître, ni l'homme."*

The humanism of Foucault's final works, then, should not be seen as contradictory to or even as a departure from the death of Man he proclaimed twenty years earlier. Once we recognize our posthuman bodies and minds, once we see ourselves for the simians and cyborgs we are, we then need to explore the vis viva, *the creative powers that animate us as they do all of nature and actualize our potentialities. This is humanism after the death of Man: what Foucault calls "le travail de soi sur soi," the continuous constituent project to create and re-create ourselves and our world.*

2.2

SOVEREIGNTY OF THE NATION-STATE

> Foreigners, please don't leave us alone with the French!
>
> Paris graffito, 1995

> We thought we were dying for the fatherland. We realized quickly it was for the bank vaults.
>
> Anatole France

As European modernity progressively took shape, machines of power were constructed to respond to its crisis, searching continually for a surplus that would resolve or at least contain the crisis. In the previous section we traced the path of one response to the crisis that led to the development of the modern sovereign state. The second approach centers on the concept of nation, a development that presupposes the first path and builds on it to construct a more perfect mechanism to reestablish order and command.

Birth of the Nation

The concept of nation in Europe developed on the terrain of the patrimonial and absolutist state. The patrimonial state was defined as the property of the monarch. In a variety of analogous forms in different countries throughout Europe, the patrimonial and absolutist state was the political form required to rule feudal social relations and relations of production.[1] Feudal property had to be delegated and its usage assigned according to the degrees of the social division of power, in the same way that levels of administration would have to be delegated in subsequent centuries. Feudal property was part of the body of the monarch, just as, if we shift our view toward the metaphysical domain, the sovereign monarchic body was part of the body of God.[2]

In the sixteenth century, in the midst of the Reformation and that violent battle among the forces of modernity, the patrimonial monarchy was still presented as the guarantee of peace and social life. It was still granted control over social development in such a way that it could absorb that process within its machine of domination. "Cujus regio, ejus religio"—or really, religion had to be subordinated to the territorial control of the sovereign. There was nothing diplomatic about this adage; on the contrary, it confided entirely to the power of the patrimonial sovereign the management of the passage to the new order. Even religion was the sovereign's property. In the seventeenth century, the absolutist reaction to the revolutionary forces of modernity celebrated the patrimonial monarchic state and wielded it as a weapon for its own purposes. At that point, however, the celebration of the patrimonial state could not but be paradoxical and ambiguous, since the feudal bases of its power were withering away. The processes of the primitive accumulation of capital imposed new conditions on all the structures of power.[3] Until the era of the three great bourgeois revolutions (the English, the American, and the French), there was no political alternative that could successfully oppose this model. The absolutist and patrimonial model survived in this period only with the support of a specific compromise of political forces, and its substance was eroding from the inside owing primarily to the emergence of new productive forces. The model did survive nonetheless, and, much more important, it was transformed through the development of some fundamental characteristics that would be bequeathed to successive centuries.

The transformation of the absolutist and patrimonial model consisted in a gradual process that replaced the theological foundation of territorial patrimony with a new foundation that was equally transcendent.[4] The spiritual identity of the nation rather than the divine body of the king now posed the territory and population as an ideal abstraction. Or rather, the physical territory and population were conceived as the extension of the transcendent essence of the nation. *The modern concept of nation thus inherited the patrimonial body of the monarchic state and reinvented it in a new form.* This new totality of power was structured in part by new capitalist productive processes on the one hand and old networks of absolutist administration on the other. This uneasy structural relationship was stabilized by the national identity: a cultural, integrating identity, founded on a biological continuity of blood relations, a spatial continuity of territory, and linguistic commonality.

It is obvious that, although this process preserved the materiality of the relationship to the sovereign, many elements changed. Most important, as the patrimonial horizon was transformed into the national horizon, the feudal order of the subject *(subjectus)* yielded to the disciplinary order of the citizen *(cives)*. The shift of the population from subjects to citizens was an index of the shift from a passive to an active role. The nation is always presented as an active force, as a generative form of social and political relations. As Benedict Anderson and others point out, the nation is often experienced as (or at least functions as if it were) a collective imagining, an active creation of the community of citizens.[5] At this point we can see both the proximity and the specific difference between the concepts of patrimonial state and national state. The latter faithfully reproduces the former's totalizing identity of both the territory and the population, but the nation and the national state propose new means of overcoming the precariousness of modern sovereignty. These concepts reify sovereignty in the most rigid way; they make the *relation* of sovereignty into a *thing* (often by naturalizing it) and thus weed out every residue of social antagonism. The nation is a kind of ideological shortcut that attempts to free the concepts of sovereignty and modernity from the antagonism and crisis that define them. National sovereignty suspends the conflictual origins of modernity (when they are not definitively destroyed), and it closes the alternative paths within modernity that had refused to concede their powers to state authority.[6]

The transformation of the concept of modern sovereignty into that of national sovereignty also required certain new material conditions. Most important, it required that a new equilibrium be established between the processes of capitalist accumulation and the structures of power. The political victory of the bourgeoisie, as the English and French revolutions show well, corresponded to the perfecting of the concept of modern sovereignty through that of national sovereignty. Behind the ideal dimension of the concept of nation there were the class figures that already dominated the processes of accumulation. "Nation" was thus at once both the hypostasis of the Rousseauian "general will" and what manufacturing ideology conceived as the "community of needs" (that is, the capitalist regulation of the market) that in the long era of primitive accumulation in Europe was more or less liberal and always bourgeois.

When in the nineteenth and twentieth centuries the concept of nation was taken up in very different ideological contexts and led popular mobilizations in regions and countries within and outside Europe that had experienced neither the liberal revolution nor the same level of primitive accumulation, it still always was presented as a concept of capitalist modernization, which claimed to bring together the interclass demands for political unity and the needs of economic development. In other words, the nation was posed as the one and only active vehicle that could deliver modernity and development. Rosa Luxemburg argued vehemently (and futilely) against nationalism in the debates internal to the Third International in the years before the First World War. Luxemburg opposed a policy of "national self-determination" for Poland as an element of the revolutionary platform, but her indictment of nationalism was much more general.[7] Her critique of the nation was not merely a critique of modernization as such, although she was no doubt keenly aware of the ambiguities involved in capitalist development; and she was not primarily concerned with the divisions that nationalisms would inevitably create within the European working class, although her own nomadic passage through central and eastern Europe certainly made her extremely sensitive to this. Luxemburg's most powerful argument, rather, was that nation means dictatorship and is thus profoundly incompatible with any attempt at democratic organization. Luxemburg recognized that national sovereignty and national mythologies effectively usurp the terrain of democratic organization by renewing the powers of territorial sovereignty and modernizing its project through the mobilization of an active community.

The process of constructing the nation, which renewed the concept of sovereignty and gave it a new definition, quickly became in each and every historical context an ideological nightmare. The crisis of modernity, which is the contradictory co-presence of the multitude and a power that wants to reduce it to the rule of one—that is, the co-presence of a new productive set of free subjectivities and a disciplinary power that wants to exploit it—is not finally pacified or resolved by the concept of nation, any more than it was by the concept of sovereignty or state. The nation can only mask the crisis ideologically, displace it, and defer its power.

The Nation and the Crisis of Modernity

Jean Bodin's work lies at the head of the road in European thought that leads to the concept of national sovereignty. His masterwork, *Les six livres de la République,* which first appeared in 1576, right in the middle of the Renaissance crisis, addressed the current civil and religious wars in France and Europe as its fundamental problem. Bodin confronted political crises, conflicts, and war, but these elements of rupture did not lead him to pose any idyllic alternative, not even in simply theoretical or utopian terms. This is why Bodin's work was not only a seminal contribution to the modern definition of sovereignty but also an effective anticipation of the subsequent development of sovereignty in national terms. By adopting a realistic standpoint, he managed to anticipate modernity's own critique of sovereignty.

Sovereignty, Bodin claimed, cannot be produced by the unity of the Prince and the multitude, the public and the private, nor can its problem be resolved so long as one holds to either a contractualist or a natural right framework. Really, the origin of political power and the definition of sovereignty consist in the victory of one side over the other, a victory that makes the one sovereign and the other subject. Force and violence create the sovereign. The physical determinations of power impose the *plenitudo potestatis* (the fullness of power). This is the plenitude and the unity of power, since "the union of [the republic's] members depends on unity under a single ruler, on whom the effectiveness of all the rest depends. A sovereign prince is therefore indispensable, for it is his power which informs all the members of the republic."[8]

After discarding the framework of natural right and the transcendental perspectives that it always in some way invokes, Bodin presents us with a figure of the sovereign, or rather the state, that realistically and thus historically constructs its own origin and structure. The modern state arose from within this transformation, and only there could it continue to develop. This is the theoretical hinge on which the theory of modern sovereignty is linked to and perfects the experience of territorial sovereignty. By taking up Roman law and drawing on its capacities to articulate the sources of right and order the forms of property, Bodin's doctrine became a theory of a united political body articulated as administration that appeared to surmount the difficulties of the crisis of modernity. The displacement of the center of theoretical consideration from the question of legitimacy to that of the life of the state and its sovereignty as a united body constituted an important advance. When Bodin spoke of "the political right of sovereignty," he already anticipated the national (and corporeal) overdetermination of sovereignty, and he thus opened an original and direct path that would stretch forward across the subsequent centuries.[9]

After Bodin, in the seventeenth and eighteenth centuries there developed in Europe simultaneously two schools of thought that also accorded the theme of sovereignty a central role and effectively anticipated the concept of national sovereignty: the natural right tradition and the realist (or historicist) tradition of state theory.[10] Both schools mediated the transcendental conception of sovereignty with a realistic methodology that grasped the terms of the material conflict; both brought together the construction of the sovereign state with the constitution of the sociopolitical community that later would be called nation. As in Bodin, both of these schools continually confronted the crisis of the theoretical conception of sovereignty, which was itself continually reopened by the antagonistic powers of modernity and the juridical and administrative construction of the figure of the state.

In the natural right school, from Grotius to Althusius and from Thomasius to Puffendorf, the transcendental figures of sovereignty were brought down to earth and grounded in the reality of the institutional and administrative processes. Sovereignty was distributed by setting in motion a system of multiple contracts designed to intervene on every node of the administrative structure of power. This process was not oriented toward the apex of the state and the mere title of sovereignty; rather, the problem of legitimation began to be addressed in terms of an *administrative machine* that functioned through the articulations of the exercise of power. The circle of sovereignty and obedience closed in on itself, duplicating itself, multiplying, and extending across social reality. Sovereignty came to be studied less from the perspective of the antagonists involved in the crisis of modernity and more as an administrative process that articulates these antagonisms and aims toward a unity in the dialectic of power, abstacting and reifying it through the historical dynamics. An important segment of the natural right school thus developed the idea of distributing and articulating the transcendent sovereignty through the real forms of administration.[11]

The synthesis that was implicit in the natural right school, however, became explicit in the context of historicism. Certainly, it would be incorrect to attribute to the historicism of the Enlightenment the thesis that was really only developed later by the reactionary schools in the period after the French Revolution—the thesis, that is, that unites the theory of sovereignty with the theory of the nation and grounds both of them in a common historical humus. And yet there are already in this early period the seeds of that later development. Whereas an important segment of the natural right school developed the idea of articulating transcendent sovereignty through the real forms of administration, the historicist thinkers of the Enlightenment attempted to conceive *the subjectivity of the historical process* and thereby find an effective ground for the title and exercise of sovereignty.[12] In the work of Giambattista Vico, for example, that terrific meteor that shot across the age of Enlightenment, the determinations of the juridical conception of sovereignty were all grounded in the power of historical development. The transcendent figures of sovereignty were translated into indexes of a providential process, which was at once both human and divine. This construction of sovereignty (or really reification of sovereignty) in history was very powerful. On this historical terrain, which forces every ideological construct to confront reality, the genetic crisis of modernity was never closed—and there was no need for it to close, because the crisis itself produced new figures that incessantly spurred on historical and political development, all still under the rule of the transcendent sovereign. What an ingenious inversion of the problematic! And yet, at the same time, what a complete mystification of sovereignty! The elements of the crisis, a continuous and unresolved crisis, were now considered active elements of progress. In effect, we can already recognize in Vico the embryo of Hegel's apologia of "effectiveness," making the present world arrangement the telos of history.[13]

What remained hints and suggestions in Vico, however, emerged as an open and radical declaration in the late German Enlightenment. In the Hannover school first, and then in the work of J. G. Herder, the modern theory of sovereignty was directed exclusively toward the analysis of what was conceived as a social and cultural continuity: the real historical continuity of the territory, the population, and the nation. Vico's argument that ideal history is located in the history of all nations became more radical in Herder so that every human perfection is, in a certain respect, national.[14] Identity is thus conceived not as the resolution of social and historical differences but as the product of a primordial unity. The nation is a complete figure of sovereignty *prior* to historical development; or better, there is no historical development that is not already prefigured in the origin. In other words, the nation sustains the concept of sovereignty by claiming to precede it.[15] It is the material engine that courses throughout history, the "genius" that works history. The nation becomes finally the condition of possibility of all human action and social life itself.

The Nation's People

Between the end of the eighteenth and the beginning of the nineteenth centuries, the concept of national sovereignty finally emerged in European thought in its completed form. At the base of this definitive figure of the concept were a trauma, the French Revolution, and the resolution of that trauma, the reactionary appropriation and celebration of the concept of nation. The fundamental elements of this swift reconfiguration of the concept of nation that made it a real political weapon can be seen in summary form in the work of Emmanuel-Joseph Sieyès. In his wonderful and libelous tract *What Is the Third Estate?* he linked the concept of nation to that of the Third Estate, that is, the bourgeoisie. Sieyès tried to lead the concept of sovereignty back to its humanist origins and rediscover its revolutionary possibilities. More important for our purposes, Sieyès's intense engagement with revolutionary activity allowed him to interpret the concept of nation as a *constructive political concept,* a constitutional mechanism. It gradually becomes clear, however, particularly in Sieyès's later work, the work of his followers, and above all that of his detractors, that although the nation was formed through politics, it was ultimately a *spiritual construction,* and the concept of nation was thus stripped away from the revolution, consigned to all the Thermidors. The nation became explicitly the concept that summarized the bourgeois hegemonic solution to the problem of sovereignty.[16]

At those points when the concept of nation has been presented as popular and revolutionary, as indeed it was during the French Revolution, one might assume that the nation has broken away from the modern concept of sovereignty and its apparatus of subjugation and domination, and is dedicated instead to a democratic notion of community. The link between the concept of nation and the concept of people was indeed a powerful innovation, and it did constitute the center of the Jacobin sensibility as well as that of other revolutionary groups. What appears as revolutionary and liberatory in this notion of national, popular sovereignty, however, is really nothing more than another turn of the screw, a further extension of the subjugation and domination that the modern concept of sovereignty has carried with it from the beginning. The precarious power of sovereignty as a solution to the crisis of modernity was first referred for support to the nation, and then when the nation too was revealed as a precarious solution, it was further referred to the people. In other words, just as the concept of nation completes the notion of sovereignty by claiming to precede it, so too the concept of the people completes that of nation through another feigned logical regression. Each logical step back functions to solidify the power of sovereignty by mystifying its basis, that is, by resting on the naturalness of the concept. The identity of the nation and even more so the identity of the people must appear natural and originary.

We, by contrast, must de-naturalize these concepts and ask what is a nation and how is it made, but also, what is a people and how is it made? Although "the people" is posed as the originary basis of the nation, *the modern conception of the people is in fact a product of the nation-state,* and survives only within its specific ideological context. Many contemporary analyses of nations and nationalism from a wide variety of perspectives go wrong precisely because they rely unquestioningly on the naturalness of the concept and identity of the people. We should note that the concept of the people is very different from that of the multitude.[17] Already in the seventeenth century, Hobbes was very mindful of this difference and its importance for the construction of sovereign order: "It is a great hindrance to civil government, especially monarchical, that men distinguish not enough between a people and a multitude. The people is somewhat that is one, having one will, and to whom one action may be attributed; none of these can be properly said of the multitude. The people rules in all governments. For even in monarchies the people commands; for the people wills by the will of one man . . . (however it seem a paradox) the king is the people."[18] The multitude is a multiplicity, a plane of singularities, an open set of relations, which is not homogeneous or identical with itself and bears an indistinct, inclusive relation to those outside of it. The people, in contrast, tends toward identity and homogeneity internally while posing its difference from and excluding what remains outside of it. Whereas the multitude is an inconclusive constituent relation, the people is a constituted synthesis that is prepared for sovereignty. The people provides a single will and action that is independent of and often in conflict with the various wills and actions of the multitude. Every nation must make the multitude into a people.

Two fundamental kinds of operations contribute to the construction of the modern concept of the people in relation to that of the nation in Europe in the eighteenth and nineteenth centuries. The more important of these are the mechanisms of colonial racism that construct the identity of European peoples in a dialectical play of oppositions with their native Others. The concepts of nation, people, and race are never very far apart.[19] The construction of an absolute racial difference is the essential ground for the conception of a homogeneous national identity. Numerous excellent studies are appearing today, when the pressures of immigration and multiculturalism are creating conflicts in Europe, to demonstrate that, despite the persistent nostalgia of some, European societies and peoples were never really pure and uniform.[20] The identity of the people was constructed on an imaginary plane that hid and/or eliminated differences, and this corresponded on the practical plane to racial subordination and social purification.

The second fundamental operation in the construction of the people, which is facilitated by the first, is the eclipse of internal differences through the *representation* of the whole population by a hegemonic group, race, or class. The representative group is the active agent that stands behind the effectiveness of the concept of nation. In the course of the French Revolution itself, between Thermidor and the Napoleonic period, the concept of nation revealed its fundamental content and served as an antidote to the concept and forces of revolution. Even in Sieyès's early work we can see clearly how the nation serves to placate the crisis and how sovereignty will be reappropriated through the representation of the bourgeoisie. Sieyès claims that a nation can have only *one* general interest: it would be impossible to establish order if the nation were to admit several different interests. Social order necessarily supposes the *unity* of ends and the concert of means.[21] The concept of nation in these early years of the French Revolution was the first hypothesis of the construction of popular hegemony and the first conscious manifesto of a social class, but it was also the final declaration of a fully accomplished secular transformation, a coronation, a final seal. Never was the concept of nation so reactionary as when it presented itself as revolutionary.[22] Paradoxically, this cannot but be a completed revolution, an end of history. The passage from revolutionary activity to the spiritual construction of the nation and the people is inevitable and implicit in the concepts themselves.[23]

National sovereignty and popular sovereignty were thus products of a spiritual construction, that is, a construction of identity. When Edmund Burke opposed Sieyès, his position was much less profoundly different than the torrid polemical climate of the age would lead us to believe. Even for Burke, in fact, national sovereignty is the product of a spiritual construction of identity. This fact can be recognized even more clearly in the work of those who carried the standard of the counterrevolutionary project on the European continent. The continental conceptions of this spiritual construction revived both the historical and the voluntarist traditions of the nation and added to the conception of historical development a transcendental synthesis in national sovereignty. This synthesis is always already accomplished in the identity of the nation and the people. Johann Gottlieb Fichte, for example, claims in more or less mythological terms that the fatherland and the people are representatives and gauges of earthly eternity; they are what here on earth can be immortal.[24] The Romantic counterrevolution was in fact more realistic than the Enlightenment revolution. It framed and fixed what was already accomplished, celebrating it in the eternal light of hegemony. The Third Estate is power; the nation is its totalizing representation; the people is its solid and natural foundation; and national sovereignty is the apex of history. Every historical alternative to bourgeois hegemony had thus been definitively surpassed through the bourgeoisie's own revolutionary history.[25]

This bourgeois formulation of the concept of national sovereignty surpassed by far all the previous formulations of modern sovereignty. It consolidated a particular and hegemonic image of modern sovereignty, the image of the victory of the bourgeoisie, which it then both historicized and universalized. National particularity is a potent universality. All the threads of a long development were woven together here. In the identity, that is, the spiritual essence, of the people and the nation, there is a territory embedded with cultural meanings, a shared history, and a linguistic community; but moreover there is the consolidation of a class victory, a stable market, the potential for economic expansion, and new spaces to invest and civilize. In short, the construction of national identity guarantees a continually reinforced legitimation, and the right and power of a sacrosanct and irrepressible unity. This is a decisive shift in the concept of sovereignty. Married to the concepts of nation and people, the modern concept of sovereignty shifts its epicenter from the mediation of conflicts and crisis to the unitary experience of a nation-subject and its imagined community.

Subaltern Nationalism

We have been focusing our attention up to this point on the development of the concept of nation in Europe while Europe was in the process of achieving world dominance. Outside of Europe, however, the concept of nation has often functioned very differently. In some respects, in fact, one might even say that the function of the concept of nation is inverted when deployed among subordinated rather than dominant groups. Stated most boldly, it appears that *whereas the concept of nation promotes stasis and restoration in the hands of the dominant, it is a weapon for change and revolution in the hands of the subordinated.*

The progressive nature of subaltern nationalism is defined by two primary functions, each of which is highly ambiguous. Most important, the nation appears as progressive insofar as it serves as a line of defense against the domination of more powerful nations and external economic, political, and ideological forces. The right to self-determination of subaltern nations is really a right to secession from the control of dominant powers.[26] Anticolonial struggles thus used the concept of nation as a weapon to defeat and expel the occupying enemy, and anti-imperialist policies similarly erected national walls to obstruct the overpowering forces of foreign capital. The concept of nation also served as an ideological weapon to ward off the dominant discourse that figured the dominated population and culture as inferior; the claim to nationhood affirmed the dignity of the people and legitimated the demand for independence and equality. In each of these cases, *the nation is progressive strictly as a fortified line of defense against more powerful external forces.* As much as those walls appear progressive in their protective function against external domination, however, they can easily play an inverse role with respect to the interior they protect. The flip side of the structure that resists foreign powers is itself a dominating power that exerts an equal and opposite internal oppression, repressing internal difference and opposition in the name of national identity, unity, and security. Protection and oppression can be hard to tell apart. This strategy of "national protection" is a double-edged sword that at times appears necessary despite its destructiveness.

The nation appears progressive in the second place insofar as it poses the commonality of a potential community. Part of the "modernizing" effects of the nation in subordinated countries has been the unification of diverse populations, breaking down religious, ethnic, cultural, and linguistic barriers. The unification of countries such as Indonesia, China, and Brazil, for example, is an ongoing process that involves overcoming innumerable such barriers—and in many cases this national unification was prepared by the European colonial power. In cases of diasporic populations, too, the nation seems at times to be the only concept available under which to imagine the community of the subaltern group—as, for example, the Aztlán is imagined as the geographical homeland of "la Raza," the spiritual Latino nation in North America. It may be true, as Benedict Anderson says, that a nation should be understood as an imagined community—but here we should recognize that the claim is inverted so that *the nation becomes the only way to imagine community!* Every imagination of a community becomes overcoded as a nation, and hence our conception of community is severely impoverished. Just as in the context of the dominant countries, here too the multiplicity and singularity of the multitude are negated in the straitjacket of the identity and homogeneity of the people. Once again, the unifying power of the subaltern nation is a double-edged sword, at once progressive and reactionary.

Both of these simultaneously progressive and regressive aspects of subaltern nationalism are present in all their ambiguity in the tradition of black nationalism in the United States. Although deprived as it is of any territorial definition (and thus undoubtedly different from the majority of other subaltern nationalisms), it too presents the two fundamental progressive functions—sometimes by striving to pose itself in an analogous position to the proper, territorially defined nations. In the early 1960s, for example, after the enormous impetus created by the Bandung Conference and the emerging African and Latin American national liberation struggles, Malcolm X attempted to redirect the focus of demands of African American struggles from "civil rights" to "human rights" and thus rhetorically shift the forum of appeal from the U.S. Congress to the U.N. General Assembly.[27] Malcolm X, like many African American leaders at least since Marcus Garvey, clearly recognized the powerful position of speaking as a nation and a people. The concept of nation here configures a defensive position of *separation* from the hegemonic "external" power and at the same time represents the *autonomous power* of the unified community, the power of the people.

More important than any such theoretical and rhetorical propositions, however, are the actual practices of black nationalism, that is, the wide variety of activities and phenomena that are conceived by the actors themselves as expressions of black nationalism: from community drill teams and parades to meal programs, separate schools, and projects of community economic development and self-sufficiency. As Wahneema Lubiano puts it, "Black nationalism is significant for the ubiquity of its presence in black American lives."[28] In all these various activities and realms of life, black nationalism names precisely the circuits of self-valorization that constitute the community and allow for its relative self-determination and self-constitution. Despite the range of disparate phenomena called black nationalism, then, we can still recognize in them the two fundamental progressive functions of subaltern nationalism: the defense and the unification of the community. Black nationalism can name any expression of the separation and autonomous power of the African American people.

In the case of black nationalism too, however, the progressive elements are accompanied inevitably by their reactionary shadows. The repressive forces of nation and people feed off the self-valorization of the community and destroy its multiplicity. When black nationalism poses the uniformity and homogeneity of the African American people as its basis (eclipsing class differences, for example) or when it designates one segment of the community (such as African American men) as de facto representatives of the whole, the profound ambiguity of subaltern nationalism's progressive functions emerges as clearly as ever.[29] Precisely the structures that play a defensive role with respect to the outside—in the interest of furthering the power, autonomy, and unity of the community—are the same that play an oppressive role internally, negating the multiplicity of the community itself.

We should emphasize, however, that these ambiguous progressive functions of the concept of nation exist primarily when nation is not effectively linked to sovereignty, that is, when the imagined nation does not (yet) exist, when the nation remains merely a dream. As soon as the nation begins to form as a sovereign state, its progressive functions all but vanish. Jean Genet was enchanted by the revolutionary desire of the Black Panthers and the Palestinians, but he recognized that becoming a sovereign nation would be the end of their revolutionary qualities. "The day when the Palestinians are institutionalized," he said, "I will no longer be at their side. The day the Palestinians become a nation like the other nations, I will no longer be there."[30] With national "liberation" and the construction of the nation-state, all of the oppressive functions of modern sovereignty inevitably blossom in full force.

Totalitarianism of the Nation-State

When the nation-state does function as an institution of sovereignty, does it finally manage to resolve the crisis of modernity? Does the concept of the people and its biopolitical displacement of sovereignty succeed in shifting the terms and the terrain of the synthesis between constituent power and constituted power, and between the dynamic of productive forces and relations of production, in such a way as to carry us beyond the crisis? A vast panorama of authors, poets, and politicians (often emerging from progressive, socialist, and anti-imperialist movements) have certainly thought so. The conversion of the nineteenth-century Jacobin Left into a national Left, the more and more intense adoption of national programs in the Second and Third Internationals, and the nationalist forms of liberation struggles in the colonial and postcolonial world all the way up to today's resistance of nations to the processes of globalization and the catastrophes they provoke: all this seems to support the view that the nation-state does afford a new dynamic beyond the historical and conceptual disaster of the modern sovereign state.[31]

We have a different perspective on the function of the nation, however, and in our view the crisis of modernity remains resolutely open under the rule of the nation and its people. When we take up again our genealogy of the concept of sovereignty in nineteenth- and twentieth-century Europe, it is clear that the state-form of modernity first fell into the nation-state-form, then the nation-state-form descended into a whole series of barbarisms. When class struggle reopened the mystified synthesis of modernity in the early decades of the twentieth century and demonstrated again the powerful antithesis between the state and the multitude and between productive forces and relations of production, that antithesis led directly to European civil war—a civil war that was nonetheless cloaked in the guise of conflicts among sovereign nation-states.[32] In the Second World War, Nazi Germany, along with the various European fascisms, stood opposed to socialist Russia. Nations were presented as mystifications of, or stand-ins for, the class subjects in conflict. If Nazi Germany is the ideal type of the transformation of modern sovereignty into national sovereignty and of its articulation in capitalist form, then Stalinist Russia is the ideal type of the transformation of popular interest and the cruel logics that follow from it into a project of national modernization, mobilizing for its own purposes the productive forces that yearn for liberation from capitalism.

Here we could analyze the national socialist apotheosis of the modern concept of sovereignty and its transformation into national sovereignty: nothing could more clearly demonstrate the coherence of this passage than the transfer of power from the Prussian monarchy to Hitler's regime, under the good auspices of the German bourgeoisie. This passage, however, is well known, as are the explosive violence of this transfer of power, the exemplary obedience of the German people, their military and civil valor in the service of the nation, and the secondary consequences that we can call, in a kind of intellectual shorthand, Auschwitz (as symbol of the Jewish holocaust) and Buchenwald (as symbol of the extermination of communists, homosexuals, Gypsies, and others). Let us leave this story to other scholars and to the disgrace of history.

We are more interested here with the other side of the national question in Europe during this era. In other words, what really happened when nationalism went hand in hand with socialism in Europe? In order to respond to this question, we have to revisit a few central moments in the history of European socialism. In particular, we must remember that not long after its inception, between the middle and end of the nineteenth century, the socialist International had to come to terms with strong nationalist movements, and through this confrontation the original internationalist passion of the workers' movement quickly evaporated. The policies of the strongest European workers' movements, in Germany, Austria, France, and above all England, immediately raised the banner of national interest. Social-democratic reformism was entirely invested in this compromise conceived in the name of the nation—a compromise between class interests, that is, between the proletariat and certain strata of the bourgeois hegemonic structure in each country. Let's not even talk about the ignoble history of betrayal in which segments of the European workers' movement supported the imperialist enterprises of the European nation-states, nor the unpardonable folly that brought together the various European reformisms in consenting to the masses' being led to slaughter in the First World War.

Social-democratic reformism did have an adequate theory for these positions. Several Austrian social-democratic professors invented it, contemporaries of Musil's Count Leinsdorf. In the idyllic atmosphere of alpine Kakania, in the gentle intellectual climate of that "return to Kant," those professors, such as Otto Bauer, insisted on the necessity of considering nationality a fundamental element of modernization.[33] In fact, they believed that from the confrontation between nationality (defined as a community of character) and capitalist development (understood as society) there would emerge a dialectic that in its unfolding would eventually favor the proletariat and its progressive hegemony in society. This program ignored the fact that the concept of nation-state is not divisible but rather organic, not transcendental but transcendent, and even in its transcendence it is constructed to oppose every tendency on the part of the proletariat to reappropriate social spaces and social wealth. What, then, could modernization mean if it is fundamentally tied to the reform of the capitalist system and inimical to any opening of the revolutionary process? These authors celebrated the nation without wanting to pay the price of this celebration. Or better, they celebrated it while mystifying the destructive power of the concept of nation. Given this perspective, support for the imperialist projects and the interimperialist war were really logical and inevitable positions for social-democratic reformism.

Bolshevism, too, entered the terrain of nationalist mythology, particularly through Stalin's celebrated prerevolutionary pamphlet on Marxism and the national question.[34] According to Stalin, nations are immediately revolutionary, and revolution means modernization: nationalism is an ineluctable stage in development. Through Stalin's translation, however, as nationalism becomes socialist, socialism becomes Russian, and Ivan the Terrible is laid to rest in the tomb beside Lenin. The Communist International is transformed into an assembly of the "fifth column" of Russian national interests. The notion of communist revolution—the deterritorializing specter that had haunted Europe and the world, and that from the Paris Commune to 1917 in Saint Petersburg and to Mao's Long March had managed to bring together deserters, internationalist partisans, striking workers, and cosmopolitan intellectuals—was finally made into a reterritorializing regime of national sovereignty. It is a tragic irony that nationalist socialism in Europe came to resemble national socialism. This is not because "the two extremes meet," as some liberals would like to think, but because the abstract machine of national sovereignty is at the heart of both.

When, in the midst of the cold war, the concept of totalitarianism was introduced into political science, it only touched on extrinsic elements of the question. In its most coherent form the concept of totalitarianism was used to denounce the destruction of the democratic public sphere, the continuation of Jacobinist ideologies, the extreme forms of racist nationalism, and the negation of market forces. The concept of totalitarianism, however, ought to delve much more deeply into the real phenomena and at the same time give a better explanation of them. In fact, totalitarianism consists not simply in totalizing the effects of social life and subordinating them to a global disciplinary norm, but also in the negation of social life itself, the erosion of its foundation, and the theoretical and practical stripping away of the very possibility of the existence of the multitude. What is totalitarian is the organic foundation and the unified source of society and the state. The community is not a dynamic collective creation but a primordial founding myth. An originary notion of the people poses an identity that homogenizes and purifies the image of the population while blocking the constructive interactions of differences within the multitude.

Sieyès saw the embryo of totalitarianism already in eighteenth-century conceptions of national and popular sovereignty, conceptions that effectively preserved the absolute power of monarchy and transferred it to national sovereignty. He glimpsed the future of what might be called totalitarian democracy.[35] In the debate over the Constitution of Year III of the French Revolution, Sieyès denounced the "bad plans for a re-total [*ré-total*] instead of a re-public [*ré-publique*], which would be fatal for freedom and ruinous for both the public realm and the private."[36] The concept of nation and the practices of nationalism are from the beginning set down on the road not to the republic but to the "re-total," the total thing, that is, the totalitarian overcoding of social life.

2.3

THE DIALECTICS OF COLONIAL SOVEREIGNTY

To Toussaint l'Ouverture

Toussaint, the most unhappy man of men!
Whether the whistling Rustic tend his plough
Within thy hearing, or thy head be now
Pillowed in some deep dungeon's earless den;—
O miserable Chieftain! where and when
Wilt thou find patience! Yet die not; do thou
Wear rather in thy bonds a cheerful brow:
Though fallen thyself, never to rise again,
Live, and take comfort. Thou hast left behind
Powers that will work for thee; air, earth, and skies;
There's not a breathing of the common wind
That will forget thee; thou hast great allies;
Thy friends are exultations, agonies,
And love, and man's unconquerable mind.

William Wordsworth

We now need to take a step back and examine the genealogy of the concept of sovereignty from the perspective of colonialism. The crisis of modernity has from the beginning had an intimate relation to racial subordination and colonization. Whereas within its domain the nation-state and its attendant ideological structures work tirelessly to create and reproduce the purity of the people, on the outside the nation-state is a machine that produces Others, creates racial difference, and raises boundaries that delimit and support the modern subject of sovereignty. These boundaries and barriers, however, are not impermeable but rather serve to regulate two-way flows between Europe and its outside. The Oriental, the African, the Amerindian are all necessary components for the negative foundation of European identity and modern sovereignty as such. The dark Other of European Enlightenment stands as its very foundation just as the productive relationship with the "dark continents" serves as the economic foundation of the European nation-states.[1] The racial conflict intrinsic to European modernity is another symptom of the permanent crisis that defines modern sovereignty. The colony stands in dialectical opposition to European modernity, as its necessary double and irrepressible antagonist. Colonial sovereignty is another insufficient attempt to resolve the crisis of modernity.

Humankind Is One and Many

The age of European discovery and the progressively intense communication among the spaces and peoples of the earth that followed have always carried with them a real utopian element. But so much blood has been spilled, so many lives and cultures destroyed, that it seems much more urgent to denounce the barbarity and horror of western European (and then also U.S., Soviet, and Japanese) expansion and control over the globe. We think it important, however, not to forget the utopian tendencies that have always accompanied the progression toward globalization, even if these tendencies have continually been defeated by the powers of modern sovereignty. The love of differences and the belief in the universal freedom and equality of humanity proper to the revolutionary thought of Renaissance humanism reappear here on a global scale. This utopian element of globalization is what prevents us from simply falling back into particularism and isolationism in reaction to the totalizing forces of imperialism and racist domination, pushing us instead to forge a project of counterglobalization, counter-Empire. This utopian moment, however, has never been unambiguous. It is a tendency that constantly conflicts with sovereign order and domination. We see three exemplary expressions of this utopianism, in all its ambiguity, in the thought of Bartolomé de Las Casas, Toussaint L'Ouverture, and Karl Marx.

In the first half-century after the European landing in the Americas at Hispaniola, Bartolomé de Las Casas witnessed with horror the barbarity of the conquistadores and colonists and their enslavement and genocide of the Amerindians. The majority of the Spanish military, administrators, and colonists, hungry for gold and power, saw the occupants of this new world as irrevocably Other, less than human, or at least naturally subordinate to Europeans—and Las Casas recounts for us how the newly arrived Europeans treated them worse than their animals. In this context it is a wonder that Las Casas, who was part of the Spanish mission, could separate himself enough from the common stream of opinion to insist on the humanity of the Amerindians and contest the brutality of the Spanish rulers. His protest arises from one simple principle: *humankind is one and equal.*

One should recognize at the same time, however, that a missionary vocation is intrinsically linked to the humanitarian project of the good bishop of Chiapas. In fact, Las Casas can think equality only in terms of sameness. The Amerindians are equal to Europeans in nature only insofar as they are potentially European, or really potentially Christian: "The nature of men is the same and all are called by Christ in the same way."[2] Las Casas cannot see beyond the Eurocentric view of the Americas, in which the highest generosity and charity would be bringing the Amerindians under the control and tutelage of the true religion and its culture. The natives are undeveloped potential Europeans. In this sense Las Casas belongs to a discourse that extends well into the twentieth century on the perfectibility of savages. For the Amerindians, just as for the Jews of sixteenth-century Spain, the path to freedom from persecution must pass first through Christian conversion. Las Casas is really not so far from the Inquisition. He recognizes that humankind is one, but cannot see that it is also simultaneously many.

More than two centuries after Las Casas, in the late eighteenth century, when Europe's domination over the Americas had changed form from conquest, massacre, and pillage to the more stable colonial structure of large-scale slave production and trade exclusives, a black slave named Toussaint L'Ouverture led the first successful independence struggle against modern slavery in the French colony of Saint Domingue (now Haiti). Toussaint L'Ouverture breathed in the rhetoric of the French Revolution emanating from Paris in its pure form. If the French revolutionaries opposing the ancien régime proclaimed the universal human right to "liberté, egalité, et fraternité," Toussaint assumed that the blacks, mulattoes, and whites of the colony were also included under the broad umbrella of the rights of citizens. He took the victory over the feudal aristocracy and the exaltation of universal values in Europe to imply also the victory over the "race aristocracy" and the abolition of slavery. All will now be free citizens, equal brothers in the new French republic. The letters of Toussaint to French military and governmental leaders pursue the rhetoric of the revolution faultlessly to its logical conclusion and thereby reveal its hypocrisy. Perhaps naively or perhaps as a conscious political tactic, Toussaint demonstrates how the leaders of the revolution betray the principles they claim to hold most dear. In a report to the Directoire on 14 Brumaire an VI (November 5, 1797), Toussaint warned the French leaders that any return to slavery, any compromise of principles, would be impossible. A declaration of freedom is irreversible: "Do you think that men who have enjoyed the blessing of liberty will calmly see it snatched away? . . . But no, the same hand that has broken our chains will not enslave us anew. France will not revoke her principles, she will not withdraw from us the greatest of her benefits."[3]

The proclamations of universal rights launched so confidently in Paris come back from Saint Domingue only to strike horror in the hearts of the French. In the voyage across the Atlantic, the universality of the ideals became more real and were put into practice. As Aimé Césaire puts it, Toussaint L'Ouverture pushed the project forward across the terrain "that separates the *only thought* from concrete reality; right from its actualization; reason from its proper truth."[4] Toussaint takes the Declaration of the Rights of Man to the letter and insists on its full translation into practice. The revolution under Toussaint does not seek liberation from European domination only to return to a lost African world or reestablish in isolation traditional forms of rule; Toussaint looks forward to the forms of liberty and equality newly made available in the increasingly interconnected world.[5]

At times, however, Toussaint writes as if the very idea of freedom had been created by the French, and as if he and his insurgent companions were free only by the grace of Paris. This may be merely a rhetorical strategy of Toussaint's, an example of his ironic obsequiousness toward the French rulers; but certainly one should not think freedom to be a European idea. The slaves of Saint Domingue had revolted against their masters ever since their capture and forced immigration from Africa. They were not granted freedom but won it through bloody and tireless battle. Neither the desire for freedom nor its conquest originated in France, and the blacks of Saint Domingue did not need the Parisians to teach them to fight for it. What Toussaint does receive and make good use of is the specific rhetoric of the French revolutionaries that gives legitimate form to his quest for liberation.

In the nineteenth century Karl Marx, like Las Casas and Toussaint L'Ouverture before him, recognized the utopian potential of the ever-increasing processes of global interaction and communication. Like Las Casas, Marx was horrified by the brutality of European conquest and exploitation. Capitalism was born in Europe through the blood and sweat of conquered and colonized non-European peoples: "The veiled slavery of the wage-labourers in Europe needed the unqualified slavery of the New World as its pedestal."[6] Like Toussaint L'Ouverture, Marx recognized human freedom as a universal project to be realized through practice and from which no population should be excluded.

This global utopian vein in Marx is nonetheless ambiguous, perhaps even more so than in the other two cases, as we can see clearly from the series of articles he wrote for the *New York Daily*

Tribune in 1853 on British rule in India. Marx's primary goal in these articles was to explain the debate going on at the time in the British Parliament over the status of the East India Company and situate the debate in the history of British colonial rule. Marx is of course quick to note the brutality of the introduction of British "civilization" into India and the havoc and suffering wrought by the rapacious greed of British capital and the British government. He immediately warns, however, in terms that bring us right back to the revolutionary face of the Renaissance, against simply reacting to the barbarity of the British by supporting blindly the status quo of Indian society. The village system that Marx understood to preexist the British colonial intrusion was nothing to be championed: "Sickening as it must be to human feeling to witness" the destruction and suffering caused by the British, "we must not forget that these idyllic village communities, inoffensive though they may appear, had always been the solid foundation of Oriental despotism, that they restrained the human mind, within the smallest possible compass, making it the unresisting tool of superstition, enslaving it beneath the traditional rules depriving it of all grandeur and historical energies."[7] Neither does the ruling structure of Indian princes deserve support, even in reaction to the British: "It is not a strange thing that the same men who denounce 'the barbarous splendors of the Crown and Aristocracy of England' are shedding tears at the downfall of Indian Nabobs, Rujahs, and Jagidars, the great majority of whom possess not even the prestige of antiquity, being generally usurpers of very recent date, set up by English intrigue."[8]

The colonial situation falls too easily into a choice between two bad alternatives: either submission to British capital and British rule or return to traditional Indian social structures and submission to Indian princes; either foreign domination or local domination. For Marx there must be another path that refuses both of these alternatives, a path of insubordination and freedom. In this sense, in creating the conditions of possibility for a new society, "whatever may have been the crimes of England, she was the unconscious tool of history in bringing about that revolution."[9] Capital can, in certain circumstances, be a force of enlightenment. Like Toussaint, then, Marx saw no use in overthrowing foreign domination simply to restore some isolated and traditional form of oppression. The alternative must look forward to a new form of freedom, connected to the expansive networks of global exchange.

The only "alternative" path Marx can imagine, however, is that same path that European society has already traveled. Marx has no conception of the difference of Indian society, the different potentials it contains. He can thus see the Indian past only as vacant and static: "Indian society has no history at all, at least no known history. What we call its history is but the history of the successive intruders who founded their empires on the passive basis of that unresisting and unchanging society."[10] The claim that Indian society has no history means not that nothing has happened in India but that the course of events has been determined exclusively by external forces, while Indian society has remained passive, "unresisting and unchanging." Certainly Marx was limited by his scant knowledge of India's present and past.[11] His lack of information, however, is not the point. The central issue is that Marx can conceive of history outside of Europe only as moving strictly along the path already traveled by Europe itself. "England has to fulfill a double mission in India," he wrote, "one destructive, the other regenerating—the annihilation of old Asiatic Society, and the laying of the material foundations of Western society in Asia."[12] India can progress only by being transformed into a Western society. All the world can move forward only by following the footsteps of Europe. Marx's Eurocentrism is in the end not so different from that of Las Casas.

The Crisis of Colonial Slavery

Although the utopian vein has continually surfaced in the historical process of the interconnection and intercommunication of the world in the modern period, it has nonetheless continually been suppressed militarily and ideologically by the forces of European domination. The primary result has been massacres on a scale never before imagined and the establishment of racial, political, and economic structures of European rule over the non-European world. The rise of European supremacy was driven in large part by the development and spread of capitalism, which fed Europe's seemingly insatiable thirst for wealth. The global expansion of capitalism, however, was neither a uniform nor a univocal process. In various regions and among different populations capitalism developed unevenly: it lurched forward, hesitated, and retreated according to a variety of diverse paths. One such circuitous path is traced by the history of large-scale colonial slave production in the Americas between the late seventeenth and mid-nineteenth centuries, a history that is not precapitalist but rather *within* the complex and contradictory developments of capital.

Large-scale plantation production with slave labor was initiated in the Caribbean in the mid-seventeenth century by English and French planters who imported African slaves to fill the void left by the native peoples killed by European weapons and disease. By the end of the eighteenth century, the products of slave labor in the Americas constituted one third of the value of European commerce.[13] European capitalism stood in a very ambiguous relation to this slave production in the Americas. One might reason logically, as many have, that since capitalism is based ideologically and materially on free labor, or really on the worker's ownership of his or her own labor power, capitalism must be antithetical to slave labor. From this perspective, colonial slavery would be seen as a preexisting form of production analogous to feudalism that capital succeeds gradually in overcoming. The capitalist ideology of freedom would in this case be an unalloyed force of enlightenment.

Capital's relationship to colonial slavery, however, is in fact much more intimate and complex. First of all, even though capitalism's ideology is indeed antithetical to slavery, in practice capital nonetheless not only subsumed and reinforced existing slave production systems throughout the world but also *created new systems of slavery* on an unprecedented scale, particularly in the Americas.[14] One might interpret capital's creation of slave systems as a kind of apprenticeship to capitalism, in which slavery would function as a transitional stage between the natural (that is, self-sufficient and isolated) economies that preexisted European intrusion and capitalism proper. Indeed, the scale and organization of the eighteenth-century Caribbean plantations did foreshadow in certain respects the nineteenth-century European industrial plant.[15] The slave production in the Americas and the African slave trade, however, were not merely or even predominantly a transition to capitalism. They were a relatively stable support, a pedestal of superexploitation on which European capitalism stood. There is no contradiction here: slave labor in the colonies made capitalism in Europe possible, and European capital had no interest in giving it up.

In the very same period when European powers constructed the bases of the slave economy across the Atlantic, there was also in Europe, principally in eastern but also in southern Europe, a refeudalization of the agrarian economy and thus a very strong tendency to block the mobility of labor and freeze the conditions of the labor market. Europe was thrown back into a second period of servitude. The point here is not simply to denounce the irrationality of the bourgeoisie, but to understand how *slavery and servitude can be perfectly compatible with capitalist production,* as mechanisms that limit the mobility of the labor force and block its movements. Slavery, servitude, and all the other guises of the coercive organization of labor—from coolieism in the Pacific and peonage in Latin America to apartheid in South Africa—are all essential elements internal to the processes of capitalist development. In this period slavery and wage labor engaged each other as dance partners in the coordinated steps of capitalist development.[16]

Certainly many noble and enlightened proponents of abolitionism in Europe and the Americas in the late eighteenth and early nineteenth centuries argued against slavery on moral grounds. The abolitionist arguments had some real force, however, only when they served the interests of capital, for example, when they served to undercut the profits of a competitor's slave production. Even then, however, their force was quite limited. In fact, neither moral arguments at home nor calculations of profitability abroad could move European capital to dismantle the slave regimes. Only the revolt and revolution of slaves themselves could provide an adequate lever. Just as capital moves forward to restructure production and employ new technologies only as a response to the organized threat of worker antagonism, so too European capital would not relinquish slave production until the organized slaves posed a threat to their power and made that system of production untenable. In other words, slavery was not abandoned for economic reasons but rather overthrown by political forces.[17] Political unrest did of course undercut the economic profitability of the system, but more important, the slaves in revolt came to constitute a real counterpower. The Haitian revolution was certainly the watershed in the modern history of slave revolt—and its specter circulated throughout the Americas in the early nineteenth century just as the specter of the October Revolution haunted European capitalism over a century later. One should not forget, however, that revolt and antagonism were a constant part of slavery throughout the Americas, from New York City to Bahia. The economy of slavery, like the economy of modernity itself, was an economy of crisis.

The claim that regimes of slavery and servitude are internal to capitalist production and development points toward the intimate relationship between the laboring subjects' desire to flee the relationship of command and capital's attempts to block the population within fixed territorial boundaries. Yann Moulier Boutang emphasizes the primacy of these lines of flight in the history of capitalist development:

> An anonymous, collective, continuous, and uncontainable force of defection is what has driven the labor market toward freedom. This same force is what has obliged liberalism to produce the apology of free labor, the right to property, and open borders. It has also forced the bourgeois economists to establish models that immobilize labor, discipline it, and disregard the elements of uninterrupted flight. All of this has

> functioned to invent and reinvent a thousand forms of slavery. This ineluctable aspect of accumulation precedes the question of the proletarianization of the liberal era. It constructs the bases of the modern state.[18]

The deterritorializing desire of the multitude is the motor that drives the entire process of capitalist development, and capital must constantly attempt to contain it.

The Production of Alterity

Colonialism and racial subordination function as a temporary solution to the crisis of European modernity, not only in economic and political terms, but also in terms of identity and culture. Colonialism constructs figures of alterity and manages their flows in what unfolds as a complex dialectical structure. The negative construction of non-European others is finally what founds and sustains European identity itself.

Colonial identity functions first of all through a Manichaean logic of exclusion. As Franz Fanon tells us, "The colonial world is a world cut in two."[19] The colonized are excluded from European spaces not only in physical and territorial terms, and not only in terms of rights and privileges, but even in terms of thought and values. The colonized subject is constructed in the metropolitan imaginary as other, and thus, as far as possible, the colonized is cast outside the defining bases of European civilized values. (We can't reason with them; they can't control themselves; they don't respect the value of human life; they only understand violence.) Racial difference is a sort of black hole that can swallow up all the capacities for evil, barbarism, unrestrained sexuality, and so forth. The dark colonized subject thus seems at first obscure and mysterious in its otherness. This colonial construction of identities rests heavily on the fixity of the boundary between metropole and colony. The purity of the identities, in both biological and cultural senses, is of utmost importance, and maintenance of the boundary is cause for considerable anxiety. "All values, in fact," Fanon points out, "are irrevocably poisoned and diseased as soon as they are allowed in contact with the colonized race."[20] The boundaries protecting this pure European space are continually under siege. Colonial law operates primarily around these boundaries, both in that it supports their exclusionary function and in that it applies differently to the subjects on the two sides of the divide. Apartheid is simply one form, perhaps the emblematic form, of the compartmentalization of the colonial world.

The barriers that divide the colonial world are not simply erected on natural boundaries, even though there are almost always physical markers that help naturalize the division. *Alterity is not given but produced.* This premise is the common point of departure for a wide range of research that has emerged in recent decades, including notably Edward's Said's seminal book: "I have begun with the assumption that the Orient is not an inert fact of nature . . . that the Orient was created—or, as I call it, 'Orientalized.' " Orientalism is not simply a scholarly project to gain more accurate knowledge of a real object, the Orient, but rather a discourse that creates its own object in the unfolding of the discourse itself. The two primary characteristics of this Orientalist project are its homogenization of the Orient from Maghreb to India (Orientals everywhere are all nearly the same) and its essentialization (the Orient and the Oriental character are timeless and unchanging identities). The result, as Said points out, is not the Orient as it is, an empirical object, but the Orient as it has been Orientalized, an object of European discourse.[21] The Orient, then, at least as we know it through Orientalism, is a creation of discourse, made in Europe and exported back to the Orient. The representation is at once a form of creation and a form of exclusion.

Among the academic disciplines involved in this cultural production of alterity, anthropology was perhaps the most important rubric under which the native other was imported to and exported from Europe.[22] From the real differences of non-European peoples, nineteenth-century anthropologists constructed an other being of a different nature; differential cultural and physical traits were construed as the essence of the African, the Arab, the Aboriginal, and so forth. When colonial expansion was at its peak and European powers were engaged in the scramble for Africa, anthropology and the study of non-European peoples became not only a scholarly endeavor but also a broad field for public instruction. The other was imported to Europe—in natural history museums, public exhibitions of primitive peoples, and so forth—and thus made increasingly available for the popular imaginary. In both its scholarly and its popular forms, nineteenth-century anthropology presented non-European subjects and cultures as undeveloped versions of Europeans and their civilization: they were signs of primitiveness that represented stages on the road to European civilization. The diachronic stages of humanity's evolution toward civilization were thus conceived as present synchronically in the various primitive peoples and cultures spread across the globe.[23] The anthropological presentation of non-European others within this evolutionary theory of civilizations served to confirm and validate the eminent position of Europeans and thereby legitimate the colonialist project as a whole.

Important segments of the discipline of history were also deeply embedded in the scholarly and popular production of alterity, and thus also in the legitimation of colonial rule. For example, upon arriving in India and finding no historiography they could use, British administrators had to write their own "Indian history" to sustain and further the interests of colonial rule. The British had to historicize the Indian past in order to have access to it and put it to work. This British creation of an Indian history, however, like the formation of the colonial state, could be achieved only by imposing European colonial logics and models on Indian reality.[24] India's past was thus annexed so as to become merely a portion of British history—or rather, British scholars and administrators created an Indian history and exported it to India. This historiography supported the Raj and in turn made the past inaccessible to Indians as history. The reality of India and Indians was thus supplanted by a powerful representation that posed them as an other to Europe, a primitive stage in the teleology of civilization.

The Dialectic of Colonialism

In the logic of colonialist representations, the construction of a separate colonized other and the segregation of identity and alterity turns out paradoxically to be at once absolute and extremely intimate. The process consists, in fact, of two moments that are dialectically related. In the first moment difference has to be pushed to the extreme. In the colonial imaginary the colonized is not simply an other banished outside the realm of civilization; rather, it is grasped or produced as Other, as the absolute negation, as the most distant point on the horizon. Eighteenth-century colonial slaveholders, for example, recognized the absoluteness of this difference clearly. "The Negro is a being, whose nature and dispositions are not merely different from those of the European, they are the *reverse* of them. Kindness and compassion excite in his breast implacable and deadly hatred; but stripes, and insults, and abuse, generate gratitude, affection, and inviolable attachment!"[25] Thus the slaveholders' mentality, according to an abolitionist pamphlet. The non-European subject acts, speaks, and thinks in a manner *exactly opposite* to the European.

Precisely because the difference of the Other is absolute, it can be inverted in a second moment as the foundation of the Self. In other words, the evil, barbarity, and licentiousness of the colonized Other are what make possible the goodness, civility, and propriety of the European Self. What first appears strange, foreign, and distant thus turns out to be very close and intimate. Knowing, seeing, and even touching the colonized is essential, even if this knowledge and contact take place only on the plane of representation and relate little to the actual subjects in the colonies and the metropole. The intimate struggle with the slave, feeling the sweat on its skin, smelling its odor, defines the vitality of the master. This intimacy, however, in no way blurs the division between the two identities in struggle, but only makes more important that the boundaries and the purity of the identities be policed. *The identity of the European Self is produced in this dialectical movement.* Once the colonial subject is constructed as absolutely Other, it can in turn be subsumed (canceled and raised up) within a higher unity. The absolute Other is reflected back into the most proper. Only through opposition to the colonized does the metropolitan subject really become itself. What first appeared as a simple logic of exclusion, then, turns out to be a negative dialectic of recognition. The colonizer does produce the colonized as negation, but, through a dialectical twist, that negative colonized identity is negated in turn to found the positive colonizer Self. Modern European thought and the modern Self are both necessarily bound to what Paul Gilroy calls the "relationship of racial terror and subordination."[26] The gilded monuments not only of European cities but also of modern European thought itself are founded on the intimate dialectical struggle with its Others.

We should be careful to note that the colonial world never really conformed to the simple two-part division of this dialectical structure. Any analysis of eighteenth-century Haitian society before the revolution, for example, cannot consider only whites and blacks but must also take into account at least the position of mulattoes, who were at times united with whites on the basis of their property and freedom, and at times united with blacks because of their nonwhite skin. Even in simple racial terms this social reality demands at least three axes of analysis—but that, too, fails to grasp the real social divisions. One must also recognize the conflict among whites of different classes and the interests of the black slaves as distinct from those of the free blacks and maroons. In short, the real social situation in the colonies never breaks down neatly into an absolute binary between pure opposing forces. Reality always presents proliferating multiplicities. Our argument here, however, is not that reality presents this facile binary structure but that colonialism, as an abstract machine that produces identities and alterities, imposes binary divisions on the colonial world. Colonialism homogenizes real social differences by creating one overriding opposition that pushes differences to the absolute and then subsumes the opposition under the identity of European civilization. *Reality is not dialectical, colonialism is.*

The work of numerous authors, such as Jean-Paul Sartre and Franz Fanon, who have recognized that colonial representations and colonial sovereignty are dialectical in form has proven useful in several respects. First of all, the dialectical construction demonstrates that there is nothing essential about the identities in struggle. The White and the Black, the European and the Oriental, the colonizer and the colonized are all representations that function only in relation to each other and (despite appearances) have no real necessary basis in nature, biology, or rationality. Colonialism is an abstract machine that produces alterity and identity. And yet in the colonial situation these differences and identities are made to function as if they were absolute, essential, and natural. The first result of the dialectical reading is thus the denaturalization of racial and cultural difference. This does not mean that once recognized as artificial constructions, colonial identities evaporate into thin air; they are real illusions and continue to function as if they were essential. This recognition is not a politics in itself, but merely the sign that an anticolonial politics is possible. In the second place, the dialectical interpretation makes clear that colonialism and colonialist representations are grounded in a violent struggle that must be continually renewed. The European Self needs violence and needs to confront its Other to feel and maintain its power, to remake itself continually. The generalized state of war that continuously subtends colonial representations is not accidental or even unwanted—violence is the necessary foundation of colonialism itself. Third, posing colonialism as a negative dialectic of recognition makes clear the potential for subversion inherent in the situation. For a thinker like Fanon, the reference to Hegel suggests that the Master can only achieve a hollow form of recognition; it is the Slave, through life-and-death struggle, who has the potential to move forward toward full consciousness.[27] The dialectic ought to imply movement, but this dialectic of European sovereign identity has fallen back into stasis. The failed dialectic suggests the possibility of a proper dialectic that through negativity will move history forward.

The Boomerang of Alterity

Many authors, particularly during the long season of intense decolonization struggles from the end of World War II through the 1960s, argued that this positive dialectic of colonialism that founds and stabilizes European sovereign identity should be challenged by a properly negative and hence revolutionary dialectic. We cannot defeat the colonialist production of alterity, these authors claimed, simply by revealing the artificiality of the identities and differences created—and thereby hoping to arrive directly at an affirmation of the authentic universality of humanity. The only possible strategy is one of reversal or inversion of the colonialist logic itself. "The unity which will come eventually, bringing all oppressed peoples together in the same struggle," Sartre proclaims, "must be preceded in the colonies by what I shall call the moment of separation or negativity: this antiracist racism is the only road that will lead to the abolition of racial differences."[28] Sartre imagines that this negative dialectic will finally set history in motion.

The negative dialectic has most often been conceived in cultural terms, for example, as the project of négritude—the quest to discover the black essence or unveil the black soul. According to this logic, the response to colonialist representations has to involve reciprocal and symmetrical representations. Even if the blackness of the colonized is recognized as a production and a mystification constructed in the colonial imaginary, it is not denied or dispelled on account of that, but rather affirmed—as essence! According to Sartre, the revolutionary poets of négritude, such as Aimé Césaire and Léopold Senghor, adopt the negative pole that they have inherited from the European dialectic and transform it into something positive, intensifying it, claiming it as a moment of self-consciousness. No longer a force of stabilization and equilibrium, the domesticated Other has become savage, truly Other—that is, capable of reciprocity and autonomous initiative. This, as Sartre announces so beautifully and ominously, is "the moment of the boomerang."[29] The negative moment is able to operate a reciprocal destruction of the European Self—precisely because European society and its values are founded on the domestication and negative subsumption of the colonized. The moment of negativity is posed as the necessary first step in a transition toward the ultimate goal of a raceless society that recognizes the equality, freedom, and common humanity of all.[30]

Despite the coherent dialectical logic of this Sartrean cultural politics, however, the strategy it proposes seems to us completely illusory. The power of the dialectic, which in the hands of colonial power mystified the reality of the colonial world, is adopted again as part of an anticolonial project as if the dialectic were itself the real form of the movement of history. Reality and history, however, are not dialectical, and no idealist rhetorical gymnastics can make them conform to the dialect.

The strategy of negativity, however, the moment of the boomerang, appears in an entirely different light when it is cast in a nondialectical form and in political rather than cultural terms. Fanon, for example, refuses the cultural politics of négritude with its consciousness of black identity and poses the revolutionary antithesis instead in terms of physical violence. The original moment of violence is that of colonialism: the domination and exploitation of the colonized by the colonizer. The second moment, the response of the colonized to this original violence, can take all sorts of perverted forms in the colonial context. "The colonized man will first manifest this aggressiveness which has been deposited in his bones against his own people."[31] The violence among the colonized population, sometimes thought to be the residues of ancient tribal or religious antagonisms, is really the pathological reflections of the violence of colonialism that most often surfaces as superstitions, myths, dances, and mental disorders. Fanon does not recommend that the colonized should flee or avoid the violence. Colonialism by its very operation perpetuates this violence, and if it is not addressed directly, it will continue to manifest itself in these destructive, pathological forms. The only path to health that Doctor Fanon can recommend is a reciprocal counterviolence.[32] Moreover, this is the only path to liberation. The slave who never struggles for freedom, who is simply granted the permission of the master, will forever remain a slave. This is precisely the "reciprocity" that Malcolm X proposed as a strategy to address the violence of white supremacy in the United States.[33]

For both Fanon and Malcolm X, however, this negative moment, this violent reciprocity, does not lead to any dialectical synthesis; it is not the upbeat that will be resolved in a future harmony. This open negativity is merely the healthy expression of a real antagonism, a direct relation of force. Because it is not the means to a final synthesis, this negativity is not a politics in itself; rather, it merely poses a separation from colonialist domination and opens the field for politics. The real political process of constitution will have to take place on this open terrain of forces with a positive logic, separate from the dialectics of colonial sovereignty.

The Poisoned Gift of National Liberation

Subaltern nationalism has indeed, as we argued in the previous section, served important progressive functions. The nation has served among subordinated groups both as a defensive weapon employed to protect the group against external domination and as a sign of the unity, autonomy, and power of the community.[34] During the period of de-colonization and after, the nation appeared as the necessary vehicle for political modernization and hence the ineluctable path toward freedom and self-determination. The promise of a global democracy among nations, including their formal equality and sovereignty, was written into the original Charter of the United Nations: "The Organization and its Members . . . shall act in accordance with . . . the principle of the sovereign equality of all its members."[35] National sovereignty means freedom from foreign domination and the self-determination of peoples, and thus signals the definitive defeat of colonialism.

The progressive functions of national sovereignty, however, are always accompanied by powerful structures of internal domination. The perils of national liberation are even clearer when viewed externally, in terms of the world economic system in which the "liberated" nation finds itself. Indeed, the equation nationalism equals political and economic modernization, which has been heralded by leaders of numerous anticolonial and anti-imperialist struggles from Gandhi and Ho Chi Minh to Nelson Mandela, really ends up being a perverse trick. This equation serves to mobilize popular forces and galvanize a social movement, but where does the movement lead and what interests does it serve? In most cases it involves a *delegated* struggle, in which the modernization project also establishes in power the new ruling group that is charged with carrying it out. The revolution is thus offered up, hands and feet bound, to the new bourgeoisie. It is a February revolution, one might say, that should be followed by an October. But the calendar has gone crazy: October never comes, the revolutionaries get bogged down in "realism," and modernization ends up lost in hierarchies of the world market. Is not the control exerted by the world market, however, the opposite of the nationalist dream of an autonomous, self-centered development? The nationalism of anticolonial and anti-imperialist struggles effectively functions in reverse, and the liberated countries find themselves subordinated in the international economic order.

The very concept of a liberatory national sovereignty is ambiguous if not completely contradictory. While this nationalism seeks to liberate the multitude from *foreign* domination, it erects *domestic* structures of domination that are equally severe. The position of the newly sovereign nation-state cannot be understood when it is viewed in terms of the rosy U.N. imaginary of a harmonious concert of equal and autonomous national subjects. The postcolonial nation-state functions as an essential and subordinated element in the global organization of the capitalist market. As Partha Chatterjee argues, national liberation and national sovereignty are not just powerless against this global capitalist hierarchy but themselves contribute to its organization and functioning:

> Nowhere in the world has nationalism qua nationalism challenged the legitimacy of the marriage between Reason and

> capital. Nationalist thought . . . does not possess the ideological means to make this challenge. The conflict between metropolitain capital and the people-nation it resolves by absorbing the political life of the nation into the body of the state. Conservatory of the passive revolution, the national state now proceeds to find for "the nation" a place in the global order of capital, while striving to keep the contradictions between capital and the people in perpetual suspension. All politics is now sought to be subsumed under the overwhelming requirements of the state-representing-the-nation.[36]

The entire logical chain of representation might be summarized like this: the people representing the multitude, the nation representing the people, and the state representing the nation. Each link is an attempt to hold in suspension the crisis of modernity. Representation in each case means a further step of abstraction and control. From India to Algeria and Cuba to Vietnam, *the state is the poisoned gift of national liberation.*

The final link that explains the necessary subordination of the postcolonial nation-state, however, is the global order of capital. The global capitalist hierarchy that subordinates the formally sovereign nation-states within its order is fundamentally different from the colonialist and imperialist circuits of international domination. The end of colonialism is also the end of the modern world and modern regimes of rule. The end of modern colonialisms, of course, has not really opened an age of unqualified freedom but rather yielded to new forms of rule that operate on a global scale. Here we have our first real glimpse of the passage to Empire.

Contagion

When Louis-Ferdinand Destouches (Céline) went to Africa, what he found was disease. In the unforgettable African passage of Journey to the End of the Night, *the narrator, through the deliriums of his own fever, saw a population permeated through and through with disease: "The natives in those parts suffered horribly from every communicable disease* [toutes les maladies attrapables]*."[1] Perhaps this is exactly what we should expect* from Doctor Destouches, given that he was sent to Africa by the League of Nations to work as a hygienist, but of course Céline was also working with a commonplace of colonial consciousness.

There are two sides to the connection between colonialism and disease. First of all, simply the fact that the indigenous population is disease-ridden is itself a justification for the colonial project: "These niggers are sick! You'll see! They're completely corrupt [tout crevés et tout pourris]! . . . They're degenerates!" (p. 142). Disease is a sign of physical and moral corruption, a sign of a lack of civilization. Colonialism's civilizing project, then, is justified by the hygiene it brings. On the other side of the coin, however, from the European perspective, the primary danger of colonialism is disease—or really contagion. In Africa, Louis-Ferdinand finds "every communicable disease." Physical contamination, moral corruption, madness: the darkness of the colonial territories and populations is contagious, and Europeans are always at risk. (This is essentially the same truth that Kurtz recognizes in Conrad's Heart of Darkness.) Once there is established the differential between the pure, civilized European and the corrupt, barbarous Other, there is possible not only a civilizing process from disease to health, but also ineluctably the reverse process, from health to disease. Contagion is the constant and present danger, the dark underside of the civilizing mission.

It is interesting in Céline's Journey that the disease of colonial territories is a sign not really of death, but of an overabundance of life. The narrator, Louis-Ferdinand, finds that not only the population but moreover the African terrain itself is "monstrous" (p. 140). The disease of the jungle is that life springs up everywhere, everything grows, without bounds. What a horror for a hygienist! The disease that the colony lets loose is the lack of boundaries on life, an unlimited contagion. If one looks back, Europe appears reassuringly sterile. (Remember in Heart of Darkness the deathly pallor of Brussels that Marlow finds on his return from the Belgian Congo, but with respect to the monstrous, unbounded overabundance of life in the colony, the sterile environment of Europe seems comforting.) The standpoint of the hygienist may in fact be the privileged position for recognizing the anxieties of colonialist consciousness. The horror released by European conquest and colonialism is a horror of unlimited contact, flow, and ex-

change—or really the horror of contagion, miscegenation, and unbounded life. Hygiene requires protective barriers. European colonialism was continually plagued by contradictions between virtuous exchange and the danger of contagion, and hence it was characterized by a complex play of flows and hygienic boundaries between metropole and colony and among colonial territories.

The contemporary processes of globalization have torn down many of the boundaries of the colonial world. Along with the common celebrations of the unbounded flows in our new global village, one can still sense also an anxiety about increased contact and a certain nostalgia for colonialist hygiene. The dark side of the consciousness of globalization is the fear of contagion. If we break down global boundaries and open universal contact in our global village, how will we prevent the spread of disease and corruption? This anxiety is most clearly revealed with respect to the AIDS pandemic.[2] The lightning speed of the spread of AIDS in the Americas, Europe, Africa, and Asia demonstrated the new dangers of global contagion. As AIDS has been recognized first as a disease and then as a global pandemic, there have developed maps of its sources and spread that often focus on central Africa and Haiti, in terms reminiscent of the colonialist imaginary: unrestrained sexuality, moral corruption, and lack of hygiene. Indeed, the dominant discourses of AIDS prevention have been all about hygiene: We must avoid contact and use protection. The medical and humanitarian workers have to throw up their hands in frustration working with these infected populations who have so little respect for hygiene! (Think of what Doctor Destouches would say!) International and supranational projects to stop the spread of AIDS have tried to establish protective boundaries at another level by requiring HIV tests in order to cross national boundaries. The boundaries of nation-states, however, are increasingly permeable by all kinds of flows. Nothing can bring back the hygienic shields of colonial boundaries. The age of globalization is the age of universal contagion.

2.4

SYMPTOMS OF PASSAGE

> Here then is the man outside our people, outside our humanity. He is continually starving, nothing belongs to him but the instant, the prolonged instant of torture . . . He always has only one thing: his suffering, but there is nothing on the entire face of the earth that could serve as a remedy for him, there is no ground on which to plant his two feet, no support for his two hands to grasp, and thus there is so much less for him than there is for the music-hall trapeze artist who is at least hanging by a thread.
>
> Franz Kafka

The end of colonialism and the declining powers of the nation are indicative of a general passage from the paradigm of modern sovereignty toward the paradigm of imperial sovereignty. The various postmodernist and postcolonialist theories that have emerged since the 1980s give us a first view of this passage, but the perspective they offer proves to be quite limited. As the prefix "post-" should indicate, postmodernist and postcolonialist theorists never tire of critiquing and seeking liberation from the past forms of rule and their legacies in the present. Postmodernists continually return to the lingering influence of the Enlightenment as the source of domination; postcolonialist theorists combat the remnants of colonialist thinking.

We suspect that postmodernist and postcolonialist theories may end up in a dead end because they fail to recognize adequately the contemporary object of critique, that is, they mistake today's real enemy. What if the modern form of power these critics (and we ourselves) have taken such pains to describe and contest no longer holds sway in our society? What if these theorists are so intent on combating the remnants of a past form of domination that they fail to recognize the new form that is looming over them in the present? What if the dominating powers that are the intended object of critique have mutated in such a way as to depotentialize any such postmodernist challenge? In short, what if a new paradigm of power, a postmodern sovereignty, has come to replace the modern paradigm and rule through differential hierarchies of the hybrid and fragmentary subjectivities that these theorists celebrate? In this case, modern forms of sovereignty would no longer be at issue, and the postmodernist and postcolonialist strategies that appear to be liberatory would not challenge but in fact coincide with and even unwittingly reinforce the new strategies of rule!

When we begin to consider the ideologies of corporate capital and the world market, it certainly appears that the postmodernist and postcolonialist theorists who advocate a politics of difference, fluidity, and hybridity in order to challenge the binaries and essentialism of modern sovereignty have been outflanked by the strategies of power. Power has evacuated the bastion they are attacking and has circled around to their rear to join them in the assault in the name of difference. These theorists thus find themselves pushing against an open door. We do not mean to suggest that postmodernist and/or postcolonialist theorists are somehow the lackeys of global capital and the world market. Anthony Appiah and Arif Dirlik are ungenerous when they cast these authors in the position of "a comprador intelligentsia" and "the intelligentsia of global capitalism."[1] There is no need to doubt the democratic, egalitarian, and even at times anticapitalist desires that motivate large segments of these fields of work, but it is important to investigate the utility of these theories in the context of the new paradigm of power. This new enemy not only is resistant to the old weapons but actually thrives on them, and thus joins its would-be antagonists in applying them to the fullest. Long live difference! Down with essentialist binaries!

To a certain extent postmodernist and postcolonialist theories are important *effects* that reflect or trace the expansion of the world market and the passage of the form of sovereignty. These theories point toward Empire, but in a vague and confused way, with no awareness of the paradigmatic leap that this passage constitutes. We have to delve deep into this passage, elaborate its terms, and make clear the lineaments that constitute the new Empire. Recognizing the value and limitations of postmodernist and postcolonialist theories is a first step in this project.

Politics of Difference

In order to appreciate fully the critical powers of postmodernist discourses, one must first focus on the modern forms of sovereignty. As we saw in the previous sections, the world of modern sovereignty is a Manichaean world, divided by a series of binary oppositions that define Self and Other, white and black, inside and outside, ruler and ruled. Postmodernist thought challenges precisely this binary logic of modernity and in this respect provides important resources for those who are struggling to challenge modern discourses of patriarchy, colonialism, and racism. In the context of postmodernist theories, the hybridity and ambivalences of our cultures and our senses of belonging seem to challenge the binary logic of Self and Other that stands behind modern colonialist, sexist, and racist constructions. Similarly, the postmodernist insistence on difference and specificity defies the totalitarianism of universalizing discourses and structures of power; the affirmation of fragmented social identities appears as a means of contesting the sovereignty of both the modern subject and the modern nation-state, along with all the hierarchies they imply. This postmodernist critical sensibility is extremely important in this regard because it constitutes the proposition (or the symptom) of a break with respect to the entire development of modern sovereignty.

It is difficult to generalize about the numerous discourses that go under the banner of postmodernism, but most of them draw at least indirectly on Jean-François Lyotard's critique of modernist master narratives, Jean Baudrillard's affirmations of cultural simulacra, or Jacques Derrida's critique of Western metaphysics. In the most basic and reductive formulation, postmodernist theories are defined by many of their proponents as sharing one single common denominator, a generalized attack on the Enlightenment.[2] From this perspective the call to action is clear: Enlightenment is the problem and postmodernism is the solution.

We should take care, however, to look more closely at what exactly is intended by "Enlightenment" or "modernity" from this postmodernist perspective.[3] We argued earlier that modernity should be understood not as uniform and homogeneous, but rather as constituted by at least two distinct and conflicting traditions. The first tradition is that initiated by the revolution of Renaissance humanism, from Duns Scotus to Spinoza, with the discovery of the place of immanence and the celebration of singularity and difference. The second tradition, the Thermidor of the Renaissance revolution, seeks to control the utopian forces of the first through the construction and mediation of dualisms, and arrives finally at the concept of modern sovereignty as a provisional solution. When postmodernists propose their opposition to a modernity and an Enlightenment that exalt the universality of reason only to sustain white male European supremacy, it should be clear that they are really attacking the second tradition of our schema (and unfortunately ignoring or eclipsing the first). It would be more accurate, in other words, to pose postmodernist theory as a challenge neither to the Enlightenment nor to modernity in toto but specifically to the tradition of modern sovereignty. More precisely still, these various theoretical contestations are brought together most coherently in a challenge to the dialectic as the central logic of modern domination, exclusion, and command—for both its relegating the multiplicity of difference to binary oppositions and its subsequent subsumption of these differences in a unitary order. If modern power itself is dialectical, the logic goes, then the postmodernist project must be nondialectical.

Once we recognize postmodernist discourses as an attack on the dialectical form of modern sovereignty, then we can see more clearly how they contest systems of domination such as racism and sexism by deconstructing the boundaries that maintain the hierarchies between white and black, masculine and feminine, and so forth. This is how postmodernists can conceive their theoretical practice as heir to an entire spectrum of modern and contemporary liberation struggles. The history of challenges to European political-economic hegemony and its colonial rule, the successes of national liberation movements, women's movements, and antiracist struggles, are all interpreted as the heritage of postmodernist politics because they, too, aim at disrupting the order and the dualisms of modern sovereignty. If the modern is the field of power of the white, the male, and the European, then in perfectly symmetrical fashion the postmodern will be the field of liberation of the non-white, the non-male, and the non-European. As bell hooks says, in its best form radical postmodernist practice, a politics of difference, incorporates the values and voices of the displaced, the marginalized, the exploited, and the oppressed.[4] The binaries and dualisms of modern sovereignty are not disrupted only to establish new ones; rather, the very power of binaries is dissolved as "we set differences to play across boundaries."[5]

Postmodernist thinking has been received by a wide range of scholars as a clarion call to a new paradigm of academic and intellectual practice, and as a real opportunity to dislodge the dominant paradigms of scholarship in their own field.[6] One of the most important examples from our perspective is the postmodernist challenge in the field of international relations.[7] Here the "modernist" paradigm of research is more or less identified with the methods of realism and neorealism, and thus centered on the concept of sovereignty, commonly understood as synonymous with the power of nation-states, the legitimate use of state violence, and territorial integrity. From a postmodernist perspective, this "modernist" international relations, because of its acceptance of and focus on these boundaries, tends to support the dominant power and the sovereignty of nation-states. Authors in this field thus make a clear connection between the critique of the binary dualisms of the "Enlightenment" developed in the context of the philosophical and literary postmodernists and the challenge to the fixed boundaries of modern state sovereignty. Postmodernist international relations theorists strive to challenge the sovereignty of states by deconstructing the boundaries of the ruling powers, highlighting irregular and uncontrolled international movements and flows, and thus fracturing stable unities and oppositions. "Discourse" and "interpretation" are presented as powerful weapons against the institutional rigidities of the modernist perspectives. The resulting postmodernist analyses point toward the possibility of a global politics of difference, a politics of deterritorialized flows across a smooth world, free of the rigid striation of state boundaries.

Although many of the various postmodernist theorists are lucid in their refusal of the logics of modern sovereignty, they are in general extremely confused about the nature of our potential liberation from it—perhaps precisely because they cannot recognize clearly the forms of power that have today come to supplant it. When they present their theories as part of a project of political liberation, in other words, postmodernists are still waging battle against the shadows of old enemies: the Enlightenment, or really modern forms of sovereignty and its binary reductions of difference and multiplicity to a single alternative between Same and Other. The affirmation of hybridities and the free play of differences across boundaries, however, is liberatory only in a context where power poses hierarchy exclusively though essential identities, binary divisions, and stable oppositions. The structures and logics of power in the contemporary world are entirely immune to the "liberatory" weapons of the postmodernist politics of difference. In fact, Empire too is bent on doing away with those modern forms of sovereignty and on setting differences to play across boundaries. Despite the best intentions, then, the postmodernist politics of difference not only is ineffective against but can even coincide with and support the functions and practices of imperial rule. The danger is that postmodernist theories focus their attention so resolutely on the old forms of power they are running from, with their heads turned backwards, that they tumble unwittingly into the welcoming arms of the new power. From this perspective the celebratory affirmations of postmodernists can easily appear naive, when not purely mystificatory.

What we find most important in the various postmodernist currents of thought is the historical phenomenon they represent: they are the symptom of a rupture in the tradition of modern sovereignty. There is, of course, a long tradition of "anti-modern" thought that opposes modern sovereignty, including the great thinkers of the Frankfurt School (along with the entire republican line we have traced back to Renaissance humanism). What is new, however, is that postmodernist theorists point to the *end* of modern sovereignty and demonstrate a new capacity to think outside the framework of modern binaries and modern identities, a thought of plurality and multiplicity. However confusedly or unconsciously, they indicate the passage toward the constitution of Empire.

The Liberation of Hybridities, or Beyond Colonial Binaries

A certain stream of postcolonial studies also proposes a global politics of difference and might be well situated in line with postmodernist theory. Our analysis of modern sovereignty in the preceding sections poses already a strong potential rationale for an accord between postcolonialist and postmodernist theories. Insofar as modern sovereignty was identified with Europe's tendency toward global domination, and more important, insofar as colonial administration and imperialist practices were central components in the constitution of modern sovereignty, postmodernist and postcolonialist theories do indeed share a common enemy. Postmodernism appears in this light to be fundamentally post-Eurocentric.

Postcolonial studies encompasses a wide and varied group of discourses, but we want to focus here on the work of Homi Bhabha because it presents the clearest and best-articulated example of the continuity between postmodernist and postcolonialist discourses. One of the primary and constant objects of Bhabha's attack are *binary divisions*. In fact, the entire postcolonial project as he presents it is defined by its refusal of the binary divisions on which the colonialist worldview is predicated. The world is not divided in two and segmented in opposing camps (center versus periphery, First versus Third World), but rather it is and has always been defined by innumerable partial and mobile differences. Bhabha's refusal to see the world in terms of binary divisions leads him to reject also theories of totality and theories of the identity, homogeneity, and essentialism of social subjects. These various refusals are very closely linked. The binary conception of the world implies the essentialism and homogeneity of the identities on its two halves, and, through the relationship across that central boundary, implies the subsumption of all experience within a coherent social totality. In short, the specter that haunts Bhabha's analysis and that coherently links together these various opponents is the Hegelian dialectic, that is, the dialectic that subsumes within a coherent totality the essential social identities that face each other in opposition. In this sense one could say that postcolonial theory (or at least this version of it) is, along with postmodernist theories, defined above all by its being nondialectical.

Bhabha's critique of the dialectic—that is, his attack on binary divisions, essential identities, and totalization—is both a sociological claim about the real nature of societies and a political project aimed at social change. The former is in fact a condition of possibility of the latter. Social identities and nations were never really coherent imagined communities; the colonized's mimicry of the colonizer's discourse rearticulates the whole notion of identity and alienates it from essence; cultures are always already partial and hybrid formations. This social fact is the basis on which a subversive political project can be conducted to destroy the binary structure of power and identity. In summary form, then, Bhabha's logic of liberation runs like this: Power, or forces of social oppression, function by imposing binary structures and totalizing logics on social subjectivities, repressing their difference. These oppressive structures, however, are never total, and differences are always in some way expressed (through mimicry, ambivalence, hybridization, fractured identities, and so forth). The postcolonial political project, then, is to affirm the multiplicity of differences so as to subvert the power of the ruling binary structures.

The utopia Bhabha points toward after the binary and totalizing structures of power have been fractured and displaced is not an isolated and fragmentary existence but a new form of community, a community of the "unhomely," a new internationalism, a gathering of people in the diaspora. The affirmation of difference and hybridity is itself, according to Bhabha, an affirmation of community: "To live in the unhomely world, to find its ambivalences and ambiguities enacted in the house of fiction, or its sundering and splitting performed in the work of art, is also to affirm a profound desire for social solidarity."[8] The seeds of the alternative community, he believes, arise out of close attention to the locality of culture, its hybridity, and its resistance to the binary structuring of social hierarchies.

We should be careful to recognize the form of the dominating power that serves as the enemy (and really the negative foundation) in this postcolonialist framework. Power is assumed to operate exclusively through a dialectical and binary structure. The only form of domination Bhabha recognizes, in other words, is that of modern sovereignty. This is why, for example, he can say "hierarchical or binary" as if the two terms were interchangeable: from his perspective hierarchy as such is necessarily grounded in binary divisions, so that the mere fact of hybridity has the power to destroy hierarchy *tout court*. Hybridity itself is a realized politics of difference, setting differences to play across boundaries. This is where the postcolonial and the postmodern most powerfully meet: in the united attack on the dialectics of modern sovereignty and the proposition of liberation as a politics of difference.

Like the postmodernist theorists, postcolonial theorists such as Bhabha interest us primarily insofar as they are symptoms of the epochal shift we are undergoing, that is, the passage to Empire. Perhaps the discourses themselves are possible only when the regimes of modern sovereignty are already on the wane. Like postmodernists too, however, postcolonialist theorists in general give a very confused view of this passage because they remain fixated on attacking an old form of power and propose a strategy of liberation that could be effective only on that old terrain. The postcolonialist perspective remains primarily concerned with colonial sovereignty. As Gyan Prakash says, "The postcolonial exists as an aftermath, as an after—after being worked over by colonialism."[9] This may make postcolonialist theory a very productive tool for rereading history, but it is entirely insufficient for theorizing contemporary global power. Edward Said, certainly one of the most brilliant to go under the label of postcolonial theory, manages to condemn the current global power structures only to the extent that they perpetuate cultural and ideological remnants of European colonialist rule.[10] He charges that "the tactics of the great empires [that is, the European imperialisms], which were dismantled after the first world war, are being replicated by the U.S."[11] What is missing here is a recognition of the novelty of the structures and logics of power that order the contemporary world. Empire is not a weak echo of modern imperialisms but a fundamentally new form of rule.

Fundamentalism and/or Postmodernism

Another symptom of the historical passage already in process in the final decades of the twentieth century is the rise of so-called fundamentalisms. Since the collapse of the Soviet Union, the great ideologues of geopolitics and the theoreticians of the end of history have consistently posed fundamentalisms as the primary danger facing global order and stability. Fundamentalism, however, is a poor and confused category that groups together widely disparate phenomena. In general, one might say that fundamentalisms, diverse though they may be, are linked by their being understood both from within and outside as anti-modernist movements, resurgences of primordial identities and values; they are conceived as a kind of historical backflow, a de-modernization. It is more accurate and more useful, however, to understand the various fundamentalism not as the re-creation of a premodern world, but rather as a powerful refusal of the contemporary historical passage in course. In this sense, then, like postmodernist and postcolonialist theories, fundamentalisms too are a symptom of the passage to Empire.

Often today in the media the term "fundamentalism" reduces the variety of social formations that go by that name and refers exclusively to Islamic fundamentalism, the complexity of which is in turn reduced to a violent and intolerant religious fanaticism that is above all "anti-Western." Islamic fundamentalism itself, of course, takes various forms and has a long history extending throughout the modern era. Islamic revivalism and reformism were strong at different times in the eighteenth and nineteenth centuries, and the current forms of Islamic radicalism bear distinct similarities to those previous movements. Islamic fundamentalisms are most coherently united, however, in their being *resolutely opposed to modernity and modernization.* Insofar as political and cultural modernization has been a process of secularization, Islamic fundamentalisms oppose it by posing sacred texts at the center of political constitutions and religious leaders, both priests and jurists, in positions of political power. In terms, too, of gender roles, family structures, and cultural forms, an unchanging, traditional religious norm is commonly meant to stand against the progressively changing secular forms of modernity. Counter to modernism's dynamic and secular society, fundamentalism seems to pose a static and religious one. In this light, then, as an anti-modernism, Islamic fundamentalisms seem to be engaged in an effort to reverse the process of social modernization, separate from the global flows of modernity, and re-create a premodern world. The Iranian revolution of 1979, for example, would from this perspective be seen as an anti-revolution, resurrecting an ancient order.

Christian fundamentalisms in the United States also present themselves as movements against social modernization, re-creating what is imagined to be a past social formation based on sacred texts. These movements should certainly be situated in line with the long U.S. tradition of projects to create in America a new Jerusalem, a Christian community separate from both the corruption of Europe and the savagery of the "uncivilized" world.[12] The most prominent social agenda of the current Christian fundamentalist groups is centered on the (re)creation of the stable and hierarchical nuclear family, which is imagined to have existed in a previous era, and thus they are driven specifically in their crusades against abortion and homosexuality. Christian fundamentalisms in the United States have also continuously been oriented (in different times and different regions more or less overtly) toward a project of white supremacy and racial purity. The new Jerusalem has almost always been imagined as a white and patriarchal Jerusalem.

These common characterizations of fundamentalisms as a return to a premodern or traditional world and its social values, however, obscure more than they illuminate. In fact, fundamentalist visions of a return to the past are generally based on historical illusions. The purity and wholesomeness of the stable, nuclear heterosexual family heralded by Christian fundamentalists, for example, never existed in the United States. The "traditional family" that serves as their ideological foundation is merely a pastiche of values and practices that derives more from television programs than from any real historical experiences within the institution of the family.[13] It is a fictional image projected on the past, like Main Street U.S.A. at Disneyland, constructed retrospectively through the lens of contemporary anxieties and fears. The "return to the traditional family" of the Christian fundamentalists is not backward-looking at all, but rather a new invention that is part of a political project against the contemporary social order.

Similarly, the current forms of Islamic fundamentalism should not be understood as a return to past social forms and values, not even from the perspective of the practitioners. According to Fazlur Rahman: "Actually it is even something of a misnomer to call such phenomena in Islam 'fundamentalist' except insofar as they emphasize the basis of Islam as being the two original sources: the Qur'an and the Sunna of the Prophet Muhammed. Otherwise they emphasize ijtihad, original thought."[14] Contemporary Islamic radicalisms are indeed primarily based on "original thought" and the invention of original values and practices, which perhaps echo those of other periods of revivalism or fundamentalism but are really directed in reaction to the present social order. In both cases, then, the fundamentalist "return to tradition" is really a new invention.[15]

The anti-modern thrust that defines fundamentalisms might be better understood, then, not as a *pre*modern but as a *post*modern project. The postmodernity of fundamentalism has to be recognized primarily in its refusal of modernity as a weapon of Euro-American hegemony—and in this regard Islamic fundamentalism is indeed the paradigmatic case. In the context of Islamic traditions, fundamentalism is postmodern insofar as it rejects the tradition of Islamic modernism for which modernity was always overcoded as assimilation or submission to Euro-American hegemony. "If modern meant the pursuit of Western education, technology and industrialization in the first flush of the post-colonial period," Akbar Ahmed writes, "postmodern would mean a reversion to traditional Muslim values and a rejection of modernism."[16] Considered simply in cultural terms, Islamic fundamentalism is a paradoxical kind of postmodernist theory—postmodern only because it chronologically follows and opposes Islamic modernism. It is more properly postmodernist, however, when considered in geopolitical terms. Rahman writes: "The current postmodernist fundamentalism, in an important way, is novel because its basic élan is anti-Western . . . Hence its condemnation of classical modernism as a purely Westernizing force."[17] Certainly, powerful segments of Islam have been in some sense "anti-Western" since the religion's inception. What is novel in the contemporary resurgence of fundamentalism is really the refusal of the powers that are emerging in the new imperial order. From this perspective, then, insofar as the Iranian revolution was a powerful rejection of the world market, we might think of it as the first postmodernist revolution.

This marriage between postmodernism and fundamentalism is certainly an odd coupling considering that postmodernist and fundamentalist discourses stand in most respects in polar opposition: hybridity versus purity, difference versus identity, mobility versus stasis. It seems to us that postmodernists and the current wave of fundamentalists have arisen not only at the same time but also in response to the same situation, only at opposite poles of the global hierarchy, according to a striking geographical distribution. Simplifying a great deal, one could argue that postmodernist discourses appeal primarily to the winners in the processes of globalization and fundamentalist discourses to the losers. In other words, the current global tendencies toward increased mobility, indeterminacy, and hybridity are experienced by some as a kind of liberation but by others as an exacerbation of their suffering. Certainly, bands of popular support for fundamentalist projects—from the Front National in France and Christian fundamentalism in the United States to the Islamic Brothers—have spread most widely among those who have been further subordinated and excluded by the recent transformations of the global economy and who are most threatened by the increased mobility of capital. The losers in the processes of globalization might indeed be the ones who give us the strongest indication of the transformation in progress.

The Ideology of the World Market

Many of the concepts dear to postmodernists and postcolonialists find a perfect correspondence in the current ideology of corporate capital and the world market. The ideology of the world market has always been the anti-foundational and anti-essentialist discourse par excellence. Circulation, mobility, diversity, and mixture are its very conditions of possibility. Trade brings differences together and the more the merrier! Differences (of commodities, populations, cultures, and so forth) seem to multiply infinitely in the world market, which attacks nothing more violently than fixed boundaries: it overwhelms any binary division with its infinite multiplicities.

As the world market today is realized ever more completely, it tends to deconstruct the boundaries of the nation-state. In a previous period, nation-states were the primary actors in the modern imperialist organization of global production and exchange, but to the world market they appear increasingly as mere obstacles. Robert

Reich, former U.S. secretary of labor, is in an excellent position to recognize and celebrate the overcoming of national boundaries in the world market. He contends that "as almost every factor of production—money, technology, factories, and equipment—moves effortlessly across borders, the very idea of a [national] economy is becoming meaningless." In the future "there will be no *national* products or technologies, no national corporations, no national industries. There will no longer be national economies, as least as we have come to understand that concept."[18] With the decline of national boundaries, the world market is liberated from the kind of binary divisions that nation-states had imposed, and in this new free space a myriad of differences appears. These differences of course do not play freely across a smooth global space, but rather are regimented in global networks of power consisting of highly differentiated and mobile structures. Arjun Appadurai captures the new quality of these structures with the analogy of landscapes, or better, seascapes: in the contemporary world he sees finanscapes, technoscapes, ethnoscapes, and so forth.[19] The suffix "-scape" allows us on the one hand to point to the fluidity and irregularity of these various fields and on the other to indicate formal commonalities among such diverse domains as finance, culture, commodities, and demography. The world market establishes a real politics of difference.

The various -scapes of the world market provide capital with potentials on a scale previously unimaginable. It should be no surprise, then, that postmodernist thinking and its central concepts have flourished in the various fields of practice and theory proper to capital, such as marketing, management organization, and the organization of production. Postmodernism is indeed the logic by which global capital operates. Marketing has perhaps the clearest relation to postmodernist theories, and one could even say that the capitalist marketing strategies have long been postmodernist, *avant la lettre*. On the one hand, marketing practices and consumer consumption are prime terrain for developing postmodernist thinking: certain postmodernist theorists, for example, see perpetual shopping and the consumption of commodities and commodified images as the paradigmatic and defining activities of postmodern experience, our collective journeys through hyperreality.[20] On the other hand, postmodernist thinking—with its emphasis on concepts such as difference and multiplicity, its celebration of fetishism and simulacra, its continual fascination with the new and with fashion—is an excellent description of the ideal capitalist schemes of commodity consumption and thus provides an opportunity to perfect marketing strategies. As a marketing theorist says, there are clear "parallels between contemporary market practices and the precepts of postmodernism."[21]

Marketing itself is a practice based on differences, and the more differences that are given, the more marketing strategies can develop. Ever more hybrid and differentiated populations present a proliferating number of "target markets" that can each be addressed by specific marketing strategies—one for gay Latino males between the ages of eighteen and twenty-two, another for Chinese-American teenage girls, and so forth. Postmodern marketing recognizes the difference of each commodity and each segment of the population, fashioning its strategies accordingly.[22] Every difference is an opportunity.

Postmodern marketing practices represent the consumption cycle of contemporary capital, its external face, but we are even more interested in the postmodernist tendencies within the cycle of capitalist production. In the productive sphere, postmodernist thinking has perhaps had the largest direct impact in the field of management and organization theory. Authors in this field argue that large and complex modern organizations, with their rigid boundaries and homogeneous units, are not adequate for doing business in the postmodern world. "The postmodern organization," one theorist writes, "has certain distinctive features—notably, an emphasis on small-to-moderate size and complexity and adoption of flexible structures and modes of interinstitutional cooperation to meet turbulent organizational and environmental conditions."[23] Postmodern organizations are thus imagined either as located on the boundaries between different systems and cultures or as internally hybrid. What is essential for postmodern management is that organizations be mobile, flexible, and able to deal with difference. Here postmodernist theories pave the way for the transformation of the internal structures of capitalist organizations.

The "culture" within these organizations has also adopted the precepts of postmodernist thinking. The great transnational corporations that straddle national boundaries and link the global system are themselves internally much more diverse and fluid culturally than the parochial modern corporations of previous years. The contemporary gurus of corporate culture who are employed by management as consultants and strategy planners preach the efficiency and profitability of diversity and multiculturalism within corporations.[24] When one looks closely at U.S. corporate ideology (and, to a lesser but still significant extent, at U.S. corporate practice), it is clear that corporations do not operate simply by excluding the gendered and/or racialized Other. In fact, the old modernist forms of racist and sexist theory are the explicit enemies of this new corporate culture. The corporations seek to include difference within their realm and thus aim to maximize creativity, free play, and diversity in the corporate workplace. People of all different races, sexes, and sexual orientations should potentially be included in the corporation; the daily routine of the workplace should be rejuvenated with unexpected changes and an atmosphere of fun. Break down the old boundaries and let one hundred flowers bloom![25] The task of the boss, subsequently, is to organize these energies and differences in the interests of profit. This project is aptly called "diversity management." In this light, the corporations appear not only "progressive" but also "postmodernist," as leaders in a very real politics of difference.

The production processes of capital have also taken forms that echo postmodernist projects. We will have ample opportunity to analyze (particularly in Section 3.4) how production has come to be organized in flexible and hybrid networks. This is, in our view, the most important respect in which the contemporary transformations of capital and the world market constitute a real process of postmodernization.

We certainly agree with those contemporary theorists, such as David Harvey and Fredric Jameson, who see postmodernity as a new phase of capitalist accumulation and commodification that accompanies the contemporary realization of the world market.[26] The global politics of difference established by the world market is defined not by free play and equality, but by the imposition of new hierarchies, or really by a constant process of hierarchization. Postmodernist and postcolonialist theories (and fundamentalisms in a very different way) are really sentinels that signal this passage in course, and in this regard are indispensable.

Truth Commissions

It is salutary to remind ourselves that postmodernist and postcolonial discourses are effective only in very specific geographical locations and among a certain class of the population. As a political discourse, postmodernism has a certain currency in Europe, Japan, and Latin America, but its primary site of application is within an elite segment of the U.S. intelligentsia. Similarly, the postcolonial theory that shares certain postmodernist tendencies has been developed primarily among a cosmopolitan set that moves among the metropolises and major universities of Europe and the United States. This specificity does not invalidate the theoretical perspectives, but it should make us pause for a moment to reflect on their political implications and practical effects. Numerous genuinely progressive and liberatory discourses have emerged throughout history among elite groups, and we have no intention here of questioning the vocation of such theorizing *tout court.* More important than the specificity of these theorists are the resonances their concepts stimulate in different geographical and class locations.

Certainly from the standpoint of many around the world, hybridity, mobility, and difference do not immediately appear as liberatory in themselves. Huge populations see mobility as an aspect of their suffering because they are displaced at an increasing speed in dire circumstances. For several decades, as part of the modernization process there have been massive migrations from rural areas to metropolitan centers within each country and across the globe. The international flow of labor has only increased in recent years, not only from south to north, in the form of legal and illegal guest workers or immigrants, but also from south to south, that is, the temporary or semipermanent worker migrations among southern regions, such as that of South Asian workers in the Persian Gulf. Even these massive worker migrations, however, are dwarfed in terms of numbers and misery by those forced from their homes and land by famine and war. Just a cursory glance around the world, from Central America to Central Africa and from the Balkans to Southeast Asia, will reveal the desperate plight of those on whom such mobility has been imposed. For them, mobility across boundaries often amounts to forced migration in poverty and is hardly liberatory. In fact, a stable and defined place in which to live, a certain immobility, can on the contrary appear as the most urgent need.

The postmodernist epistemological challenge to "the Enlightenment"—its attack on master narratives and its critique of truth—also loses its liberatory aura when transposed outside the elite intellectual strata of Europe and North America. Consider, for example, the mandate of the Truth Commission formed at the end of the civil war in El Salvador, or the similar institutions that have been established in the post-dictatorial and post-authoritarian regimes of Latin America and South Africa. In the context of state terror and mystification, clinging to the primacy of the concept of truth can be a powerful and necessary form of resistance. Establishing and making public the truth of the recent past—attributing responsibility to state officials for specific acts and in some cases exacting retribution—appears here as the ineluctable precondition for any democratic future. The master narratives of the Enlightenment do not seem particularly repressive here, and the concept of truth is not fluid or unstable—on the contrary! The truth is that this general ordered the torture and assassination of that union leader, and this colonel led the massacre of that village. Making public such truths is an exemplary Enlightenment project of modernist politics, and the critique of it in these contexts could serve only to aid the mystificatory and repressive powers of the regime under attack.

In our present imperial world, the liberatory potential of the postmodernist and postcolonial discourses that we have described only resonates with the situation of an elite population that enjoys certain rights, a certain level of wealth, and a certain position in the global hierarchy. One should not take this recognition, however, as a complete refutation. It is not really a matter of either/or. Difference, hybridity, and mobility are not liberatory in themselves, but neither are truth, purity, and stasis. The real revolutionary practice refers to the level of *production.* Truth will not make us free, but taking control of the production of truth will. Mobility and hybridity are not liberatory, but taking control of the production of mobility and stasis, purities and mixtures is. The real truth commissions of Empire will be constituent assemblies of the multitude, social factories for the production of truth.

The Poor

In each and every historical period a social subject that is ever-present and everywhere the same is identified, often negatively but nonetheless urgently, around a common living form. This form is not that of the powerful and the rich: they are merely partial and localized figures, quantitate signatae. *The only non-localizable "common name" of pure difference in all eras is that of the poor. The poor is destitute, excluded, repressed, exploited—and yet living! It is the common denominator of life, the foundation of the multitude. It is strange, but also illuminating, that postmodernist authors seldom adopt this figure in their theorizing. It is strange because the poor is in a certain respect an eternal postmodern figure: the figure of a transversal, omnipresent, different, mobile subject; the testament to the irrepressible aleatory character of existence.*

This common name, the poor, is also the foundation of every possibility of humanity. As Niccolò Machiavelli pointed out, in the "return to beginnings" that characterizes the revolutionary phase of the religions and ideolo-

gies of modernity, the poor is almost always seen to have a prophetic capacity: not only is the poor in *the world, but the poor itself is the very possibility of the world. Only the poor lives radically the actual and present being, in destitution and suffering, and thus only the poor has the ability to renew being. The divinity of the multitude of the poor does not point to any transcendence. On the contrary, here and only here in this world, in the existence of the poor, is the field of immanence presented, confirmed, consolidated, and opened. The poor is god on earth.*

Today there is not even the illusion of a transcendent God. The poor has dissolved that image and recuperated its power. Long ago modernity was inaugurated with Rabelais's laugh, with the realistic supremacy of the belly of the poor, with a poetics that expresses all that there is in destitute humanity "from the belt on down." Later, through the processes of primitive accumulation, the proletariat emerged as a collective subject that could express itself in materiality and immanence, a multitude of poor that not only prophesied but produced, and that thus opened possibilities that were not virtual but concrete. Finally today, in the biopolitical regimes of production and in the processes of postmodernization, the poor is a subjugated, exploited figure, but nonetheless a figure of production. This is where the novelty lies. Everywhere today, at the basis of the concept and the common name of the poor, there is a relationship of production. Why are the postmodernists unable to read this passage? They tell us that a regime of transversal linguistic relations of production has entered into the unified and abstract universe of value. But who is the subject that produces "transversally," who gives a creative meaning to language—who if not the poor, who are subjugated and desiring, impoverished and powerful, always more powerful? Here, within this reign of global production, the poor is distinguished no longer only by its prophetic capacity but also by its indispensable presence in the production of a common wealth, always more exploited and always more closely indexed to the wages of rule. The poor itself is power. There is World Poverty, but there is above all World Possibility, and only the poor is capable of this.

Vogelfrei, *"bird free," is the term Marx used to describe the proletariat, which at the beginning of modernity in the processes of primitive accumulation was freed twice over: in the first place, it was freed from being the property of the master (that is, freed from servitude); and in the second place, it was "freed" from the means of production, separated from the soil, with nothing to sell but its own labor power. In this sense, the proletariat was forced to become the pure possibility of wealth. The dominant stream of the Marxist tradition, however, has always hated the poor, precisely for their being "free as birds," for being immune to the discipline of the factory and the discipline necessary for the construction of socialism. Consider how, when in the early 1950s Vittorio De Sica and Cesare Zavattini set the poor to fly away on broomsticks at the end of their beautiful film* Miracle in Milan, *they were so violently denounced for utopianism by the spokesmen of socialist realism.*

The Vogelfrei *is an angel or an intractable demon. And here, after so many attempts to transform the poor into proletarians and proletarians into a liberation army (the idea of army weighed heavily on that of liberation), once again in postmodernity emerges in the blinding light of clear day the multitude, the common name of the poor. It comes out fully in the open because in postmodernity the subjugated has absorbed the exploited. In other words, the poor, every poor person, the multitude of poor people, have eaten up and digested the multitude of proletarians. By that fact itself the poor have become productive. Even the prostituted body, the destitute person, the hunger of the multitude—all forms of the poor have become productive. And the poor have therefore become ever more important: the life of the poor invests the planet and envelops it with its desire for creativity and freedom. The poor is the condition of every production.*

The story goes that at the root of the postmodernist sensibility and the construction of the concept of postmodernism are those French socialist philosophers who in their youth celebrated factory discipline and the shining horizons of real socialism, but who became repentant after the crisis of 1968 and gave up, proclaiming the futility of the pretense of communism to reappropriate social wealth. Today these same philosophers cynically deconstruct, banalize, and laugh at every social struggle that contests the universal triumph of exchange value. The media and the culture of the media tell us that those philosophers are the ones who recognized this new era of the world, but that is not true. The discovery of postmodernity consisted in the reproposition of the poor at the center of the political and productive terrain.

What was really prophetic was the poor, bird-free laugh of Charlie Chaplin when, free from any utopian illusions and above all from any discipline *of liberation, he interpreted the "modern times" of poverty, but at the same time linked the name of the poor to that of life, a liberated life and a liberated productivity.*

2.5

NETWORK POWER: U.S. SOVEREIGNTY AND THE NEW EMPIRE

> I am persuaded no constitution was ever before so well calculated as ours for extensive empire and self government.
>
> Thomas Jefferson

> Our Constitution is so simple and practical that it is possible always to meet extraordinary needs by changes in emphasis and arrangement without loss of essential form.
>
> Franklin D. Roosevelt

In order to articulate the nature of imperial sovereignty, we must first take a step back in time and consider the political forms that prepared its terrain and constitute its prehistory. The American Revolution represents a moment of great innovation and rupture in the genealogy of modern sovereignty. The U.S. constitutional project, emerging from the struggles for independence and formed through a rich history of alternative possibilities, bloomed like a rare flower in the tradition of modern sovereignty. Tracing the original developments of the notion of sovereignty in the United States will allow us to recognize its significant differences from the modern sovereignty we have described thus far and discern the bases on which a new imperial sovereignty has been formed.

The American Revolution and the Model of Two Romes

The American Revolution and the "new political science" proclaimed by the authors of the *Federalist* broke from the tradition of modern sovereignty, "returning to origins" and at the same time developing new languages and new social forms that mediate between the one and the multiple. Against the tired transcendentalism of modern sovereignty, presented either in Hobbesian or in Rousseauian form, the American constituents thought that only the republic can give order to democracy, or really that the order of the multitude must be born not from a transfer of the title of power and right, but from an arrangement internal to the multitude, from a democratic interaction of powers linked together in networks. The new sovereignty can arise, in other words, only from the constitutional formation of limits and equilibria, checks and balances, which both constitutes a central power and maintains power in the hands of the multitude. There is no longer any necessity or any room here for the transcendence of power. "The science of politics," the authors of the *Federalist* write,

> like most other sciences, has received great improvement. The efficacy of various principles is now well understood, which were either not known at all, or imperfectly known to the ancients. The regular distribution of power into distinct departments; the introduction of legislative balances and checks; the institution of courts composed of judges, holding their offices during good behaviour; the representation of the people in the legislature, by deputies of their own election; these are either wholly new discoveries, or have made their principal progress towards perfection in modern times. They are means, and powerful means, by which the excellencies of republican government may be retained, and its imperfections lessened or avoided.[1]

What takes shape here is an extraordinarily secular and immanentist idea, despite the profound religiousness that runs throughout the texts of the Founding Fathers. It is an idea that rediscovers the revolutionary humanism of the Renaissance and perfects it as a political and constitutional science. Power can be constituted by a whole series of powers that regulate themselves and arrange themselves in networks. Sovereignty can be exercised within a vast horizon of activities that subdivide it without negating its unity and that subordinate it continually to the creative movement of the multitude.

Contemporary historians, such as J. G. A. Pocock, who link the development of the U.S. Constitution and its notion of political sovereignty to the Machiavellian tradition, go a long way toward understanding this deviation from the modern concept of sovereignty.[2] They link the U.S. Constitution not to baroque and counterreformist Machiavellianism, which constructs an apologia of state reason and all the injustices that derive from it, but to the tradition of republican Machiavellianism that, after having inspired the protagonists of the English Revolution, was reconstructed in the Atlantic exodus among European democrats who were defeated but not vanquished.[3] This republican tradition does have a solid foundation in Machiavelli's own texts. First of all, there is the Machiavellian concept of power as a *constituent power*—that is, as a product of an internal and immanent social dynamic. For Machiavelli, power is always republican; it is always the product of the life of the multitude and constitutes its fabric of expression. The free city of Renaissance humanism is the utopia that anchors this revolutionary principle. The second Machiavellian principle at work here is that the social base of this democratic sovereignty is always conflictual. Power is organized through the emergence and the interplay of counterpowers. The city is thus a constituent power that is formed through plural social conflicts articulated in continuous constitutional processes. This is how Machiavelli read the organization of republican ancient Rome, and this is how the Renaissance notion of the city served as the foundation for a realist political theory and practice: social conflict is the basis of the stability of power and the logic of the city's expansion. Machiavelli's thought inaugurated a Copernican revolution that reconfigured politics as perpetual movement. These are the primary teachings that the Atlantic doctrine of democracy derived from the republican Machiavelli.[4]

This republican Rome was not the only Rome that fascinated Machiavelli and guided the Atlantic republicans. Their new "science of politics" was also inspired by imperial Rome, particularly as it was presented in the writings of Polybius. In the first place, Polybius' model of imperial Rome grounded more solidly the republican process of the mediation of social powers and brought it to a conclusion in a synthesis of diverse forms of government. Polybius conceived the perfect form of power as structured by a mixed constitution that combines monarchic power, aristocratic power, and democratic power.[5] The new political scientists in the United States organized these three powers as the three branches of the republican constitution. Any disequilibrium among these powers, and this is the second sign of Polybius' influence, is a symptom of corruption. The Machiavellian Constitution of the United States is a structure poised against corruption—the corruption of both factions and individuals, of groups and the state. The Constitution was designed to resist any cyclical decline into corruption by activating the entire multitude and organizing its constituent capacity in networks of organized counterpowers, in flows of diverse and equalized functions, and in a process of dynamic and expansive self-regulation.

These ancient models, however, go only so far in characterizing the U.S. experience, because in many respects it was truly new and original. In very different periods, Alexis de Tocqueville and Hannah Arendt both grasped the novelty of this new ideology and new form of power. Tocqueville was the more cautious of the two. Although he recognized the vitality of the new political world in the United States and saw how the synthesis of diverse forms of government had been forged into a regulated mass democracy, he also claimed to have seen in America the democratic revolution reach its natural limits. His judgment about whether American democracy can avoid the old cycle of corruption was thus mixed when not outright pessimistic.[6] Hannah Arendt, by contrast, unreservedly celebrated American democracy as the site of the invention of modern politics itself. The central idea of the American Revolution, she claimed, is the establishment of freedom, or really the foundation of a political body that guarantees the space where freedom can operate.[7] Arendt puts the accent on the *establishment* of this democracy in society, that is, the fixity of its foundation and the stability of its functioning. The revolution succeeds in her estimation to the extent that it puts an end to the dynamic of constituent powers and establishes a stable constituted power.

Later we will critique this notion of network power contained in the U.S. Constitution, but here we want simply to highlight its originality. Against the modern European conceptions of sovereignty, which consigned political power to a transcendent realm and thus estranged and alienated the sources of power from society, here the concept of sovereignty refers to a power entirely within society. Politics is not opposed to but integrates and completes society.

Extensive Empire

Before moving on to analyze how in the course of U.S. history this new principle of sovereignty developed and was transformed, let us concentrate our attention for a moment on the nature of the concept itself. The first characteristic of the U.S. notion of sovereignty is that it poses an idea of the immanence of power in opposition to the transcendent character of modern European sovereignty. This idea of immanence is based on an idea of productivity. If it were not, the principle would be impotent: in immanence alone, nothing allows society to become political. The multitude that constitutes society is productive. U.S. sovereignty does not consist, then, in the regulation of the multitude but arises, rather, as the result of the productive synergies of the multitude. The humanist revolution of the Renaissance and the subsequent experiences of sectarian Protestantism all developed this idea of productivity. In line with the Protestant ethic, one might say that only the productive power of the multitude demonstrates the existence of God and the presence of divinity on earth.[8] Power is not something that lords over us but something that we make. The American Declaration of Independence celebrates this new idea of power in the clearest terms. The emancipation of humanity from every transcendent power is grounded on the multitude's power to construct its own political institutions and constitute society.

This principle of constituent production, however, yields to or is explained by a procedure of self-reflection in a kind of dialectical ballet. This is the second characteristic of the U.S. notion of sovereignty. In the process of the constitution of sovereignty on the plane of immanence, there also arises an experience of finitude that results from the conflictive and plural nature of the multitude itself. The new principle of sovereignty seems to produce its own internal limit. To prevent these obstacles from disrupting order and completely emptying out the project, sovereign power must rely on the exercise of control. In other words, after the first moment of affirmation comes a dialectical negation of the constituent power of the multitude that preserves the teleology of the project of sovereignty. Are we thus faced with a point of crisis in the elaboration of the new concept? Does transcendence, first refused in the definition of the source of power, return through the back door in the exercise of power, when the multitude is posed as finite and thus demanding special instruments of correction and control?

That outcome is a constant threat, but after having recognized these internal limits, the new U.S. concept of sovereignty opens with extraordinary force toward the outside, almost as if it wanted to banish the idea of control and the moment of reflection from its own Constitution. The third characteristic of this notion of sovereignty is its tendency toward an open, expansive project operating on an unbounded terrain. Although the text of the U.S. Constitution is extremely attentive to the self-reflective moment, the life and exercise of the Constitution are instead, throughout their jurisprudential and political history, decidedly open to expansive movements, to the renewed declaration of the democratic foundation of power. The principle of expansion continually struggles against the forces of limitation and control.[9]

It is striking how strongly this American experiment resembles the ancient constitutional experience, and specifically the political theory inspired by imperial Rome! In that tradition the conflict between limit and expansion was always resolved in favor of expansion. Machiavelli defined as expansive those republics whose democratic foundations led to both the continuous production of conflicts and the appropriation of new territories. Polybius conceived expansiveness as the reward for the perfect synthesis of the three forms of government, because the eminent form of such a power encourages the democratic pressure of the multitude to surpass every limit and every control. Without expansion the republic constantly risks being absorbed into the cycle of corruption.[10]

This democratic expansive tendency implicit in the notion of network power must be distinguished from other, purely expansionist and imperialist forms of expansion. The fundamental difference is that the expansiveness of the immanent concept of sovereignty is inclusive, not exclusive. In other words, when it expands, this new sovereignty does not annex or destroy the other powers it faces but on the contrary opens itself to them, including them in the network. What opens is the basis of consensus, and thus, through the constitutive network of powers and counterpowers, the entire sovereign body is continually reformed. Precisely because of this expansive tendency, the new concept of sovereignty is profoundly reformist.[11]

We can now distinguish clearly the *expansive tendency* of the democratic republic from the *expansionism* of the transcendent sovereigns—or from, because this is primarily what is at issue, the expansionism of modern nation-states. The idea of sovereignty as an expansive power in networks is poised on the hinge that links the principle of a democratic republic to the idea of Empire. Empire can only be conceived as a universal republic, a network of powers and counterpowers structured in a boundless and inclusive architecture. This imperial expansion has nothing to do with imperialism, nor with those state organisms designed for conquest, pillage, genocide, colonization, and slavery. Against such imperialisms, Empire extends and consolidates the model of network power. Certainly, when we consider these imperial processes historically (and we will soon focus on them in U.S. history), we see clearly that the expansive moments of Empire have been bathed in tears and blood, but this ignoble history does not negate the difference between the two concepts.

Perhaps the fundamental characteristic of imperial sovereignty is that *its space is always open.* As we saw in earlier sections, the modern sovereignty that developed in Europe from the sixteenth century onward conceived space as bounded, and its boundaries were always policed by the sovereign administration. Modern sovereignty resides precisely on the limit. In the imperial conception, by contrast, power finds the logics of its order always renewed and always re-created in expansion. This definition of imperial power raises numerous paradoxes: the indifference of the subjects coupled with the singularization of productive networks; the open and expansive space of Empire together with its continuous reterritorializations; and so forth. The idea of an Empire that is also a democratic republic, however, is formed precisely by linking and combining the extreme terms of these paradoxes. The tension of these conceptual paradoxes will run throughout the articulation and establishment of imperial sovereignty in practice.

Finally, we should note that an idea of peace is at the basis of the development and expansion of Empire. This is an immanent idea of peace that is dramatically opposed to the transcendent idea of peace, that is, the peace that only the transcendent sovereign can impose on a society whose nature is defined by war. Here, on the contrary, nature is peace. Virgil gives us perhaps the highest expression of this Roman peace: "The final age that the oracle foretold has arrived; / The great order of the centuries is born again."[12]

Open Frontiers

The realization of the imperial notion of sovereignty was a long process that developed through the different phases of U.S. constitutional history. As a written document, of course, the U.S. Constitution has remained more or less unchanged (except for a few extremely important amendments), but the Constitution should also be understood as a material regime of juridical interpretation and practice that is exercised not only by jurists and judges but also by subjects throughout the society. This material, social constitution has indeed changed radically since the founding of the republic. U.S. constitutional history, in fact, should be divided into four distinct phases or regimes.[13] A first phase extends from the Declaration of Independence to the Civil War and Reconstruction; a second, extremely contradictory, phase corresponds to the Progressive era, straddling the turn of the century, from the imperialist doctrine of Theodore Roosevelt to Woodrow Wilson's international reformism; a third phase moves from the New Deal and the Second World War through the height of the cold war; and finally, a fourth phase is inaugurated with the social movements of the 1960s and continues through the dissolution of the Soviet Union and its Eastern European bloc. Each of these phases of U.S. constitutional history marks a step toward the realization of imperial sovereignty.

In the first phase of the Constitution, between the presidencies of Thomas Jefferson and Andrew Jackson, the open space of the frontier became the conceptual terrain of republican democracy: this opening afforded the Constitution its first strong definition. The declarations of freedom made sense in a space where the constitution of the state was seen as an open process, a collective self-making.[14] Most important, this American terrain was free of the forms of centralization and hierarchy typical of Europe. Tocqueville and Marx, from opposite perspectives, agree on this point: American civil society does not develop within the heavy shackles of feudal and aristocratic power but starts off from a separate and very different foundation.[15] An ancient dream seems newly possible. An unbounded territory is open to the desire *(cupiditas)* of humanity, and this humanity can thus avoid the crisis of the relationship between virtue *(virtus)* and fortune *(fortuna)* that had ambushed and derailed the humanist and democratic revolution in Europe. From the perspective of the new United States, the obstacles to human development are posed by nature, not history—and nature does not present insuperable antagonisms or fixed social relationships. It is a terrain to transform and traverse.

Already in this first phase, then, a new principle of sovereignty is affirmed, different from the European one: liberty is made sovereign and sovereignty is defined as radically democratic within an open and continuous process of expansion. The frontier is a frontier of liberty. How hollow the rhetoric of the Federalists would have been and how inadequate their own "new political science" had they not presupposed this vast and mobile threshold of the frontier! The very idea of scarcity that—like the idea of war—had been at the center of the European concept of modern sovereignty is a priori stripped away from the constitutive processes of the American experience. Jefferson and Jackson both understood the materiality of the frontier and recognized it as the basis that supported the expansiveness of democracy.[16] Liberty and the frontier stand in a relationship of reciprocal implication: every difficulty, every limit of liberty is an obstacle to overcome, a threshold to pass through. From the Atlantic to the Pacific extended a terrain of wealth and freedom, constantly open to new lines of flight. In this framework there is at least a partial displacement or resolution of that ambiguous dialectic we saw developing within the American Constitution that subordinated the immanent principles of the Declaration of Independence to a transcendent order of constitutional self-reflection. Across the great open spaces the constituent tendency wins out over the constitutional decree, the tendency of the immanence of the principle over regulative reflection, and the initiative of the multitude over the centralization of power.

This utopia of open spaces that plays such an important role in the first phase of American constitutional history, however, already hides ingenuously a brutal form of subordination. The North American terrain can be imagined as empty only by willfully ignoring the existence of the Native Americans—or really conceiving them as a different order of human being, as subhuman, part of the natural environment. Just as the land must be cleared of trees and rocks in order to farm it, so too the terrain must be cleared of the native inhabitants. Just as the frontier people must gird themselves against the severe winters, so too they must arm themselves against the indigenous populations. Native Americans were regarded as merely a particularly thorny element of nature, and a continuous war was aimed at their expulsion and/or elimination. Here we are faced with a contradiction that could not be absorbed within the constitutional machine: the Native Americans could not be integrated in the expansive movement of the frontier as part of the constitutional tendency; rather, they had to be excluded from the terrain to open its spaces and make expansion possible. If they had been recognized, there would have been no real frontier on the continent and no open spaces to fill. They existed outside the Constitution as its negative foundation: in other words, their exclusion and elimination were essential conditions of the functioning of the Constitution itself. This contradiction may not even properly be conceived as a crisis since Native Americans are so dramatically excluded from and external to the workings of the constitutional machine.

In this first phase that runs from the founding of the democratic republic to the Civil War, the constitutional dynamic did go into crisis as a result of an internal contradiction. Whereas Native Americans were cast outside the Constitution, African Americans were from the beginning posed within it. The conception of frontier and the idea and practice of an open space of democracy were in fact woven together with an equally open and dynamic concept of people, multitude, and *gens*. The republican people is a new people, *a people in exodus* populating the empty (or emptied) new territories. From the beginning, American space was not only an extensive, unbounded space but also an intensive space: a space of crossings, a "melting pot" of continuous hybridization. The first real crisis of American liberty was determined on this internal, intensive space. Black slavery, a practice inherited from the colonial powers, was an insurmountable barrier to the formation of a free people. The great American *anticolonial* constitution had to integrate this paradigmatic *colonial* institution at its very heart. Native Americans could be excluded because the new republic did not depend on their labor, but black labor was an essential support of the new United States: African Americans had to be included in the Constitution but could not be included equally. (Women, of course, occupied a very similar position.) The Southern constitutionalists had no trouble demonstrating that the Constitution, in its dialectical, self-reflective, and "federalist" moment, permitted, and even demanded, this perverse interpretation of the social division of labor that ran completely counter to the affirmation of equality expressed in the Declaration of Independence.

The delicate nature of this contradiction is indicated by the bizarre compromise in the drafting of the Constitution, arrived at only through tortuous negotiation, whereby the slave population does count in the determination of the number of representatives for each state in the House of Representatives, but at a ratio whereby one slave equals three-fifths of a free person. (Southern states fought to make this ratio as high as possible to increase their congressional power, and Northerners fought to lower it.) The constitutionalists were forced in effect to *quantify* the constitutional value of different races. The framers thus declared that the number of representatives "shall be determined by adding to the whole Number of free Persons, including those bound to Service for a Term of Years, and excluding Indians not taxed, three fifths of all other persons."[17] One for white and zero for Native Americans poses relatively little problem, but three fifths is a very awkward number for a Constitution. African American slaves could be neither completely included nor entirely excluded. Black slavery was paradoxically both an exception to and a foundation of the Constitution.

This contradiction posed a crisis for the newly developed U.S. notion of sovereignty because it blocked the free circulation, mixing, and equality that animate its foundation.[18] Imperial sovereignty must always overcome barriers and boundaries both within its domain and at the frontiers. This continuous overcoming is what makes the imperial space open. The enormous internal barriers between black and white, free and slave, blocked the imperial integration machine and deflated the ideological pretense to open spaces.

Abraham Lincoln was certainly right when, conducting the Civil War, he thought of himself as refounding the nation. The passage of the Fourteenth Amendment inaugurated more than a century of juridical struggles over civil rights and African American equality. Furthermore, the debate over slavery was inextricably tied to the debates over the new territories. What was in play was a redefinition of the *space* of the nation. At stake was the question whether the free exodus of the multitude, unified in a plural community, could continue to develop, perfect itself, and realize a new configuration of public space. The new democracy had to destroy the transcendental idea of the nation with all its racial divisions and create its own people, defined not by old heritages but by a new ethics of the construction and expansion of the community. The new nation could not but be the product of the political and cultural management of hybrid identities.

The Closure of Imperial Space

The great open American spaces eventually ran out. Even pushing Native Americans farther and farther away, into smaller and smaller confines, was not enough. In the nineteenth and twentieth centuries, American liberty, its new model of network power, and its alternative conception to modern sovereignty all ran up against the recognition that open terrain was limited. The development of the U.S. Constitution would be from this moment on constantly poised on a contradictory border. Every time the expansiveness of the constitutional project ran up against its limits, the republic was tempted to engage in a European-style imperialism. There was always, however, another option: to return to the project of imperial sovereignty and articulate it in a way consistent with the original "Roman" mission of the United States. This new drama of the U.S. political project was played out in the Progressive era, from the 1890s to the First World War.

This was the same period in which class struggle rose to center stage in the United States. Class struggle posed the problem of scarcity, not in absolute terms, but in terms proper to the history of capitalism: that is, as the inequity of the division of the goods of development along the lines of the social division of labor. Class division emerged as a limit that threatened to destabilize the expansive equilibria of the constitution. At the same time, capital's great trusts began to organize new forms of financial power, delinking wealth from productivity and money from the relations of production. Whereas in Europe this was experienced as a relatively continuous development—because finance capital was built on the social position of land rent and the aristocracy—in the United States it was an explosive event. It jeopardized the very possibility of a constitution in network, because when a power becomes monopolistic, the network itself is destroyed. Since the expansion of space was no longer possible and thus could no longer be used as a strategy to resolve conflicts, social conflict appeared directly as a violent and irreconcilable event. The entrance on the scene of the great U.S. workers' movement confirmed the closure of the constitutional space of mediation and the impossibility of the spatial displacement of conflicts. The Haymarket Square riot and the Pullman strike stated it loud and clear: there is no more open space, and thus conflict will result in a direct clash, right here.[19] In effect, when power ran up against its spatial limits, it was constrained to fold back on itself. This was the new context in which all actions had to be played out.

The closure of space posed a serious challenge to the original American constitutional spirit, and the path to address this challenge was treacherous. Never was the drive stronger to transform the United States into something like a European-style sovereignty. Our concepts of "reaction," "active counterrevolution," "preventive police," and "Pinkerton State" were all developed in the United States in this period. U.S. class repression had no reason to be jealous of the various kaisers and czars of Europe. Today that ferocious period of capitalist and state repression still lives on, even if the names of its primary perpetrators (such as Frick, Carnegie, Mellon, and Morgan) now only serve to grace the mantels of philanthropic foundations. How ferocious that repression was—and the stronger it was, the stronger the resistance! This is what really matters. If things had gone differently, if the resistance to repression had not been so strong, this book on Empire, as a form of rule different from imperialism, would have had no reason to be written.

The possible lines of response to address the closure of space on the North American continent were diverse, contradictory, and conflicting. The two proposals that most strongly determined the tendency of the subsequent development of the Constitution were both elaborated within the framework of U.S. "progressivism" at the beginning of the twentieth century. The first was put forward by Theodore Roosevelt, the second by Woodrow Wilson; the first exercised a completely traditional European-style imperialist ideology, and the second adopted an internationalist ideology of peace as an expansion of the constitutional conception of network power. Both of these proposals were intended as responses to the same problem: the crisis of the social relationship and consequently the crisis of Jeffersonian space. For both, the second element of importance was the corruption of the network power of the Constitution through the formation of powerful trusts. Both of their presidential administrations were marked by the passage of important progressivist antitrust legislation, from the regulation of the railroads under Roosevelt to broad regulation of business and finance under Wilson. Their common problem was understanding how class antagonism, which by this time had all but destroyed the model of network power, could be placated. They recognized that within the bounds of the system itself—and this is the third point in common—it was impossible. The open terrain had been used up, and even if it were not completely depleted, any room for movement could not be managed in democratic terms.

Since an internal solution to the closing of space was impossible, the progressivism of American ideology had to be realized with reference to the outside. The two responses both emphasized this move outward, but Wilson's project was so much more utopian that Roosevelt's. For Roosevelt, the Spanish-American War and the Rough Riders' rally up San Juan Hill constituted the prototype of the solution, and that image became even more central as he underwent his populist conversion. Roosevelt's solution to the limits of space involved abandoning the original features of the U.S. model and instead following goals and methods similar to the populist colonial imperialism of a Cecil Rhodes and the progressive imperialism of the French Third Republic.[20] This imperialist path led to the colonialist experience of the United States in the Philippines. "It is our duty toward the people living in barbarism," Roosevelt proclaimed, "to see that they are freed from their chains." Any concession to liberation struggles that allowed uncivilized populations like the Filipinos to govern themselves would thus be "an international crime."[21] Roosevelt, along with generations of European ideologues before him, relied on the notion of "civilization" as an adequate justification for imperialist conquest and domination.

Wilson's solution to the crisis of space took an entirely different path. His project of the international extension of the network power of the Constitution was a concrete political utopia. Nowhere was Wilson's interpretation of American ideology derided more strongly than it was in Europe in the period of the Treaty of Versailles, but it was not very well appreciated in the United States, either. It is true that the League of Nations, the crowning glory of the Wilsonian project for European and world peace, never got past the veto power of Congress; but his concept of world order based on the extension of the U.S. constitutional project, the idea of peace as product of a new world network of powers, was a powerful and long-lasting proposal.[22] This proposal corresponded to the original logic of the U.S. Constitution and its idea of expansive Empire. European modernists could not help mocking this proposal of a postmodern Empire: the chronicles are full of the ironies and insults of Georges Clemenceau and Lloyd George, along with the fascists, who all declared that the refusal of the Wilsonian project was a central element of their projects of dictatorship and war. Yet poor maligned Wilson appears today in a rather different light: a utopian, yes, but lucid in his foresight of the horrible future that awaited the Europe of nations in the coming years; the inventor of a world government of peace, which was certainly unrealizable, but the vision proved nonetheless an efficient promoter of the passage to Empire. This is all true even if Wilson did not recognize it. Here in fact we begin to touch concretely the difference between imperialism and Empire, and we can see in those Wilsonian utopias the intelligence and foresight of a great idiot.

American Imperialism

The third phase or regime of the U.S. Constitution might be seen as taking effect fully with the passage of the New Deal legislation such as the National Industrial Relations Act, but for our purposes it is better to mark its inception earlier, even as early as the Bolshevik Revolution of 1917 and the period when its threat echoed across the United States and throughout the world. In retrospect, in those first decades after the October Revolution we can already recognize the roots of the cold war—the bipolar division of the territories of the globe and the frantic competition between the two systems. The New Deal legislation itself, along with the construction of comparable welfare systems in Western Europe, might be cast as a response to the threat conjured up by the Soviet experience, that is, to the increasing power of workers' movements both at home and abroad.[23] The United States found itself increasingly driven by the need to placate class antagonism, and thus anticommunism became the overriding imperative. Cold war ideology gave rise to the most exaggerated forms of Manichaean division, and as a result, some of the central elements we have seen defining modern European sovereignty reappeared in the United States.

It became increasingly evident during this phase, and throughout the course of the twentieth century, that the United States, far from being that singular and democratic nation its founders imagined it to be, an Empire of Liberty, was the author of direct and brutal imperialist projects, both domestically and abroad. The figure of the U.S. government as the world cop and mastermind of the repression of liberation struggles throughout the world was not really born in the 1960s, nor even with the inception of the cold war proper, but stretches back to the Soviet revolution, and maybe even earlier. Perhaps what we have presented as *exceptions* to the development of imperial sovereignty should instead be linked together as a real tendency, an alternative within the history of the U.S. Constitution. In other words, perhaps the root of these imperialist practices should be traced back to the very origins of the country, to black slavery and the genocidal wars against the Native Americans.

Earlier we considered black slavery as a constitutional problem in the antebellum period, but racial subordination and the super-exploitation of black labor continued well after the passage of the Thirteenth, Fourteenth, and Fifteenth Amendments. The ideological and physical barriers erected around African Americans have always contradicted the imperial notion of open spaces and mixed populations. In particular, the position of black labor in the United States strongly paralleled the position of colonial labor in European regimes in terms of the division of labor, working conditions, and wage structure. Indeed, the super-exploitation of black labor gives us one example, an internal example, of the imperialist tendency that has run throughout U.S. history.

A second example of this imperialist tendency, an external example, can be seen in the history of the Monroe Doctrine and the U.S. efforts to exert control over the Americas. The doctrine, announced by President James Monroe in 1823, was presented first and foremost as a defensive measure against European colonialism: the free and independent American continents "are henceforth not to be considered as subjects for future colonization by a European power."[24] The United States assumed the role of protector of all the nations of the Americans against European aggression, a role that was eventually made explicit with the Theodore Roosevelt corollary to the doctrine, claiming for the United States "an international police power." One would be hard-pressed, however, to characterize the numerous U.S. military interventions in the Americas simply in terms of defense against European aggression.[25] Yanqui politics is a strong tradition of imperialism dressed in anti-imperialist clothing.

During the cold war this imperialist temptation—or really the ambiguity between protector and dominator—became more intense and more extensive. In other words, protecting countries across the entire world from communism (or, more accurately, Soviet imperialism) became indistinguishable from dominating and exploiting them with imperialist techniques. The U.S. involvement in Vietnam might well be considered the pinnacle of this tendency. From one perspective, and certainly within the U.S. government's elaboration of cold war ideology, the war in Vietnam fit into a global political strategy to defend the "free world" against communism, to contain its advances. The war, however, could not but also be, in practice, a continuation of European imperialism on the part of the United States. By the 1960s, the European colonial powers were losing crucial battles and their control was waning. Like aging prizefighters they began to bow out of the ring, and the United States stepped in as the new champion. The U.S. military never doubted that it was strong enough to avoid the kind of humiliation that the French suffered at Dien Bien Phu. The Americans acted during their brief tenure in Vietnam with all the violence, brutality, and barbarity befitting any European imperialist power. It seemed that the United States would declare itself the rightful heir to the declining European powers, donning their imperialist mantle and outdoing them at their own imperialist practices.

The U.S. adventure in Vietnam, of course, ended in defeat. In an extraordinary feat of unparalleled strength and courage, the Vietnamese combated two imperialist powers in succession and emerged victorious—although the fruits of that victory have since proven to be exceedingly bitter. From the perspective of the United States, however, and in terms of our brief constitutional history, the Vietnam War might be seen as the final moment of the imperialist tendency and thus a point of passage to a new regime of the Constitution. The path of European-style imperialism had become once and for all impassable, and henceforth the United States would have to both turn back and leap forward to a properly imperial rule.

As a kind of historical shorthand, we could locate the end of the third and beginning of the fourth regime of the U.S. Constitution in 1968.[26] The Tet offensive in January marked the irreversible military defeat of the U.S. imperialist adventures. More important, however, as is the case before each shift of constitutional regimes, the pressure for a return to republican principles and the original constitutional spirit was already prepared by the powerful internal social movements. Just when the United States was most deeply embroiled in an imperialist venture abroad, when it had strayed farthest from its original constitutional project, that constituent spirit bloomed most strongly at home—not only in the antiwar movements themselves, but also in the civil rights and Black Power movements, the student movements, and eventually the second-wave feminist movements. The emergence of the various components of the New Left was an enormous and powerful affirmation of the principle of constituent power and the declaration of the reopening of social spaces.

Beyond the Cold War

During the cold war, when the United States ambiguously adopted the mantle of imperialism, it subordinated the old imperialist powers to its own regime. The cold war waged by the United States did not defeat the socialist enemy, and perhaps that was never really its primary goal. The Soviet Union collapsed under the burden of its own internal contradictions. The cold war at the most produced some of the conditions of isolation that, reverberating within the Soviet bloc itself, multiplied those explosive contradictions. The most important effect of the cold war was to reorganize the lines of hegemony within the imperialist world, accelerating the decline of the old powers and raising up the U.S. initiative of the constitution of an imperial order. The United States would not have been victorious at the end of the cold war had a new type of hegemonic initiative not already been prepared. This imperial project, a global project of network power, defines the fourth phase or regime of U.S. constitutional history.

In the waning years and wake of the cold war, the responsibility of exercising an international police power "fell" squarely on the shoulders of the United States. The Gulf War was the first time the United States could exercise this power in its full form. Really, the war was an operation of repression of very little interest from the point of view of the objectives, the regional interests, and the political ideologies involved. We have seen many such wars conducted directly by the United States and its allies. Iraq was accused of having broken international law, and it thus had to be judged and punished. The importance of the Gulf War derives rather from the fact that it presented the United States as the only power able to manage international justice, *not as a function of its own national motives but in the name of global right.* Certainly, many powers have falsely claimed to act in the universal interest before, but this new role of the United States is different. Perhaps it is most accurate to say that this claim to universality may also be false, but it is false in a new way. The U.S. world police acts not in imperialist interest but in imperial interest. In this sense the Gulf War did indeed, as George Bush claimed, announce the birth of a new world order.

Legitimation of the imperial order, however, cannot be based on the mere effectiveness of legal sanction and the military might to impose it. It must be developed through the production of international juridical norms that raise up the power of the hegemonic actor in a durable and legal way. Here the constitutional process that had originated with Wilson finally reaches maturity and emerges again. Between the First and Second World Wars, between Wilson's messianism and the international economic-political initiatives of the New Deal (which we will return to in Section 3.2), a series of international organizations was built that produced what in the traditional contractual terms of international right is called a surplus of normativity and efficacy. This surplus was given an expansive and tendentially universal basis in the spirit of the San Francisco accords that founded the United Nations. The unifying, internal process was hindered by the cold war, but not completely blocked by it. Through the years of the cold war there was both a multiplication of international organisms capable of producing right and a reduction of the resistances to their functioning. We emphasized in Section 1.1 how the proliferation of these different international organisms and their consolidation in a set of symbiotic relationships—as if the one asked the other for its own legitimation—pushed beyond a conception of international right based in contract or negotiation, and alluded instead to a central authority, a legitimate supranational motor of juridical action. The objective process was thus given a subjective face. The great international institutions, which had been born on the limited basis of negotiations and pacts, led to a proliferation of organisms and actors that began to act as if there were a central authority sanctioning right.

With the end of the cold war, the United States was called to serve the role of guaranteeing and adding juridical efficacy to this complex process of the formation of a new supranational right. Just as in the first century of the Christian era the Roman senators asked Augustus to assume imperial powers of the administration for the public good, so too today the international organizations (the United Nations, the international monetary organizations, and even the humanitarian organizations) ask the United States to assume the central role in a new world order. In all the regional conflicts of the late twentieth century, from Haiti to the Persian Gulf and Somalia to Bosnia, the United States is called to intervene militarily—and these calls are real and substantial, not merely publicity stunts to quell U.S. public dissent. Even if it were reluctant, the U.S. military would have to answer the call in the name of peace and order. This is perhaps one of the central characteristics of Empire—that is, it resides in a world context that continually calls it into existence. The United States is the peace police, but only in the final instance, when the supranational organizations of peace call for an organizational activity and an articulated complex of juridical and organizational initiatives.

There are many reasons for the United States' privileged position in the new global constitution of imperial authority. It can be explained in part by the continuity of the United States' role (particularly its military role) from the central figure in the struggle against the USSR to the central figure in the newly unified world order. From the perspective of the constitutional history we are tracing here, however, we can see that the United States is privileged in a more important way by the imperial tendency of its own Constitution. The U.S. Constitution, as Jefferson said, is the one best calibrated for extensive Empire. We should emphasize once again that this Constitution is imperial and not imperialist. It is imperial because (in contrast to imperialism's project always to spread its power linearly in closed spaces and invade, destroy, and subsume subject countries within its sovereignty) the U.S. constitutional project is constructed on the model of rearticulating an open space and reinventing incessantly diverse and singular relations in networks across an unbounded terrain.

The contemporary idea of Empire is born through the global expansion of the internal U.S. constitutional project. It is in fact through the extension of *internal* constitutional processes that we enter into a constituent process of Empire. International right always had to be a negotiated, contractual process among *external* parties—in the ancient world that Thucydides portrayed in the Melian Dialogue, in the era of state reason, and in the modern relations among nations. Today right involves instead an internal and constitutive institutional process. The networks of agreements and associations, the channels of mediation and conflict resolution, and the coordination of the various dynamics of states are all institutionalized within Empire. We are experiencing a first phase of the transformation of the global frontier into an open space of imperial sovereignty.

2.6

IMPERIAL SOVEREIGNTY

> The new men of Empire are the ones who believe in fresh starts, new chapters, new pages; I struggle on with the old story, hoping that before it is finished it will reveal to me why it was that I thought it worth the trouble.
>
> J. M. Coetzee

There is a long tradition of modern critique dedicated to denouncing the dualisms of modernity. The standpoint of that critical tradition, however, is situated in the paradigmatic place of modernity itself, both "inside" and "outside," at the threshold or the point of crisis. What has changed in the passage to the imperial world, however, is that this border place no longer exists, and thus the modern critical strategy tends no longer to be effective.

Consider, for example, the responses offered in the history of modern European philosophy from Kant to Foucault to the question "What is Enlightenment?" Kant provides the classic modernist characterization of the mandate of the Enlightenment: *Sapere aude* (dare to know), emerge from the present state of "immaturity," and celebrate the public use of reason at the center of the social realm.[1] Foucault's version, when we situate it historically, is not really all that different. Foucault was dealing not with Fredrick II's despotism, which Kant wanted to guide toward more reasonable political positions, but rather with the political system of the French Fifth Republic, in which a large public sphere for political exchange was taken for granted. His response nonetheless insists once again on the necessity of straddling the border that links what traditionally would be considered the "inside" of subjectivity and the "outside" of the public sphere—even though in Foucault's terms the division is inverted so as to divide the "inside" of the system from the "outside" of subjectivity.[2] The rationality of modern critique, its center of gravity, is posed on this border.

Foucault does add another line of inquiry that seeks to go beyond these boundaries and the modern conception of the public sphere. "What is at stake . . . is this: How can the growth of capabilities [*capacités*] be disconnected from the intensification of power relations?" And this new task requires a new method: "We have to move beyond the outside-inside alternative." Foucault's response, however, is quite traditional: "We have to be at the frontiers."[3] In the end, Foucault's philosophical critique of the Enlightenment returns to the same Enlightenment standpoint. In this ebb and flow between inside and outside, the critique of modernity does not finally go beyond its terms and limits, but rather stands poised on its boundaries.

This same notion of a border place that serves as the standpoint for the critique of the system of power—a place that is both inside and outside—also animates the critical tradition of modern political theory. Modern republicanism has long been characterized by a combination of realistic foundations and utopian initiatives. Republican projects are always solidly rooted within the dominant historical process, but they seek to transform the realm of politics that thus creates an outside, a new space of liberation. The three highest examples of this critical tradition of modern political theory, in our opinion, are Machiavelli, Spinoza, and Marx. Their thought is always grounded within the real processes of the constitution of modern sovereignty, attempting to make its contradictions explode and open the space for an alternative society. The outside is constructed from within.

For Machiavelli, the constituent power that is to found a democratic politics is born out of the rupture of the medieval order and through the necessity of regulating the chaotic transformations of modernity. The new democratic principle is a utopian initiative that responds directly to the real historical process and the demands of the epochal crisis. In Spinoza, too, the critique of modern sovereignty emerges from within the historical process. Against the deployments of monarchy and aristocracy, which can only remain limited forms, Spinoza defines democracy as the absolute form of government because in democracy all of society, the entire multitude, rules; in fact, democracy is the only form of government in which the absolute can be realized. For Marx, finally, every liberatory initiative, from wage struggles to political revolutions, proposes the independence of use value against the world of exchange value, against the modalities of capitalist development—but that independence exists only within capitalist development itself. In all these cases the critique of modernity is situated *within* the historical evolution of the forms of power, *an inside that searches for an outside.* Even in the most radical and extreme forms of the call for an outside, the inside is still assumed as foundation—albeit sometimes a negative foundation—of the project. In Machiavelli's constituent formation of a new republic, Spinoza's democratic liberation of the multitude, and Marx's revolutionary abolition of the state, the inside continues to live in an ambiguous but no less determinate way in the outside that is projected as utopia.

We do not want to suggest here that modern critiques of modernity have never reached a real point of rupture that allows a shift of perspective, nor that our project cannot profit from these modern critical foundations. Machiavellian freedom, Spinozist desire, and Marxian living labor are all concepts that contain real transformative power: the power to confront reality and go beyond the given conditions of existence. The force of these critical concepts, which extends well beyond their ambiguous relation to modern social structures, consists primarily in their being posed as ontological demands.[4] The power of the modern critique of modernity resides precisely where the blackmail of bourgeois realism is refused—in other words, where utopian thought, going beyond the pressures of homology that always limit it to what already exists, is given a new constituent form.

The limitations of these critiques become clear when we question their power to transform not only the objective we are aiming for, but also the standpoint of critique. One brief example should be sufficient to illustrate this difficulty. The fifth part of Spinoza's *Ethics* is perhaps the highest development of the modern critique of modernity. Spinoza takes on the theoretical challenge to establish full knowledge of truth and discover the path of the liberation of the body and the mind, positively, in the absolute. All other modern metaphysical positions, particularly those transcendental positions of which Descartes and Hobbes are the first major representatives, are inessential and mystificatory with respect to this project of liberation. Spinoza's primary objective is the ontological development of the unity of true knowledge and the powerful body along with the absolute construction of singular and collective immanence. Never before had philosophical thought so radically undermined the traditional dualisms of European metaphysics, and never before, consequently, had it so powerfully challenged the political practices of transcendence and domination. Every ontology that does not bear the stamp of human creativity is cast aside. The desire *(cupiditas)* that rules the course of the existence and action of nature and humans is made love *(amor)*—which invests at once both the natural and the divine. And yet, in this final part of the *Ethics,* this utopia has only an abstract and indefinite relation to reality. At times, setting out from this high level of ontological development, Spinoza's thought does attempt to confront reality, but the ascetic proposal halts, stumbles, and disappears in the mystical attempt to reconcile the language of reality and divinity. Finally, in Spinoza as in the other great modern critics of modernity, the search for an outside seems to run aground and propose merely phantasms of mysticism, negative intuitions of the absolute.

There Is No More Outside

The domains conceived as inside and outside and the relationship between them are configured differently in a variety of modern discourses.[5] The spatial configuration of inside and outside itself, however, seems to us a general and foundational characteristic of modern thought. In the passage from modern to postmodern and from imperialism to Empire there is progressively less distinction between inside and outside.

This transformation is particularly evident when viewed in terms of the notion of sovereignty. Modern sovereignty has generally been conceived in terms of a (real or imagined) territory and the relation of that territory to its outside. Early modern social theorists, for example, from Hobbes to Rousseau, understood the civil order as a limited and interior space that is opposed or contrasted to the external order of nature. The bounded space of civil order, its place, is defined by its separation from the external spaces of nature. In an analogous fashion, the theorists of modern psychology understood drives, passions, instincts, and the unconscious metaphorically in spatial terms as an outside within the human mind, a continuation of nature deep within us. Here the sovereignty of the Self rests on a dialectical relation between the natural order of drives and the civil order of reason or consciousness. Finally, modern anthropology's various discourses on primitive societies function as the outside that defines the bounds of the civil world. The process of modernization, in all these varied contexts, is the internalization of the outside, that is, the civilization of nature.

In the imperial world, this dialectic of sovereignty between the civil order and the natural order has come to an end. This is one precise sense in which the contemporary world is postmodern. "Postmodernism," Fredric Jameson tells us, "is what you have when the modernization process is complete and nature is gone for good."[6] Certainly we continue to have forests and crickets and thunderstorms in our world, and we continue to understand our psyches as driven by natural instincts and passions; but we have no nature in the sense that these forces and phenomena are no longer understood as outside, that is, they are not seen as original and independent of the artifice of the civil order. In a postmodern world all phenomena and forces are artificial, or, as some might say, part of history. The modern dialectic of inside and outside has been replaced by a play of degrees and intensities, of hybridity and artificiality.

The outside has also declined in terms of a rather different modern dialectic that defined the relation between public and private in liberal political theory. The public spaces of modern society, which constitute the place of liberal politics, tend to disappear in the postmodern world. According to the liberal tradition, the modern individual, at home in its private spaces, regards the public as its outside. The outside is the place proper to politics, where the action of the individual is exposed in the presence of others and there seeks recognition.[7] In the process of postmodernization, however, such public spaces are increasingly becoming privatized. The urban landscape is shifting from the modern focus on the common square and the public encounter to the closed spaces of malls, freeways, and gated communities. The architecture and urban planning of megalopolises such as Los Angeles and São Paolo have tended to limit public access and interaction in such a way as to avoid the chance encounter of diverse populations, creating a series of protected interior and isolated spaces.[8] Alternatively, consider how the banlieu of Paris has become a series of amorphous and indefinite spaces that promote isolation rather than any interaction or communication. Public space has been privatized to such an extent that it no longer makes sense to understand social organization in terms of a dialectic between private and public spaces, between inside and outside. The place of modern liberal politics has disappeared, and thus from this perspective our postmodern and imperial society is characterized by a deficit of the political. In effect, the place of politics has been de-actualized.

In this regard, Guy Debord's analysis of the society of the spectacle, more than thirty years after its composition, seems ever more apt and urgent.[9] In imperial society the spectacle is a virtual place, or more accurately, a *non-place* of politics. The spectacle is at once unified and diffuse in such a way that it is impossible to distinguish any inside from outside—the natural from the social, the private from the public. The liberal notion of the public, the place outside where we act in the presence of others, has been both universalized (because we are always now under the gaze of others, monitored by safety cameras) and sublimated or de-actualized in the virtual spaces of the spectacle. The end of the outside is the end of liberal politics.

Finally, there is no longer an outside also in a military sense. When Francis Fukuyama claims that the contemporary historical passage is defined by the end of history, he means that the era of major conflicts has come to an end: sovereign power will no longer confront its Other and no longer face its outside, but rather will progressively expand its boundaries to envelop the entire globe as its proper domain.[10] The history of imperialist, interimperialist, and anti-imperialist wars is over. The end of that history has ushered in the reign of peace. Or really, we have entered the era of minor and internal conflicts. Every imperial war is a civil war, a police action—from Los Angeles and Granada to Mogadishu and Sarajevo. In fact, the separation of tasks between the external and the internal arms of power (between the army and the police, the CIA and the FBI) is increasingly vague and indeterminate.

In our terms, the end of history that Fukuyama refers to is the end of the crisis at the center of modernity, the coherent and defining conflict that was the foundation and raison d'être for modern sovereignty. History has ended precisely and only to the extent that it is conceived in Hegelian terms—as the movement of a dialectic of contradictions, a play of absolute negations and subsumption. The binaries that defined modern conflict have become blurred. The Other that might delimit a modern sovereign Self has become fractured and indistinct, and there is no longer an outside that can bound the place of sovereignty. The outside is what gave the crisis its coherence. Today it is increasingly difficult for the ideologues of the United States to name a single, unified enemy; rather, there seem to be minor and elusive enemies everywhere.[11] The end of the crisis of modernity has given rise to a proliferation of minor and indefinite crises, or, as we prefer, to an omni-crisis.

It is useful to remember here (and we will develop this point further in Section 3.1) that the capitalist market is one machine that has always run counter to any division between inside and outside. It is thwarted by barriers and exclusions; it thrives instead by including always more within its sphere. Profit can be generated only through contact, engagement, interchange, and commerce. The realization of the world market would constitute the point of arrival of this tendency. In its ideal form there is no outside to the world market: the entire globe is its domain.[12] We might thus use the form of the world market as a model for understanding imperial sovereignty. Perhaps, just as Foucault recognized the panopticon as the diagram of modern power, the world market might serve adequately—even though it is not an architecture but really an anti-architecture—as the diagram of imperial power.[13]

The striated space of modernity constructed *places* that were continually engaged in and founded on a dialectical play with their outsides. The space of imperial sovereignty, in contrast, is smooth. It might appear to be free of the binary divisions or striation of modern boundaries, but really it is crisscrossed by so many fault lines that it only appears as a continuous, uniform space. In this sense, the clearly defined crisis of modernity gives way to an omni-crisis in the imperial world. In this smooth space of Empire, there is no *place* of power—it is both everywhere and nowhere. Empire is an *ou-topia,* or really a *non-place.*

Imperial Racism

The passage from modern sovereignty to imperial sovereignty shows one of its faces in the shifting configurations of racism in our societies. We should note first of all that it has become increasingly difficult to identify the general lines of racism. In fact, politicians, the media, and even historians continually tell us that racism has steadily receded in modern societies—from the end of slavery to decolonization struggles and civil rights movements. Certain specific traditional practices of racism have undoubtedly declined, and one might be tempted to view the end of the apartheid laws in South

Africa as the symbolic close of an entire era of racial segregation. From our perspective, however, it is clear that racism has not receded but actually progressed in the contemporary world, both in extent and in intensity. It appears to have declined only because its form and strategies have changed. If we take Manichaean divisions and rigid exclusionary practices (in South Africa, in the colonial city, in the southeastern United States, or in Palestine) as the paradigm of *modern* racisms, we must now ask what is the *postmodern* form of racism and what are its strategies in today's imperial society.

Many analysts describe this passage as a shift in the dominant theoretical form of racism, from a racist theory based on biology to one based on culture. The dominant modern racist theory and the concomitant practices of segregation are centered on essential biological differences among races. Blood and genes stand behind the differences in skin color as the real substance of racial difference. Subordinated peoples are thus conceived (at least implicitly) as other than human, as a different order of being. These modern racist theories grounded in biology imply or tend toward an ontological difference—a necessary, eternal, and immutable rift in the order of being. In response to this theoretical position, then, modern anti-racism positions itself against the notion of biological essentialism, and insists that differences among the races are constituted instead by social and cultural forces. These modern anti-racist theorists operate on the belief that social constructivism will free us from the straitjacket of biological determinism: if our differences are socially and culturally determined, then all humans are in principle equal, of one ontological order, one nature.

With the passage to Empire, however, biological differences have been replaced by sociological and cultural signifiers as the key representation of racial hatred and fear. In this way imperial racist theory attacks modern anti-racism from the rear, and actually co-opts and enlists its arguments. Imperial racist theory agrees that races do not constitute isolable biological units and that nature cannot be divided into different human races. It also agrees that the behavior of individuals and their abilities or aptitudes are not the result of their blood or their genes, but are due to their belonging to different historically determined cultures.[14] Differences are thus not fixed and immutable but contingent effects of social history. Imperial racist theory and modern anti-racist theory are really saying very much the same thing, and it is difficult in this regard to tell them apart. In fact, it is precisely because this relativist and culturalist argument is assumed to be necessarily anti-racist that the dominant ideology of our entire society can appear to be against racism, and that imperial racist theory can appear not to be racist at all.

We should look more closely, however, at how imperial racist theory operates. Étienne Balibar calls the new racism a differentialist racism, a racism without race, or more precisely a racism that does not rest on a biological concept of race. Although biology is abandoned as the foundation and support, he says, culture is made to fill the role that biology had played.[15] We are accustomed to thinking that nature and biology are fixed and immutable but that culture is plastic and fluid: cultures can change historically and mix to form infinite hybrids. From the perspective of imperial racist theory, however, there are rigid limits to the flexibility and compatibility of cultures. Differences between cultures and traditions are, in the final analysis, insurmountable. It is futile and even dangerous, according to imperial theory, to allow cultures to mix or insist that they do so: Serbs and Croats, Hutus and Tutsis, African Americans and Korean Americans must be kept separate.

As a theory of social difference, the cultural position is no less "essentialist" than the biological one, or at least it establishes an equally strong theoretical ground for social separation and segregation. Nonetheless, it is a pluralist theoretical position: all cultural identities are equal in principle. This pluralism accepts all the differences of who we are so long as we agree to act on the basis of these differences of identity, so long as we act our race. Racial differences are thus contingent in principle, but quite necessary in practice as markers of social separation. The theoretical substitution of culture for race or biology is thus transformed paradoxically into a theory of the preservation of race.[16] This shift in racist theory shows us how imperial theory can adopt what is traditionally thought to be an anti-racist position and still maintain a strong principle of social separation.

We should be careful to note at this point that imperial racist theory in itself is a theory of segregation, not a theory of hierarchy. Whereas modern racist theory poses a hierarchy among the races as the fundamental condition that makes segregation necessary, imperial theory has nothing to say about the superiority or inferiority of different races or ethnic groups in principle. It regards that as purely contingent, a practical matter. In other words, racial hierarchy is viewed not as cause but as effect of social circumstances. For example, African American students in a certain region register consistently lower scores on aptitude tests than Asian American students. Imperial theory understands this as attributable not to any racial inferiority but rather to cultural differences: Asian American culture places a higher importance on education, encourages students to study in groups, and so forth. The hierarchy of the different races is determined only a posteriori, as an effect of their cultures—that is, on the basis of their performance. According to imperial theory, then, racial supremacy and subordination are not a theoretical question, but arise through free competition, a kind of market meritocracy of culture.

Racist practice, of course, does not necessarily correspond to the self-understandings of racist theory, which is all we have considered up to this point. It is clear from what we have seen, however, that imperial racist practice has been deprived of a central support: it no longer has a theory of racial superiority that was seen as grounding the modern practices of racial exclusion. According to Gilles Deleuze and Félix Guattari, though, "European racism . . . has never operated by exclusion, or by the designation of someone as Other . . . Racism operates by the determination of degrees of deviance in relation to the White-Man face, which endeavors to integrate nonconforming traits into increasingly eccentric and backward waves . . . From the viewpoint of racism, there is no exterior, there are no people on the outside."[17] Deleuze and

Guattari challenge us to conceive racist practice not in terms of binary divisions and exclusion but as a strategy of differential inclusion. No identity is designated as Other, no one is excluded from the domain, there is no outside. Just as imperial racist theory cannot pose as a point of departure any essential differences among human races, imperial racist practice cannot begin by an exclusion of the racial Other. White supremacy functions rather through first engaging alterity and then subordinating differences according to degrees of deviance from whiteness. This has nothing to do with the hatred and fear of the strange, unknown Other. It is a hatred born in proximity and elaborated through the degrees of difference of the neighbor.

This is not to say that our societies are devoid of racial exclusions; certainly they are crisscrossed with numerous lines of racial barriers, across each urban landscape and across the globe. The point, rather, is that racial exclusion arises generally as a result of differential inclusion. In other words, it would be a mistake today, and perhaps it is also misleading when we consider the past, to pose the apartheid or Jim Crow laws as the paradigm of racial hierarchy. Difference is not written in law, and the imposition of alterity does not go to the extreme of Otherness. Empire does not think differences in absolute terms; it poses racial differences never as a difference of nature but always as a difference of degree, never as necessary but always as accidental. Subordination is enacted in regimes of everyday practices that are more mobile and flexible but that create racial hierarchies that are nonetheless stable and brutal.

The form and strategies of imperial racism help to highlight the contrast between modern and imperial sovereignty more generally. Colonial racism, the racism of modern sovereignty, first pushes difference to the extreme and then recuperates the Other as negative foundation of the Self (see Section 2.3). The modern construction of a people is intimately involved in this operation. A people is defined not simply in terms of a shared past and common desires or potential, but primarily in dialectical relation to its Other, its outside. A people (whether diasporic or not) is always defined in terms of a *place* (be it virtual or actual). Imperial order, in contrast, has nothing to do with this dialectic. Imperial racism, or differential racism, integrates others with its order and then orchestrates those differences in a system of control. Fixed and biological notions of peoples thus tend to dissolve into a fluid and amorphous multitude, which is of course shot through with lines of conflict and antagonism, but none that appear as fixed and eternal boundaries. The surface of imperial society continuously shifts in such a way that it destabilizes any notion of place. The central moment of modern racism takes place on its boundary, in the global antithesis between inside and outside. As Du Bois said nearly one hundred years ago, the problem of the twentieth century is the problem of the color line. Imperial racism, by contrast, looking forward perhaps to the twenty-first century, rests on the play of differences and the management of micro-conflictualities within its continually expanding domain.

On the Generation and Corruption of Subjectivity

The progressive lack of distinction between inside and outside has important implications for the social production of subjectivity. One of the central and most common theses of the institutional analyses proposed by modern social theory is that subjectivity is not pre-given and original but at least to some degree formed in the field of social forces. In this sense, modern social theory progressively emptied out any notion of a presocial subjectivity and instead grounded the production of subjectivity in the functioning of major social institutions, such as the prison, the family, the factory, and the school.

Two aspects of this production process should be highlighted. First, subjectivity is a constant social process of generation. When the boss hails you on the shop floor, or the high school principal hails you in the school corridor, a subjectivity is formed. The material practices set out for the subject in the context of the institution (be they kneeling down to pray or changing hundreds of diapers) are the production processes of subjectivity. In a reflexive way, then, through its own actions, the subject is acted on, generated. Second, the institutions provide above all a discrete *place* (the home, the chapel, the classroom, the shop floor) where the production of subjectivity is enacted. The various institutions of modern society should be viewed as an archipelago of factories of subjectivity. In the course of a life, an individual passes linearly into and out of these various institutions (from the school to the barracks to the factory) and is formed by them. The relation between inside and outside is fundamental. Each institution has its own rules and logics of subjectivation: "School tells us, 'You're not at home anymore'; the army tells us, 'You're not in school anymore.' "[18] Nevertheless, within the walls of each institution the individual is at least partially shielded from the forces of the other institutions; in the convent one is normally safe from the apparatus of the family, at home one is normally out of reach of factory discipline. This clearly delimited *place* of the institutions is reflected in the regular and fixed *form* of the subjectivities produced.

In the passage to imperial society, the first aspect of the modern condition is certainly still the case, that is, subjectivities are still produced in the social factory. In fact, the social institutions produce subjectivity in an ever more intense way. We might say that postmodernism is what you have when the modern theory of social constructivism is taken to its extreme and all subjectivity is recognized as artificial. How is this possible, however, when today, as nearly everyone says, the institutions in question are everywhere in crisis and continually breaking down? This general crisis does not necessarily mean that the institutions no longer produce subjectivity. What has changed, rather, is the second condition: that is, the place of the production of subjectivity is no longer defined in this same way. The crisis means, in other words, that today the enclosures that used to define the limited space of the institutions have broken down so that the logic that once functioned primarily within the institutional walls now spreads across the entire social terrain. Inside and outside are becoming indistinguishable.

This omni-crisis of the institutions looks very different in different cases. For example, continually decreasing proportions of the U.S. population are involved in the nuclear family, while steadily increasing proportions are confined to prisons. Both institutions, however, the nuclear family and the prison, are equally in crisis, in the sense that the place of their effectivity is increasingly indeterminate. One should not think that the crisis of the nuclear family has brought a decline in the forces of patriarchy. On the contrary, discourses and practices of "family values" seem to be everywhere across the social field. The old feminist slogan "The personal is the political" has been reversed in such a way that the boundaries between public and private have fractured, unleashing circuits of control throughout the "intimate public sphere."[19] In a similar way the crisis of the prison means that carceral logics and techniques have increasingly spread to other domains of society. The production of subjectivity in imperial society tends not to be limited to any specific places. One is always still in the family, always still in school, always still in prison, and so forth. In the general breakdown, then, the functioning of the institutions is both more intensive and more extensive. The institutions work even though they are breaking down—and perhaps they work all the better the more they break down. The indefiniteness of the *place* of the production corresponds to the indeterminacy of the *form* of the subjectivities produced. The imperial social institutions might be seen, then, in a fluid process of the generation and corruption of subjectivity.

This passage is not isolated to the dominant countries and regions, but tends to be generalized to different degrees across the world. The apologia of colonial administration always celebrated its establishment of social and political institutions in the colonies, institutions that would constitute the backbone of a new civil society. Whereas in the process of modernization the most powerful countries export institutional forms to the subordinated ones, in the present process of postmodernization, *what is exported is the general crisis of the institutions.* The Empire's institutional structure is like a software program that carries a virus along with it, so that it is continually modulating and corrupting the institutional forms around it. The imperial society of control is tendentially everywhere the order of the day.

The Triple Imperative of Empire

The general apparatus of imperial command actually consists of three distinct moments: one inclusive, another differential, and a third managerial. The first moment is the magnanimous, liberal face of Empire. All are welcome within its boundaries, regardless of race, creed, color, gender, sexual orientation, and so forth. In its inclusionary moment Empire is blind to differences; it is absolutely indifferent in its acceptance. It achieves universal inclusion by setting aside differences that are inflexible or unmanageable and thus might give rise to social conflict.[20] Setting aside differences requires us to regard differences as inessential or relative and imagine a situation not in which they do not exist but rather in which we are ignorant of them. A veil of ignorance prepares a universal acceptance. When Empire is blind to these differences and when it forces its constituents to set them aside, there can exist an overlapping consensus across the entire imperial space. Setting aside differences means, in effect, taking away the potential of the various constituent subjectivities. The resulting public space of power neutrality makes possible the establishment and legitimation of a universal notion of right that forms the core of the Empire. The law of inclusionary neutral indifference is a universal foundation in the sense that it applies equally to all subjects that exist and that could exist under imperial rule. In this first moment, then, the Empire is a machine for universal integration, an open mouth with infinite appetite, inviting all to come peacefully within its domain. (Give me your poor, your hungry, your downtrodden masses . . .) The Empire does not fortify its boundaries to push others away, but rather pulls them within its pacific order, like a powerful vortex. With boundaries and differences suppressed or set aside, the Empire is a kind of smooth space across which subjectivities glide without substantial resistance or conflict.

The second moment of imperial control, its differential moment, involves the affirmation of differences accepted within the imperial realm. While from the juridical perspective differences must be set aside, from the cultural perspective differences are celebrated. Since these differences are considered now to be cultural and contingent rather than biological and essential, they are thought not to impinge on the central band of commonality or overlapping consensus that characterizes the Empire's inclusionary mechanism. They are nonconflictual differences, the kind of differences we might set aside when necessary. For example, since the end of the cold war, ethnic identities have been actively (re)created in the socialist and formerly socialist countries with the firm support of the United States, the U.N., and other global bodies. Local languages, traditional place-names, arts, handcrafts, and so forth are celebrated as important components of the transition from socialism to capitalism.[21] These differences are imagined to be "cultural" rather than "political," under the assumption that they will not lead to uncontrollable conflicts but will function, rather, as a force of peaceful regional identification. In a similar fashion, many official promotions of multiculturalism in the United States involve the celebration of traditional ethnic and cultural differences under the umbrella of universal inclusion. In general, Empire does not create differences. It takes what it is given and works with it.

The differential moment of imperial control must be followed by the management and hierarchization of these differences in a general economy of command. Whereas colonial power sought to fix pure, separate identities, Empire thrives on circuits of movement and mixture. The colonial apparatus was a kind of mold that forged fixed, distinct castings, but the imperial society of control functions through modulation, "like a self-deforming cast that changes continually, from one instant to the next, or like a sieve whose pattern changes from one point to the next."[22] The colonial poses a simple equation with a unique solution; the imperial is faced by multiple complex variables that change continuously and admit a variety of always incomplete but nonetheless effective solutions.

In a certain sense, then, the colonial might be considered more ideological and the imperial more pragmatic. Consider as an example of imperial strategy the practice of New England factories and Appalachian coal mines at the beginning of the twentieth century. The factories and mines were dependent on the labor of recent immigrants from various European countries, many of whom carried with them traditions of intense worker militancy. Bosses, however, did not shy away from bringing together this potentially explosive mixture of workers. They found, in fact, that carefully managed proportions of workers from different national backgrounds in each workshop and each mine proved to be a powerful formula of command. The linguistic, cultural, and ethnic differences within each work force were stabilizing because they could be used as a weapon to combat worker organization. It was in the bosses' interest that the melting pot not dissolve identities and that each ethnic group continue to live in a separate community maintaining its differences.

A very similar strategy can be seen in the more recent practices of labor management on a Central American banana plantation.[23] Multiple ethnic divisions among the workers function as an element of control in the labor process. The transnational corporation addresses with different methods and degrees of exploitation and repression each of the ethnic groups of workers—variously of European and African descent and from different Amerindian groups. Antagonisms and divisions among the workers along the various lines of ethnicity and identification prove to enhance profit and facilitate control. Complete cultural assimilation (in contrast to juridical integration) is certainly not a priority of imperial strategy. The reemergence of ethnic and national differences at the end of the twentieth century, not only in Europe but also in Africa, Asia, and the Americas, has presented Empire with an even more complex equation containing a myriad of variables that are in a constant state of flux. That this equation does not have a unique solution is not really a problem—on the contrary. Contingency, mobility, and flexibility are Empire's real power. The imperial "solution" will not be to negate or attenuate these differences, but rather to affirm them and arrange them in an effective apparatus of command.

"Divide and conquer" is thus not really the correct formulation of imperial strategy. More often than not, the Empire does not create division but rather recognizes existing or potential differences, celebrates them, and manages them within a general economy of command. The triple imperative of the Empire is incorporate, differentiate, manage.

From Crisis to Corruption

At the beginning of Part 2 we elaborated a notion of modern sovereignty as crisis: a crisis defined in the continual conflict between, on the one hand, the plane of immanent forces of the desire and cooperation of the multitude and, on the other hand, the transcendent authority that seeks to contain these forces and impose an order on them. We can now see that imperial sovereignty, in contrast, is organized not around one central conflict but rather through a flexible network of microconflicts. The contradictions of imperial society are elusive, proliferating, and nonlocalizable: the contradictions are everywhere. Rather than crisis, then, the concept that defines imperial sovereignty might be omni-crisis, or, as we prefer, corruption. It is a commonplace of the classical literature on Empire, from Polybius to Montesquieu and Gibbon, that Empire is from its inception decadent and corrupt.

This terminology might easily be misunderstood. It is important to make clear that we in no way intend our definition of imperial sovereignty as corruption to be a moral charge. In its contemporary and modern usage, corruption has indeed become a poor concept for our purposes. It now commonly refers only to the perverted, that which strays from the moral, the good, the pure. We intend the concept rather to refer to a more general process of decomposition or mutation with none of the moral overtones, drawing on an ancient usage that has been largely lost. Aristotle, for example, understands corruption as a becoming of bodies that is a process complementary to generation.[24] We might think of corruption, then, as de-generation—a reverse process of generation and composition, a moment of metamorphosis that potentially frees spaces for change. We have to forget all the commonplace images that come to mind when we refer to imperial decadence, corruption, and degeneration. Such moralism is completely misplaced here. More important is a strict argument about form, in other words, that Empire is characterized by a fluidity of form—an ebb and flow of formation and deformation, generation and degeneration.

To say that imperial sovereignty is defined by corruption means, on the one hand, that Empire is impure or hybrid and, on the other, that imperial rule functions by breaking down. (Here the Latin etymology is precise: *cum-rumpere,* to break.) Imperial society is always and everywhere breaking down, but this does not mean that it is necessarily heading to ruin. Just as the crisis of modernity in our characterization did not point to any imminent or necessary collapse, so too the corruption of Empire does not indicate any teleology or any end in sight. In other words, the crisis of modern sovereignty was not temporary or exceptional (as one would refer to the stock market crash of 1929 as a crisis), but rather the norm of modernity. In a similar way, corruption is not an aberration of imperial sovereignty but its very essence and modus operandi. The imperial economy, for example, functions precisely through corruption, and it cannot function otherwise. There is certainly a tradition that views corruption as the tragic flaw of Empire, the accident without which Empire would have triumphed: think of Shakespeare and Gibbon as two very different examples. We see corruption, rather, not as accidental but as necessary. Or, more accurately, Empire requires that all relations be accidental. Imperial power is founded on the rupture of every determinate ontological relationship. Corruption is simply the sign of the absence of any ontology. In the ontological vacuum, corruption becomes necessary, objective. Imperial sovereignty thrives on the proliferating contradictions corruption gives rise to; it is stabilized by its instabilities, by its impurities and admixture; it is calmed by the panic and anxieties it continually engenders. Corruption names the perpetual process of alteration and metamorphosis, the antifoundational foundation, the deontological mode of being.

We have thus arrived at a series of distinctions that conceptually mark the passage from modern to imperial sovereignty: from the people to the multitude, from dialectical opposition to the management of hybridities, from the place of modern sovereignty to the non-place of Empire, from crisis to corruption.

Refusal

Bartleby would prefer not to. The mystery of Herman Melville's classic story is the absoluteness of the refusal. When his boss asks him to perform his duties, Bartleby calmly repeats over and over, "I would prefer not to." Melville's character fits in with a long tradition of the refusal of work. Any worker with any sense, of course, wants to refuse the authority of the boss, but Bartleby takes it to the extreme. He does not object to this or that task, nor does he offer any reason for his refusal—he just passively and absolutely declines. Bartleby's behavior is indeed disarming, in part because he is so calm and serene, but moreover because his refusal is so indefinite that it becomes absolute. He simply prefers not to.

Given Melville's great penchant for metaphysics, it is no wonder that Bartleby solicits ontological interpretations.[1] *His refusal is so absolute that Bartleby appears completely blank, a man without qualities or, as Renaissance philosophers would say,* homo tantum, *mere man and nothing more. Bartleby in his pure passivity and his refusal of any particulars presents us with a figure of generic being, being as such, being and nothing more. And in the course of the story he strips down so much—approximating ever more closely naked humanity, naked life, naked being—that eventually he withers away, evaporates in the bowels of the infamous Manhattan prison, the Tombs.*

Michael K, the central character in J. M. Coetzee's wonderful novel The Life and Times of Michael K, *is also a figure of absolute refusal. But whereas Bartleby is immobile, almost petrified in his pure passivity, K is always on his feet, always moving. Michael K is a gardener, a simple man, so simple that he appears to be not of this world. In a fictional country divided by civil war, he is continually stopped by the cages, barriers, and checkpoints erected by authority, but he manages quietly to refuse them, to keep moving. Michael K does not keep moving just for the sake of perpetual motion. The barriers do not just block motion, they seem to stop life, and thus he refuses them absolutely in order to keep life in motion. What he really wants is to grow pumpkins and tend to their wandering vines. K's refusal of authority is as absolute as Bartleby's, and that very absoluteness and simplicity situate him, too, on a level of ontological purity. K also approaches the level of naked universality: "a human soul above and beneath classification,"*[2] *being simply* homo tantum.

These simple men and their absolute refusals cannot but appeal to our hatred of authority. The refusal of work and authority, or really the refusal of voluntary servitude, is the beginning of liberatory politics. Long ago Étienne de La Boétie preached just such a politics of refusal: "Resolve to serve no more, and you are at once freed. I do not ask that you place hands upon the tyrant to topple him over, but simply that you support him no longer; then you will behold him, like a great Colossus whose pedestal has been pulled away, fall of his own weight and break into pieces."[3] *La Boétie recognized the political power of refusal, the power of subtracting ourselves from the relationship of domination, and through our exodus subverting the sovereign power that lords over us. Bartleby and Michael K continue La Boétie's politics of the refusal of voluntary servitude, carrying it to the absolute.*

This refusal certainly is the beginning of a liberatory politics, but it is only a beginning. The refusal in itself is empty. Bartleby and Michael K may be beautiful souls, but their being in its absolute purity hangs on the edge of an abyss. Their lines of flight from authority are completely solitary, and they continuously tread on the verge of suicide. In political terms, too, refusal in itself (of work, authority, and voluntary servitude) leads only to a kind of social suicide. As Spinoza says, if we simply cut the tyrannical head off the social body, we will be left with the deformed corpse of society. What we need is to create a new social body, which is a project that goes well beyond refusal. Our lines of flight, our exodus must be constituent and create a real alternative. Beyond the simple refusal, or as part of that refusal, we need also to construct a new mode of life and above all a new community. This project leads not toward the naked life of homo tantum *but toward* homohomo, *humanity squared, enriched by the collective intelligence and love of the community.*

INTERMEZZO

COUNTER-EMPIRE

> While this Heavenly City is on pilgrimage on earth, it calls out all peoples and so collects a society of aliens, speaking all languages.
>
> Saint Augustine

> We want to destroy all the ridiculous monuments "to those who have died for the fatherland" that stare down at us in every village, and in their place erect monuments to the deserters. The monuments to the deserters will represent also those who died in the war because every one of them died cursing the war and envying the happiness of the deserter. Resistance is born of desertion.
>
> Antifascist partisan, Venice, 1943

We have now arrived at a turning point in our argument. The trajectory we have traced up until now—from our recognition of modernity as crisis to our analyses of the first articulations of a new imperial form of sovereignty—has allowed us to understand the transformations of the constitution of world order. But that *order* would be merely a hollow husk if we were not to designate also a new regime of *production.* Furthermore, we have not yet been able to give any coherent indication of what type of political subjectivities might contest and overthrow the forces of Empire, because those subjectivities will arrive only on the terrain of production. It is as if at this point we can see only shadows of the figures that will animate our future. Let us therefore descend into the hidden abode of production to see the figures at work there.

Even when we manage to touch on the productive, ontological dimension of the problematic and the resistances that arise there, however, we will still not be in the position—not even at the end of this book—to point to any already existing and concrete elaboration of a political alternative to Empire. And no such effective blueprint will ever arise from a theoretical articulation such as ours. It will arise only in practice. At a certain point in his thinking Marx needed the Paris Commune in order to make the leap and conceive communism in concrete terms as an effective alternative to capitalist society. Some such experiment or series of experiments advanced through the genius of collective practice will certainly be necessary today to take that next concrete step and create a new social body beyond Empire.

One Big Union!

Our study set out from the hypothesis that the power of Empire and the mechanisms of imperial sovereignty can be understood only when confronted on the most general scale, in their globality. We believe that toward the end of challenging and resisting Empire and its world market, it is necessary to pose any alternative at an equally global level. Any proposition of a particular community in isolation, defined in racial, religious, or regional terms, "delinked" from Empire, shielded from its powers by fixed boundaries, is destined to end up as a kind of ghetto. Empire cannot be resisted by a project aimed at a limited, local autonomy. We cannot move back to any previous social form, nor move forward in isolation. Rather, we must push through Empire to come out the other side. Deleuze and Guattari argued that rather than resist capital's globalization, we have to accelerate the process. "But which," they ask, "is the revolutionary path? Is there one?—To withdraw from the world market . . ? Or might it be to go in the opposite direction? To go still further, that is, in the movement of the market, of decoding and deterritorialization?"[1] Empire can be effectively contested only on its own level of generality and by pushing the processes that it offers past their present limitations. We have to accept that challenge and learn to think globally and act globally. Globalization must be met with a counter-globalization, Empire with a counter-Empire.

In this regard we might take inspiration from Saint Augustine's vision of a project to contest the decadent Roman Empire. No limited community could succeed and provide an alternative to imperial rule; only a universal, catholic community bringing together all populations and all languages in a common journey could accomplish this. The divine city is a universal city of aliens, coming together, cooperating, communicating. Our pilgrimage on earth, however, in contrast to Augustine's, has no transcendent telos beyond; it is and remains absolutely immanent. Its continuous movement, gathering aliens in community, making this world its home, is both means and end, or rather a means without end.

From this perspective the Industrial Workers of the World (IWW) is the great Augustinian project of modern times. In the first decades of the twentieth century the Wobblies, as they were called, organized powerful strikes and rebellions across the United States, from Lawrence, Massachusetts, and Paterson, New Jersey, to Everett, Washington.[2] The perpetual movement of the Wobblies was indeed an immanent pilgrimage, creating a new society in the shell of the old, without establishing fixed and stable structures of rule. (In fact, the primary criticism of the IWW from the official Left was and continues to be that its strikes, though powerful and often victorious, never left behind durable union structures.) The Wobblies had extraordinary success among the vast and mobile immigrant populations because they spoke all the languages of that hybrid labor force. The two accepted stories of the derivation of the name "Wobbly" illustrate these two central characteristics of the movement, its organizational mobility and its ethnic-linguistic hybridity: first, Wobbly is supposed to refer to the lack of a center, the flexible and unpredictable pilgrimage of IWW militancy; and second, the name is said to derive from the mispronunciation of a Chinese cook in Seattle, "I Wobbly Wobbly." The primary focus of the IWW was the universality of its project. Workers of all languages and races across the world (although in fact they only made it as far as Mexico) and workers of all trades should come together in "One Big Union."

Taking our cue from the IWW, and clearly departing from Augustine in this regard, we would cast our political vision in line with the radical republican tradition of modern democracy. What does it mean to be republican today? What sense can it have in the postmodern era to take up that antagonistic position that constituted a radically democratic alternative within modernity? Where is the standpoint from which critique can be possible and effective? In this passage from modernity to postmodernity, is there still a *place* from which we can launch our critique and construct an alternative? Or, if we are consigned to the non-place of Empire, can we construct a powerful non-place and realize it concretely, as the terrain of a postmodern republicanism?

The Non-Place of Exploitation

In order to address this problematic, allow us a brief digression. We mentioned earlier that Marx's theoretical method, in line with the tradition of modern critiques of modernity, is situated in the dialectic between inside and outside. Proletarian struggles constitute—in real, ontological terms—the motor of capitalist development. They constrain capital to adopt ever higher levels of technology and thus transform labor processes.[3] The struggles force capital continually to reform the relations of production and transform the relations of domination. From manufacturing to large-scale industry, from finance capital to transnational restructuring and the globalization of the market, it is always the initiatives of organized labor power that determine the figure of capitalist development. Through this history the place of exploitation is a dialectically determined site. Labor power is the most internal element, the very source of capital. At the same time, however, labor power represents capital's outside, that is, the place where the proletariat recognizes its own use value, its own autonomy, and where it grounds its hope for liberation. The refusal of exploitation—or really resistance, sabotage, insubordination, rebellion, and revolution—constitutes the motor force of the reality we live, and at the same time is its living opposition. In Marx's thought the relationship between the inside and the outside of capitalist development is completely determined in the dual standpoint of the proletariat, both inside and outside capital. This spatial configuration has led to many political positions founded on the dream of affirming the place of use value, pure and separate from exchange value and capitalist relations.

In the contemporary world this spatial configuration has changed. On the one hand, the relations of capitalist exploitation are expanding everywhere, not limited to the factory but tending to occupy the entire social terrain. On the other hand, social relations completely invest the relations of production, making impossible any externality between social production and economic production. The dialectic between productive forces and the system of domination no longer has a *determinate place.* The very qualities of labor power (difference, measure, and determination) can no longer be grasped, and similarly, exploitation can no longer be localized and quantified. In effect, the object of exploitation and domination tend not to be specific productive activities but the universal capacity to produce, that is, abstract social activity and its comprehensive power. This abstract labor is an activity without place, and yet it is very powerful. It is the cooperating set of brains and hands, minds and bodies; it is both the non-belonging and the creative social diffusion of living labor; it is the desire and the striving of the multitude of mobile and flexible workers; and at the same time it is intellectual energy and linguistic and communicative construction of the multitude of intellectual and affective laborers.[4]

The inside defined by use value and the outside of exchange value are nowhere to be found, and hence any politics of use value, which was always based on an illusion of separability, is now definitely inconceivable. That does not mean, however, that production and exploitation have ceased. Neither have innovation and development nor the continuous restructuring of relations of power come to an end. On the contrary, today more than ever, as productive forces tend to be completely de-localized, completely universal, they produce not only commodities but also rich and powerful social relationships. These new productive forces have no place, however, because they occupy all places, and they produce and are exploited in this indefinite non-place. The universality of human creativity, the synthesis of freedom, desire, and living labor, is what takes place in the non-place of the postmodern relations of production. Empire is the non-place of world production where labor is exploited. By contrast, and with no possible homology with Empire, here we find again the revolutionary formalism of modern republicanism. This is still a formalism because it is without place, but it is a potent formalism now that it is recognized not as abstracted from the individual and collective subjects but as the general power that constitutes their bodies and minds. The non-place has a brain, heart, torso, and limbs, globally.

Being-Against: Nomadism, Desertion, Exodus

This recognition takes us back to the initial question: What does it mean to be republican today? We have already seen that the modern critical response of opening the dialectic between inside and outside is no longer possible. An effective notion of postmodern republicanism will have to be constructed *au milieu,* on the basis of the lived experience of the global multitude. One element we can put our finger on at the most basic and elemental level is *the will to be against.* In general, the will to be against does not seem to require much explanation. Disobedience to authority is one of the most natural and healthy acts. To us it seems completely obvious that those who are exploited will resist and—given the necessary conditions—rebel. Today, however, this may not be so obvious. A long tradition of political scientists has said the problem is not why people rebel but why they do not. Or rather, as Deleuze and Guattari say, "the fundamental problem of political philosophy is still precisely the one that Spinoza saw so clearly (and that Wilhelm Reich rediscovered): 'Why do men fight *for* their servitude as stubbornly as though it were their salvation?' "[5] The first question of political philosophy today is not if or even why there will be resistance and rebellion, but rather how to determine the enemy against which to rebel. Indeed, often the inability to identify the enemy is what leads the will to resistance around in such paradoxical circles. The identification of the enemy, however, is no small task given that exploitation tends no longer to have a specific place and that we are immersed in a system of power so deep and complex that we can no longer determine specific difference or measure. We suffer exploitation, alienation, and command as enemies, but we do not know where to locate the production of oppression. And yet we still resist and struggle.

One should not exaggerate these logical paradoxes. Even though on the new terrain of Empire exploitation and domination often cannot be defined in specific places, they nonetheless exist. The globality of the command they impose represents the inverted image—something like a photo negative—of the generality of the multitude's productive activities. And yet, this inverted relation between imperial power and the power of the multitude does not indicate any homology. In effect, imperial power can no longer discipline the powers of the multitude; it can only impose control over their general social and productive capacities. From the economic point of view, the wage regime is replaced, as a function of regulation, by a flexible and global monetary system; normative command is replaced by the procedures of control and the police; and the exercise of domination is formed through communicative networks. This is how exploitation and domination constitute a general non-place on the imperial terrain. Although exploitation and domination are still experienced concretely, on the flesh of the multitude, they are nonetheless amorphous in such a way that it seems there is no place left to hide. If there is no longer a place that can be recognized as outside, we must be against in every place. This being-against becomes the essential key to every active political position in the world, every desire that is effective—perhaps of democracy itself. The first anti-fascist partisans in Europe, armed deserters confronting their traitorous governments, were aptly called "against-men."[6] Today the generalized being-against of the multitude must recognize imperial sovereignty as the enemy and discover the adequate means to subvert its power.

Here we see once again the republican principle in the very first instance: desertion, exodus, and nomadism. Whereas in the disciplinary era *sabotage* was the fundamental notion of resistance, in the era of imperial control it may be *desertion*. Whereas being-against in modernity often meant a direct and/or dialectical opposition of forces, in postmodernity being-against might well be most effective in an oblique or diagonal stance. Battles against the Empire might be won through subtraction and defection. This desertion does not have a place; it is the evacuation of the places of power.

Throughout the history of modernity, the mobility and migration of the labor force have disrupted the disciplinary conditions to which workers are constrained. And power has wielded the most extreme violence against this mobility. In this respect slavery can be considered on a continuum with the various wage labor regimes as the most extreme repressive apparatus to block the mobility of the labor force. The history of black slavery in the Americas demonstrates both the vital need to control the mobility of labor and the irrepressible desire to flee on the part of the slaves: from the closed ships of the Middle Passage to the elaborate repressive techniques employed against escaped slaves. Mobility and mass worker nomadism always express a refusal and a search for liberation: the resistance against the horrible conditions of exploitation and the search for freedom and new conditions of life. It would be interesting, in fact, to write a general history of the modes of production from the standpoint of the workers' desire for mobility (from the country to the city, from the city to the metropolis, from one state to another, from one continent to another) rather than running through that development simply from the standpoint of capital's regulation of the technological conditions of labor. This history would substantially reconfigure the Marxian conception of the stages of the organization of labor, which has served as the theoretical framework for numerous authors up to Polanyi.[7]

Today the mobility of labor power and migratory movements is extraordinarily diffuse and difficult to grasp. Even the most significant population movements of modernity (including the black and white Atlantic migrations) constitute lilliputian events with respect to the enormous population transfers of our times. A specter haunts the world and it is the specter of migration. All the powers of the old world are allied in a merciless operation against it, but the movement is irresistible. Along with the flight from the so-called Third World there are flows of political refugees and transfers of intellectual labor power, in addition to the massive movements of the agricultural, manufacturing, and service proletariat. The legal and documented movements are dwarfed by clandestine migrations: the borders of national sovereignty are sieves, and every attempt at complete regulation runs up against violent pressure. Economists attempt to explain this phenomenon by presenting their equations and models, which even if they were complete would not explain that irrepressible desire for free movement. In effect, what pushes from behind is, negatively, desertion from the miserable cultural and material conditions of imperial reproduction; but positively, what pulls forward is the wealth of desire and the accumulation of expressive and productive capacities that the processes of globalization have determined in the consciousness of every individual and social group—and thus a certain hope. Desertion and exodus are a powerful form of class struggle within and against imperial postmodernity. This mobility, however, still constitutes a spontaneous level of struggle, and, as we noted earlier, it most often leads today to a new rootless condition of poverty and misery.

A new nomad horde, a new race of barbarians, will arise to invade or evacuate Empire. Nietzsche was oddly prescient of their destiny in the nineteenth century. "Problem: where are the *barbarians* of the twentieth century? Obviously they will come into view and consolidate themselves only after tremendous socialist crises."[8] We cannot say exactly what Nietzsche foresaw in his lucid delirium, but indeed what recent event could be a stronger example of the power of desertion and exodus, the power of the nomad horde, than the fall of the Berlin Wall and the collapse of the entire Soviet bloc? In the desertion from "socialist discipline," savage mobility and mass migration contributed substantially to the collapse of the system. In fact, the desertion of productive cadres disorganized and struck at the heart of the disciplinary system of the bureaucratic Soviet world. The mass exodus of highly trained workers from Eastern Europe played a central role in provoking the collapse of the Wall.[9] Even though it refers to the particularities of the socialist state system, this example demonstrates that the mobility of the labor force can indeed express an open political conflict and contribute to the destruction of the regime. What we need, however, is more. We need a force capable of not only organizing the destructive capacities of the multitude, but also constituting through the desires of the multitude an alternative. The counter-Empire must also be a new global vision, a new way of living in the world.

Numerous republican political projects in modernity assumed mobility as a privileged terrain for struggle and organization: from the so-called Socians of the Renaissance (Tuscan and Lombard artisans and apostles of the Reform who, banished from their own country, fomented sedition against the Catholic nations of Europe, from Italy to Poland) up to the seventeenth-century sects that organized trans-Atlantic voyages in response to the massacres in Europe; and from the agitators of the IWW across the United States in the 1910s up to the European autonomists in the 1970s. In these modern examples, mobility became an active politics and established a political position. This mobility of the labor force and this political exodus have a thousand threads that are interwoven—old traditions and new needs are mixed together, just as the republicanism of modernity and modern class struggle were woven together. Post-modern republicanism, if it is to arise, must face a similar task.

New Barbarians

Those who are against, while escaping from the local and particular constraints of their human condition, must also continually attempt to construct a new body and a new life. This is a necessarily violent, barbaric passage, but as Walter Benjamin says, it is a positive barbarism: "Barbarisms? Precisely. We affirm this in order to introduce a new, positive notion of barbarism. What does the poverty of experience oblige the barbarian to do? To begin anew, to begin from the new." The new barbarian "sees nothing permanent. But for this very reason he sees ways everywhere. Where others encounter walls or mountains, there, too, he sees a way. But because he sees a way everywhere, he has to clear things from it everywhere . . . Because he sees ways everywhere, he always positions himself at crossroads. No moment can know what the next will bring. What exists he reduces to rubble, not for the sake of the rubble, but for that of the way leading through it."[10] The new barbarians destroy with an affirmative violence and trace new paths of life through their own material existence.

These barbaric deployments work on human relations in general, but we can recognize them today first and foremost in corporeal relations and configurations of gender and sexuality.[11] Conventional norms of corporeal and sexual relations between and within genders are increasingly open to challenge and transformation. Bodies themselves transform and mutate to create new posthuman bodies.[12] The first condition of this corporeal transformation is the recognition that human nature is in no way separate from nature as a whole, that there are no fixed and necessary boundaries between the human and the animal, the human and the machine, the male and the female, and so forth; it is the recognition that nature itself is an artificial terrain open to ever new mutations, mixtures, and hybridizations.[13] Not only do we consciously subvert the traditional boundaries, dressing in drag, for example, but we also move in a creative, indeterminate zone *au milieu,* in between and without regard for those boundaries. Today's corporeal mutations constitute an *anthropological exodus* and represent an extraordinarily important, but still quite ambiguous, element of the configuration of republicanism "against" imperial civilization. The anthropological exodus is important primarily because here is where the positive, constructive face of the mutation begins to appear: an ontological mutation in action, the concrete invention of a first *new place in the non-place.* This creative evolution does not merely occupy any existing place, but rather invents a new place; it is a desire that creates a new body; a metamorphosis that breaks all the naturalistic homologies of modernity.

This notion of anthropological exodus is still very ambiguous, however, because its methods, hybridization and mutation, are themselves the very methods employed by imperial sovereignty. In the dark world of cyberpunk fiction, for example, the freedom of self-fashioning is often indistinguishable from the powers of an all-encompassing control.[14] We certainly do need to change our bodies and ourselves, and in perhaps a much more radical way than the cyberpunk authors imagine. In our contemporary world, the now common aesthetic mutations of the body, such as piercings and tattoos, punk fashion and its various imitations, are all initial indications of this corporeal transformation, but in the end they do not hold a candle to the kind of radical mutation needed here. The will to be against really needs a body that is completely incapable of submitting to command. It needs a body that is incapable of adapting to family life, to factory discipline, to the regulations of a traditional sex life, and so forth. (If you find your body refusing these "normal" modes of life, don't despair—realize your gift!)[15] In addition to being radically unprepared for normalization, however, the new body must also be able to create a new life. We must go much further to define that new place of the non-place, well beyond the simple experiences of mixture and hybridization, and the experiments that are conducted around them. We have to arrive at constituting a coherent political artifice, an *artificial becoming* in the sense that the humanists spoke of a *homohomo* produced by art and knowledge, and that Spinoza spoke of a powerful body produced by that highest consciousness that is infused with love. The infinite paths of the barbarians must form a new mode of life.

Such transformations will always remain weak and ambiguous, however, so long as they are cast only in terms of form and order. Hybridity itself is an empty gesture, and the mere refusal of order simply leaves us on the edge of nothingness—or worse, these gestures risk reinforcing imperial power rather than challenging it. The new politics is given real substance only when we shift our focus from the question of form and order to the regimes and practices of production. On the terrain of production we will be able to recognize that this mobility and artificiality do not merely represent the exceptional experiences of small privileged groups but indicate, rather, the common productive experience of the multitude. As early as the nineteenth century, proletarians were recognized as the nomads of the capitalist world.[16] Even when their lives remain fixed in one geographical location (as is most often the case), their creativity and productivity define corporeal and ontological migrations. The anthropological metamorphoses of bodies are established through the common experience of labor and the new technologies that have constitutive effects and ontological implications. Tools have always functioned as human prostheses, integrated into our bodies through our laboring practices as a kind of anthropological mutation both in individual terms and in terms of collective social life. The contemporary form of exodus and the new barbarian life demand that tools become poietic prostheses, liberating us from the conditions of modern humanity. To go back to the Marxian digression we made earlier, when the dialectic between inside and outside comes to an end, and when the separate place of use value disappears from the imperial terrain, the new forms of labor power are charged with the task of producing anew the human (or really the posthuman). This task will be accomplished primarily through the new and increasingly immaterial forms of affective and intellectual labor power, in the community that they constitute, in the artificiality that they present as a project.

With this passage the deconstructive phase of critical thought, which from Heidegger and Adorno to Derrida provided a powerful instrument for the exit from modernity, has lost its effectiveness.[17] It is now a closed parenthesis and leaves us faced with a new task: constructing, in the non-place, a new place; constructing ontologically new determinations of the human, of living—a powerful artificiality of being. Donna Haraway's cyborg fable, which resides at the ambiguous boundary between human, animal, and machine, introduces us today, much more effectively than deconstruction, to these new terrains of possibility—but we should remember that this is a fable and nothing more. The force that must instead drive forward theoretical practice to actualize these terrains of potential metamorphosis is still (and ever more intensely) the common experience of the new productive practices and the concentration of productive labor on the plastic and fluid terrain of the new communicative, biological, and mechanical technologies.

Being republican today, then, means first of all struggling within and constructing against Empire, on its hybrid, modulating terrains. And here we should add, against all moralisms and all positions of resentment and nostalgia, that this new imperial terrain provides greater possibilities for creation and liberation. The multitude, in its will to be-against and its desire for liberation, must push through Empire to come out the other side.

PART 3

PASSAGES OF PRODUCTION

3.1

THE LIMITS OF IMPERIALISM

> The world is nearly all parceled out, and what there is left of it is being divided up, conquered, and colonised. To think of these stars that you see overhead at night, these vast worlds which we can never reach. I would annex the planets if I could; I often think of that. It makes me sad to see them so clear and yet so far.
>
> Cecil Rhodes

For a large portion of the twentieth century, the critique of imperialism has been among the most active and urgent arenas of Marxist theory.[1] Many of these arguments are today certainly outdated and the situation they refer to is utterly transformed. This does not mean, however, that we have nothing to learn from them. These critiques of imperialism can help us understand the passage from imperialism to Empire because in certain respects they anticipated that passage.

One of the central arguments of the tradition of Marxist thinking on imperialism is that there is an intrinsic relation between capitalism and expansion, and that capitalist expansion inevitably takes the political form of imperialism. Marx himself wrote very little about imperialism, but his analyses of capitalist expansion are central to the entire tradition of critique. What Marx explained most clearly is that capital constantly operates through a reconfiguration of the boundaries of the inside and the outside. Indeed, capital does not function within the confines of a fixed territory and population, but always overflows its borders and internalizes new spaces: "The tendency to create the world market is directly given in the concept of capital itself. Every limit appears as a barrier to be overcome."[2] This restive character of capital constitutes an ever-present point of crisis that pertains to the essence of capital itself: constant expansion is its always inadequate but nonetheless necessary attempt to quench an insatiable thirst. We do not mean to suggest that this crisis and these barriers will necessarily lead capital to collapse. On the contrary, as it is for modernity as a whole, crisis is for capital a normal condition that indicates not its end but its tendency and mode of operation. Capital's construction of imperialism and its move beyond it are both given in the complex play between limits and barriers.

The Need for an Outside

Marx analyzes capital's constant need for expansion first by focusing on the process of *realization* and thus on the unequal quantitative relationship between the worker as producer and the worker as consumer of commodities.[3] The problem of realization is one of the factors that drives capital beyond its boundaries and poses the tendency toward the world market. In order to understand the problem we have to start out from exploitation. "To begin with," we read in the *Grundrisse,* "capital forces the workers beyond necessary labour to surplus labour. Only in this way does it realize itself, and create surplus value" (p. 421). The wage of the worker (corresponding to necessary labor) must be less than the total value produced by the worker. This surplus value, however, must find an adequate market in order to be realized. Since each worker must produce more value than he or she consumes, the demand of the worker as consumer can never be an adequate demand for the surplus value. In a closed system, the capitalist production and exchange process is thus defined by a series of barriers: "Capital, then, posits necessary labour time as the barrier to the exchange value of living labour capacity; surplus labour time as the barrier to necessary labour time; and surplus value as the barrier to surplus labour time" (p. 422). All these barriers flow from a single barrier defined by the unequal relationship between the worker as producer and the worker as consumer.

Certainly, the capitalist class (along with the other classes that share in its profits) will consume some of this excess value, but it cannot consume all of it, because if it did there would be no surplus value left to reinvest. Instead of consuming all the surplus value, capitalists must practice abstinence, which is to say, they must accumulate.[4] Capital itself demands that capitalists renounce pleasures and abstain as much as possible from "wasting" the surplus value on their own consumption.

This cultural explanation of capitalist morality and abstinence, however, is just a symptom of the real economic barriers posed within capitalist production. On the one hand, if there is to be profit, then the workers must produce more value than they consume. On the other hand, if there is to be accumulation, the capitalist class and its dependents cannot consume all of that surplus value. If the working class together with the capitalist class and its dependents cannot form an adequate market and buy all the commodities produced, then even though exploitation has taken place and surplus value has been extracted, that value cannot be realized.[5]

Marx points out further that this barrier is continually exacerbated as labor becomes ever more productive. With the increase of productivity and the consequent rise in the composition of capital, variable capital (that is, the wage paid the workers) constitutes an increasingly small part of the total value of the commodities. This means that the workers' power of consumption is increasingly small with respect to the commodities produced: "The more productivity develops, the more it comes into conflict with the narrow basis on which the relations of consumption rest."[6] The realization of capital is thus blocked by the problem of the "narrow basis" of the powers of consumption. We should note that this barrier has nothing to do with the absolute power of production of a population or its absolute power of consumption (undoubtedly the proletariat could and wants to consume more), but rather it refers to *the relative power of consumption* of a population within the capitalist relations of production and reproduction.

In order to realize the surplus value generated in the production process and avoid the devaluation resulting from overproduction,

Marx argues that capital must expand its realm: "A precondition of production based on capital is therefore the production of a constantly widening sphere of circulation, whether the sphere itself is directly expanded or whether more points within it are created as points of production" (p. 407). Expanding the sphere of circulation can be accomplished by intensifying existing markets within the capitalist sphere through new needs and wants; but the quantity of the wage available to workers for spending and the capitalists' need to accumulate pose a rigid barrier to this expansion. Alternatively, additional consumers can be created by drafting new populations into the capitalist relationship, but this cannot stabilize the basically unequal relationship between supply and demand, between the value created and the value that can be consumed by the population of proletarians and capitalists involved.[7] On the contrary, new proletarians will themselves always be an inadequate market for the value of what they produce, and thus they will always only reproduce the problem on a larger scale.[8] The only effective solution is for capital to look outside itself and discover noncapitalist markets in which to exchange the commodities and realize their value. Expansion of the sphere of circulation outside the capitalist realm displaces the destabilizing inequality.

Rosa Luxemburg developed Marx's analysis of the problem of realization, but she changed the inflection of that analysis. Luxemburg casts the fact that "outside consumers qua other-than-capitalist are really essential" (pp. 365–66) in order for capital to realize its surplus value as an indication of capital's dependence on its outside. Capitalism is "the first mode of economy which is unable to exist by itself, which needs other economic systems as a medium and a soil."[9] Capital is an organism that cannot sustain itself without constantly looking beyond its boundaries, feeding off its external environment. Its outside is essential.

Perhaps this need constantly to expand its sphere of control is the sickness of European capital, but perhaps it is also the motor that drove Europe to the position of world dominance in the modern era. "Perhaps then the merit of the West, confined as it was on its narrow 'Cape of Asia,' " Fernand Braudel supposes, "was to have needed the world, to have needed to venture outside its own front door."[10] Capital from its inception tends toward being a world power, or really *the* world power.

Internalizing the Outside

Capital expands not only to meet the needs of realization and find new markets but also to satisfy the requirements of the subsequent moment in the cycle of accumulation, that is, the process of *capitalization.* After surplus value has been realized in the form of money (through intensified markets in the capitalist domain and through reliance on noncapitalist markets), that realized surplus value must be reinvested in production, that is, turned back into capital. The capitalization of realized surplus value requires that for the subsequent cycle of production the capitalist will have to secure for purchase additional supplies of constant capital (raw materials, machinery, and so forth) and additional variable capital (that is, labor power)—and eventually in turn this will require an even greater extension of the market for further realization.

The search for additional constant capital (in particular, more and newer materials) drives capital toward a kind of imperialism characterized by pillage and theft. Capital, Rosa Luxemburg asserts, "ransacks the whole world, it procures its means of production from all corners of the earth, seizing them, if necessary by force, from all levels of civilisation and from all forms of society . . . It becomes necessary for capital progressively to dispose ever more fully of the whole globe, to acquire an unlimited choice of means of production, with regard to both quality and quantity, so as to find productive employment for the surplus value it has realised."[11] In the acquisition of additional means of production, capital does relate to and rely on its noncapitalist environment, but it does not internalize that environment—or rather, it does not necessarily make that environment capitalist. The outside remains outside. For example, gold and diamonds can be extracted from Peru and South Africa or sugarcane from Jamaica and Java perfectly well while those societies and that production continue to function through noncapitalist relations.

The acquisition of additional variable capital, the engagement of new labor power and creation of proletarians, by contrast, implies a capitalist imperialism. Extending the working day of existing workers in the capitalist domain can, of course, create additional labor power, but there is a limit to this increase. For the remainder of this new labor power, capital must continually create and engage new proletarians among noncapitalist groups and countries. The progressive proletarianization of the noncapitalist environment is the continual reopening of the processes of primitive accumulation—and thus the *capitalization* of the noncapitalist environment itself. Luxemburg sees this as the real historical novelty of capitalist conquest: "All conquerors pursued the aim of dominating and exploiting the country, but none was interested in robbing the people of their productive forces and in destroying their social organisation."[12] In the process of capitalization *the outside is internalized.*

Capital must therefore not only have open exchange with noncapitalist societies or only appropriate their wealth; it must also actually transform them into capitalist societies themselves. This is what is central in Rudolf Hilferding's definition of the export of capital: "By 'export of capital' I mean the export of value which is intended to breed surplus value abroad."[13] What is exported is a relation, a social form that will breed or replicate itself. Like a missionary or vampire, capital touches what is foreign and makes it proper. "The bourgeoisie," Marx and Engels write, "compels all nations, on pain of extinction, to adopt the bourgeois mode of production; it compels them to introduce what it calls civilisation into their midst, i.e., to become bourgeois themselves. In one word, it creates the world after its own image."[14] In economic terms, this civilization and modernization mean capitalization, that is, incorporation within the expanding cycle of capitalist production and accumulation. In this way the noncapitalist environment (territory, social forms, cultures, productive processes, labor power, and so forth) is subsumed formally under capital.

We should note here that European capital does not really remake noncapitalist territories "after its own image," as if all were becoming homogeneous. Indeed, when the Marxist critics of imperialism have recognized the processes of the internalization of capital's outside, they have generally underestimated the significance of the uneven development and geographical difference implicit in them.[15] Each segment of the noncapitalist environment is transformed *differently,* and all are integrated *organically* into the expanding body of capital. In other words, the different segments of the outside are internalized not on a model of similitude but as different organs that function together in one coherent body.

At this point we can recognize the fundamental contradiction of capitalist expansion: capital's reliance on its outside, on the noncapitalist environment, which satisfies the need to realize surplus value, conflicts with the internalization of the noncapitalist environment, which satisfies the need to capitalize that realized surplus value. Historically these two processes have often taken place in sequence. A territory and population are first made accessible as an outside for exchange and realization, and then subsequently brought into the realm of capitalist production proper. The important point, however, is that once a segment of the environment has been "civilized," once it has been organically incorporated into the newly expanded boundaries of the domain of capitalist production, it can no longer be the outside necessary to realize capital's surplus value. In this sense, capitalization poses a barrier to realization and vice versa; or better, internalization contradicts the reliance on the outside. Capital's thirst must be quenched with new blood, and it must continually seek new frontiers.

It is logical to assume that there would come a time when these two moments of the cycle of accumulation, realization and capitalization, come into direct conflict and undermine each other. In the nineteenth century, the field for capitalist expansion (in material resources, labor power, and markets) seemed to stretch indefinitely, both in Europe and elsewhere. In Marx's time, capitalist production accounted for very little of global production. Only a few countries had substantial capitalist production (England, France, and Germany), and even these countries still had large segments of noncapitalist production—peasant-based agriculture, artisanal production, and so forth. Luxemburg argues, however, that since the earth is finite, the logical conflict will eventually become a real contradiction: "The more violently, ruthlessly and thoroughly imperialism brings about the decline of non-capitalist civilisations, the more rapidly it cuts the ground from under the feet of capitalist accumulation. Though imperialism is the historical method for prolonging the career of capitalism, it is also the sure means of bringing it to a swift conclusion."[16] This contradictory tension is present throughout the development of capital, but it is revealed in full view only at the limit, at the point of crisis—when capital is faced with the finitude of humanity and the earth. Here the great imperialist Cecil Rhodes appears as the paradigmatic capitalist. The spaces of the globe are closing up and capital's imperialist expansion is confronting its limits. Rhodes, ever the adventurer, gazes wistfully and yearningly at the stars above, frustrated by the cruel temptation of those new frontiers, so close and yet so far.

Even though their critiques of imperialism and capitalist expansion are often presented in strictly quantitative, economic terms, the stakes for Marxist theorists are primarily *political.* This does not mean that the economic calculations (and the critiques of them) should not be taken seriously; it means, rather, that the economic relationships must be considered as they are really articulated in the historical and social context, as part of political relations of rule and domination.[17] The most important political stake for these authors in the question of economic expansion is to demonstrate the ineluctable relationship between capitalism and imperialism. If capitalism and imperialism are essentially related, the logic goes, then any struggle against imperialism (and the wars, misery, impoverishment, and enslavement that follow from it) must also be a direct struggle against capitalism. Any political strategy aimed at reforming the contemporary configuration of capitalism to make it nonimperialist is vain and naive because the core of capitalist reproduction and accumulation necessarily implies imperialist expansion. Capital cannot behave otherwise—this is its nature. The evils of imperialism cannot be confronted except by destroying capitalism itself.

Equalization and Subsumption

Lenin's book on imperialism is cast primarily as a synthesis of the analyses of other authors to make them accessible to a wide public.[18] Lenin's text, however, also makes its own original contributions, the most important of which is to pose the critique of imperialism from the subjective standpoint and thus link it to the Marxist notion of the revolutionary potential of crises. He gave us a toolbox, a set of machines for the production of anti-imperialist subjectivity.

Lenin often presents his arguments by way of polemic. His analysis of imperialism is articulated primarily by challenging the theses of Rudolf Hilferding and Karl Kautsky. In order to develop his critiques, however, Lenin considered carefully, and at times assumed as his own, the theoretical assumptions of both these authors. Most important, Lenin adopted Hilferding's fundamental thesis that as capital expands through the imperialist construction of the world market, there emerge ever greater obstacles to the *Ausgleichung* (the equalization) of rates of profit among various branches and sectors of production. Peaceful capitalist development, however, depends on at least a tendency toward equalized economic conditions: equal prices for equal commodities, equal profit for equal capital, equal wages and equal exploitation for equal work, and so forth. Hilferding recognized that imperialism—which structures the nations and territories of capitalist development in an ever more rigid way and assigns authority to national monopolies—impedes the formation of an equalized rate of profit and thus undermines the possibility of a successful capitalist mediation of international development.[19] In effect, the domination and division of the world market by monopolies had made the process of equalization virtually impossible. Only if the national central banks were to intervene, or better, if a unified international bank were to intervene, could this contradiction, which portends both trade wars and fighting wars, be equalized and placated. In short, Lenin adopted

Hilferding's hypothesis that capital had entered a new phase of international development defined by monopoly and that this led to both an increase of contradictions and a crisis of equalization. He did not accept, however, that the utopia of a unified international bank could be taken seriously and that a still capitalist *Aufhebung* (subsumption) of the crisis could ever come about.

Lenin regarded the position of Kautsky, who also took Hilferding's work as his point of departure, as even more utopian and damaging. Kautsky proposed, in effect, that capitalism could achieve a real political and economic unification of the world market. The violent conflicts of imperialism could be followed by a new peaceful phase of capitalism, an "ultra-imperialist" phase. The magnates of capital could unite in a single world trust, substituting an internationally united finance capital for the competition and struggle between nationally based finance capitals. We can thus imagine a phase in the future, he claimed, in which capital achieves a peaceful subsumption and resolution in which not a unified bank but market forces and monopolies more or less regulated by states could succeed somehow in determining the global equalization of the rate of profit.[20] Lenin agreed with Kautsky's basic thesis that there is a trend in capitalist development toward the international cooperation of the various national finance capitals and possibly toward the construction of a single world trust. What he objected to so strongly was the fact that Kautsky used this vision of a peaceful future to negate the dynamics of the present reality; Lenin thus denounced his "profoundly reactionary desire to blunt the contradictions" of the present situation.[21] Rather than waiting for some peaceful ultra-imperialism to arrive in the future, revolutionaries should act now on the contradictions posed by capital's present imperialist organization.

Thus, while generally adopting these authors' analytical propositions, Lenin rejected their political positions. Although he fundamentally agreed with Hilferding's analysis of the tendency toward a world market dominated by monopolies, he denied that such a system was already in effect in such a way that it could mediate and equalize the rate of profit. He denied this not so much theoretically as politically. Lenin maintained that capitalist development in the monopoly phase would be plagued by a series of contradictions and that communists had to act on them. It was the responsibility of the workers' movement to oppose every capitalist attempt at organizing an effective equalization of imperialist rates of profit, and it was the task of the revolutionary party to intervene in and deepen the objective contradictions of development. What had to be avoided most was the realization of the tendency toward "ultra-imperialism," which would monstrously increase the power of capital and take away for a long period to come the possibility of struggles on the most contradictory and thus weakest links in the chain of domination. Lenin writes, either as hope or as prediction, "This development proceeds in such circumstances, at such a pace, through such contradictions, conflicts and upheavals—not only economic but political, national, etc.—that inevitably imperialism will burst and capitalism will be transformed into its opposite *long before* one world trust materialises, before the 'ultra-imperialist,' world-wide amalgamation of national finance capitals takes place."[22]

Lenin's logical démarche here between analytical propositions and political positions was certainly tortuous. Nevertheless, his reasoning was very effective from the subjective point of view. As Ilya Babel said, Lenin's thought ran along "the mysterious curve of the straight line" that carried the analysis of the reality of the working class to the necessity of its political organization. Lenin recognized the untimely element of the definition of imperialism and grasped in the subjective practices of the working class not only the potential obstacles to the linear solution of the crises of capitalist realization (which Luxemburg emphasized too), but also the existing and concrete possibility that these practices—struggles, insurrections, and revolutions—could destroy imperialism itself.[23] In this sense Lenin took the critique of imperialism from theory to practice.

From Imperialism to Empire

One of the most remarkable aspects of Lenin's analysis is his critique of imperialism as a political concept. Lenin brought together the problematic of modern sovereignty and that of capitalist development under the lens of one unified critique, and by weaving together the different lines of critique, he was able to glimpse beyond modernity. In other words, through his political re-elaboration of the concept of imperialism, Lenin, more than any other Marxist, was able to anticipate the passage to a new phase of capital beyond imperialism and identify the place (or really the non-place) of emerging imperial sovereignty.

When Lenin studied imperialism, he focused his attention not only on the work of the various recent Marxist authors but also further back to the work of John Hobson and his bourgeois populist version of the critique of imperialism.[24] Lenin learned a great deal from Hobson—which, incidentally, he could have learned equally well from the German, French, or Italian populist theorists of imperialism. In particular, he learned that the modern European nation-states use imperialism to transfer outside their own borders the political contradictions that arise within each single country. The nation-state asks imperialism to resolve or really displace class struggle and its destabilizing effects. Cecil Rhodes expressed the essence of this function of imperialism most clearly: "My cherished idea is a solution for the social problem, i.e., in order to save the 40,000,000 inhabitants of the United Kingdom from a bloody civil war, we colonial statesmen must acquire new lands to settle the surplus population, to provide new markets for the goods produced by them in the factories and mines. The Empire, as I have always said, is a bread and butter question. If you want to avoid civil war, you must become imperialists."[25] Through imperialism, the modern state exports class struggle and civil war in order to preserve order and sovereignty at home.

Lenin saw imperialism as a structural stage in the evolution of the modern state. He imagined a necessary and linear historical progression from the first forms of the modern European state to the nation-state and then to the imperialist state. At each stage in this development the state had to invent new means of constructing popular consensus, and thus the imperialist state had to find a way to incorporate the multitude and its spontaneous forms of class struggle within its ideological state structures; it had to transform the multitude into a people. This analysis is the initial political articulation of the concept of hegemony that would later become central to Gramsci's thought.[26] Lenin thus interpreted imperialist populism as simply another variant of the proposition of sovereignty as a solution for the crisis of modernity.

On the basis of this interpretation of imperialism as a hegemonic element of sovereignty, Lenin could account for the structuring effects and totalitarian consequences of imperialist politics. He understood with great clarity the centripetal dynamic of imperialism that progressively undermined the distinction between the "inside" and the "outside" of capitalist development. The standpoint of Luxemburg's critique of imperialism was rooted in the "outside," that is, in the resistances that could reorganize the noncapitalist use values of the multitude in both the dominant and the subordinate countries. From Lenin's perspective, however, that standpoint and that strategy are not tenable. The structural transformations imposed by imperialist politics tend to eliminate any possibility of being outside, in either the dominant or the subordinate countries. The standpoint of critique had to be located not outside but within the crisis of modern sovereignty. Lenin believed that with World War I, in which the imperialist stage of modern sovereignty had led directly to mortal conflict among nation-states, the point of crisis had arrived.

Lenin recognized finally that, although imperialism and the monopoly phase were indeed expressions of the global expansion of capital, the imperialist practices and the colonial administrations through which they were often pursued had come to be obstacles to the further development of capital. He emphasized the fact, noted by many critics of imperialism, that competition, essential for the functioning and expansion of capital, declines necessarily in the imperialist phase in proportion to the growth of monopolies. Imperialism, with its trade exclusives and protective tariffs, its national and colonial territories, is continually posing and reinforcing fixed boundaries, blocking or channeling economic, social, and cultural flows. As we saw earlier in cultural terms (in Section 2.3), and as Luxemburg argues in economic terms, imperialism rests heavily on these fixed boundaries and the distinction between inside and outside. Imperialism actually creates a straitjacket for capital—or, more precisely, at a certain point the boundaries created by imperialist practices obstruct capitalist development and the full realization of its world market. Capital must eventually overcome imperialism and destroy the barriers between inside and outside.

It would be an exaggeration to say that, on the basis of these intuitions, Lenin's analysis of imperialism and its crisis leads directly to the theory of Empire. It is true, nonetheless, that his revolutionary standpoint revealed the fundamental node of capitalist development—or better, the Gordian knot that had to be undone. Even though Lenin's practical and political proposal for world revolution was defeated (and soon we will focus on the reasons for this defeat), something like the transformation he foresaw was nonetheless necessary. Lenin's analysis of the crisis of imperialism had the same power and necessity as had Machiavelli's analysis of the crisis of the medieval order: the reaction had to be revolutionary. This is the alternative implicit in Lenin's work: *either world communist revolution or Empire,* and there is a profound analogy between these two choices.

The Missing Volumes of *Capital*

In order to understand the passage from imperialism to Empire, in addition to looking at the development of capital itself, we must also understand the genealogy from the perspective of class struggle. This point of view is in fact probably more central to the real historical movements. Theories of the passages to and beyond imperialism that privilege the pure critique of the dynamics of capital risk undervaluing the power of the real efficient motor that drives capitalist development from its deepest core: the movements and struggles of the proletariat. This motor can be very difficult to recognize, often because it is masked by the ideology of the state and the dominant classes, but even when it appears only faintly or sporadically, it is nonetheless effective. History has a logic only when subjectivity rules it, only when (as Nietzsche says) the emergence of subjectivity reconfigures efficient causes and final causes in the development of history. The power of the proletariat consists precisely in this.

We thus arrive at the delicate passage through which the subjectivity of class struggle transforms imperialism into Empire. In this third part of our book we will trace the genealogy of the economic order of Empire so as to reveal the global nature of proletarian class struggle and its ability to anticipate and prefigure the developments of capital toward the realization of the world market. We still need to identify, however, a theoretical schema that can sustain us in this inquiry. The old analyses of imperialism will not be sufficient here because in the end they stop at the threshold of the analysis of subjectivity and concentrate rather on the contradictions of capital's own development. We need to identify a theoretical schema that puts the subjectivity of the social movements of the proletariat at center stage in the processes of globalization and the constitution of global order.

There is a paradox in Marx's thought that may be particularly illuminating for resolving the problems we are facing here. In his outlines for the drafting of *Capital,* Marx planned three volumes that were never written: one on the wage, a second on the state, and a third on the world market.[27] One could say that the content of the volume on the wage, insofar as it was really to be a volume on wage earners, was in part contained in Marx's political and historical writings, such as *The Eighteenth Brumaire, The Class Struggles in France,* and the writings on the Paris Commune.[28] The situation of the volumes on the state and the world market, however, is completely different. Marx's various notes on these questions are scattered and entirely insufficient; not even outlines of these volumes exist. The comments Marx did make about the concept of the state are directed less toward a general theoretical discussion than toward specific analyses of national politics: on English parliamentarianism, on French Bonapartism, on Russian autocracy, and so forth. The national limits of these situations are what made a general theory impossible. The constitutional characteristics of each nation-state were, in Marx's view, conditioned by the difference in the rates of profit in the different national economies along with the differences in the regimes of exploitation—in short, by particular state overdeterminations of the processes of valorization in the different national sites of development. *The nation-state was a singular organization of the limit.* In these conditions a general theory of the state could not but be aleatory and conceived only in the most abstract terms. Marx's difficulties in writing the volumes of *Capital* on the state and the world market were thus fundamentally linked: the volume on the state could not be written until the world market had been realized.

Marx's thinking, however, was oriented toward a moment when capitalist valorization and the political processes of command would converge and overlap on the world level. The nation-state played only an ephemeral role in his work. Processes of capitalist development determine valorization and exploitation as functions of a global system of production, and every obstacle that appears on that terrain tends to be surpassed in the long run. "The tendency to create the world market," he wrote, "is directly given in the concept of capital itself. Every limit appears as a barrier to be overcome."[29] A Marxian theory of the state can be written only when all such fixed barriers are overcome and when the state and capital effectively coincide. In other words, the decline of nation-states is in a profound sense the full realization of the relationship between the state and capital. "Capitalism only triumphs," as Fernand Braudel says, "when it becomes identified with the state, when it is the state."[30] Today it is perhaps finally possible (if one still feels the need) to draft Marx's two missing volumes; or rather, following the spirit of his method and gathering together Marx's insights about the state and the world market, one could attempt to write a revolutionary critique of Empire.

The analyses of the state and the world market also become possible in Empire for another reason, because at this point in development class struggle acts *without limit* on the organization of power. Having achieved the global level, capitalist development is faced directly with the multitude, without mediation. Hence the dialectic, or really the science of the limit and its organization, evaporates. Class struggle, pushing the nation-state toward its abolition and thus going beyond the barriers posed by it, proposes the constitution of Empire as the site of analysis and conflict. Without that barrier, then, the situation of struggle is completely open. Capital and labor are opposed in a directly antagonistic form. This is the fundamental condition of every political theory of communism.

Cycles

From imperialism to Empire and from the nation-state to the political regulation of the global market: what we are witnessing, considered from the point of view of historical materialism, is a qualitative passage in modern history. When we are incapable of expressing adequately the enormous importance of this passage, we sometimes quite poorly define what is happening as the entry into postmodernity. We recognize the poverty of this description, but we sometimes prefer it to others because at least postmodernity indicates the epochal shift in contemporary history.[1] *Other authors, however, seem to undervalue the difference of our situation and lead the analysis back to the categories of a cyclical understanding of historical evolution. What we are living today, in their view, would merely be another phase in the regularly repeating cycles of the forms of economic development or forms of government.*

We are familiar with numerous theories of historical cycles, from those concerning the forms of government that we inherited from Greco-Roman antiquity to those of the cyclical development and decline of civilization in twentieth-century authors such as Oswald Spengler and José Ortega y Gasset. There are, of course, enormous differences between Plato's cyclical evaluation of the forms of government and Polybius' apologia for the Roman Empire, or between Spengler's Nazi ideology and the strong historicism of Fernand Braudel. We find this entire mode of reasoning completely inadequate, however, because every theory of cycles seems to laugh at the fact that history is a product of human action by imposing an objective law that rules over the intentions and resistances, the defeats and the victories, the joys and the suffering of humans. Or worse, it makes human actions dance to the rhythm of the cyclical structures.

Giovanni Arrighi adopted the methodology of long cycles to write a rich and fascinating analysis of "the long twentieth century."[2] *The book is focused primarily on understanding how the crisis of United States hegemony and accumulation in the 1970s (indicated, for example, by the decoupling of the dollar from the gold standard in 1971 and by the defeat of the U.S. military in Vietnam) is a fundamental turning point in the history of world capitalism. In order to approach the contemporary passage, however, Arrighi believes that we need to step back and situate this crisis in the long history of cycles of capitalist accumulation. Following the methodology of Fernand Braudel, Arrighi constructs an enormous historical and analytical apparatus of four great systemic cycles of capitalist accumulation, four "long centuries," that situate the United States in line after the Genoese, the Dutch, and the British.*

This historical perspective leads Arrighi to demonstrate how everything returns, or specifically how capitalism always returns. The crisis of the 1970s, then, is really nothing new. What is happening to the capitalist system led by the United States today happened to the British one hundred years ago, to the Dutch before them, and earlier to the Genoese. The crisis indicated a passage, which is the turning point in every systemic cycle of accumulation, from a first phase of material expansion (investment in production) to a second phase of financial expansion (including speculation). This passage toward financial expansion, which Arrighi claims has characterized the U.S. economy since the early 1980s, always has an autumnal character; it signals the end of a cycle. It indicates specifically the end of U.S. hegemony over the world capitalist system, because the end of each long cycle always indicates a geographical shift of the epicenter of systemic processes of capital accumulation. "Shifts of this kind," he writes, "have occurred in all the crises and financial expansions that have marked the transition from one systemic cycle of accumulation to another."[3] *Arrighi claims that the United States has passed the torch to Japan to lead the next long cycle of capitalist accumulation.*

We are not interested in discussing whether or not Arrighi is right to advance this hypothesis about the decline of the United States and the rise of Japan. What concerns us more is that in the context of Arrighi's cyclical argument it is impossible to recognize a rupture of the system, a paradigm shift, an event. Instead, everything must always return, and the history of capitalism thus becomes the eternal return of the same. In the end, such a cyclical analysis masks the motor of the process of crisis and restructuring. Even though Arrighi himself has done extensive research on working-class conditions and movements throughout the world, in the context of this book, and under the weight of its historical apparatus, it seems that the crisis of the 1970s was simply part of the objective and inevitable cycles of capitalist accumulation, rather than the result of proletarian and anticapitalist attack both in the dominant and in the subordinated countries. The accumulation of these struggles was the motor of the crisis, and they determined the terms and nature of capitalist restructuring. More important than any historical debate about the crisis of the 1970s, however, are the possibilities of rupture today. We have to recognize where in the transnational networks of production, the circuits of the world market, and the global structures of capitalist rule there is the potential for rupture and the motor for a future that is not simply doomed to repeat the past cycles of capitalism.

3.2

DISCIPLINARY GOVERNABILITY

> It seems politically impossible for a capitalist democracy to organize expenditure on the scale necessary to make the grand experiment which would prove my case—except in war conditions.
>
> John Maynard Keynes, July 29, 1940

> The old imperialism—exploitation for foreign profit—has no place in our plans.
>
> President Harry S. Truman, January 20, 1949

The first major wave of Marxist theoretical analyses of imperialism was clustered around the period of World War I. This period too was the beginning of some profound changes in the world capitalist system. Coming out of the Soviet Revolution of 1917 and the first great interimperialist war, capitalist development, it was clear, could not proceed as before. There was, as we said, a clear choice: either world communist revolution or the transformation of capitalist imperialism toward Empire. Capital had to respond to this challenge, but conditions throughout the world were not very favorable. In the 1920s the disorder of capitalist development in the imperialist countries had reached its peak. The growth and concentration of industrial production, which the war had pushed to an extreme, continued at a rapid pace in the dominant capitalist countries, and the spread of Taylorism allowed for increasingly high levels of productivity. This rational organization of labor, however, did not lead to the rational organization of markets, but instead only increased their anarchy. Wage regimes in the dominant countries became ever stronger and more rigid along the Fordist model. The fixed regimes of high wages functioned in part as a response to the threat conjured up by the October Revolution, an inoculation against the spread of the communist disease. Meanwhile, colonial expansion continued unabated as the spoils of the German, Austrian, and Turkish territories were divided among the victors under the dirty sheets of the League of Nations.

This set of factors underlay the great economic crisis of 1929—a crisis of both capitalist overinvestment and proletarian underconsumption in the dominant capitalist countries.[1] When Wall Street's "Black Friday" officially declared the crisis open, the rulers had to face the general problems of the capitalist system and search for a solution, if one was still possible. What they should have done at Versailles during the peace negotiations—deal with the *causes* of the interimperialist war rather than simply punish the losers[2]—now had to be done within each individual country. Capitalism had to be transformed radically. The governments of the primary imperialist countries, however, were not able to accomplish this. In Great Britain and France, reform never really took place, and the few attempts got bogged down in the face of the conservative reaction. In Italy and Germany, the project to restructure capitalist relations eventually evolved into Nazism and fascism.[3] In Japan, too, capitalist growth took the form of militarism and imperialism.[4] Only in the United States was capitalist reform put into effect and proposed as a democratic New Deal. The New Deal constituted a real departure from the previous forms of the bourgeois regulation of economic development. For our analysis, the importance of the New Deal should be gauged not only in terms of its capacity to restructure the relations of production and power within a single dominant capitalist country but also, above all, in terms of its effects throughout the world—effects that were not direct or straightforward but nonetheless profound. With the New Deal the real process of surpassing imperialism began to take root.

A New Deal for the World

In the United States, the New Deal was supported by a strong political subjectivity among both popular forces and the elite. The continuity of the liberal and populist faces of American progressivism from the beginning of the century converged in Franklin Delano Roosevelt's action program. One could rightly say that FDR resolved the contradictions of American progressivism by forging a synthesis of the American imperialist vocation and reformist capitalism, represented by Theodore Roosevelt and Woodrow Wilson.[5] This subjectivity was the driving force that transformed U.S. capitalism and renewed U.S. society in the process. The state was celebrated not only as mediator of conflicts but also as motor of social movement. The transformations of the state's juridical structure set in motion procedural mechanisms that could allow for the strong participation and expression of a broad plurality of social forces. The state took the central role in economic regulation, too, as Keynesianism was applied to labor and monetary policies. U.S. capitalism was spurred forward by these reforms, and it developed in a regime of high wages, high consumption, and also high conflictuality. Out of this development came the trinity that would constitute the modern welfare state: a synthesis of Taylorism in the organization of labor, Fordism in the wage regime, and Keynesianism in the macroeconomic regulation of society.[6] It was not a welfare state that was the product of economic and social policies that mixed public assistance and imperialist incentives, as had been the case in Europe, but rather one that invested social relations in their entirety, imposing a regime of discipline accompanied by greater participation in the processes of accumulation. It was a capitalism that wanted to be transparent, regulated by a state that exercised liberal planning.

We should make clear that our apologia of Roosevelt's welfare state is somewhat exaggerated here in order to demonstrate our central thesis: that the New Deal model (responding to the crisis common to all the dominant capitalist states after the First World War) was the first instance of a strong subjectivity that tended in the direction of Empire. The New Deal produced the highest form of *disciplinary* government. When we speak of disciplinary government, we are not referring simply to the juridical and political forms that organize it. We are referring primarily to the fact that in a disciplinary society, the entire society, with all its productive and reproductive articulations, is subsumed under the command of capital and the state, and that the society tends, gradually but with unstoppable continuity, to be ruled solely by criteria of capitalist production. *A disciplinary society is thus a factory-society.*[7] Disciplinarity is at once a form of production and a form of government such that disciplinary production and disciplinary society tend to coincide completely. In this new factory-society, productive subjectivities are forged as one-dimensional functions of economic development. The figures, structures, and hierarchies of the division of social labor become ever more widespread and minutely defined as civil society is increasingly absorbed into the state: the new rules of subordination and the disciplinary capitalist regimes are extended across the entire social terrain.[8] It is precisely when the disciplinary regime is pushed to its highest level and most complete application that it is revealed as the extreme limit of a social arrangement, a society in the process of being overcome. This is certainly due in large part to the motor behind the process, the subjective dynamics of resistance and revolt, which we will return to in the next section.

The New Deal model, then, was first of all a development proper to U.S. politics, a response to the domestic economic crisis, but it also became a flag that the U.S. Army raised throughout the course of the Second World War. Several explanations were given for why the United States entered the war. Roosevelt always claimed to have been dragged in unwillingly by the dynamics of international politics. Keynes and the economists thought instead that the needs of the New Deal—confronted as it was in 1937 by a new type of crisis, challenged by the political pressure of workers' demands—had obliged the U.S. government to choose the path of war. Facing an international struggle for the new repartition of the world market, the United States could not avoid the war, in particular because with the New Deal, the U.S. economy had entered into another expansive phase. In either case, the U.S. entry into World War II tied the New Deal indissolubly to the crisis of European imperialisms and projected the New Deal on the scene of world government as an alternative, successor model. From that point on, the effects of the New Deal reforms would be felt over the entire global terrain.

In the aftermath of the war, many viewed the New Deal model as the only path to global recovery (under the pacific powers of U.S. hegemony). As one U.S. commentator wrote, "Only a New Deal for the world, more far reaching and consistent than our faltering New Deal, can prevent the coming of World War III."[9] The economic reconstruction projects launched after the Second World War did in fact impose on all the dominant capitalist countries, both the victorious Allies and the defeated powers, adhesion to the expansive model of disciplinary society according to the model constructed by the New Deal. The previous European and Japanese forms of state-based public assistance and the development of the corporativist state (in both its liberal and national-socialist forms) were thus substantially transformed. The "social state" was born, or really the global disciplinary state, which took into account more widely and deeply the life cycles of populations, ordering their production and reproduction within a scheme of collective bargaining fixed by a stable monetary regime. With the extension of U.S. hegemony, the dollar became king. The initiative of the dollar (through the Marshall Plan in Europe and the economic reconstruction in Japan) was the ineluctable path to postwar reconstruction; the establishment of the dollar's hegemony (through the Bretton Woods accords) was tied to the stability of all the standards of value; and U.S. military power determined the ultimate exercise of sovereignty with respect to each of the dominant and subordinate capitalist countries. All the way up to the 1960s this model was expanded and perfected. It was the Golden Age of the New Deal reform of capitalism on the world stage.[10]

Decolonization, Decentering, and Discipline

As a result of the project of economic and social reform under U.S. hegemony, the imperialist politics of the dominant capitalist countries was transformed in the postwar period. The new global scene was defined and organized primarily around three mechanisms or apparatuses: (1) the process of decolonization that gradually recomposed the world market along hierarchical lines branching out from the United States; (2) the gradual decentralization of production; and (3) the construction of a framework of international relations that spread across the globe the disciplinary productive regime and disciplinary society in its successive evolutions. Each of these aspects constitutes a step in the evolution from imperialism toward Empire.

Decolonization, the first mechanism, was certainly a bitter and ferocious process. We have already dealt with it briefly in Section 2.3, and we have seen its convulsive movements from the point of view of the colonized in struggle. Here we must historicize the process from the standpoint of the dominant powers. The colonial territories of defeated Germany, Italy, and Japan, of course, were completely dissolved or absorbed by the other powers. By this time, however, the colonial projects of the victors, too (Britain, France, Belgium, and Holland), had come to a standstill.[11] In addition to facing growing liberation movements in the colonies, they also found themselves stymied by the bipolar divide between the United States and the Soviet Union. The decolonization movements too were seized immediately in the jaws of this cold war vise, and the movements that had been focused on their independence were forced to negotiate between the two camps.[12] What Truman said in 1947 during the Greek crisis remained true for the decolonizing and postcolonial forces throughout the cold war: "At the present moment in world history nearly every nation must choose between alternative ways of life."[13]

The linear trajectory of decolonization was thus interrupted by the necessity of selecting a global adversary and lining up behind one of the two models of international order. The United States, which was by and large favorable to decolonization, was forced by the necessities of the cold war and the defeat of the old imperialisms to assume the primary role as international guardian of capitalism and hence ambiguous heir of the old colonizers. From both the side of the anticolonial subjects and the side of the United States, decolonization was thus distorted and diverted. The United States inherited a global order, but one whose forms of rule conflicted with its own constitutional project, its imperial form of sovereignty. The Vietnam War was the final episode of the United States' ambiguous inheritance of the old imperialist mantle, and it ran the risk of blocking any possible opening of an imperial "new frontier" (see Section 2.5). This phase was the final obstacle to the maturation of the new imperial design, which would eventually be built on the ashes of the old imperialisms. Little by little, after the Vietnam War the new world market was organized: a world market that destroyed the fixed boundaries and hierarchical procedures of European imperialisms. In other words, the completion of the decolonization process signaled the point of arrival of a new world hierarchization of the relations of domination—and the keys were firmly in the hands of the United States. The bitter and ferocious history of the first period of decolonization opened onto a second phase in which the army of command wielded its power less through military hardware and more through the dollar. This was an enormous step forward toward the construction of Empire.

The second mechanism is defined by a process of decentering the sites and flows of production.[14] Here, as in decolonization, two phases divide the postwar period. A first, neocolonial phase involved the continuity of the old hierarchical imperialist procedures and the maintenance if not deepening of the mechanisms of unequal exchange between subordinated regions and dominant nation-states. This first period, however, was a brief transitional phase, and, in effect, in the arc of twenty years the scene changed radically. By the end of the 1970s, or really by the end of the Vietnam War, transnational corporations began to establish their activities firmly across the globe, in every corner of the planet. The transnationals became the fundamental motor of the economic and political transformation of postcolonial countries and subordinated regions. In the first place, they served to transfer the technology that was essential for constructing the new productive axis of the subordinate countries; second, they mobilized the labor force and local productive capacities in these countries; and finally, the transnationals collected the flows of wealth that began to circulate on an enlarged base across the globe. These multiple flows began to converge essentially toward the United States, which guaranteed and coordinated, when it did not directly command, the movement and operation of the transnationals. This was a decisive constituent phase of Empire. Through the activities of the transnational corporations, the mediation and equalization of the rates of profit were unhinged from the power of the dominant nation-states. Furthermore, the constitution of capitalist interests tied to the new postcolonial nation-states, far from opposing the intervention of transnationals, developed on the terrain of the transnationals themselves and tended to be formed under their control. Through the decentering of productive flows, new regional economies and a new global division of labor began to be determined.[15] There was no global order yet, but an order was being formed.

Along with the decolonization process and the decentering of flows, a third mechanism involved the spread of disciplinary forms of production and government across the world. This process was highly ambiguous. In the postcolonial countries, discipline required first of all transforming the massive popular mobilization for liberation into a mobilization for production. Peasants throughout the world were uprooted from their fields and villages and thrown into the burning forge of world production.[16] The ideological model that was projected from the dominant countries (particularly from the United States) consisted of Fordist wage regimes, Taylorist methods of the organization of labor, and a welfare state that would be modernizing, paternalistic, and protective. From the standpoint of capital, the dream of this model was that eventually every worker in the world, sufficiently disciplined, would be interchangeable in the global productive process—a global factory-society and a global Fordism. The high wages of a Fordist regime and the accompanying state assistance were posed as the workers' rewards for accepting disciplinarity, for entering the global factory. We should be careful to point out, however, that these specific relations of production, which were developed in the dominant countries, were never realized in the same forms in the subordinated regions of the global economy. The regime of high wages that characterizes Fordism and the broad social assistance that characterizes the welfare state were realized only in fragmentary forms and for limited populations in the subordinated capitalist countries. All this, however, did not really have to be realized; its promise served rather as the ideological carrot to ensure sufficient consensus for the modernizing project. The real substance of the effort, the real take-off toward modernity, which was in fact achieved, was the spread of the disciplinary regime throughout the social spheres of production and reproduction.

The leaders of the socialist states agreed in substance on this disciplinary project. Lenin's renowned enthusiasm for Taylorism was later outdone by Mao's modernization projects.[17] The official socialist recipe for decolonization also followed the essential logic dictated by the capitalist transnationals and the international agencies: each postcolonial government had to create a labor force adequate to the disciplinary regime. Numerous socialist economists (especially those who were in the position to plan the economies of countries recently liberated from colonialism) claimed that industrialization was the ineluctable path to development[18] and enumerated the benefits of the extension of "peripheral Fordist" economies.[19] The benefits were really an illusion, and the illusion did not last long, but that could not significantly alter the course of these postcolonial countries along the path of modernization and disciplinarization. This seemed to be the only path open to them.[20] Disciplinarity was everywhere the rule.

These three mechanisms—decolonization, decentering of production, and disciplinarity—characterize the imperial power of the New Deal, and demonstrate how far it moved beyond the old practices of imperialism. Certainly the original formulators of the New Deal policies in the United States in the 1930s never imagined such a wide application of their ideas, but already in the 1940s, in the midst of war, world leaders began to recognize its role and power in the establishment of global economic and political order. By the time of Harry Truman's inauguration, he understood that finally the old European-style imperialism could have no part in their plans. No, the new era had something new in store.

Into and Out of Modernity

The cold war was the dominant figure on the global scene during the period of decolonization and decentralization, but from today's vantage point we have the impression that its role was really secondary. Although the specular oppositions of the cold war strangled both the U.S. imperial project and the Stalinist project of socialist modernization, these were really minor elements of the entire process. The truly important element, whose significance goes well beyond the history of the cold war, was the gigantic postcolonial transformation of the Third World under the guise of modernization and development. In the final analysis, that project was relatively independent of the dynamics and constraints of the cold war, and one could almost claim, *post factum,* that in the Third World the competition between the two world power blocs merely accelerated the processes of liberation.

It is certainly true that the Third World elites who led the anticolonial and anti-imperialist struggles during this period were ideologically tied to one or the other side of the cold war divide, and in both cases they defined the mass project of liberation in terms of modernization and development. For us, however, poised as we are at the far border of modernity, it is not difficult to recognize the tragic lack of perspective involved in the translation of liberation into modernization. The myth of modernity—and thus of sovereignty, the nation, the disciplinary model, and so forth—was virtually the exclusive ideology of the elites, but this is not the most important factor here.

The revolutionary processes of liberation determined by the multitude actually pushed beyond the ideology of modernization, and in the process revealed an enormous new production of subjectivity. This subjectivity could not be contained in the bipolar U.S.-

USSR relationship, nor in the two competing regimes, which both merely reproduced modernity's modalities of domination. When Nehru, Sukarno, and Chou En-lai came together at the Bandung Conference in 1955 or when the nonalignment movement first formed in the 1960s, what was expressed was not so much the enormity of their nations' misery nor the hope of repeating the glories of modernity but rather the enormous potential for liberation that the subaltern populations themselves produced.[21] This non-aligned perspective gave a first glimpse of a new and generalized desire.

The question what to do after liberation so as not to fall under the domination of one camp or the other remained unanswered. What were clear and full of potential, by contrast, were the subjectivities that pushed beyond modernity. The utopian image of the Soviet and Chinese revolutions as alternatives for development vanished when those revolutions could no longer go forward, or rather when they failed to find a way to go beyond modernity. The U.S. model of development appeared equally closed, since throughout the postwar period the United States presented itself more as the police force of the old imperialisms than the agent of a new hope. The struggle of subaltern populations for their liberation remained an explosive and uncontainable mixture. By the end of the 1960s the liberation struggles, whose influence had come to be felt in every interstice of world space, assumed a force, a mobility, and a plasticity of form that drove the project of capitalist modernization (in both its liberal and its socialist guises) out into an open sea, where it lost its bearings. Behind the façade of the bipolar U.S.-Soviet divide they could discern a single disciplinary model, and against this model the enormous movements struggled, in forms that were more or less ambiguous, more or less mystified, but nonetheless real. This enormous new subjectivity alluded to and made necessary a paradigm shift.

The inadequacy of the theory and practice of modern sovereignty became evident at this point. By the 1960s and 1970s, even though the model of disciplinary modernization had been imposed across the world, even though the welfarist policies set in motion by the dominant countries had become unstoppable and were naively championed by leaders in the subordinated countries, and even in this new world of communicative media and networks, the mechanisms of modern sovereignty were no longer sufficient to rule the new subjectivities. We should point out here that as the paradigm of modern sovereignty lost its effectiveness, so too the classical theories of imperialism and anti-imperialism lost whatever explanatory powers they had. In general, when these theories conceived the surpassing of imperialism, they saw it as a process that would be in perfect continuity with the paradigm of modernization and modern sovereignty. What happened, however, was exactly the opposite. Massified subjectivities, populations, oppressed classes, in the very moment when they entered the processes of modernization, began to transform them and go beyond them. The struggles for liberation, in the very moment when they were situated and subordinated in the world market, recognized insufficient and tragic keystone of modern sovereignty. Exploitation and domination could no longer be imposed in their modern forms. As these enormous new subjective forces emerged from colonization and reached modernity, they recognized that *the primary task is not getting into but getting out of modernity.*

Toward a New Global Paradigm

A paradigm shift in the world economic and political order was taking place. One important element of this passage was the fact that the world market as a structure of hierarchy and command became more important and decisive in all the zones and regions in which the old imperialisms had previously operated. The world market began to appear as the centerpiece of an apparatus that could regulate global networks of circulation. This unification was still posed only at a formal level. The processes that arose on the conflictual terrain of liberation struggles and expanding capitalist circulation were not necessarily or immediately compatible with the new structures of the world market. Integration proceeded unevenly and at different speeds. In different regions and often within the same region, diverse forms of labor and production coexisted, as did also different regimes of social reproduction. What might have seemed like a coherent central axis of the restructuring of global production was shattered into a thousand particular fragments and the unifying process was experienced everywhere singularly. Far from being unidimensional, the process of restructuring and unifying command over production was actually an explosion of innumerable different productive systems. The processes of the unification of the world market operated paradoxically through diversity and diversification, but its tendency was nonetheless real.

Several important effects follow from the tendency toward the unification of the world market. On the one hand, the wide spread of the disciplinary model of the organization of labor and society outward from the dominant regions produced in the rest of the world a strange effect of proximity, simultaneously pulling it closer and isolating it away in a ghetto. That is, liberation struggles found themselves "victorious" but nonetheless consigned to the ghetto of the world market—a vast ghetto with indeterminate borders, a shantytown, a favela. On the other hand, huge populations underwent what might be called *wage emancipation* as a result of these processes. Wage emancipation meant the entrance of great masses of workers into the disciplinary regime of modern capitalist production, whether it be in the factory, the fields, or some other site of social production, and hence these populations were liberated from the semi-servitude that imperialism had perpetuated. Entry into the wage system can be bloody (and it has been); it can reproduce systems of ferocious repression (and it has done so); but even in the shacks of the new shantytowns and favelas, the wage relation does determine the constitution of new needs, desires, and demands. For example, the peasants who become wage workers and who are subjected to the discipline of the new organization of labor in many cases suffer worse living conditions, and one cannot say that they are more free than the traditional territorialized laborer, but they do become infused with *a new desire for liberation*. When the new disciplinary regime constructs the tendency toward a global market of labor power, it constructs also the possibility of its antithesis. It constructs the desire to escape the disciplinary regime and tendentially an undisciplined multitude of workers who want to be free.

The increasing mobility of large portions of the global proletariat is another important consequence of the tendential unification of the world market. In contrast to the old imperialist regimes in which the currents of labor mobility were primarily regulated vertically between colony and metropole, the world market opens up wider horizontal paths. The constitution of a global market organized along a disciplinary model is traversed by tensions that open mobility in every direction; it is a transversal mobility that is rhizomatic rather than arborescent. Our interest here is not only in giving a phenomenological description of the existing situation, but also in recognizing the possibilities inherent in that situation. The new transversal mobility of disciplined labor power is significant because it indicates a real and powerful search for freedom and the formation of new, nomadic desires that cannot be contained and controlled within the disciplinary regime.[22] It is true that many workers across the world are subject to forced migrations in dire circumstances that are hardly liberatory in themselves. It is true, too, that this mobility rarely increases the cost of labor power; in fact, it most often decreases it, increasing instead the competition among workers. The mobility does carry for capital a high price, however, which is the increased desire for liberation.

Some significant macroeconomic effects follow from the new mobility introduced by capital's global disciplinary paradigm. The mobility of populations makes it increasingly difficult to manage national markets (particularly national labor markets) individually. The adequate domain for the application of capitalist command is no longer delimited by national borders or by the traditional international boundaries. Workers who flee the Third World to go to the First for work or wealth contribute to undermining the boundaries between the two worlds. The Third World does not really disappear in the process of unification of the world market but enters into the First, establishes itself at the heart as ghetto, shantytown, favela, always again produced and reproduced. In turn, the First World is transferred to the Third in the form of stock exchanges and banks, transnational corporations and icy skyscrapers of money and command. Economic geography and political geography both are destabilized in such a way that the boundaries among the various zones are themselves fluid and mobile. As a result, the entire world market tends to be the only coherent domain for the effective application of capitalist management and command.

At this point the capitalist regimes have to undergo a process of reform and restructuring in order to ensure their capacity to organize the world market. This tendency emerges clearly only in the 1980s (and is established definitively after the collapse of the Soviet model of modernization), but already at the moment of its first appearance its principal features are clearly defined. It has to be a new mechanism of the general control of the global process and thus a mechanism that can coordinate politically the new dynamics of the global domain of capital and the subjective dimensions of the actors; it has to be able to articulate the imperial dimension of command and the transversal mobility of the subjects. We will see in the next section how this process was realized historically, and thus we will begin to address directly the processes of the constitution of a global apparatus of government.

Real Subsumption and the World Market

Before we move on, the expository development of our study demands that we look more closely at the relationship between this tendency toward the realization of the world market and the paradigm of disciplinary production and government. How does the spread of disciplinary regimes throughout the world represent a fundamental genealogical moment of Empire? We can give one explanation why this is the case by linking Marx's description of the phases of the capitalist subsumption of society together with his analyses of the tendency toward the world market. The two movements actually coincide at a certain point, or really the capitalist subsumption of society tends to be completed in the construction of the world market.

Earlier we saw that the practices of imperialism involve capital's internalization of its outside and are thus processes of the *formal subsumption* of labor under capital. Marx uses the term "formal subsumption" to name processes whereby capital incorporates under its own relations of production laboring practices that originated outside its domain.[23] The processes of formal subsumption are thus intrinsically related to the extension of the domain of capitalist production and capitalist markets. At a certain point, as capitalist expansion reaches its limit, the processes of formal subsumption can no longer play the central role. The processes of the *real subsumption* of labor under capital do not rely on the outside and do not involve the same processes of expansion. Through the real subsumption, the integration of labor into capital becomes more intensive than extensive and society is ever more completely fashioned by capital. There are certainly processes of real subsumption without a world market, but there cannot be a fully realized world market without the processes of real subsumption. In other words, the realization of the world market and the general equalization or at least management of rates of profit on a world scale cannot be the result simply of financial or monetary factors but must come about through a transformation of social and productive relations. Discipline is the central mechanism of this transformation. When a new social reality is formed, integrating both the development of capital and the proletarianization of the population into a single process, the political form of command must itself be modified and articulated in a manner and on a scale adequate to this process, a global quasi-state of the disciplinary regime.

Marx's intuitions of the processes of real subsumption do not furnish us with the key we need. The passage from the formal subsumption to the real must be explained through the practices of active subjective forces. In other words, disciplinarity pushed to its extreme, imposed by the global Taylorization of labor processes, cannot actually determine the need for a new form of command except through the expression of active social subjectivities. The globalization of markets, far from being simply the horrible fruit of capitalist entrepreneurship, was actually the result of the desires and demands of Taylorist, Fordist, and disciplined labor power across the world. In this sense, the processes of the formal subsumption anticipated and carried through to maturity the real subsumption, not because the latter was the product of the former (as Marx himself seemed to believe), but because in the former were constructed conditions of liberation and struggle that only the latter could control. The movements of desiring subjectivities forced the development to go forward—and proclaimed that there was no turning back. In response to these movements in both the dominant and the subordinated countries, a new form of control had to be posed in order to establish command over what was no longer controllable in disciplinary terms.

Primitive Accumulations

Just when the proletariat seems to be disappearing from the world stage, the proletariat is becoming the universal figure of labor. This claim is not actually as paradoxical as it may seem. What has disappeared is the hegemonic position of the industrial working class, which has not disappeared or even declined in numbers—it has merely lost its hegemonic position and shifted geographically. We understand the concept "proletariat," however, to refer not just to the industrial working class but to all those who are subordinated to, exploited by, and produce under the rule of capital. From this perspective, then, as capital ever more globalizes its relations of production, all forms of labor tend to be proletarianized. In each society and across the entire world the proletariat is the ever more general figure of social labor.

Marx described the processes of proletarianization in terms of primitive accumulation, *the prior or previous accumulation necessary before capitalist production and reproduction can begin to take place. What is necessary is not merely an accumulation of wealth or property, but a* social *accumulation, the creation of capitalists and proletarians. The essential historical process, then, involves first of all divorcing the producer from the means of production. For Marx it was sufficient to describe the English example of this social transformation, since England represented the "highest point" of capitalist development at the time. In England, Marx explains, proletarianization was accomplished first by the enclosures of the common lands and the clearing of peasants from the estates, and then by the brutal punishment of vagabondage and vagrancy. The English peasant was thus "freed" from all previous means of subsistence, herded toward the new manufacturing towns, and made ready for the wage relation and the discipline of capitalist production. The central motor for the creation of capitalists, by contrast, came from outside England, from commerce—or really from conquest, the slave trade, and the colonial system. "The treasures captured outside Europe by undisguised looting, enslavement and murder," Marx writes, "flowed back to the mother-country and were turned into capital there."*[1] *The enormous influx of wealth overflowed the capacities of the old feudal relations of production. English capitalists sprang up to embody the new regime of command that could exploit this new wealth.*

It would be a mistake, however, to take the English experience of becoming-proletarian and becoming-capitalist as representative of all the others. Over the last three hundred years, as capitalist relations of production and reproduction have spread across the world, although primitive accumulation has always involved separating the producer from the means of production and thereby creating classes of proletarians and capitalists, each process of social transformation has nonetheless been unique. In each case the social and productive relations that preexisted were different, the processes of the transition were different, and even the form of the resulting capitalist relations of production and especially those of reproduction were different in line with specific cultural and historical differences.

Despite these important differences, it is still useful to group the modern processes of primitive accumulation under two general models that highlight the relationship between wealth and command, and between inside and outside. *In all cases, the primitive accumulation of capital requires a new combination of wealth and command. What is distinctive about the first model, which Marx described for England and which applies generally to Europe as a whole, is that the new wealth for the primitive accumulation of capital comes from the outside (from the colonial territories) and the command arises internally (through the evolution of English and European relations of production). According to the second model, which characterizes most of the modern processes of primitive accumulation outside Europe, the terms are reversed, such that the new wealth arises from within and command comes from the outside (usually European capital). This inversion of wealth/command and inside/outside in the two models leads to a whole series of differences in the economic, political, and social formations of capital across the world. Many of these differences deriving from the two models were described adequately by theorists of underdevelopment in terms of central and peripheral capitalist formations.*[2]

As we pass from modernity to postmodernity, the processes of primitive accumulation do indeed continue. Primitive accumulation is not a process that happens once and then is done with; rather, capitalist relations of production and social classes have to be reproduced continually. What has changed is the model or mode of primitive accumulation. First of all, the play between inside and outside that distinguishes the two modern models has progressively declined. More important, the nature of the labor and wealth accumulated is changing. In postmodernity the social wealth accumulated is increasingly immaterial; it involves social relations, communication systems, information, and affective networks. Correspondingly, social labor is increasingly more immaterial; it simultaneously produces and reproduces directly all aspects of social life. As the proletariat is becoming the universal figure of labor, the object of proletarian labor is becoming equally universal. Social labor produces life itself.

We should emphasize the central role that informational accumulation plays in the processes of postmodern primitive accumulation and the ever greater socialization of production. As the new informational economy emerges, a certain accumulation of information is necessary before capitalist production can take place. Information carries through its networks both the wealth and the command of production, disrupting previous conceptions of inside and outside, but also reducing the temporal progression that had previously defined primitive accumulation. In other words, informational accumulation (like the primitive accumulation Marx analyzed) destroys or at least destructures the previously existing productive processes, but (differently than Marx's primitive accumulation) it immediately integrates those productive processes in its own networks and generates across the different realms of production the highest levels of productivity. The temporal sequence of development is thus reduced to immediacy as the entire society tends to be integrated in some way into the networks of informational production. Information networks tend toward something like a simultaneity of social production. *The revolution of informational accumulation therefore requires an enormous leap forward in the greater socialization of production. This increased socialization, along with the reduction of social space and temporality, is a process that no doubt benefits capital with increased productivity, but is one also that points beyond the era of capital toward a new social mode of production.*

3.3

RESISTANCE, CRISIS, TRANSFORMATION

> The continuity of struggle is easy: the workers need only themselves and the boss in front of them. But the continuity of organization is a rare and complex thing: as soon as it is institutionalized it quickly becomes used by capitalism, or by the workers' movement in the service of capitalism.
>
> Mario Tronti

> The New Left sprang . . . from Elvis's gyrating pelvis.
>
> Jerry Rubin

Earlier we posed the Vietnam War as a deviation from the U.S. constitutional project and its tendency toward Empire. The war was also, however, an expression of the desire for freedom of the Vietnamese, an expression of peasant and proletarian subjectivity—a fundamental example of resistance against both the final forms of imperialism and the international disciplinary regime. The Vietnam War represents a real turning point in the history of contemporary capitalism insofar as the Vietnamese resistance is conceived as the symbolic center of a whole series of struggles around the world that had up until that point remained separate and distant from one another. The peasantry who were being subsumed under multinational capital, the (post)colonial proletariat, the industrial working class in the dominant capitalist countries, and the new strata of intellectual proletariat everywhere all tended toward a common site of exploitation in the factory-society of the globalized disciplinary regime. The various struggles converged against one common enemy: *the international disciplinary order.* An objective unity was established, sometimes with the consciousness of those in struggle and sometimes without. The long cycle of struggles against the disciplinary regimes had reached maturity and forced capital to modify its own structures and undergo a paradigm shift.

Two, Three, Many Vietnams

In the late 1960s the international system of capitalist production was in crisis.[1] Capitalist crisis, as Marx tells us, is a situation that requires capital to undergo a general devaluation and a profound rearrangement of the relations of production as a result of the downward pressure that the proletariat puts on the rate of profit. In other words, capitalist crisis is not simply a function of capital's own dynamics but is caused directly by proletarian conflict.[2] This Marxian notion of crisis helps bring to light the most important features of the crisis of the late 1960s. The fall of the rate of profit and the disruption of relations of command in this period are best understood when seen as a *result* of the confluence and accumulation of proletarian and anticapitalist attacks against the international capitalist system.

In the dominant capitalist countries, this period witnessed a worker attack of the highest intensity directed primarily against the disciplinary regimes of capitalist labor. The attack was expressed, first of all, as a general refusal of work and specifically as a refusal of factory work. It was aimed against productivity and against any model of development based on increasing the productivity of factory labor. The refusal of the disciplinary regime and the affirmation of the sphere of non-work became the defining features of a new set of collective practices and a new form of life.[3] Second, the attack served to subvert the capitalist divisions of the labor market. The three primary characteristics of the labor market—the separation of social groups (by class strata, race, ethnicity, or sex), the fluidity of the labor market (social mobility, tertiarization, new relations between directly and indirectly productive labor, and so forth), and the hierarchies of the market of abstract labor—were all threatened by the rising rigidity and commonality of worker demands. The increasing socialization of capital led also toward the social unification of the proletariat. This increasingly unified voice posed the general demand for a guaranteed social wage and a very high level of welfare.[4] Third, and finally, the worker attack was waged directly against capitalist command. The refusal of work and the social unification of the proletariat came together in a frontal attack against the coercive organization of social labor and the disciplinary structures of command. This worker attack was completely political—even when many mass practices, particularly of youth, seemed decidedly apolitical—insofar as it exposed and struck the political nerve centers of the economic organization of capital.

The peasant and proletarian struggles in the subordinate countries also imposed reform on local and international political regimes. Decades of revolutionary struggle—from the Chinese Revolution to Vietnam and from the Cuban Revolution to the numerous liberation struggles throughout Latin America, Africa, and the Arab world—had pushed forward a proletarian wage demand that various socialist and/or nationalist reformist regimes had to satisfy and that directly destabilized the international economic system. The ideology of modernization, even when it did not bring "development," created new desires that exceeded the established relations of production and reproduction. The sudden increase in the costs of raw materials, energy, and certain agricultural commodities in the 1960s and 1970s was a symptom of these new desires and the rising pressure of the international proletariat on the wage. The effects of these struggles not only were a quantitative matter but also determined a qualitatively new element that profoundly marked the intensity of the crisis. For more than one hundred years the practices of imperialism had worked to subsume all forms of production throughout the world under the command of capital, and that tendency was only intensified in this period of transition. The tendency created necessarily a potential or virtual unity of the international proletariat. This *virtual unity* was never fully actualized as a *global political unity,* but it nonetheless had substantial effects. In other words, the few instances of the actual and conscious international organization of labor are not what seem most important here, but rather the *objective* coincidence of struggles that overlap precisely because, despite their radical diversity, they were all directed against the international disciplinary regime of capital. The growing coincidence determined what we call an accumulation of struggles.

This accumulation of struggles undermined the capitalist strategy that had long relied on the hierarchies of the international divisions of labor to block any global unity among workers. Already in the nineteenth century, before European imperialism had fully bloomed, Engels was bemoaning the fact that the English proletariat was put in the position of a "labor aristocracy" because its interests lay with the project of British imperialism rather than with the ranks of colonial labor power. In the period of the decline of imperialisms, strong international divisions of labor certainly remained, but the imperialist advantages of any national working class had begun to wither away. The common struggles of the proletariat in the subordinate countries took away the possibility of the old imperialist strategy of transferring the crisis from the metropolitan terrain to its subordinate territories. It was no longer feasible to rely on Cecil Rhodes's old strategy of placating the domestic dangers of class struggle in Europe by shifting the economic pressures to the still peaceful order of the dominated imperialist terrain maintained with brutally effective techniques. The proletariat formed on the imperialist terrain was now itself organized, armed, and dangerous. There was thus a tendency toward the unity of the international or multinational proletariat in one common attack against the capitalist disciplinary regime.[5] The resistance and initiative of the proletariat in the subordinate countries resonated as a symbol and model both above and within the proletariat of the dominant capitalist countries. By virtue of this convergence, the worker struggles throughout the domain of international capital already decreed the end of the division between First and Third Worlds and the potential political integration of the entire global proletariat. The convergence of struggles posed on an international scale the problem of transforming laboring cooperation into revolutionary organization and actualizing the virtual political unity.

With this objective convergence and accumulation of struggles, Third Worldist perspectives, which may earlier have had a limited utility, were now completely useless. We understand Third Worldism to be defined by the notion that the primary contradiction and antagonism of the international capitalist system is between the capital of the First World and the labor of the Third.[6] The potential for revolution thus resides squarely and exclusively in the Third World. This view has been evoked implicitly and explicitly in a variety of dependency theories, theories of underdevelopment, and world system perspectives.[7] The limited merit of the Third Worldist perspective was that it directly countered the "First Worldist" or Eurocentric view that innovation and change have always originated, and can only originate, in Euro-America. Its specular opposition of this false claim, however, leads only to a position that is equally false. We find this Third Worldist perspective inadequate because it ignores the innovations and antagonisms of labor in the First and Second Worlds. Furthermore, and most important for our argument here, the Third Worldist perspective is blind to the real convergence of struggles across the world, in the dominant and subordinate countries alike.

Capitalist Response to the Crisis

As the global confluence of struggles undermined the capitalist and imperialist capacities of discipline, the economic order that had dominated the globe for almost thirty years, the Golden Age of U.S. hegemony and capitalist growth, began to unravel. The form and substance of the capitalist management of international development for the postwar period were dictated at the conference at Bretton Woods, New Hampshire, in 1944.[8] The Bretton Woods system was based on three fundamental elements. Its first characteristic was the comprehensive economic hegemony of the United States over all the nonsocialist countries. This hegemony was secured through the strategic choice of a liberal development based on relatively free trade and moreover by maintaining gold (of which the United States possessed about one third of the world total) as the guarantee of the power of the dollar. The dollar was "as good as gold." Second, the system demanded the agreement for monetary stabilization between the United States and the other dominant capitalist countries (first Europe then Japan) over the traditional territories of European imperialisms, which had been dominated previously by the British pound and the French franc. Reform in the dominant capitalist countries could thus be financed by a surplus of exports to the United States and guaranteed by the monetary system of the dollar. Finally, Bretton Woods dictated the establishment of a quasi-imperialist relationship of the United States over all the subordinate nonsocialist countries. Economic development within the United States and stabilization and reform in Europe and Japan were all guaranteed by the United States insofar as it accumulated imperialist superprofits through its relationship to the subordinate countries.

The system of U.S. monetary hegemony was a fundamentally new arrangement because, whereas the control of previous international monetary systems (notably the British) had been firmly in the hands of private bankers and financiers, Bretton Woods gave control to a series of governmental and regulatory organizations, including the International Monetary Fund, the World Bank, and ultimately the U.S. Federal Reserve.[9] Bretton Woods might thus be understood as the monetary and financial face of the hegemony of the New Deal model over the global capitalist economy.

The Keynesian and pseudo-imperialist mechanisms of Bretton Woods eventually went into crisis when the continuity of the workers' struggles in the United States, Europe, and Japan raised the costs of stabilization and reformism, and when anti-imperialist and anticapitalist struggles in subordinate countries began to undermine the extraction of superprofits.[10] When the imperialist motor could no longer move forward and the workers' struggles become ever more demanding, the U.S. trade balance began to lean heavily in the direction of Europe and Japan. A first phase of crisis—creeping rather than rampant—extended from the early to the late 1960s. Since the controls provided by Bretton Woods made the dollar de facto inconvertible, the monetary mediation of international production and trade developed through a phase characterized by the relatively free circulation of capital, the construction of a strong Eurodollar market, and the fixing of political parity more or less everywhere in the dominant countries.[11] The explosion of 1968 in Europe, the United States, and Japan, coupled with the Vietnamese military victory over the United States, however, completely dissolved this provisory stabilization. Stagflation gave way to rampant inflation. The second phase of the crisis might be thought of as beginning on August 17, 1971, when President Nixon decoupled the dollar from the gold standard, making the dollar inconvertible de jure and adding a 10 percent surcharge to all imports from Europe to the United States.[12] The entire U.S. debt was effectively pushed onto Europe. This operation was accomplished only by virtue of the economic and political power of the United States, which thus reminded the Europeans of the initial terms of the agreement, of its hegemony as the highest point of exploitation and capitalist command.

In the 1970s the crisis became official and structural. The system of political and economic equilibria invented at Bretton Woods had been completely thrown into disarray, and what remained was only the brute fact of U.S. hegemony. The declining effectiveness of the Bretton Woods mechanisms and the decomposition of the monetary system of Fordism in the dominant countries made it clear that the reconstruction of an international system of capital would have to involve a comprehensive restructuring of economic relations and a paradigm shift in the definition of world command. Such a crisis, however, is not always an entirely negative or unwelcome event from the perspective of capital. Marx claims that capital does indeed have a fundamental interest in economic crisis for its transformative power. With respect to the overall system, individual capitalists are conservative. They are focused primarily on maximizing their individual profits in the short term even when this leads down a ruinous path for collective capital in the long term. Economic crisis can overcome these resistances, destroy unprofitable sectors, restructure the organization of production, and renew its technologies. In other words, economic crisis can push forward a transformation that reestablishes a high general rate of profit, thus responding effectively on the very terrain defined by the worker attack. Capital's general devaluation and its efforts to destroy worker organization serve to transform the substance of the crisis—the disequilibria of circulation and overproduction—into a reorganized apparatus of command that rearticulates the relationship between development and exploitation.

Given the intensity and coherence of the struggles of the 1960s and 1970s, two paths were open to capital for accomplishing the tasks of placating the struggles and restructuring command, and it tried each of them in turn. The first path, which had only a limited effectiveness, was *the repressive option*—a fundamentally conservative operation. Capital's repressive strategy was aimed at completely reversing the social process, separating and disaggregating the labor market, and reestablishing control over the entire cycle of production. Capital thus privileged the organizations that represented a guaranteed wage for a limited portion of the work force, fixing that segment of the population within their structures and reinforcing the separation between those workers and more marginalized populations. The reconstruction of a system of hierarchical compartmentalization, both within each nation and internationally, was accomplished by controlling social mobility and fluidity. The repressive use of technology, including the automation and computerization of production, was a central weapon wielded in this effort. The previous fundamental technological transformation in the history of capitalist production (that is, the introduction of the assembly line and the mass manufacturing regime) involved crucial modifications of the immediate productive processes (Taylorism) and an enormous step forward in the regulation of the social cycle of reproduction (Fordism). The technological transformations of the

1970s, however, with their thrust toward automatic rationalization, pushed these regimes to the extreme limit of their effectiveness, to the breaking point. Taylorist and Fordist mechanisms could no longer control the dynamic of productive and social forces.[13] Repression exercised through the old framework of control could perhaps keep a lid on the destructive powers of the crisis and the fury of the worker attack, but it was ultimately also a self-destructive response that would suffocate capitalist production itself.

At the same time, then, a second path had to come into play, one that would involve a technological transformation aimed no longer only at repression but rather at *changing the very composition of the proletariat,* and thus integrating, dominating, and profiting from its new practices and forms. In order to understand the emergence of this second path of capitalist response to the crisis, however, the path that constitutes a paradigm shift, we have to look beyond the immediate logic of capitalist strategy and planning. The history of capitalist forms is always necessarily a *reactive* history: left to its own devices capital would never abandon a regime of profit. In other words, capitalism undergoes systemic transformation only when it is forced to and when its current regime is no longer tenable. In order to grasp the process from the perspective of its active element, we need to adopt the standpoint of the other side—that is, the standpoint of the proletariat along with that of the remaining non-capitalist world that is progressively being drawn into capitalist relations. The power of the proletariat imposes limits on capital and not only determines the crisis but also dictates the terms and nature of the transformation. *The proletariat actually invents the social and productive forms that capital will be forced to adopt in the future.*

We can get a first hint of this determinant role of the proletariat by asking ourselves how throughout the crisis the United States was able to maintain its hegemony. The answer lies in large part, perhaps paradoxically, not in the genius of U.S. politicians or capitalists, but in the power and creativity of the U.S. proletariat. Whereas earlier, from another perspective, we posed the Vietnamese resistance as the symbolic center of the struggles, now, in terms of the paradigm shift of international capitalist command, the U.S. proletariat appears as the subjective figure that expressed most fully the desires and needs of international or multinational workers.[14] Against the common wisdom that the U.S. proletariat is weak because of its low party and union representation with respect to Europe and elsewhere, perhaps we should see it as strong for precisely those reasons. Working-class power resides not in the representative institutions but in the antagonism and autonomy of the workers themselves.[15] This is what marked the real power of the U.S. industrial working class. Moreover, the creativity and conflictuality of the proletariat resided also, and perhaps more important, in the laboring populations outside the factories. Even (and especially) those who actively refused work posed serious threats and creative alternatives.[16] In order to understand the continuation of U.S. hegemony, then, it is not sufficient to cite the relations of force that U.S. capitalism wielded over the capitalists in other countries. U.S. hegemony was actually sustained by the antagonistic power of the U.S. proletariat.

The new hegemony that seemed to remain in the hands of the United States was still limited at this point, closed within the old mechanisms of disciplinary restructuring. A paradigm shift was needed to design the restructuring process along the lines of the political and technological shift. In other words, capital had to confront and respond to *the new production of subjectivity of the proletariat.* This new production of subjectivity reached (beyond the struggle over welfare, which we have already mentioned) what might be called an ecological struggle, a struggle over the mode of life, that was eventually expressed in the developments of immaterial labor.

The Ecology of Capital

We are still not yet in a position to understand the nature of the second path of capital's response to the crisis, the paradigm shift that will move it beyond the logics and practices of disciplinary modernization. We need to step back once again and examine the limitations imposed on capital by the international proletariat and the noncapitalist environment that both made the transformation necessary and dictated its terms.

At the time of the First World War it seemed to many observers, and particularly to the Marxist theorists of imperialism, that the death knell had sounded and capital had reached the threshold of a fatal disaster. Capitalism had pursued decades-long crusades of expansion, used up significant portions of the globe for its accumulation, and for the first time been forced to confront the limits of its frontiers. As these limits approached, imperialist powers inevitably found themselves in mortal conflict with one another. Capital depended on its outside, as Rosa Luxemburg said, on its noncapitalist environment, in order to realize and capitalize its surplus value and thus continue its cycles of accumulation. In the early twentieth century it appeared that the imperialist adventures of capitalist accumulation would soon deplete the surrounding noncapitalist nature and capital would starve to death. Everything outside the capitalist relation—be it human, animal, vegetable, or mineral—was seen from the perspective of capital and its expansion as nature.[17] The critique of capitalist imperialism thus expressed an ecological consciousness—ecological precisely insofar as it recognized the real limits of nature and the catastrophic consequences of its destruction.[18]

Well, as we write this book and the twentieth century draws to a close, capitalism is miraculously healthy, its accumulation more robust than ever. How can we reconcile this fact with the careful analyses of numerous Marxist authors at the beginning of the century who pointed to the imperialist conflicts as symptoms of an impending ecological disaster running up against the limits of nature? There are three ways we might approach this mystery of capital's continuing health. First, some claim that capital is no longer imperialist, that it has reformed, turned back the clock to its salad days of free competition, and developed a conservationist, ecological relationship with its noncapitalist environment. Even if theorists from Marx to Luxemburg had not demonstrated that such a process runs counter to the essence of capitalist accumulation itself, merely a cursory glance at contemporary global political economy should persuade anyone to dismiss this explanation out of hand. It is quite clear that capitalist expansion continued at an increasing pace in the latter half of the twentieth century, opening new territories to the capitalist market and subsuming noncapitalist productive processes under the rule of capital.

A second hypothesis might be that the unforeseen persistence of capitalism involves simply a continuation of the same processes of expansion and accumulation that we analyzed earlier, only that the complete depletion of the environment was not yet imminent, and that the moment of confronting limits and of ecological disaster is still to come. The global resources of the noncapitalist environment have indeed proved to be vast. Although the so-called Green Revolution has subsumed within capitalism a large portion of the world's noncapitalist agriculture, and other modernization projects have incorporated new territories and civilizations into the cycle of capitalist accumulation, there still remain enormous (if, of course, limited) basins of labor power and material resources to be subsumed in capitalist production and potential sites for expanding markets. For example, the collapse of the socialist regimes in the Soviet Union and Eastern Europe, along with the opening of the Chinese economy in the post-Mao era, has provided global capital access to huge territories of noncapitalist environment—prefabricated for capitalist subsumption by years of socialist modernization. Even in regions already securely integrated into the world capitalist system, there are still ample opportunities for expansion. In other words, according to this second hypothesis, noncapitalist environments continue to be subsumed formally under capital's domain, and thus accumulation can still function at least in part through this formal subsumption: the prophets of capital's imminent doom were not wrong but merely spoke too early. The limitations of the noncapitalist environment, however, are real. Sooner or later the once abundant resources of nature will run out.

A third hypothesis, which may be seen as complementary to the second, is that today capital continues to accumulate through subsumption in a cycle of expanded reproduction, but that increasingly it subsumes not the noncapitalist environment but its own capitalist terrain—that is, that the subsumption is no longer *formal* but *real*. Capital no longer looks outside but rather inside its domain, and its expansion is thus intensive rather than extensive. This passage centers on a qualitative leap in the technological organization of capital. Previous stages of the industrial revolution introduced machine-made consumer goods and then machine-made machines, but now we find ourselves confronted with machine-made raw materials and foodstuffs—in short, machine-made nature and machine-made culture.[19] We might say, then, following Fredric Jameson, that postmodernization is the economic process that emerges when mechanical and industrial technologies have expanded to invest the entire world, when the modernization process is complete, and when the formal subsumption of the noncapitalist environment has reached its limit. Through the processes of modern technological transformation, all of nature has become capital, or at least has become subject to capital.[20] Whereas modern accumulation is based on the formal subsumption of the noncapitalist environment, postmodern accumulation relies on the real subsumption of the capitalist terrain itself. This seems to be the real capitalist response to the threat of "ecological disaster," a response that looks to the future.[21] The completion of the industrialization of society and nature, however, the completion of modernization, poses only the precondition for the passage to postmodernization and grasps the transformation only in negative terms, as *post-*. In the next section we will confront directly the real processes of postmodernization, or the informatization of production.

Assault on the Disciplinary Regime

To understand this passage more deeply, we have to touch somehow on its determinant foundation, which resides in the subjective transformations of labor power. In the period of crisis, throughout the 1960s and 1970s, the expansion of welfare and the universalization of discipline in both the dominant and the subordinate countries created a new margin of freedom for the laboring multitude. In other words, workers made use of the disciplinary era, and above all its moments of dissent and its phases of political destabilization (such as the period of the Vietnam crisis), in order to expand the social powers of labor, increase the value of labor power, and redesign the set of needs and desires to which the wage and welfare had to respond. In Marx's terminology, one would say that the value of necessary labor had risen enormously—and of course most important from the perspective of capital, as necessary labor time increases, surplus labor time (and hence profit) decreases correspondingly. From the standpoint of the capitalist, the value of necessary labor appears as an objective economic quantity—the price of labor power, like the price of grain, oil, and other commodities—but really it is determined socially and is the index of a whole series of social struggles. The definition of the set of social needs, the quality of the time of non-work, the organization of family relationships, the accepted expectations of life are all in play and effectively represented by the costs of reproducing the worker. The enormous rise in the social wage (in terms of both working wages and welfare) during the period of crisis in the 1960s and 1970s resulted directly from the accumulation of social struggles on the terrain of reproduction, the terrain of non-work, the terrain of life.

The social struggles not only raised the costs of reproduction and the social wage (hence decreasing the rate of profit), but also and more important forced a change in the quality and nature of labor itself. Particularly in the dominant capitalist countries, where the margin of freedom afforded to and won by workers was greatest, the refusal of the disciplinary regime of the social factory was accompanied by a reevaluation of the social value of the entire set of productive activities. The disciplinary regime clearly no longer succeeded in containing the needs and desires of young people. The prospect of getting a job that guarantees regular and stable work for eight hours a day, fifty weeks a year, for an entire working life, the prospect of entering the normalized regime of the social factory, which had been a dream for many of their parents, now appeared as a kind of death. The mass refusal of the disciplinary regime, which took a variety of forms, was not only a negative expression but also a moment of creation, what Nietzsche calls a transvaluation of values.

The various forms of social contestation and experimentation all centered on a refusal to value the kind of fixed program of material production typical of the disciplinary regime, its mass factories, and its nuclear family structure.[22] The movements valued instead a more flexible dynamic of creativity and what might be considered more *immaterial* forms of production. From the standpoint of the traditional "political" segments of the U.S. movements of the 1960s, the various forms of cultural experimentation that blossomed with a vengeance during that period all appeared as a kind of distraction from the "real" political and economic struggles, but what they failed to see was that *the "merely cultural" experimentation had very profound political and economic effects.*

"Dropping out" was really a poor conception of what was going on in Haight-Ashbury and across the United States in the 1960s. The two essential operations were the refusal of the disciplinary regime and the experimentation with new forms of productivity. The refusal appeared in a wide variety of guises and proliferated in thousands of daily practices. It was the college student who experimented with LSD instead of looking for a job; it was the young woman who refused to get married and make a family; it was the "shiftless" African-American worker who moved on "CP" (colored people's) time, refusing work in every way possible.[23] The youth who refused the deadening repetition of the factory-society invented new forms of mobility and flexibility, new styles of living. Student movements forced a high social value to be accorded to knowledge and intellectual labor. Feminist movements that made clear the political content of "personal" relationships and refused patriarchal discipline raised the social value of what has traditionally been considered women's work, which involves a high content of affective or caring labor and centers on services necessary for social reproduction.[24] The entire panoply of movements and the entire emerging counterculture highlighted the social value of cooperation and communication. This massive transvaluation of the values of social production and production of new subjectivities opened the way for a powerful transformation of labor power. In the next section we will see in detail how the indexes of the value of the movements—mobility, flexibility, knowledge, communication, cooperation, the affective—would define the transformation of capitalist production in the subsequent decades.

The various analyses of "new social movements" have done a great service in insisting on the political importance of cultural movements against narrowly economic perspectives that minimize their significance.[25] These analyses, however, are extremely limited themselves because, just like the perspectives they oppose, they perpetuate narrow understandings of the economic and the cultural. Most important, they fail to recognize *the profound economic power of the cultural movements,* or really the increasing indistinguishability of economic and cultural phenomena. On the one hand, capitalist relations were expanding to subsume all aspects of social production and reproduction, the entire realm of life; and on the other hand, cultural relations were redefining production processes and economic structures of value. A regime of production, and above all a regime of the production of subjectivity, was being destroyed and another invented by the enormous accumulation of struggles.

These new circuits of the production of subjectivity, which were centered on the dramatic modifications of value and labor, were realized within and against the final period of the disciplinary organization of society. The movements anticipated the capitalist awareness of a need for a paradigm shift in production and dictated its form and nature. If the Vietnam War had not taken place, if there had not been worker and student revolts in the 1960s, if there had not been 1968 and the second wave of the women's movements, if there had not been the whole series of anti-imperialist struggles, capital would have been content to maintain its own arrangement of power, happy to have been saved the trouble of shifting the paradigm of production! It would have been content for several good reasons: because the natural limits of development served it well; because it was threatened by the development of immaterial labor; because it knew that the transversal mobility and hybridization of world labor power opened the potential for new crises and class conflicts on an order never before experienced. The restructuring of production, from Fordism to post-Fordism, from modernization to postmodernization, was anticipated by the rise of a new subjectivity.[26] The passage from the phase of perfecting the disciplinary regime to the successive phase of shifting the productive paradigm was driven from below, by a proletariat whose composition had already changed. Capital did not need to invent a new paradigm (even if it were capable of doing so) because *the truly creative moment had already taken place.* Capital's problem was rather to dominate a new composition that had already been produced autonomously and defined within a new relationship to nature and labor, a relationship of autonomous production.

At this point the disciplinary system has become completely obsolete and must be left behind. Capital must accomplish a negative mirroring and an inversion of the new quality of labor power; it must adjust itself so as to be able to command once again. We suspect that for this reason the industrial and political forces that have relied most heavily and with the most intelligence on the extreme modernization of the disciplinary productive model (such as the major elements of Japanese and East Asian capital) are the ones that will suffer most severely in this passage. The only configurations of capital able to thrive in the new world will be those that adapt to and govern the new immaterial, cooperative, communicative, and affective composition of labor power.

The Death Throes of Soviet Discipline

Now that we have given a first approximation of the conditions and forms of the new paradigm, we want to examine briefly one gigantic subjective effect that the paradigm shift determined in the course of its movement: the collapse of the Soviet system. Our thesis, which we share with many scholars of the Soviet world,[27] is that the system went into crisis and fell apart because of its structural incapacity to go beyond the model of disciplinary governability, with respect to both its mode of production, which was Fordist and Taylorist, and its form of political command, which was Keynesian-socialist and thus simply modernizing internally and imperialist externally. This lack of flexibility in adapting its deployments of command and its productive apparatus to the changes of labor power exacerbated the difficulties of the transformation. The heavy bureaucracy of the Soviet state, inherited from a long period of intense modernization, placed Soviet power in an impossible position when it had to react to the new demands and desires that the globally emerging subjectivities expressed, first within the process of modernization and then at its outer limits.

The challenge of postmodernity was posed primarily not by the enemy powers but by the new subjectivity of labor power and its new intellectual and communicative composition. The regime, particularly in its illiberal aspects, was unable to respond adequately to these subjective demands. The system could have continued, and for a certain period did continue, to work on the basis of the model of disciplinary modernization, but it could not combine modernization with the new mobility and creativity of labor power, the fundamental conditions for breathing life into the new paradigm and its complex mechanisms. In the context of Star Wars, the nuclear arms race, and space exploration, the Soviet Union may still have been able to keep up with its adversaries from the technological and military point of view, but the system could not manage to sustain the competitive conflict on the subjective front. It could not compete, in other words, precisely where the real power conflicts were being played out, and it could not face the challenges of the comparative productivity of economic systems, because advanced technologies of communication and cybernetics are efficient only when they are rooted in subjectivity, or better, when they are animated by productive subjectivities. For the Soviet regime, managing the power of the new subjectivities was a matter of life and death.

According to our thesis, then, after the dramatic final years of Stalin's rule and Khrushchev's abortive innovations, Brezhnev's regime imposed a freeze on a productive civil society that had reached a high level of maturity and that, after the enormous mobilizations for war and productivity, was asking for social and political recognition. In the capitalist world, the massive cold war propaganda and the extraordinary ideological machine of falsification and misinformation prevented us from seeing the real developments in Soviet society and the political dialectics that unfolded there. Cold war ideology called that society totalitarian, but in fact it was a society criss-crossed by extremely strong instances of creativity and freedom, just as strong as the rhythms of economic development and cultural modernization. The Soviet Union was better understood not as a totalitarian society but rather as a bureaucratic dictatorship.[28] And only if we leave these distorted definitions behind can we see how political crisis was produced and reproduced in the Soviet Union, to the point finally of burying the regime.

Resistance to the bureaucratic dictatorship is what drove the crisis. The Soviet proletariat's refusal of work was in fact the very same method of struggle that the proletariat in the capitalist countries deployed, forcing their governments into a cycle of crisis, reform, and restructuring. This is our point: despite the delays of development of Russian capitalism, despite the massive losses in World War II, despite the relative cultural isolation, the relative exclusion from the world market, the cruel policies of imprisonment, starvation, and murder of the population, despite all this, and despite their enormous differences with the dominant capitalist countries, the proletariat in Russia and the other countries of the Soviet bloc managed by the 1960s and 1970s to pose the very same problems as the proletariat in the capitalist countries.[29] Even in Russia and the other countries under Soviet control, the demand for higher wages and greater freedom grew continuously along with the rhythm of modernization. And just as in the capitalist countries, there was defined a new figure of labor power, which now expressed enormous productive capacities on the basis of a new development of the intellectual powers of production. This new productive reality, this living intellectual multitude, is what the Soviet leaders tried to lock in the cages of a disciplinary war economy (a war that was continually conjured up rhetorically) and corral in the structures of a socialist ideology of labor and economic development, that is, a socialist management of capital that no longer made any sense. The Soviet bureaucracy was not able to construct the armory necessary for the *postmodern* mobilization of the new labor power. It was frightened by it, terrorized by the collapse of disciplinary regimes, by the transformations of the Taylorized and Fordist subjects that had previously animated production. This was the point where the crisis became irreversible and, given the immobility of the Brezhnevian hibernation, catastrophic.

What we find important was not so much the lack of or the offenses against the individual and formal freedoms of workers, but rather the waste of the productive energy of a multitude that had exhausted the potential of modernity and now wanted to be liberated from the socialist management of capitalist accumulation in order to express a higher level of productivity. This repression and this energy were the forces that, from opposite sides, made the Soviet world collapse like a house of cards. Glasnost and perestroika certainly did represent a self-criticism of Soviet power and posed the necessity of a democratic passage as the condition for a renewed productivity of the system, but they were employed too late and too timidly to stop the crisis. The Soviet machine turned in on itself and ground to a halt, without the fuel that only new productive subjectivities can produce. The sectors of intellectual and immaterial labor withdrew their consensus from the regime, and their exodus condemned the system to death: death from the socialist victory of modernization, death from the incapacity to use its effects and surpluses, death from a definitive asphyxia that strangled the subjective conditions which demanded a passage to postmodernity.

3.4

POSTMODERNIZATION, OR THE INFORMATIZATION OF PRODUCTION

> Postmodernism is not something we can settle once and for all and then use with a clear conscience. The concept, if there is one, has to come at the end, and not at the beginning, of our discussions of it.
>
> Fredric Jameson

> The good news from Washington is that every single person in Congress supports the concept of an information superhighway. The bad news is that no one has any idea what that means.
>
> Congressman Edward Markey

It has now become common to view the succession of economic paradigms since the Middle Ages in three distinct moments, each defined by the dominant sector of the economy: a first paradigm in which agriculture and the extraction of raw materials dominated the economy, a second in which industry and the manufacture of durable goods occupied the privileged position, and a third and current paradigm in which providing services and manipulating information are at the heart of economic production.[1] The dominant position has thus passed from primary to secondary to tertiary production. Economic *modernization* involves the passage from the first paradigm to the second, from the dominance of agriculture to that of industry. Modernization means industrialization. We might call the passage from the second paradigm to the third, from the domination of industry to that of services and information, a process of economic *postmodernization,* or better, *informatization.*

The most obvious definition and index of the shifts among these three paradigms appear first in quantitative terms, in reference either to the percentage of the population engaged in each of these productive domains or to the percentage of the total value produced by the various sectors of production. The changes in employment statistics in the dominant capitalist countries during the past one hundred years do indeed indicate dramatic shifts.[2] This quantitative view, however, can lead to serious misunderstandings of these economic paradigms. Quantitative indicators cannot grasp either the *qualitative* transformation in the progression from one paradigm to another or the *hierarchy* among the economic sectors in the context of each paradigm. In the process of modernization and the passage toward the paradigm of industrial dominance, not only did agricultural production decline quantitatively (both in percentage of workers employed and in proportion of the total value produced), but also, more important, agriculture itself was transformed. When agriculture came under the domination of industry, even when agriculture was still predominant in quantitative terms, it became subject to the social and financial pressures of industry, and moreover agricultural production itself was industrialized. Agriculture, of course, did not disappear; it remained an essential component of modern industrial economies, but it was now a transformed, industrialized agriculture.

The quantitative perspective also fails to recognize hierarchies among national or regional economies in the global system, which leads to all kinds of historical misrecognitions, posing analogies where none exist. From a quantitative perspective, for example, one might assume a twentieth-century society with the majority of its labor force occupied in agriculture or mining and the majority of its value produced in these sectors (such as India or Nigeria) to be in a position analogous to a society that existed sometime in the past with the same percentage of workers or value produced in those sectors (such as France or England). The historical illusion casts the analogy in a dynamic sequence so that one economic system occupies the same position or stage in a sequence of development that another had held in a previous period, as if all were on the same track moving forward in line. From the qualitative perspective, that is, in terms of their position in global power relationships, however, the economies of these societies occupy entirely incomparable positions. In the earlier case (France or England of the past), the agricultural production existed as the dominant sector in its economic sphere, and in the later (twentieth-century India or Nigeria), it is subordinated to industry in the world system. The two economies are not on the same track but in radically different and even divergent situations—of dominance and subordination. In these different positions of hierarchy, a host of economic factors is completely different—exchange relationships, credit and debt relationships, and so forth.[3] In order for the latter economy to realize a position analogous to that of the former, it would have to invert the power relationship and achieve a position of dominance in its contemporary economic sphere, as Europe did, for example, in the medieval economy of the Mediterranean world. Historical change, in other words, has to be recognized in terms of the power relationships throughout the economic sphere.

Illusions of Development

The discourse of economic *development,* which was imposed under U.S. hegemony in coordination with the New Deal model in the postwar period, uses such false historical analogies as the foundation for economic policies. This discourse conceives the economic history of all countries as following one single pattern of development, each at different times and according to different speeds. Countries whose economic production is not presently at the level of the dominant countries are thus seen as developing countries, with the idea that if they continue on the path followed previously by the dominant countries and repeat their economic policies and strategies, they will eventually enjoy an analogous position or stage. The developmental view fails to recognize, however, that the economies of the so-called developed countries are defined not only by certain quantitative factors or by their internal structures, but also and more important by *their dominant position in the global system.*

The critiques of the developmentalist view that were posed by underdevelopment theories and dependency theories, which were born primarily in the Latin American and African contexts in the 1960s, were useful and important precisely because they emphasized the fact that the evolution of a regional or national economic system depends to a large extent on its place within the hierarchy and power structures of the capitalist world-system.[4] The dominant regions will continue to develop and the subordinate will continue to underdevelop as mutually supporting poles in the global power structure. To say that the subordinate economies do not develop does not mean that they do not change or grow; it means, rather, that *they remain subordinate in the global system* and thus never achieve the promised form of a dominant, developed economy. In some cases individual countries or regions may be able to change their position in the hierarchy, but the point is that, regardless of who fills which position, the hierarchy remains the determining factor.[5]

The theorists of underdevelopment themselves, however, also repeat a similar illusion of economic development.[6] Summarizing in schematic terms, we could say that their logic begins with two valid historical claims but then draws from them an erroneous conclusion. First, they maintain that, through the imposition of colonial regimes and/or other forms of imperialist domination, the underdevelopment of subordinated economies was created and sustained by their integration into the global network of dominant capitalist economies, their partial articulation, and thus their real and continuing dependence on those dominant economies. Second, they claim that the dominant economies themselves had originally developed their fully articulated and independent structures in relative isolation, with only limited interaction with other economies and global networks.[7]

From these two more or less acceptable historical claims, however, they then deduce an invalid conclusion: if the developed economies achieved full articulation in relative isolation and the underdeveloped economies became disarticulated and dependent through their integration into global networks, then a project for the relative isolation of the underdeveloped economies will result in their development and full articulation. In other words, as an alternative to the "false development" pandered by the economists of the dominant capitalist countries, the theorists of underdevelopment promoted "real development," which involves delinking an economy from its dependent relationships and articulating in relative isolation an autonomous economic structure. Since this is how the dominant economies developed, it must be the true path to escape the cycle of underdevelopment. This syllogism, however, asks us to believe that the laws of economic development will somehow transcend the differences of historical change.

The alternative notion of development is based paradoxically on the same historical illusion central to the dominant ideology of development it opposes. The tendential realization of the world market should destroy any notion that today a country or region could isolate or delink itself from the global networks of power in order to re-create the conditions of the past and develop as the dominant capitalist countries once did. Even the dominant countries are now dependent on the global system; the interactions of the world market have resulted in a generalized disarticulation of all economies. Increasingly, any attempt at isolation or separation will mean only a more brutal kind of domination by the global system, a reduction to powerlessness and poverty.

Informatization

The processes of modernization and industrialization transformed and redefined all the elements of the social plane. When agriculture was modernized as industry, the farm progressively became a factory, with all of the factory's discipline, technology, wage relations, and so forth. Agriculture was modernized as industry. More generally, society itself slowly became industrialized even to the point of transforming human relations and human nature. Society became a factory. In the early twentieth century, Robert Musil reflected beautifully on the transformation of humanity in the passage from the pastoral agricultural world to the social factory: "There was a time when people grew naturally into the conditions they found waiting for them and that was a very sound way of becoming oneself. But nowadays, with all this shaking up of things, when everything is becoming detached from the soil it grew in, even where the production of soul is concerned one really ought, as it were, to replace the traditional handicrafts by the sort of intelligence that goes with the machine and the factory."[8] The processes of becoming human and the nature of the human itself were fundamentally transformed in the passage defined by modernization.

In our times, however, *modernization has come to an end.* In other words, industrial production is no longer expanding its dominance over other economic forms and social phenomena. A symptom of this shift is manifest in the quantitative changes in employment. Whereas the process of modernization was indicated by a migration of labor from agriculture and mining (the primary sector) to industry (the secondary), the process of postmodernization or informatization has been demonstrated through the migration from industry to service jobs (the tertiary), a shift that has taken place in the dominant capitalist countries, and particularly in the United States, since the early 1970s. Services cover a wide range of activities from health care, education, and finance to transportation, entertainment, and advertising. The jobs for the most part are highly mobile and involve flexible skills. More important, they are characterized in general by the central role played by knowledge, information, affect, and communication. In this sense many call the postindustrial economy an informational economy.

The claim that modernization is over and that the global economy is today undergoing a process of postmodernization toward an informational economy does not mean that industrial production will be done away with or even that it will cease to play an important role, even in the most dominant regions of the globe. Just as the processes of industrialization transformed agriculture and made it more productive, so too the informational revolution will transform industry by redefining and rejuvenating manufacturing processes. The new managerial imperative operative here is, "Treat manufacturing as a service."[9] In effect, as industries are transformed, the division between manufacturing and services is becoming blurred.[10] Just as through the process of modernization all production tended to become industrialized, so too through the process of postmodernization all production tends toward the production of services, toward becoming informationalized.

Not all countries, of course, even among the dominant capitalist countries, have embarked on the project of postmodernization along the same path. On the basis of the change of employment statistics in the G-7 countries since 1970, Manuel Castells and Yuko Aoyama have discerned two basic models or paths of informatization.[11] Both models involve the increase of employment in postindustrial services, but they emphasize different kinds of services and different relations between services and manufacturing. The first path tends toward a *service economy model* and is led by the United States, the United Kingdom, and Canada. This model involves a rapid decline in industrial jobs and a corresponding rise in service-sector jobs. In particular, the financial services that manage capital come to dominate the other service sectors. In the second model, the *info-industrial model,* typified by Japan and Germany, industrial employment declines more slowly than it does in the first model, and, more important, the process of informatization is closely integrated into and serves to reinforce the strength of existing industrial production. Services related directly to industrial production thus remain more important in this model relative to other services. The two models represent two strategies to manage and gain an advantage in the economic transition, but it should be clear that they both move resolutely in the direction of the informatization of the economy and the heightened importance of productive flows and networks.

Although the subordinated countries and regions of the world are not capable of implementing such strategies, the processes of postmodernization nonetheless impose irreversible changes on them. The fact that informatization and the shift toward services have taken place thus far primarily in the dominant capitalist countries and not elsewhere should not lead us back to an understanding of the contemporary global economic situation in terms of linear stages of development. It is true that as industrial production has declined in the dominant countries, it has been effectively exported to subordinated countries, from the United States and Japan, for example, to Mexico and Malaysia. Such geographical shifts and displacements might lead some to believe that there is a new global organization of economic stages whereby the dominant countries are informational service economies, their first subordinates are industrial economies, and those further subordinated are agricultural. From the perspective of stages of development, for example, one might think that through the contemporary export of industrial production, an auto factory built by Ford in Brazil in the 1990s might be comparable to a Ford factory in Detroit in the 1930s because both instances of production belong to the same industrial stage.

When we look more closely, however, we can see that the two factories are not comparable, and the differences are extremely important. First of all, the two factories are radically different in terms of technology and productive practices. When fixed capital is exported, it is exported generally at its highest level of productivity. The Ford factory in 1990s Brazil, then, would not be built with the technology of the Ford factory of 1930s Detroit, but would be based on the most advanced and most productive computer and informational technologies available. The technological infrastructure of the factory itself would locate it squarely within the informational economy. Second, and perhaps more important, the two factories stand in different relations of dominance with respect to the global economy as a whole. The Detroit auto factory of the 1930s stood at the pinnacle of the global economy in the dominant position and producing the highest value; the 1990s auto factory, whether in São Paulo, Kentucky, or Vladivostok, occupies a subordinate position in the global economy—subordinated to the high-value production of services. Today all economic activity tends to come under the dominance of the informational economy and to be qualitatively transformed by it. The geographical differences in the global economy are not signs of the co-presence of different stages of development but lines of the new global hierarchy of production.

It is becoming increasingly clear from the perspective of subordinated regions that modernization is no longer the key to economic advancement and competition. The most subordinated regions, such as areas of sub-Saharan Africa, are effectively excluded from capital flows and new technologies, and they thus find themselves on the verge of starvation.[12] Competition for the middle-level positions in the global hierarchy is conducted not through the industrialization but through the informatization of production. Large countries with varied economies, such as India and Brazil, can support simultaneously all levels of productive processes: information-based production of services, modern industrial production of goods, and traditional handicraft, agricultural, and mining production. There does not need to be an orderly historical progression among these forms, but rather they mix and coexist. All of the forms of production exist within the networks of the world market and under the domination of the informational production of services.

The transformations of the Italian economy since the 1950s demonstrate clearly that relatively backward economies do not simply follow the same stages the dominant regions experience, but evolve through alternative and mixed patterns. After World War II, Italy was still a predominantly peasant-based society, but in the 1950s and 1960s it went through furious if incomplete modernization and industrialization, a first economic miracle. Then, however, in the 1970s and 1980s, when the processes of industrialization were still not complete, the Italian economy embarked on another transformation, a process of postmodernization, and achieved a second economic miracle. These Italian miracles were not really leaps forward that allowed it to catch up with the dominant economies; rather, they represented mixtures of different incomplete economic forms. What is most significant here, and what might usefully pose the Italian case as the general model for all other backward economies, is that *the Italian economy did not complete one stage (industrialization) before moving on to another (informatization).* According to two contemporary economists, the recent Italian transformation reveals "an interesting transition from proto-industrialism to proto-informationalism."[13] Various regions will evolve to have peasant elements mixed with partial industrialization and partial informatization. The economic stages are thus all present at once, merged into a hybrid, composite economy that varies not in kind but in degree across the globe.

Just as modernization did in a previous era, postmodernization or informatization today marks a new mode of becoming human. Where the production of soul is concerned, as Musil would say, one really ought to replace the traditional techniques of industrial machines with the cybernetic intelligence of information and communication technologies. We must invent what Pierre Levy calls an anthropology of cyberspace.[14] This shift of metaphors gives us a first glimpse of the transformation, but we need to look more closely to see clearly the changes in our notion of the human and in humanity itself that emerge in the passage toward an informational economy.

The Sociology of Immaterial Labor

The passage toward an informational economy necessarily involves a change in the quality and nature of labor. This is the most immediate sociological and anthropological implication of the passage of economic paradigms. Today information and communication have come to play a foundational role in production processes.

A first aspect of this transformation is recognized by many in terms of the change in factory labor—using the auto industry as a central point of reference—from the Fordist model to the Toyotist model.[15] The primary structural change between these models involves the system of communication between the production and the consumption of commodities, that is, the passage of information between the factory and the market. The Fordist model constructed a relatively "mute" relationship between production and consumption. The mass production of standardized commodities in the Fordist era could count on an adequate demand and thus had little need to "listen" to the market. A feedback circuit from consumption to production did allow changes in the market to spur changes in productive engineering, but this communication circuit was restricted (owing to the fixed and compartmentalized channels of planning and design structures) and slow (owing to the rigidity of the technologies and procedures of mass production).

Toyotism is based on an inversion of the Fordist structure of communication between production and consumption. Ideally, according to this model, production planning will communicate with markets constantly and immediately. Factories will maintain zero stock, and commodities will be produced just in time according to the present demand of the existing markets. This model thus involves not simply a more rapid feedback loop but an inversion of the relationship because, at least in theory, the production decision actually comes after and in reaction to the market decision. In the most extreme cases the commodity is not produced until the consumer has already chosen and purchased it. In general, however, it would be more accurate to conceive the model as striving toward a continual interactivity or rapid communication between production and consumption. This industrial context provides a first sense in which communication and information have come to play a newly central role in production. One might say that instrumental action and communicative action have become intimately interwoven in the informationalized industrial process, but one should quickly add that this is an impoverished notion of communication as the mere transmission of market data.[16]

The service sectors of the economy present a richer model of productive communication. Most services indeed are based on the continual exchange of information and knowledges. Since the production of services results in no material and durable good, we define the labor involved in this production as *immaterial labor*—that is, labor that produces an immaterial good, such as a service, a cultural product, knowledge, or communication.[17] One face of immaterial labor can be recognized in analogy to the functioning of a computer. The increasingly extensive use of computers has tended progressively to redefine laboring practices and relations, along with, indeed, all social practices and relations. Familiarity and facility with computer technology is becoming an increasingly general primary qualification for work in the dominant countries. Even when direct contact with computers is not involved, the manipulation of symbols and information along the model of computer operation is extremely widespread. In an earlier era workers learned how to act like machines both inside and outside the factory. We even learned (with the help of Muybridge's photos, for example) to recognize human activity in general as mechanical. Today we increasingly think like computers, while communication technologies and their model of interaction are becoming more and more central to laboring activities. One novel aspect of the computer is that it can continually modify its own operation through its use. Even the most rudimentary forms of artificial intelligence allow the computer to expand and perfect its operation based on its interaction with its user and its environment. The same kind of continual interactivity characterizes a wide range of contemporary productive activities, whether computer hardware is directly involved or not. The computer and communication revolution of production has transformed laboring practices in such a way that they all tend toward the model of information and communication technologies.[18] Interactive and cybernetic machines become a new prosthesis integrated into our bodies and minds and a lens through which to redefine our bodies and minds themselves. The anthropology of cyberspace is really a recognition of the new human condition.

Robert Reich calls the kind of immaterial labor involved in computer and communication work "symbolic-analytical services"—tasks that involve "problem-solving, problem-identifying, and strategic brokering activities."[19] This type of labor claims the highest value, and thus Reich identifies it as the key to competition in the new global economy. He recognizes, however, that the growth of these knowledge-based jobs of creative symbolic manipulation implies a corresponding growth of low-value and low-skill jobs of routine symbol manipulation, such as data entry and word processing. Here begins to emerge a fundamental division of labor within the realm of immaterial production.

We should note that one consequence of the informatization of production and the emergence of immaterial labor has been a real homogenization of laboring processes. From Marx's perspective in the nineteenth century, the concrete practices of various laboring activities were radically heterogeneous: tailoring and weaving involved incommensurable concrete actions. Only when abstracted from their concrete practices could different laboring activities be brought together and seen in a homogeneous way, no longer as tailoring and weaving but as the expenditure of human labor power in general, as *abstract labor*.[20] With the computerization of production today, however, the heterogeneity of concrete labor has tended to be reduced, and the worker is increasingly further removed from the object of his or her labor. The labor of computerized tailoring and the labor of computerized weaving may involve exactly the same concrete practices—that is, manipulation of symbols and information. Tools, of course, have always abstracted labor power from the object of labor to a certain degree. In previous periods, however, the tools generally were related in a relatively inflexible way to certain tasks or certain groups of tasks; different tools corresponded to different activities—the tailor's tools, the weaver's tools, or later a sewing machine and a power loom. The computer proposes itself, in contrast, as the universal tool, or rather as the central tool, through which all activities might pass. Through the computerization of production, then, labor tends toward the position of abstract labor.

The model of the computer, however, can account for only one face of the communicational and immaterial labor involved in the production of services. The other face of immaterial labor is the *affective labor* of human contact and interaction. Health services, for example, rely centrally on caring and affective labor, and the entertainment industry is likewise focused on the creation and manipulation of affect. This labor is immaterial, even if it is corporeal and affective, in the sense that its products are intangible, a feeling of ease, well-being, satisfaction, excitement, or passion. Categories such as "in-person services" or services of proximity are often used to identify this kind of labor, but what is really essential to it are the creation and manipulation of affect. Such affective production, exchange, and communication are generally associated with human contact, but that contact can be either actual or virtual, as it is in the entertainment industry.

This second face of immaterial labor, its affective face, extends well beyond the model of intelligence and communication defined by the computer. Affective labor is better understood by beginning from what feminist analyses of "women's work" have called "labor in the bodily mode."[21] Caring labor is certainly entirely immersed in the corporeal, the somatic, but the affects it produces are nonetheless immaterial. What affective labor produces are social networks, forms of community, biopower. Here one might recognize once again that the instrumental action of economic production has been united with the communicative action of human relations; in this case, however, communication has not been impoverished, but production has been enriched to the level of complexity of human interaction.

In short, we can distinguish three types of immaterial labor that drive the service sector at the top of the informational economy. The first is involved in an industrial production that has been informationalized and has incorporated communication technologies in a way that transforms the production process itself. Manufacturing is regarded as a service, and the material labor of the production of durable goods mixes with and tends toward immaterial labor. Second is the immaterial labor of analytical and symbolic tasks, which itself breaks down into creative and intelligent manipulation on the one hand and routine symbolic tasks on the other. Finally, a third type of immaterial labor involves the production and manipulation of affect and requires (virtual or actual) human contact, labor in the bodily mode. These are the three types of labor that drive the postmodernization of the global economy.

We should point out before moving on that in each of these forms of immaterial labor, cooperation is completely inherent in the labor itself. Immaterial labor immediately involves social interaction and cooperation. In other words, the cooperative aspect of immaterial labor is not imposed or organized from the outside, as it was in previous forms of labor, but rather, *cooperation is completely immanent to the laboring activity itself.*[22] This fact calls into question the old notion (common to classical and Marxian political economics) by which labor power is conceived as "variable capital," that is, a force that is activated and made coherent only by capital, because the cooperative powers of labor power (particularly immaterial labor power) afford labor the possibility of valorizing itself. Brains and bodies still need others to produce value, but the others they need are not necessarily provided by capital and its capacities to orchestrate production. Today productivity, wealth, and the creation of social surpluses take the form of cooperative interactivity through linguistic, communicational, and affective networks. In the expression of its own creative energies, immaterial labor thus seems to provide the potential for a kind of spontaneous and elementary communism.

Network Production

The first geographical consequence of the passage from an industrial to an informational economy is a dramatic decentralization of production. The processes of modernization and the passage to the industrial paradigm provoked the intense aggregation of productive forces and mass migrations of labor power toward centers that became factory cities, such as Manchester, Osaka, and Detroit. Efficiency of mass industrial production depended on the concentration and proximity of elements in order to create the factory site and facilitate transportation and communication. The informatization of industry and the rising dominance of service production, however, have made such concentration of production no longer necessary. Size and efficiency are no longer linearly related; in fact, large scale has in many cases become a hindrance. Advances in telecommunications and information technologies have made possible a deterritorialization of production that has effectively dispersed the mass factories and evacuated the factory cities. Communication and control can be exercised efficiently at a distance, and in some cases immaterial products can be transported across the world with minimal delay and expense. Several different production facilities can be coordinated in the simultaneous production of a single commodity in such a way that factories can be dispersed to various locations. In some sectors even the factory site itself can be done away with as its workers communicate exclusively through new information technologies.[23]

In the passage to the informational economy, the assembly line has been replaced by *the network* as the organizational model of production, transforming the forms of cooperation and communication within each productive site and among productive sites. The mass industrial factory defined the circuits of laboring cooperation primarily through the physical deployments of workers on the shop floor. Individual workers communicated with their neighboring workers, and communication was generally limited to physical proximity. Cooperation among productive sites also required physical proximity both to coordinate the productive cycles and to minimize the transportation costs and time of the commodities being produced. For example, the distance between the coal mine and the steel mill, and the efficiency of the lines of transportation and communication between them, are significant factors in the overall efficiency of steel production. Similarly, for automobile production the efficiency of communication and transportation among the series of subcontractors involved is crucial in the overall efficiency of the system. The passage toward informational production and the network structure of organization, in contrast, make productive cooperation and efficiency no longer dependent to such a degree on proximity and centralization. Information technologies tend to make distances less relevant. Workers involved in a single process can effectively communicate and cooperate from remote locations without consideration to proximity. In effect, the network of laboring cooperation requires no territorial or physical center.

The tendency toward the deterritorialization of production is even more pronounced in the processes of immaterial labor that involve the manipulation of knowledge and information. Laboring processes can be conducted in a form almost entirely compatible with communication networks, for which location and distance have very limited importance. Workers can even stay at home and log on to the network. The labor of informational production (of both services and durable goods) relies on what we can call *abstract cooperation.* Such labor dedicates an ever more central role to communication of knowledges and information among workers, but those cooperating workers need not be present and can even be relatively unknown to one another, or known only through the productive information exchanged. The circuit of cooperation is consolidated in the network and the commodity at an abstract level. Production sites can thus be deterritorialized and tend toward a virtual existence, as coordinates in the communication network. As opposed to the old vertical industrial and corporate model, production now tends to be organized in horizontal network enterprises.[24]

The information networks also release production from territorial constraints insofar as they tend to put the producer in direct contact with the consumer regardless of the distance between them. Bill Gates, the co-founder of the Microsoft Corporation, takes this tendency to an extreme when he predicts a future in which networks will overcome entirely the barriers to circulation and allow an ideal, "friction-free" capitalism to emerge: "The information highway will extend the electronic marketplace and make it the ultimate go-between, the universal middleman."[25] If Gates's vision were to be realized, the networks would tend to reduce all distance and make transactions immediate. Sites of production and sites of consumption would then be present to one another, regardless of geographical location.

These tendencies toward the deterritorialization of production and the increased mobility of capital are not absolute, and there are significant countervailing tendencies, but to the extent that they do proceed, they place labor in a weakened bargaining position. In the era of the Fordist organization of industrial mass production, capital was bound to a specific territory and thus to dealing contractually with a limited laboring population. The informatization of production and the increasing importance of immaterial production have tended to free capital from the constraints of territory and bargaining. Capital can withdraw from negotiation with a given local population by moving its site to another point in the global network—or merely by using the potential to move as a weapon in negotiations. Entire laboring populations, which had enjoyed a certain stability and contractual power, have thus found themselves in increasingly precarious employment situations. Once the bargaining position of labor has been weakened, network production can accommodate various old forms of non-guaranteed labor, such as freelance work, home work, part-time labor, and piecework.[26]

The decentralization and global dispersal of productive processes and sites, which is characteristic of the postmodernization or informatization of the economy, provokes a corresponding centralization of the control over production. The centrifugal movement of production is balanced by the centripetal trend of command. From the local perspective, the computer networks and communications technologies internal to production systems allow for more extensive monitoring of workers from a central, remote location. Control of laboring activity can potentially be individualized and continuous in the virtual panopticon of network production. The centralization of control, however, is even more clear from a global perspective. The geographical dispersal of manufacturing has created a demand for increasingly centralized management and planning, and also for a new centralization of specialized producer services, especially financial services.[27] Financial and trade-related services in a few key cities (such as New York, London, and Tokyo) manage and direct the global networks of production. As a mass demographic shift, then, the decline and evacuation of industrial cities has corresponded to the rise of global cities, or really cities of control.

Information Highways

The structure and management of communication networks are essential conditions for production in the informational economy.

These global networks must be constructed and policed in such a way as to guarantee order and profits. It should come as no surprise, then, that the U.S. government poses the establishment and regulation of a global information infrastructure as one of its highest priorities, and that communications networks have become the most active terrain of mergers and competition for the most powerful transnational corporations.

An adviser to the Federal Communications Commission, Peter Cowhey, provides an interesting analogy for the role these networks play in the new paradigm of production and power. The construction of the new information infrastructure, he says, provides the conditions and terms of global production and government just as road construction did for the Roman Empire.[28] The wide distribution of Roman engineering and technology was indeed both the most lasting gift to the imperial territories and the fundamental condition for exercising control over them. Roman roads, however, did not play a central role in the imperial production processes but only facilitated the circulation of goods and technologies. Perhaps a better analogy for the global information infrastructure might be the construction of railways to further the interests of nineteenth- and twentieth-century imperialist economies. Railways in the dominant countries consolidated their national industrial economies, and the construction of railroads in colonized and economically dominated regions opened those territories to penetration by capitalist enterprises, allowing for their incorporation into imperialist economic systems. Like Roman roads, however, railways played only an external role in imperialist and industrial production, extending its lines of communication and transportation to new raw materials, markets, and labor power. *The novelty of the new information infrastructure is the fact that it is embedded within and completely immanent to the new production processes.* At the pinnacle of contemporary production, information and communication are the very commodities produced; the network itself is the site of both production and circulation.

In political terms, the global information infrastructure might be characterized as the combination of a *democratic* mechanism and an *oligopolistic* mechanism, which operate along different models of network systems. The democratic network is a completely horizontal and deterritorialized model. The Internet, which began as a project of DARPA (the U.S. Defense Department Advanced Research Projects Agency), but has now expanded to points throughout the world, is the prime example of this democratic network structure. An indeterminate and potentially unlimited number of interconnected nodes communicate with no central point of control; all nodes regardless of territorial location connect to all others through a myriad of potential paths and relays. The Internet thus resembles the structure of telephone networks, and indeed it generally incorporates them as its own paths of communication, just as it relies on computer technology for its points of communication. The development of cellular telephony and portable computers, unmooring in an even more radical way the communicating points in the network, has intensified the process of deterritorialization. The original design of the Internet was intended to withstand military attack. Since it has no center and almost any portion can operate as an autonomous whole, the network can continue to function even when part of it has been destroyed. The same design element that ensures survival, the decentralization, is also what makes control of the network so difficult. Since no one point in the network is necessary for communication among others, it is difficult for it to regulate or prohibit their communication. This democratic model is what Deleuze and Guattari call a rhizome, a nonhierarchical and noncentered network structure.[29]

The oligopolistic network model is characterized by broadcast systems. According to this model, for example in television or radio systems, there is a unique and relatively fixed point of emission, but the points of reception are potentially infinite and territorially indefinite, although developments such as cable television networks fix these paths to a certain extent. The broadcast network is defined by its centralized production, mass distribution, and one-way communication. The entire culture industry—from the distribution of newspapers and books to films and video cassettes—has traditionally operated along this model. A relatively small number of corporations (or in some regions a single entrepreneur, such as Rupert Murdoch, Silvio Berlusconi, or Ted Turner) can effectively dominate all of these networks. This oligopolistic model is not a rhizome but a tree structure that subordinates all of the branches to the central root.

The networks of the new information infrastructure are a hybrid of these two models. Just as in a previous era Lenin and other critics of imperialism recognized a consolidation of international corporations into quasi-monopolies (over railways, banking, electric power, and the like), today we are witnessing a competition among transnational corporations to establish and consolidate quasi-monopolies over the new information infrastructure. The various telecommunication corporations, computer hardware and software manufacturers, and information and entertainment corporations are merging and expanding their operations, scrambling to partition and control the new continents of productive networks. There will, of course, remain democratic portions or aspects of this consolidated web that will resist control owing to the web's interactive and decentralized structure; but there is already under way a massive centralization of control through the (de facto or de jure) unification of the major elements of the information and communication power structure: Hollywood, Microsoft, IBM, AT&T, and so forth. The new communication technologies, which hold out the promise of a new democracy and a new social equality, have in fact created new lines of inequality and exclusion, both within the dominant countries and especially outside them.[30]

Commons

There has been a continuous movement throughout the modern period to privatize public property. In Europe the great common lands created with the break-up of the Roman Empire and the rise of Christianity were eventually transferred to private hands in the course of capitalist primitive accumulation. Throughout the world what remains of the vast public spaces are now only the stuff of legends: Robin Hood's forest, the Great Plains of the Amerindians, the steppes of the nomadic tribes, and so forth. During the consolidation of industrial society, the construction and destruction of public spaces developed in an ever more powerful spiral. It is true that when it was dictated by the necessities of accumulation (in order to foster an acceleration or leap in development, to concentrate and mobilize the means of production, to make war, and so forth), public property was expanded by expropriating large sectors of civil society and transferring wealth and property to the collectivity. That public property, however, was soon reappropriated in private hands. In each process the communal possession, which is considered natural, is transformed at public expense into a second and third nature that functions finally for private profit. A second nature was created, for example, by damming the great rivers of western North America and irrigating the dry valleys, and then this new wealth was handed over to the magnates of agribusiness. Capitalism sets in motion a continuous cycle of private reappropriation of public goods: the expropriation of what is common.

The rise and fall of the welfare state in the twentieth century is one more cycle in this spiral of public and private appropriations. The crisis of the welfare state has meant primarily that the structures of public assistance and distribution, which were constructed through public funds, are being privatized and expropriated for private gain. The current neoliberal trend toward the privatization of energy and communication services is another turn of the spiral. This consists in granting to private businesses the networks of energy and communication that were built through enormous expenditures of public monies. Market regimes and neoliberalism survive off these private appropriations of second, third, and nth nature. The commons, which once were considered the basis of the concept of the public, are expropriated for private use and no one can lift a finger. The public is thus dissolved, privatized, even as a concept. Or really, the immanent relation between the public and the common is replaced by the transcendent power of private property.

We do not intend here to weep over the destruction and expropriation that capitalism continually operates across the world, even though resisting its force (and in particular resisting the expropriation of the welfare state) is certainly an eminently ethical and important task. We want to ask, rather, what is the operative notion of the common today, in the midst of postmodernity, the information revolution, and the consequent transforma-

tions of the mode of production. It seems to us, in fact, that today we participate in a more radical and profound commonality than has ever been experienced in the history of capitalism. The fact is that we participate in a productive world made up of communication and social networks, interactive services, and common languages. Our economic and social reality is defined less by the material objects that are made and consumed than by co-produced services and relationships. Producing increasingly means constructing cooperation and communicative commonalities.

The concept of private property itself, understood as the exclusive right to use a good and dispose of all wealth that derives from the possession of it, becomes increasingly nonsensical in this new situation. There are ever fewer goods that can be possessed and used exclusively in this framework; it is the community that produces and that, while producing, is reproduced and redefined. The foundation of the classic modern conception of private property is thus to a certain extent dissolved in the postmodern mode of production.

One should object, however, that this new social condition of production has not at all weakened the juridical and political regimes of private property. The conceptual crisis of private property does not become a crisis in practice, and instead the regime of private expropriation has tended to be applied universally. This objection would be valid if not for the fact that, in the context of linguistic and cooperative production, labor and the common property tend to overlap. Private property, despite its juridical powers, cannot help becoming an ever more abstract and transcendental concept and thus ever more detached from reality.

A new notion of "commons" will have to emerge on this terrain. Deleuze and Guattari claim in *What Is Philosophy?* that in the contemporary era, and in the context of communicative and interactive production, the construction of concepts is not only an epistemological operation but equally an ontological project. Constructing concepts and what they call "common names" is really an activity that combines the intelligence and the action of the multitude, making them work together. Constructing concepts means making exist in reality a project that is a community. There is no other way to construct concepts but to work in a common way. This commonality is, from the standpoint of the phenomenology of production, *from the standpoint of the epistemology of the concept, and from the standpoint of practice, a project in which the multitude is completely invested.* The commons is the incarnation, the production, and the liberation of the multitude. *Rousseau said that the first person who wanted a piece of nature as his or her own exclusive possession and transformed it into the transcendent form of private property was the one who invented evil. Good, on the contrary, is what is common.*

3.5

MIXED CONSTITUTION

> One of the wonderful things about the information highway is that virtual equity is far easier to achieve than real-world equity . . . We are all created equal in the virtual world.
>
> Bill Gates

The paradigm shift of production toward the network model has fostered the growing power of transnational corporations beyond and above the traditional boundaries of nation-states. The novelty of this relationship has to be recognized in terms of the long-standing power struggle between capitalists and the state. The history of this conflict is easily misunderstood. One should understand that, most significantly, despite the constant antagonism between capitalists and the state, the relationship is really conflictive only when capitalists are considered individually.

Marx and Engels characterize the state as the executive board that manages the interests of capitalists; by this they mean that although the action of the state will at times contradict the immediate interests of individual capitalists, it will always be in the long-term interest of the collective capitalist, that is, the collective subject of social capital as a whole.[1] Competition among capitalists, the reasoning goes, however free, does not guarantee the common good of the collective capitalist, for their immediate egoistic drive for profit is fundamentally myopic. The state is required for prudence to mediate the interests of individual capitalists, raising them up in the collective interest of capital. Capitalists will thus all combat the powers of the state even while the state is acting in their own collective interests. This conflict is really a happy, virtuous dialectic from the perspective of total social capital.

When Giants Rule the Earth

The dialectic between the state and capital has taken on different configurations in the different phases of capitalist development. A quick and rough periodization will help us pose at least the most basic features of this dynamic. In the eighteenth and nineteenth centuries, as capitalism established itself fully in Europe, the state managed the affairs of the total social capital but required relatively unobtrusive powers of intervention. This period has come to be viewed in retrospect (with a certain measure of distortion) as the golden age of European capitalism, characterized by free trade among relatively small capitalists. Outside the European nation-state in this period, before the full deployment of powerful colonial administrations, European capital operated with even fewer constraints. To a large extent the capitalist companies were sovereign when operating in colonial or precolonial territories, establishing their own monopoly of force, their own police, their own courts. The Dutch East India Company, for example, ruled the territories it exploited in Java until the end of the eighteenth century with its own structures of sovereignty. Even after the company was dissolved in 1800, capital ruled relatively free of state mediation or control.[2] The situation was much the same for the capitalists operating in the British South Asian and African colonies. The sovereignty of the East India Company lasted until the East India Act of 1858 brought the company under the rule of the queen, and in southern Africa the free reign of capitalist adventurers and entrepreneurs lasted at least until the end of the century.[3] This period was thus characterized by relatively little need of state intervention at home and abroad: within the European nation-states individual capitalists were ruled (in their own collective interest) without great conflict, and in the colonial territories they were effectively sovereign.

The relationship between state and capital changed gradually in the nineteenth and early twentieth centuries when crises increasingly threatened the development of capital. In Europe and the United States, corporations, trusts, and cartels grew to establish quasi-monopolies over specific industries and clusters of industries extending far across national boundaries. The monopoly phase posed a direct threat to the health of capitalism because it eroded the competition among capitalists that is the lifeblood of the system.[4] The formation of monopolies and quasi-monopolies also undermined the managerial capacities of the state, and thus the enormous corporations gained the power to impose their particular interests over the interest of the collective capitalist. Consequently there erupted a whole series of struggles in which the state sought to establish its command over the corporations, passing antitrust laws, raising taxes and tariffs, and extending state regulation over industries. In the colonial territories, too, the uncontrolled activities of the sovereign companies and the adventurer capitalists led increasingly toward crisis. For example, the 1857 Indian rebellion against the powers of the East India Company alerted the British government to the disasters the colonial capitalists were capable of if left uncontrolled. The India Act passed by the British Parliament the next year was a direct response to the potential for crisis. The European powers gradually established fully articulated and fully functioning administrations over the colonial territories, effectively recuperating colonial economic and social activity securely under the jurisdiction of the nation-states and thus guaranteeing the interests of total social capital against crises. Internally and externally, the nation-states were forced to intervene more strongly to protect the interests of total social capital against individual capitalists.

Today a third phase of this relationship has fully matured, in which large transnational corporations have effectively surpassed the jurisdiction and authority of nation-states. It would seem, then, that this centuries-long dialectic has come to an end: *the state has been defeated and corporations now rule the earth!* In recent years numerous studies have emerged on the Left that read this phenomenon in apocalyptic terms as endangering humanity at the hands of unrestrained capitalist corporations and that yearn for the old protective powers of nation-states.[5] Correspondingly, proponents of capital celebrate a new era of deregulation and free trade. If this really were the case, however, if the state really had ceased to manage the affairs of collective capital and the virtuous dialectic of conflict between state and capital were really over, then the capitalists ought to be the ones most fearful of the future! Without the state, social capital has no means to project and realize its collective interests.

The contemporary phase is in fact not adequately characterized by the victory of capitalist corporations over the state. Although transnational corporations and global networks of production and circulation have undermined the powers of nation-states, state functions and constitutional elements have effectively been displaced to other levels and domains. We need to take a much more nuanced look at how the relationship between state and capital has changed. We need to recognize first of all the crisis of political relations in the national context. As the concept of national sovereignty is losing its effectiveness, so too is the so-called autonomy of the political.[6] Today a notion of politics as an independent sphere of the determination of consensus and a sphere of mediation among conflicting social forces has very little room to exist. Consensus is determined more significantly by economic factors, such as the equilibria of the trade balances and speculation on the value of currencies. Control over these movements is not in the hands of the political forces that are traditionally conceived as holding sovereignty, and consensus is determined not through the traditional political mechanisms but by other means. Government and politics come to be completely integrated into the system of transnational command. Controls are articulated through a series of international bodies and functions. This is equally true for the mechanisms of political mediation, which really function through the categories of bureaucratic mediation and managerial sociology rather than through the traditional political categories of the mediation of conflicts and the reconciliation of class conflict. Politics does not disappear; what disappears is any notion of the autonomy of the political.

The decline of any autonomous political sphere signals the decline, too, of any independent space where revolution could emerge in the national political regime, or where social space could be transformed using the instruments of the state. The traditional idea of counter-power and the idea of resistance against modern sovereignty in general thus becomes less and less possible. This situation resembles in certain respects the one that Machiavelli faced in a different era: the pathetic and disastrous defeat of "humanistic" revolution or resistance at the hands of the powers of the sovereign principality, or really the early modern state. Machiavelli recognized that the actions of individual heroes (in the style of Plutarch's heroes) were no longer able even to touch the new sovereignty of the principality. A new type of resistance would have to be found that would be adequate to the new dimensions of sovereignty. Today, too, we can see that the traditional forms of resistance, such as the institutional workers' organizations that developed through the major part of the nineteenth and twentieth centuries, have begun to lose their power. Once again a new type of resistance has to be invented.

Finally, the decline of the traditional spheres of politics and resistance is complemented by the transformation of the democratic state such that its functions have been integrated into mechanisms of command on the global level of the transnational corporations. The national democratic model of state-managed exploitation functioned in the dominant capitalist countries so long as it was able to regulate the growing conflictuality in a dynamic fashion—so long, in other words, as it was able to keep alive the potential of the development and the utopia of state planning, so long, above all, as the class struggle in the individual countries determined a sort of dualism of power over which the unitary state structures could situate themselves. To the extent that these conditions have disappeared, in both real and ideological terms, the national democratic capitalist state has self-destructed. The unity of single governments has been disarticulated and invested in a series of separate bodies (banks, international organisms of planning, and so forth, in addition to the traditional separate bodies), which all increasingly refer for legitimacy to the transnational level of power.

The recognition of the rise of the transnational corporations above and beyond the constitutional command of the nation-states should not, however, lead us to think that constitutional mechanisms and controls as such have declined, that transnational corporations, relatively free of nation-states, tend to compete freely and manage themselves. Instead, the constitutional functions have been displaced to another level. Once we recognize the decline of the traditional national constitutional system, we have to explore how power is constitutionalized on a supranational level—in other words, how the constitution of Empire begins to form.

The Pyramid of Global Constitution

At first glance and on a level of purely empirical observation, the new world constitutional framework appears as a disorderly and even chaotic set of controls and representative organizations. These global constitutional elements are distributed in a wide spectrum of bodies (in nation-states, in associations of nation-states, and in international organizations of all kinds); they are divided by function and content (such as political, monetary, health, and educational organisms); and they are traversed by a variety of productive activities. If we look closely, however, this disorderly set does nonetheless contain some points of reference. More than ordering elements, these are rather matrixes that delimit relatively coherent horizons in the disorder of global juridical and political life. When we analyze the configurations of global power in its various bodies and organizations, we can recognize a pyramidal structure that is composed of three progressively broader tiers, each of which contains several levels.

At the narrow pinnacle of the pyramid there is one superpower, the United States, that holds hegemony over the global use of force—a superpower that can act alone but prefers to act in collaboration with others under the umbrella of the United Nations. This singular status was posed definitively with the end of the cold war and first confirmed in the Gulf War. On a second level, still within this first tier, as the pyramid broadens slightly, a group of nation-states control the primary global monetary instruments and thus have the ability to regulate international exchanges. These nation-states are bound together in a series of organisms—the G7, the

Paris and London Clubs, Davos, and so forth. Finally, on a third level of this first tier a heterogeneous set of associations (including more or less the same powers that exercise hegemony on the military and monetary levels) deploy cultural and biopolitical power on a global level.

Below the first and highest tier of unified global command there is a second tier in which command is distributed broadly across the world, emphasizing not so much unification as articulation. This tier is structured primarily by the networks that transnational capitalist corporations have extended throughout the world market—networks of capital flows, technology flows, population flows, and the like. These productive organizations that form and supply the markets extend transversally under the umbrella and guarantee of the central power that constitutes the first tier of global power. If we were to take up the old Enlightenment notion of the construction of the senses by passing a rose in front of the face of the statue, we could say that the transnational corporations bring the rigid structure of the central power to life. In effect, through the global distribution of capitals, technologies, goods, and populations, the transnational corporations construct vast networks of communication and provide the satisfaction of needs. The single and univocal pinnacle of world command is thus articulated by the transnational corporations and the organization of markets. The world market both homogenizes and differentiates territories, rewriting the geography of the globe. Still on the second tier, on a level that is often subordinated to the power of the transnational corporations, reside the general set of sovereign nation-states that now consist essentially in local, territorialized organizations. The nation-states serve various functions: political mediation with respect to the global hegemonic powers, bargaining with respect to the transnational corporations, and redistribution of income according to biopolitical needs within their own limited territories. Nation-states are filters of the flow of global circulation and regulators of the articulation of global command; in other words, they capture and distribute the flows of wealth to and from the global power, and they discipline their own populations as much as this is still possible.

The third and broadest tier of the pyramid, finally, consists of groups that represent popular interests in the global power arrangement. The multitude cannot be incorporated directly into the structures of global power but must be filtered through mechanisms of representation. Which groups and organizations fulfill the contestatory and/or legitimating function of popular representation in the global power structures? Who represents the People in the global constitution? Or, more important, what forces and processes transform the multitude into a People that can then be represented in the global constitution? In many instances nation-states are cast in this role, particularly the collective of subordinated or minor states. Within the United Nations General Assembly, for example, collections of subordinate nation-states, the majority numerically but the minority in terms of power, function as an at least symbolic constraint on and legitimation of the major powers. In this sense the entire world is conceived as being represented on the floor of the U.N. General Assembly and in other global forums. Here, since the nation-states themselves are presented (both in the more or less democratic countries and in the authoritarian regimes) as representing the will of their People, the representation of nation-states on a global scale can only lay claim to the popular will at two removes, through two levels of representation: the nation-state representing the People representing the multitude.

Nation-states, however, are certainly not the only organizations that construct and represent the People in the new global arrangement. Also on this third tier of the pyramid, the global People is represented more clearly and directly not by governmental bodies but by a variety of organizations that are at least relatively independent of nation-states and capital. These organizations are often understood as functioning as the structures of a global civil society, channeling the needs and desires of the multitude into forms that can be represented within the functioning of the global power structures. In this new global form we can still recognize instances of the traditional components of civil society, such as the media and religious institutions. The media have long positioned themselves as the voice or even the conscience of the People in opposition to the power of states and the private interests of capital. They are cast as a further check and balance on governmental action, providing an objective and independent view of all the People want or need to know. It has long been clear, however, that the media are in fact often not very independent from capital on the one hand and states on the other.[7] Religious organizations are an even more long-standing sector of non-governmental institutions that represent the People. The rise of religious fundamentalisms (both Islamic and Christian) insofar as they represent the People against the state should perhaps be understood as components of this new global civil society—but when such religious organizations stand against the state, they often tend to become the state themselves.

The newest and perhaps most important forces in the global civil society go under the name of non-governmental organizations (NGOs). The term NGO has not been given a very rigorous definition, but we would define it as any organization that purports to represent the People and operate in its interest, separate from (and often against) the structures of the state. Many in fact regard NGOs as synonymous with "people's organizations" because the People's interest is defined in distinction from state interest.[8] These organizations operate at local, national, and supranational levels. The term NGO thus groups together an enormous and heterogeneous set of organizations: in the early 1990s there were reported to be more than eighteen thousand NGOs worldwide. Some of these organizations fulfill something like the traditional syndicalist function of trade unions (such as the Self-Employed Women's Association of Ahmedabad, India); others continue the missionary vocation of religious sects (such as Catholic Relief Services); and still others seek to represent populations that are not represented by nation-states (such as the World Council of Indigenous Peoples). It would be futile to try to characterize the functioning of this vast and heterogeneous set of organizations under one single definition.[9]

Some critics assert that NGOs, since they are outside and often in conflict with state power, are compatible with and serve the neoliberal project of global capital. While global capital attacks the powers of the nation-state from above, they argue, the NGOs function as a "parallel strategy 'from below' " and present the "community face" of neoliberalism.[10] It may indeed be true that the activities of many NGOs serve to further the neoliberal project of global capital, but we should be careful to point out that this cannot adequately define the activities of all NGOs categorically. The fact of being non-governmental or even opposed to the powers of nation-states does not in itself line these organizations up with the interests of capital. There are many ways to be outside and opposed to the state, of which the neoliberal project is only one.

For our argument, and in the context of Empire, we are most interested in a subset of NGOs that strive to represent the least among us, those who cannot represent themselves. These NGOs, which are sometimes characterized broadly as humanitarian organizations, are in fact the ones that have come to be among the most powerful and prominent in the contemporary global order. Their mandate is not really to further the particular interests of any limited group but rather to represent directly global and universal human interests. Human rights organizations (such as Amnesty International and Americas Watch), peace groups (such as Witness of Peace and Shanti Sena), and the medical and famine relief agencies (such as Oxfam and Médecins sans frontières) all defend human life against torture, starvation, massacre, imprisonment, and political assassination. Their political action rests on a universal moral call—what is at stake is life itself. In this regard it is perhaps inaccurate to say that these NGOs represent those who cannot represent themselves (the warring populations, the starving masses, and so forth) or even that they represent the global People in its entirety. They go further than that. What they really represent is the vital force that underlies the People, and thus they transform politics into a question of generic life, life in all its generality. These NGOs extend far and wide in the humus of biopower; they are the capillary ends of the contemporary networks of power, or (to return to our general metaphor) they are the broad base of the triangle of global power.

Here, at this broadest, most universal level, the activities of these NGOs coincide with the workings of Empire "beyond politics," on the terrain of biopower, meeting the needs of life itself.

Polybius and Imperial Government

If we take a step back from the level of empirical description, we can quickly recognize that the tripartite division of functions and elements that has emerged allows us to enter directly into the problematic of Empire. In other words, the contemporary empirical situation resembles the theoretical description of imperial power as the supreme form of government that Polybius constructed for Rome and the European tradition handed down to us.[11] For Polybius, the Roman Empire represented the pinnacle of political development because it brought together the three "good" forms of power—monarchy, aristocracy, and democracy, embodied in the persons of the Emperor, the Senate, and the popular *comitia*. The Empire prevented these good forms from descending into the vicious cycle of corruption in which monarchy becomes tyranny, aristocracy becomes oligarchy, and democracy becomes ochlocracy or anarchy.

According to Polybius' analysis, monarchy anchors the unity and continuity of power. It is the foundation and ultimate instance of imperial rule. Aristocracy defines justice, measure, and virtue, and articulates their networks throughout the social sphere. It oversees the reproduction and circulation of imperial rule. Finally, democracy organizes the multitude according to a representational schema so that the People can be brought under the rule of the regime and the regime can be constrained to satisfy the needs of the People. Democracy guarantees discipline and redistribution. The Empire we find ourselves faced with today is also—mutatis mutandis—constituted by a functional equilibrium among these three forms of power: the monarchic unity of power and its global monopoly of force; aristocratic articulations through transnational corporations and nation-states; and democratic-representational *comitia,* presented again in the form of nation-states along with the various kinds of NGOs, media organizations, and other "popular" organisms. One might say that the coming imperial constitution brings together the three good traditional classifications of government in a relationship that is formally compatible with Polybius' model, even though certainly its contents are very different from the social and political forces of the Roman Empire.

We can recognize the ways in which we are close to and distant from the Polybian model of imperial power by situating ourselves in the genealogy of interpretations of Polybius in the history of European political thought. The major line of interpretation comes down to us through Machiavelli and the Italian Renaissance; it animated the Machiavellian tradition in debates preceding and following the English Revolution, and finally found its highest application in the thought of the Founding Fathers and the drafting of the U.S. Constitution.[12] The key shift to come about in the course of this interpretive tradition was the transformation of Polybius' classical *tripartite* model into a *trifunctional* model of constitutional construction. In a still medieval, proto-bourgeois society such as Machiavelli's Florence or even prerevolutionary England, the Polybian synthesis was conceived as an edifice uniting three distinct class bodies: to monarchy belonged the union and force, to aristocracy the land and the army, and to the bourgeoisie the city and money. If the state were to function properly, every possible conflict among these bodies had to be resolved in the interest of the totality. In modern political science, however, from Montesquieu to the Federalists, this synthesis was transformed into a model that regulated *not bodies but functions*.[13] Social groups and classes were themselves considered embodying functions: the executive, the judiciary, and the representative. These functions were abstracted from the collective social subjects or classes that enacted them and presented instead as pure juridical elements. The three functions were then organized in an equilibrium that was formally the same as the equilibrium that had previously supported the interclass solution. It was an equilibrium of checks and balances, of weights and counterweights, that continually managed to reproduce the unity of the state and the coherence of its parts.[14]

It seems to us that in certain respects the original ancient Polybian model of the constitution of Empire is closer to our reality than the modern liberal tradition's transformation of it. Today we are once again in a genetic phase of power and its accumulation, in which functions are seen primarily from the angle of the relations and materiality of force rather than from the perspective of a possible equilibrium and the formalization of the total definitive arrangement. In this phase of the constitution of Empire, the demands expressed by the modern development of constitutionalism (such as the division of powers and the formal legality of procedures) are not given the highest priority (see Section 1.1).

One could even argue that our experience of the constitution (in formation) of Empire is really the development and coexistence of the "bad" forms of government rather than the "good" forms, as the tradition pretends. All the elements of the mixed constitution appear at first sight in fact as through a distorting lens. Monarchy, rather than grounding the legitimation and transcendent condition of the unity of power, is presented as a global police force and thus as a form of tyranny. The transnational aristocracy seems to prefer financial speculation to entrepreneurial virtue and thus appears as a parasitical oligarchy. Finally, the democratic forces that in this framework ought to constitute the active and open element of the imperial machine appear rather as corporative forces, as a set of superstitions and fundamentalisms, betraying a spirit that is conservative when not downright reactionary.[15] Both within the individual states and on the international level, this limited sphere of imperial "democracy" is configured as a *People* (an organized particularity that defends established privileges and properties) rather than as a *multitude* (the universality of free and productive practices).

Hybrid Constitution

The Empire that is emerging today, however, is not really a throwback to the ancient Polybian model, even in its negative, "bad" form. The contemporary arrangement is better understood in postmodern terms, that is, as an evolution beyond the modern, liberal model of a mixed constitution. The framework of juridical formalization, the constitutional mechanism of guarantees, and the schema of equilibrium are all transformed along two primary axes in the passage from the modern to the postmodern terrain.

The first axis of transformation involves the nature of the mixture in the constitution—a passage from the ancient and modern model of a *mixtum* of separate bodies or functions to a process of the hybridization of governmental functions in the current situation. The processes of the real subsumption, of subsuming labor under capital and absorbing global society within Empire, force the figures of power to destroy the spatial measure and distance that had defined their relationships, merging the figures in hybrid forms. This mutation of spatial relationships transforms the exercise of power itself. First of all, postmodern imperial monarchy involves rule over the unity of the world market, and thus it is called on to guarantee the circulation of goods, technologies, and labor power—to guarantee, in effect, the collective dimension of the market. The processes of the globalization of monarchic power, however, can make sense only if we consider them in terms of the series of hybridizations that monarchy operates with the other forms of power. Imperial monarchy is not located in a separate isolable place—and our postmodern Empire has no Rome. The monarchic body is itself multiform and spatially diffuse. This process of hybridization is even more clear with respect to the development of the aristocratic function, and specifically the development and articulation of productive networks and markets. In fact, aristocratic functions tend to merge inextricably with monarchic functions. In the case of postmodern aristocracy, the problem consists not only in creating a vertical conduit between a center and a periphery for producing and selling commodities, but also in continuously putting in relation a wide horizon of producers and consumers within and among markets. This omnilateral relationship between production and consumption becomes all the more important when the production of commodities tends to be defined predominantly by immaterial services embedded in network structures. Here hybridization becomes a central and conditioning element of the formation of circuits of production and circulation.[16] Finally, the democratic functions of Empire are determined within these same monarchic and aristocratic hybridizations, shifting their relations in certain respects and introducing new relations of force. On all three levels, what was previously conceived as mixture, which was really the organic interaction of functions that remained separate and distinct, now tends toward a hybridization of the functions themselves. We might thus pose this first axis of transformation as a passage from *mixed constitution* to *hybrid constitution.*

A second axis of constitutional transformation, which demonstrates both a displacement of constitutional theory and a new quality of the constitution itself, is revealed by the fact that in the present phase, command must be exercised to an ever greater extent over the temporal dimensions of society and hence over the dimension of subjectivity. We have to consider how the monarchic moment functions both as a unified world government over the circulation of goods and as a mechanism of the organization of collective social labor that determines the conditions of its reproduction.[17] The aristocratic moment must deploy its hierarchical command and its ordering functions over the transnational articulation of production and circulation, not only through traditional monetary instruments, but also to an ever greater degree through the instruments and dynamics of the cooperation of social actors themselves. The processes of social cooperation have to be constitutionally formalized as an aristocratic function. Finally, although both the monarchic and the aristocratic functions allude to the subjective and productive dimensions of the new hybrid constitution, the key to these transformations resides in the democratic moment, and the temporal dimension of the democratic moment has to refer ultimately to the multitude. We should never forget, however, that we are dealing here with the imperial overdetermination of democracy, in which the multitude is captured in flexible and modulating apparatuses of control. This is precisely where the most important qualitative leap must be recognized: from the disciplinary paradigm to the control paradigm of government.[18] Rule is exercised directly over the movements of productive and cooperating subjectivities; institutions are formed and redefined continually according to the rhythm of these movements; and the topography of power no longer has to do primarily with spatial relations but is inscribed, rather, in the temporal displacements of subjectivities. Here we find once again the non-place of power that our analysis of sovereignty revealed earlier. The non-place is the site where the hybrid control functions of Empire are exercised.

In this imperial non-place, in the hybrid space that the constitutional process constructs, we still find the continuous and irrepressible presence of subjective movements. Our problematic remains something like that of the mixed constitution, but now it is infused with the full intensity of the displacements, modulations, and hybridizations involved in the passage to postmodernity. Here the movement from the social to the political and the juridical that always defines constituent processes begins to take shape; here the reciprocal relationships between social and political forces that demand a formal recognition in the constitutional process begin to emerge; and finally, here the various functions (monarchy, aristocracy, and democracy) measure the force of the subjectivities that constitute them and attempt to capture segments of their constituent processes.

Struggle over the Constitution

Our ultimate objective in this analysis of the constitutional processes and figures of Empire is to recognize the terrain on which contestation and alternatives might emerge. In Empire, as indeed was also the case in modern and ancient regimes, the constitution itself is a site of struggle, but today the nature of that site and that struggle is by no means clear. The general outlines of today's imperial constitution can be conceived in the form of a rhizomatic and universal communication network in which relations are established to and from all its points or nodes. Such a network seems paradoxically to be at once completely open and completely closed to struggle and intervention. On the one hand, the network formally allows all possible subjects in the web of relations to be present simultaneously, but on the other hand, the network itself is a real and proper non-place. The struggle over the constitution will have to be played out on this ambiguous and shifting terrain.

There are three key variables that will define this struggle, variables that act in the realm between the common and the singular, between the axiomatic of command and the self-identification of the subject, and between the production of subjectivity by power and the autonomous resistance of the subjects themselves. The first variable involves the guarantee of the network and its general control, in such a way that (positively) the network can always function and (negatively) it cannot function against those in power.[19] The second variable concerns those who distribute services in the network and the pretense that these services are remunerated equitably, so that the network can sustain and reproduce a capitalist economic system and at the same time produce the social and political segmentation that is proper to it.[20] The third variable, finally, is presented within the network itself. It deals with the mechanisms by which differences among subjectivities are produced and with the ways in which these differences are made to function within the system.

According to these three variables, each subjectivity must become a subject that is ruled in the general networks of control (in the early modern sense of the one who is subject [*subdictus*] to a sovereign power), and at the same time each must also be an independent agent of production and consumption within networks. Is this double articulation really possible? Is it possible for the system to sustain simultaneously political subjection and the subjectivity of the producer/consumer? It does not really seem so. In effect, the fundamental condition of the existence of the *universal network,* which is the central hypothesis of this constitutional framework, is that it be *hybrid,* and that is, for our purposes, that the political subject be fleeting and passive, while the producing and consuming agent is present and active. This means that, far from being a simple repetition of a traditional equilibrium, the formation of the new mixed constitution leads to a fundamental disequilibrium among the established actors and thus to a new social dynamic that liberates the producing and consuming subject from (or at least makes ambiguous its position within) the mechanisms of political subjection. Here is where the primary site of struggle seems to emerge, on the terrain of the production and regulation of subjectivity.

Is this really the situation that will result from the capitalist transformation of the mode of production, the cultural developments of postmodernism, and the processes of political constitution of Empire? We are certainly not yet in the position to come to that conclusion. We can see, nonetheless, that in this new situation the strategy of equilibrated and regulated participation, which the liberal and imperial mixed constitutions have always followed, is confronted by new difficulties and by the strong expression of autonomy by the individual and collective productive subjectivities involved in the process. On the terrain of the production and regulation of subjectivity, and in the disjunction between the political subject and the economic subject, it seems that we can identify a real field of struggle in which all the gambits of the constitution and the equilibria among forces can be reopened—a true and proper situation of crisis and maybe eventually of revolution.

Spectacle of the Constitution

The open field of struggle that seems to appear from this analysis, however, quickly disappears when we consider the new mechanisms by which these hybrid networks of participation are manipulated from above.[21] In effect, the glue that holds together the diverse functions and bodies of the hybrid constitution is what Guy Debord called the spectacle, an integrated and diffuse apparatus of images and ideas that produces and regulates public discourse and opinion.[22] In the society of the spectacle, what was once imagined as the public sphere, the open terrain of political exchange and participation, completely evaporates. The spectacle destroys any collective form of sociality—individualizing social actors in their separate automobiles and in front of separate video screens—and at the same time imposes a new mass sociality, a new uniformity of action and thought. On this spectacular terrain, traditional forms of struggle over the constitution become inconceivable.

The common conception that the media (and television in particular) have destroyed politics is false only to the extent that it seems based on an idealized notion of what democratic political discourse, exchange, and participation consisted of in the era prior to this media age. The difference of the contemporary manipulation of politics by the media is not really a difference of nature but a difference of degree. In other words, there have certainly existed previously numerous mechanisms for shaping public opinion and public perception of society, but contemporary media provide enormously more powerful instruments for these tasks. As Debord says, in the society of the spectacle only what appears exists, and the major media have something approaching a monopoly over what appears to the general population. This law of the spectacle clearly reigns in the realm of media-driven electoral politics, an art of manipulation perhaps developed first in the United States but now spread throughout the world. The discourse of electoral seasons focuses almost exclusively on how candidates appear, on the timing and circulation of images. The major media networks conduct a sort of second-order spectacle that reflects on (and undoubtedly shapes in part) the spectacle mounted by the candidates and their political parties. Even the old calls for a focus less on image and more on issues and substance in political campaigns that we heard not so long ago seem hopelessly naive today. Similarly, the notions that politicians function as celebrities and that political campaigns operate on the logic of advertising—hypotheses that seemed radical and scandalous thirty years ago—are today taken for granted. Political discourse is an articulated sales pitch, and political participation is reduced to selecting among consumable images.

When we say that the spectacle involves the *media manipulation* of public opinion and political action, we do not mean to suggest that there is a little man behind the curtain, a great Wizard of Oz who controls all that is seen, thought, and done. There is no single locus of control that dictates the spectacle. The spectacle, however, generally functions *as if* there were such a point of central control. As Debord says, the spectacle is both diffuse and integrated. Conspiracy theories of governmental and extragovernmental plots of global control, which have certainly proliferated in recent decades, should thus be recognized as both true and false. As Fredric Jameson explains wonderfully in the context of contemporary film, conspiracy theories are a crude but effective mechanism for approximating the functioning of the totality.[23] The spectacle of politics functions *as if* the media, the military, the government, the transnational corporations, the global financial institutions, and so forth were all consciously and explicitly directed by a single power even though in reality they are not.

The society of the spectacle rules by wielding an age-old weapon. Hobbes recognized long ago that for effective domination "the Passion to be reckoned upon, is Fear."[24] For Hobbes, fear is what binds and ensures social order, and still today fear is the primary mechanism of control that fills the society of the spectacle.[25] Although the spectacle seems to function through desire and pleasure (desire for commodities and pleasure of consumption), it really works through the communication of fear—or rather, the spectacle creates forms of desire and pleasure that are intimately wedded to fear. In the vernacular of early modern European philosophy, the communication of fear was called *superstition*. And indeed the politics of fear has always been spread through a kind of superstition. What has changed are the forms and mechanisms of the superstitions that communicate fear.

The spectacle of fear that holds together the postmodern, hybrid constitution and the media manipulation of the public and politics certainly takes the ground away from a struggle over the imperial constitution. It seems as if there is no place left to stand, no weight to any possible resistance, but only an implacable machine of power. It is important to recognize the power of the spectacle and the impossibility of traditional forms of struggle, but this is not the end of the story. As the old sites and forms of struggle decline, new and more powerful ones arise. The spectacle of imperial order is not an ironclad world, but actually opens up the real possibility of its overturning and new potentials for revolution.

3.6

CAPITALIST SOVEREIGNTY, OR ADMINISTERING THE GLOBAL SOCIETY OF CONTROL

> As long as society is founded on money we won't have enough of it.
>
> Leaflet, Paris strike, December 1995

> This is the abolition of the capitalist mode of production within the capitalist mode of production itself, and hence a self-abolishing contradiction, which presents itself *prima facie* as a mere point of transition to a new form of production.
>
> Karl Marx

Capital and sovereignty might well appear to be a contradictory coupling. Modern sovereignty relies fundamentally on the *transcendence* of the sovereign—be it the Prince, the state, the nation, or even the People—over the social plane. Hobbes established the spatial metaphor of sovereignty for all modern political thought in his unitary Leviathan that rises above and overarches society and the multitude. The sovereign is the surplus of power that serves to resolve or defer the crisis of modernity. Furthermore, modern sovereignty operates, as we have seen in detail, through the creation and maintenance of fixed boundaries among territories, populations, social functions, and so forth. Sovereignty is thus also a surplus of code, an overcoding of social flows and functions. In other words, sovereignty operates through the striation of the social field.

Capital, on the contrary, operates on the plane of *immanence,* through relays and networks of relationships of domination, without reliance on a transcendent center of power. It tends historically to destroy traditional social boundaries, expanding across territories and enveloping always new populations within its processes. Capital functions, according to the terminology of Deleuze and Guattari, through a generalized decoding of fluxes, a massive deterritorialization, and then through conjunctions of these deterritorialized and decoded fluxes.[1] We can understand the functioning of capital as deterritorializing and immanent in three primary aspects that Marx himself analyzed. First, in the processes of primitive accumulation, capital separates populations from specifically coded territories and sets them in motion. It clears the Estates and creates a "free" proletariat. Traditional cultures and social organizations are destroyed in capital's tireless march through the world to create the networks and pathways of a single cultural and economic system of production and circulation. Second, capital brings all forms of value together on one common plane and links them all through money, their general equivalent. Capital tends to reduce all previously established forms of status, title, and privilege to the level of the cash nexus, that is, to quantitative and commensurable economic terms. Third, the laws by which capital functions are not separate and fixed laws that stand above and direct capital's operations from on high, but historically variable laws that are immanent to the very functioning of capital: the laws of the rate of profit, the rate of exploitation, the realization of surplus value, and so forth.

Capital therefore demands not a transcendent power but a mechanism of control that resides on the plane of immanence. Through the social development of capital, the mechanisms of modern sovereignty—the processes of coding, overcoding, and recoding that imposed a transcendent order over a bounded and segmented social terrain—are progressively replaced by an *axiomatic:* that is, a set of equations and relationships that determines and combines variables and coefficients immediately and equally across various terrains without reference to prior and fixed definitions or terms.[2] The primary characteristic of such an axiomatic is that relations are prior to their terms. In other words, within an axiomatic system, postulates "are not propositions that can be true or false, since they contain relatively indeterminate *variables*. Only when we give these variables particular values, or in other words, when we substitute constants for them, do the postulates become propositions, true or false, according to the constants chosen."[3] Capital operates through just such an axiomatic of propositional functions. The general equivalence of money brings all elements together in quantifiable, commensurable relations, and then the immanent laws or equations of capital determine their deployment and relation according to the particular constants that are substituted for the variables of the equations. Just as an axiomatic destabilizes any terms and definitions prior to the relations of logical deduction, so too capital sweeps clear the fixed barriers of precapitalist society—and even the boundaries of the nation-state tend to fade into the background as capital realizes itself in the world market. Capital tends toward a smooth space defined by uncoded flows, flexibility, continual modulation, and tendential equalization.[4]

The transcendence of modern sovereignty thus conflicts with the immanence of capital. Historically, capital has relied on sovereignty and the support of its structures of right and force, but those same structures continually contradict in principle and obstruct in practice the operation of capital, finally obstructing its development. The entire history of modernity that we have traced thus far might be seen as the evolution of the attempts to negotiate and mediate this contradiction. The historical process of mediation has been not an equal give and take, but rather a one-sided movement from sovereignty's transcendent position toward capital's plane of immanence. Foucault traces this movement in his analysis of the passage in European rule between the seventeenth and eighteenth centuries from "sovereignty" (an absolute form of sovereignty centralized in the will and person of the Prince) and "governmentality" (a form of sovereignty expressed through a decentralized economy of rule and management of goods and populations).[5] This passage between forms of sovereignty coincides importantly with the early development and expansion of capital. Each of the modern paradigms of sovereignty indeed supports capital's operation for a specific historical period, but at the same time they pose obstacles to capital's development that eventually have to be overcome. This evolving relationship is perhaps the central problematic to be confronted by any theory of the capitalist state.

Civil society served for one historical period as mediator between the immanent forces of capital and the transcendent power of modern sovereignty. Hegel adopted the term "civil society" from his reading of British economists, and he understood it as a mediation between the self-interested endeavors of a plurality of economic individuals and the unified interest of the state. Civil society mediates between the (immanent) Many and the (transcendent) One. The institutions that constitute civil society functioned as passageways that channel flows of social and economic forces, raising them up toward a coherent unity and, flowing back, like an irrigation network, distribute the command of the unity throughout the immanent social field. These non-state institutions, in other words, organized capitalist society under the order of the state and in turn spread state rule throughout society. In the terms of our conceptual framework, we might say that civil society was the terrain of the becoming-immanent of modern state sovereignty (down to capitalist society) and at the same time inversely the becoming-transcendent of capitalist society (up to the state).

In our times, however, civil society no longer serves as the adequate point of mediation between capital and sovereignty. The structures and institutions that constitute it are today progressively withering away. We have argued elsewhere that this withering can be grasped clearly in terms of the decline of the dialectic between the capitalist state and labor, that is, in the decline of the effectiveness and role of labor unions, the decline of collective bargaining with labor, and the decline of the representation of labor in the constitution.[6] The withering of civil society might also be recognized as concomitant with the passage from disciplinary society to the society of control (see Section 2.6). Today the social institutions that constitute disciplinary society (the school, the family, the hospital, the factory), which are in large part the same as or closely related to those understood as civil society, are everywhere in crisis. As the walls of these institutions break down, the logics of subjectification that previously operated within their limited spaces now spread out, generalized across the social field. The breakdown of the institutions, the withering of civil society, and the decline of disciplinary society all involve a smoothing of the striation of modern social space. Here arise the networks of the society of control.[7]

With respect to disciplinary society and civil society, the society of control marks a step toward the plane of immanence. The disciplinary institutions, the boundaries of the effectivity of their logics, and their striation of social space all constitute instances of verticality or transcendence over the social plane. We should be careful, however, to locate where exactly this transcendence of disciplinary society resides. Foucault was insistent on the fact, and this was the brilliant core of his analysis, that the exercise of discipline is absolutely immanent to the subjectivities under its command. In other words, discipline is not an external voice that dictates our practices from on high, overarching us, as Hobbes would say, but rather something like an inner compulsion indistinguishable from our will, immanent to and inseparable from our subjectivity itself. The institutions that are the condition of possibility and that define spatially the zones of effectivity of the exercise of discipline, however, do maintain a certain separation from the social forces produced and organized. They are in effect an instance of sovereignty, or rather a point of mediation with sovereignty. The walls of the prison both enable and limit the exercise of carceral logics. They differentiate social space.

Foucault negotiates with enormous subtlety this distance between the transcendent walls of the institutions and the immanent exercise of discipline through his theories of the *dispositif* and the diagram, which articulate a series of stages of abstraction.[8] In somewhat simplified terms, we can say that the *dispositif* (which is translated as either mechanism, apparatus, or deployment) is the general strategy that stands behind the immanent and actual exercise of discipline. Carceral logic, for example, is the unified dispositif that oversees or subtends—and is thus abstracted and distinct from—the multiplicity of prison practices. At a second level of abstraction, the *diagram* enables the deployments of the disciplinary dispositif. For example, the carceral architecture of the panopticon, which makes inmates constantly visible to a central point of power, is the diagram or virtual design that is actualized in the various disciplinary dispositifs. Finally, the institutions themselves instantiate the diagram in particular and concrete social forms as well. The prison (its walls, administrators, guards, laws, and so forth) does not rule its inmates the way a sovereign commands its subjects. It creates a space in which inmates, through the strategies of carceral dispositifs and through actual practices, *discipline themselves*. It would be more precise to say, then, that the disciplinary institution is not itself sovereign, but its abstraction from or transcendence above the social field of the production of subjectivity constitutes the key element in the exercise of sovereignty in disciplinary society. Sovereignty has become virtual (but it is for that no less real), and it is actualized always and everywhere through the exercise of discipline.

Today the collapse of the walls that delimited the institutions and the smoothing of social striation are symptoms of the flattening of these vertical instances toward the horizontality of the circuits of control. The passage to the society of control does not in any way mean the end of discipline. In fact, the immanent exercise of discipline—that is, the self-disciplining of subjects, the incessant whisperings of disciplinary logics within subjectivities themselves—is extended even more generally in the society of control. What has changed is that, along with the collapse of the institutions, the disciplinary dispositifs have become less limited and bounded spatially in the social field. Carceral discipline, school discipline, factory discipline, and so forth interweave in a hybrid production of subjectivity. In effect, in the passage to the society of control, the elements of transcendence of disciplinary society decline while the immanent aspects are accentuated and generalized.

The immanent production of subjectivity in the society of control corresponds to the axiomatic logic of capital, and their resemblance indicates a new and more complete compatibility between sovereignty and capital. The production of subjectivity in civil society and disciplinary society did in a certain period further the rule and facilitate the expansion of capital. The modern social institutions produced social identities that were much more mobile and flexible than the previous subjective figures. The subjectivities produced in the modern institutions were like the standardized machine parts produced in the mass factory: the inmate, the mother, the worker, the student, and so forth. Each part played a specific role in the assembled machine, but it was standardized, produced en masse, and thus replaceable with any part of its type. At a certain point, however, the fixity of these standardized parts, of the identities produced by the institutions, came to pose an obstacle to the further progression toward mobility and flexibility. The passage toward the society of control involves a production of subjectivity that is not fixed in identity but hybrid and modulating. As the walls that defined and isolated the effects of the modern institutions progressively break down, subjectivities tend to be produced simultaneously by numerous institutions in different combinations and doses. Certainly in disciplinary society each individual had many identities, but to a certain extent the different identities were defined by different places and different times of life: one was mother or father at home, worker in the factory, student at school, inmate in prison, and mental patient in the asylum. In the society of control, it is precisely these places, these discrete sites of applicability, that tend to lose their definition and delimitations. A hybrid subjectivity produced in the society of control may not carry the identity of a prison inmate or a mental patient or a factory worker, but may still be constituted simultaeously by all of their logics. It is factory worker outside the factory, student outside school, inmate outside prison, insane outside the asylum—all at the same time. It belongs to no identity and all of them—outside the institutions but even more intensely ruled by their disciplinary logics.[9] Just like imperial sovereignty, the subjectivities of the society of control have mixed constitutions.

A Smooth World

In the passage of sovereignty toward the plane of immanence, the collapse of boundaries has taken place both within each national context and on a global scale. The withering of civil society and the general crisis of the disciplinary institutions coincide with the decline of nation-states as boundaries that mark and organize the divisions in global rule. The establishment of a global society of control that smooths over the striae of national boundaries goes hand in hand with the realization of the world market and the real subsumption of global society under capital.

In the nineteenth and early twentieth centuries, imperialism contributed to capital's survival and expansion (see Section 3.1). The partition of the world among the dominant nation-states, the establishment of colonial administrations, the imposition of trade exclusives and tariffs, the creation of monopolies and cartels, differentiated zones of raw material extraction and industrial production, and so forth all aided capital in its period of global expansion. Imperialism was a system designed to serve the needs and further the interests of capital in its phase of global conquest. And yet, as most of the (communist, socialist, *and* capitalist) critics of imperialism have noted, imperialism also from its inception conflicted with capital. It was a medicine that itself threatened the life of the patient. Although imperialism provided avenues and mechanisms for capital to pervade new territories and spread the capitalist mode of production, it also created and reinforced rigid boundaries among the various global spaces, strict notions of inside and outside that effectively blocked the free flow of capital, labor, and goods—thus necessarily precluding the full realization of the world market.

Imperialism is a machine of global striation, channeling, coding, and territorializing the flows of capital, blocking certain flows and facilitating others. The world market, in contrast, requires a smooth space of uncoded and deterritorialized flows. This conflict between the striation of imperialism and the smooth space of the capitalist world market gives us a new perspective that allows us to reconsider Rosa Luxemburg's prediction of capitalist collapse: "Though imperialism is the historical method for prolonging the career of capitalism, it is also the sure means of bringing it to a swift conclusion."[10] The international order and striated space of imperialism did indeed serve to further capitalism, but it eventually became a fetter to the deterritorializing flows and smooth space of capitalist development, and ultimately it had to be cast aside. Rosa Luxemburg was essentially right: *imperialism would have been the death of capital had it not been overcome.* The full realization of the world market is necessarily the end of imperialism.

The decline of the power of nation-states and the dissolution of the international order bring with them the definitive end of the effectiveness of the term "Third World." One could tell this story as a very simple narrative. The term was coined as the complement to the bipolar cold war division between the dominant capitalist nations and the major socialist nations, such that the Third World was conceived as what was outside this primary conflict, the free space or frontier over which the first two worlds would compete. Since the cold war is now over, the logic of this division is no longer effective. This is true, but the neat closure of this simple narrative fails to account for the real history of the term in its important uses and effects.

Many argued, beginning at least as early as the 1970s, that the Third World never really existed, in the sense that the conception attempts to pose as a homogeneous unit an essentially diverse set of nations, failing to grasp and even negating the significant social, economic, and cultural differences between Paraguay and Pakistan, Morocco and Mozambique. Recognizing this real multiplicity, however, should not blind us to the fact that, from the point of view of capital in its march of global conquest, such a unitary and homogenizing conception did have a certain validity. For example,

Rosa Luxemburg clearly takes the standpoint of capital when she divides the world into the capitalist domain and the noncapitalist environment. The various zones of that environment are undoubtedly radically different from one another, but from the standpoint of capital it is all the outside: potential terrain for its expanded accumulation and its future conquest. During the cold war, when the regions of the Second World were effectively closed, Third World meant to the dominant capitalist nations the remaining open space, the terrain of possibility. The diverse cultural, social, and economic forms could all potentially be subsumed formally under the dynamic of capitalist production and the capitalist markets. From the standpoint of this potential subsumption, despite the real and substantial differences among nations, the Third World was really one.

It is similarly logical when Samir Amin, Immanuel Wallerstein, and others differentiate within the capitalist domain among central, peripheral, and semi-peripheral countries.[11] Center, periphery, and semi-periphery are distinguished by different social, political, and bureaucratic forms, different productive processes, and different forms of accumulation. (The more recent conceptual division between North and South is not significantly different in this regard.) Like the First–Second–Third World conception, the division of the capitalist sphere into center, periphery, and semi-periphery homogenizes and eclipses real differences among nations and cultures, but does so in the interest of highlighting a tendential unity of political, social, and economic forms that emerge in the long imperialist processes of formal subsumption. In other words, Third World, South, and periphery all homogenize real differences to highlight the unifying processes of capitalist development, but also and more important, they name *the potential unity of an international opposition, the potential confluence of anticapitalist countries and forces.*

The geographical divisions among nation-states or even between central and peripheral, northern and southern clusters of nation-states are no longer sufficient to grasp the global divisions and distribution of production, accumulation, and social forms.

Through the decentralization of production and the consolidation of the world market, the international divisions and flows of labor and capital have fractured and multiplied so that it is no longer possible to demarcate large geographical zones as center and periphery, North and South. In geographical regions such as the Southern Cone of Latin America or Southeast Asia, all levels of production can exist simultaneously and side by side, from the highest levels of technology, productivity and accumulation to the lowest, with a complex social mechanism maintaining their differentiation and interaction. In the metropolises, too, labor spans the continuum from the heights to the depths of capitalist production: the sweatshops of New York and Paris can rival those of Hong Kong and Manila. If the First World and the Third World, center and periphery, North and South were ever really separated along national lines, today they clearly infuse one another, distributing inequalities and barriers along multiple and fractured lines. This is not to say that the United States and Brazil, Britain and India are now identical territories in terms of capitalist production and circulation, but rather that between them are no differences of nature, only differences of degree. The various nations and regions contain different proportions of what was thought of as First World and Third, center and periphery, North and South. The geography of uneven development and the lines of division and hierarchy will no longer be found along stable national or international boundaries, but in fluid infra- and supranational borders.

Some may protest, with a certain justification, that the dominant voices of the global order are proclaiming the nation-state dead just when "the nation" has emerged as a revolutionary weapon for the subordinated, for the wretched of the earth. After the victory of national liberation struggles and after the emergence of potentially destabilizing international alliances, which matured for decades after the Bandung Conference, what better way to undermine the power of Third World nationalism and internationalism than to deprive it of its central and guiding support, the nation-state! In other words, according to this view, which provides at least one plausible narrative for this complex history, the nation-state, which had been the guarantor of international order and the keystone to imperialist conquest and sovereignty, became through the rise and organization of anti-imperialist forces the element that most endangered the international order. Thus imperialism in retreat was forced to abandon and destroy the prize of its own armory before the weapon could be wielded against it.

We believe, however, that it is a grave mistake to harbor any nostalgia for the powers of the nation-state or to resurrect any politics that celebrates the nation. First of all, these efforts are in vain because the decline of the nation-state is not simply the result of an ideological position that might be reversed by an act of political will: it is a structural and irreversible process. The nation was not only a cultural formulation, a feeling of belonging, and a shared heritage, but also and perhaps primarily a juridico-economic structure. The declining effectiveness of this structure can be traced clearly through the evolution of a whole series of global juridico-economic bodies, such as GATT, the World Trade Organization, the World Bank, and the IMF. The globalization of production and circulation, supported by this supranational juridical scaffolding, supersedes the effectiveness of national juridical structures. Second, and more important, even if the nation were still to be an effective weapon, the nation carries with it a whole series of repressive structures and ideologies (as we argued in Section 2.2), and any strategy that relies on it should be rejected on that basis.

The New Segmentations

The general equalization or smoothing of social space, however, in both the withering of civil society and the decline of national boundaries, does not indicate that social inequalities and segmentations have disappeared. On the contrary, they have in many respects become more severe, but under a different form. It might be more accurate to say that center and periphery, North and South no longer define an international order but rather have moved closer to one another. Empire is characterized by the close proximity of extremely unequal populations, which creates a situation of permanent social danger and requires the powerful apparatuses of the society of control to ensure separation and guarantee the new management of social space.

Trends in urban architecture in the world's megalopolises demonstrate one aspect of these new segmentations. Where the extremes of wealth and poverty have increased and the physical distance between rich and poor has decreased in global cities such as Los Angeles, São Paulo, and Singapore, elaborate measures have to be taken to maintain their separation. Los Angeles is perhaps the leader in the trend toward what Mike Davis calls "fortress architecture," in which not only private homes but also commercial centers and government buildings create open and free environments internally by creating a closed and impenetrable exterior.[12] This tendency in urban planning and architecture has established in concrete, physical terms what we called earlier the end of the outside, or rather the decline of public space that had allowed for open and unprogrammed social interaction.

Architectural analysis, however, can give only a first introduction to the problematic of the new separations and segmentations. The new lines of division are more clearly defined by the politics of labor. The computer and informational revolution that has made it possible to link together different groups of labor power in real time across the world has led to furious and unrestrained competition among workers. Information technologies have been used to weaken the structural resistances of labor power, in terms of both the rigidity of wage structures and cultural and geographical differences. Capital has thus been able to impose both temporal flexibility and spatial mobility. It should be clear that this process of weakening the resistances and rigidities of labor power has become a completely political process oriented toward a form of management that maximizes economic profit. This is where the theory of imperial administrative action becomes central.

The imperial politics of labor is designed primarily to lower the price of labor. This is, in effect, something like a process of primitive accumulation, a process of reproletarianization. The regulation of the working day, which was the real keystone to socialist politics throughout the past two centuries, has been completely overturned. Working days are often twelve, fourteen, sixteen hours long without weekends or vacations; there is work for men, women, and children alike, and for the old and the handicapped. Empire has work for everyone! The more unregulated the regime of exploitation, the more work there is. This is the basis on which the new segmentations of work are created. They are determined (in the language of the economists) by the different levels of productivity, but we could summarize the change simply by saying that there is more work and lower wages. Like God's broom sweeping across society (this is how Hegel described the imposition of barbarian law, principally at the hands of Attila the Hun), the new norms of productivity differentiate and segment the workers. There are still places in the world where poverty allows for the reproduction of labor power at a lower cost, and there are still places in the metropolises where differences of consumption force a lower class to sell itself for less, or really to submit itself to a more brutal regime of capitalist exploitation.

Financial and monetary flows follow more or less the same global patterns as the flexible organization of labor power. On the one hand, speculative and finance capital goes where the price of labor power is lowest and where the administrative force to guarantee exploitation is highest. On the other hand, the countries that still maintain the rigidities of labor and oppose its full flexibility and mobility are punished, tormented, and finally destroyed by global monetary mechanisms. The stock market drops when the unemployment rate goes down, or really when the percentage of workers who are not immediately flexible and mobile rises. The same happens when the social policies in a country do not completely accommodate the imperial mandate of flexibility and mobility—or better, when some elements of the welfare state are preserved as a sign of the persistence of the nation-state. Monetary policies enforce the segmentations dictated by labor policies.

Fear of violence, poverty, and unemployment is in the end the primary and immediate force that creates and maintains these new segmentations. What stands behind the various politics of the new segmentations is a politics of communication. As we argued earlier, the fundamental content of the information that the enormous communication corporations present is fear. The constant fear of poverty and anxiety over the future are the keys to creating a struggle among the poor for work and maintaining conflict among the imperial proletariat. Fear is the ultimate guarantee of the new segmentations.

Imperial Administration

After we have seen how traditional social barriers are lowered in the formation of Empire and how at the same time new segmentations are created, we must also investigate the administrative modalities through which these various developments unfold. It is easy to see that these processes are full of contradictions. When power is made immanent and sovereignty transforms into governmentality, the functions of rule and regimes of control have to develop on a continuum that flattens differences to a common plane. We have seen, however, that differences are, on the contrary, accentuated in this process, in such a way that imperial integration determines new mechanisms of the separation and segmentation of different strata of the population. The problem of imperial administration is thus to manage this process of integration and therefore to pacify, mobilize, and control the separated and segmented social forces.

In these terms, however, the problem is still not clearly posed. The segmentation of the multitude has in fact been the condition of political administration throughout history. The difference today lies in the fact that, whereas in modern regimes of national sovereignty, administration worked toward a *linear* integration of conflicts and toward a coherent apparatus that could repress them, that is, toward the rational normalization of social life with respect to both the administrative goal of equilibrium and the development of administrative reforms, in the imperial framework administration becomes *fractal* and aims to integrate conflicts not by imposing a coherent social apparatus but by controlling differences. It is no longer possible to understand imperial administration in the terms of a Hegelian definition of administration, which is grounded on the mediations of bourgeois society that constitute the spatial center of social life; but it is equally impossible to understand it according to a Weberian definition, that is, a rational definition that is based on continuous temporal mediation and an emerging principle of legitimacy.

A first principle that defines imperial administration is that in it *the management of political ends tends to be separate from the management of bureaucratic means.* The new paradigm is thus not only different from but opposed to the old public administration model of the modern state, which continually strove to coordinate its system of bureaucratic means with its political ends. In the imperial regime, bureaucracies (and administrative means in general) are considered not according to the linear logics of their functionality to goals, but according to differential and multiple instrumental logics. The problem of administration is not a problem of unity but one of instrumental multifunctionality. Whereas for the legitimation and administration of the modern state the universality and equality of administrative actions were paramount, in the imperial regime what is fundamental is the singularity and adequacy of the actions to specific ends.

From this first principle, however, there arises what seems to be a paradox. Precisely to the extent that administration is singularized and no longer functions simply as the actor for centralized political and deliberative organs, it becomes increasingly autonomous and engages more closely with various social groups: business and labor groups, ethnic and religious groups, legal and criminal groups, and so forth. Instead of contributing to social integration, *imperial administration acts rather as a disseminating and differentiating mechanism.* This is the second principle of imperial administration. Administration will thus tend to present specific procedures that allow the regime to engage directly with the various social singularities, and the administration will be more effective the more direct its contact with the different elements of social reality. Hence administrative action becomes increasingly autocentric and thus functional only to the specific problems that it has to resolve. It becomes more and more difficult to recognize a continuous line of administrative action across the set of relays and networks of the imperial regime. In short, the old administrative principle of universality, treating all equally, is replaced by the differentiation and singularization of procedures, treating each differently.

Even though it is difficult now to trace a coherent and universal line of procedure, such as the one that characterized modern sovereign systems, this does not mean that the imperial apparatus is not unified. The autonomy and unity of administrative action is constructed in other ways, by means neither of the normative deduction of continental European juridical systems nor of the procedural formalism of Anglo-Saxon systems. Rather, it is created by conforming to the structural logics that are active in the construction of Empire, such as the police and military logics (or really the repression of potential subversive forces in the context of imperial peace), the economic logics (the imposition of the market, which in turn is ruled by the monetary regime), and the ideological and communicative logics. The only way that administrative action gains its autonomy and legitimate authority in the imperial regime is by following along the differentiating lines of these logics. This authorization, however, is not direct. Administration is not strategically oriented toward the realization of the imperial logics. It submits to them, insofar as they animate the great military, monetary, and communicative means that authorize administration itself. *Administrative action has become fundamentally non-strategic, and thus it is legitimated through heterogeneous and indirect means.* This is the third principle of administrative action in the imperial regime.

Once we have recognized these three "negative" principles of imperial administrative action—its instrumental character, its procedural autonomy, and its heterogeneity—we have to ask what allows it to function without continually opening violent social antagonisms. What virtue affords this disarticulated system of control, inequality, and segmentation a sufficient measure of consent and legitimation? This leads to the fourth principle, the "positive" characteristic of imperial administration. The unifying matrix and the most dominant value of imperial administration lie in its *local effectiveness*.

To understand how this fourth principle can support the administrative system as a whole, consider the kind of administrative relationships that were formed between the feudal territorial organizations and the monarchic power structures in Europe in the Middle Ages, or between mafia organizations and state structures in the modern period. In both cases the procedural autonomy, differential application, and territorialized links to various segments of the population, together with the specific and limited exercise of legitimate violence, were not generally in contradiction with the principle of a coherent and unified ordering. These systems of the distribution of administrative power were held together by the local effectiveness of a series of specific deployments of military, financial, and ideological powers. In the European medieval system, the vassal was required to contribute armed men and money when the monarch needed them (whereas ideology and communication were controlled in large part by the church). In the mafia system, the administrative autonomy of the extended family and the deployment of police-like violence throughout the social territory guaranteed the adherence to the primary principles of the capitalist system and supported the ruling political class. As in these medieval and mafia examples, the autonomy of localized administrative bodies does not contradict imperial administration—on the contrary, it aids and expands its global effectiveness.

Local autonomy is a fundamental condition, the sine qua non of the development of the imperial regime. In fact, given the mobility of populations in Empire, it would not be possible to claim a principle of legitimate administration if its autonomy did not also march a nomad path with the populations. It would likewise be impossible to order the segments of the multitude through processes that force it to be more mobile and flexible in hybrid cultural forms and in multicolored ghettos if this administration were not equally flexible and capable of specific and continuous procedural revisions and differentiations. Consent to the imperial regime is not something that descends from the transcendentals of good administration, which were defined in the modern rights states. Consent, rather, is formed through the local effectiveness of the regime.

We have sketched here only the most general outlines of imperial administration. A definition of imperial administration that focuses only on the autonomous local effectiveness of administrative action cannot in itself guarantee the system against eventual threats, riots, subversions, and insurrections, or even against the normal conflicts among local segments of the administration. This argument, however, does manage to transform the discussion into one about the "royal prerogatives" of imperial government—once we have established the principle that the regulation of conflict and the recourse to the exercise of legitimate violence must be resolved in terms of self-regulation (of production, money, and communication) and by the internal police forces of Empire. This is where the question of administration is transformed into a question of command.

Imperial Command

Whereas modern regimes tended to bring administration increasingly in line with command to the point of making the two indistinguishable, imperial command remains separate from administration. In both the modern and the imperial regimes, the internal contradictions along with the risks and possible deviations of a non-centralized administration demand the guarantee of a supreme command. The early theorists of the juridical foundations of the modern state conceive of this as an originary appeal to a supreme power, but the theory of imperial command has no need for such fables about its genealogy. It is not the appeals of a multitude perpetually at war that demand a pacifying supreme power (as in Hobbes), nor the appeals of a commercial class that demand the security of contracts (as in Locke and Hume). Imperial command is rather the result of a social eruption that has overturned all the old relationships that constituted sovereignty.

Imperial command is exercised no longer through the disciplinary modalities of the modern state but rather through the modalities of biopolitical control. These modalities have as their basis and their object a productive multitude that cannot be regimented and normalized, but must nonetheless be governed, even in its autonomy. The concept of the People no longer functions as the organized subject of the system of command, and consequently the identity of the People is replaced by the mobility, flexibility, and perpetual differentiation of the multitude. This shift demystifies and destroys the circular modern idea of the legitimacy of power by which power constructs from the multitude a single subject that could then in turn legitimate that same power. That sophistic tautology no longer works.

The multitude is governed with the instruments of the postmodern capitalist system and within the social relations of the real subsumption. The multitude can only be ruled along internal lines, in production, in exchanges, in culture—in other words, in the biopolitical context of its existence. In its deterritorialized autonomy, however, this biopolitical existence of the multitude has the potential to be transformed into an autonomous mass of intelligent productivity, into an absolute democratic power, as Spinoza would say. If that were to happen, capitalist domination of production, exchange, and communication would be overthrown. Preventing this is the first and primary task of imperial government. We should keep in mind, however, that the constitution of Empire depends for its own existence on the forces that pose this threat, the autonomous forces of productive cooperation. Their powers must be controlled but not destroyed.

The guarantee that Empire offers to globalized capital does not involve a micropolitical and/or microadministrative management of populations. The apparatus of command has no access to the local spaces and the determinate temporal sequences of life where the administration functions; it does not manage to put its hands on the singularities and their activity. What imperial command seeks substantially to invest and protect, and what it guarantees for capitalist development, are rather the general equilibria of the global system.

Imperial control operates through three global and absolute means: the bomb, money, and ether. The panoply of thermonuclear weapons, effectively gathered at the pinnacle of Empire, represents the continuous possibility of the destruction of life itself. This is an operation of absolute violence, a new metaphysical horizon, which completely changes the conception whereby the sovereign state had a monopoly of legitimate physical force. At one time, in modernity, this monopoly was legitimated either as the expropriation of weapons from the violent and anarchic mob, the disordered mass of individuals who tend to slaughter one another, or as the instrument of defense against the enemy, that is, against other peoples organized in states. Both these means of legitimation were oriented finally toward the survival of the population. Today they are no longer effective. The expropriation of the means of violence from a supposedly self-destructive population tends to become merely administrative and police operations aimed at maintaining the segmentations of productive territories. The second justification becomes less effective too as nuclear war between state powers becomes increasingly unthinkable. The development of nuclear technologies and their imperial concentration have limited the sovereignty of most of the countries of the world insofar as it has taken away from them the power to make decisions over war and peace, which is a primary element of the traditional definition of sovereignty. Furthermore, the ultimate threat of the imperial bomb has reduced every war to a limited conflict, a civil war, a dirty war, and so forth. It has made every war the exclusive domain of administrative and police power. From no other standpoint is the passage from modernity to postmodernity and from modern sovereignty to Empire more evident than it is from the standpoint of the bomb. Empire is defined here in the final instance as the "non-place" of life, or, in other words, as the absolute capacity for destruction. Empire is the ultimate form of biopower insofar as it is the absolute inversion of the power of life.

Money is the second global means of absolute control. The construction of the world market has consisted first of all in the monetary deconstruction of national markets, the dissolution of national and/or regional regimes of monetary regulation, and the subordination of those markets to the needs of financial powers. As national monetary structures tend to lose any characteristics of sovereignty, we can see emerging through them the shadows of a new unilateral monetary reterritorialization that is concentrated at the political and financial centers of Empire, the global cities. This is not the construction of a universal monetary regime on the basis of new productive localities, new local circuits of circulation, and thus new values; instead, it is a monetary construction based purely on the political necessities of Empire. Money is the imperial arbiter, but just as in the case of the imperial nuclear threat, this arbiter has neither a determinate location nor a transcendent status. Just as the nuclear threat authorizes the generalized power of the police, so too the monetary arbiter is continually articulated in relation to the productive functions, measures of value, and allocations of wealth that constitute the world market. Monetary mechanisms are the primary means to control the market.[13]

Ether is the third and final fundamental medium of imperial control. The management of communication, the structuring of the education system, and the regulation of culture appear today more than ever as sovereign prerogatives. All of this, however, dissolves in the ether. The contemporary systems of communication are not subordinated to sovereignty; on the contrary, sovereignty seems to be subordinated to communication—or actually, sovereignty is articulated through communications systems. In the field of communication, the paradoxes that bring about the dissolution of territorial and/or national sovereignty are more clear than ever. The deterritorializing capacities of communication are unique: communication is not satisfied by limiting or weakening modern territorial sovereignty; rather it attacks the very possibility of linking an order to a space. It imposes a continuous and complete circulation of signs. Deterritorialization is the primary force and circulation the form through which social communication manifests itself. In this way and in this ether, languages become functional to circulation and dissolve every sovereign relationship. Education and culture too cannot help submitting to the circulating society of the spectacle. Here we reach an extreme limit of the process of the dissolution of the relationship between order and space. At this point we cannot conceive this relationship except in *another space,* an elsewhere that cannot in principle be contained in the articulation of sovereign acts.

The space of communication is completely deterritorialized. It is absolutely other with respect to the residual spaces that we have been analyzing in terms of the monopoly of physical force and the definition of monetary measure. Here it is a question not of residue but of *metamorphosis:* a metamorphosis of all the elements of political economy and state theory. Communication is the form of capitalist production in which capital has succeeded in submitting society entirely and globally to its regime, suppressing all alternative paths. If ever an alternative is to be proposed, it will have to arise from within the society of the real subsumption and demonstrate all the contradictions at the heart of it.

These three means of control refer us again to the three tiers of the imperial pyramid of power. The bomb is a monarchic power, money aristocratic, and ether democratic. It might appear in each of these cases as though the reins of these mechanisms were held by the United States. It might appear as if the United States were the new Rome, or a cluster of new Romes: Washington (the bomb), New York (money), and Los Angeles (ether). Any such territorial conception of imperial space, however, is continually destabilized by the fundamental flexibility, mobility, and deterritorialization at the core of the imperial apparatus. Perhaps the monopoly of force and the regulation of money can be given partial territorial determinations, but communication cannot. Communication has become the central element that establishes the relations of production, guiding capitalist development and also transforming productive forces. This dynamic produces an extremely open situation: here the centralized locus of power has to confront the power of productive subjectivities, the power of all those who contribute to the interactive production of communication. Here in this circulating domain of imperial domination over the new forms of production, communication is most widely disseminated in capillary forms.

Big Government Is Over!

"Big government is over" is the battle cry of conservatives and neoliberals throughout Empire. The Republican Congress of the United States, led by Newt Gingrich, fought to demystify the fetish of big government by calling it "totalitarian" and "fascist" (in a session of Congress that wanted to be imperial but ended up being carnivalesque). It appeared as though we had returned to the times of the great diatribes of Henry Ford against Franklin D. Roosevelt! Or rather to the much less grand times of Margaret Thatcher's first administration, when she frenetically, and with a sense of humor that only the British can muster, sought to sell off the public goods of the nation, from communications systems to the water supply, from the rail system and oil to the universities and hospitals. In the United States, however, the representatives of the most avid conservative wing finally went too far, and in the end everyone recognized it. The bottom line and brutal irony was that they sounded the attack on big government just when the development of the postmodern informational revolution most needed big government to support its efforts—for the construction of information highways, the control of the equilibria of the stock exchanges despite the wild fluctuations of speculation, the firm maintenance of monetary values, public investment in the military-industrial system to help transform the mode of production, the reform of the educational system to adapt to these new productive networks, and so forth. Precisely at this time, after the Soviet Union had collapsed, the imperial tasks facing the U.S. government were most urgent and big government was most needed.

When the proponents of the globalization of capital cry out against big government, they are being not only hypocritical but also ungrateful. Where would capital be if it had not put its hands on big government and made it work for centuries in its exclusive interest? And today where would imperial capital be if big government were not big enough to wield the power of life and death over the entire global multitude? Where would capital be without a big government capable of printing money to produce and reproduce a global order that guarantees capitalist power and wealth? Or without the communications networks that expropriate the cooperation of the productive multitude? Every morning when they wake up, capitalists and their representatives across the world, instead of reading the curses against big government in the Wall Street Journal, *ought to get down on their knees and praise it!*

Now that the most radical conservative opponents of big government have collapsed under the weight of the paradox of their position, we want to pick up their banners where they left them in the mud. It is our turn now to cry "Big government is over!" Why should that slogan be the exclusive property of the conservatives? Certainly, having been educated in class struggle, we know well that big government has also been an instrument for the redistribution of social wealth and that, under the pressure of working-class struggle, it has served in the fight for equality and democracy. Today, however, those times are over. In imperial postmodernity big government has become merely the despotic means of domination and the totalitarian production of subjectivity. Big government conducts the great orchestra of subjectivities reduced to commodities. And it is consequently the determination of the limits of desire: these are in fact the lines that, in the biopolitical Empire, establish the new division of labor across the global horizon, in the interest of reproducing the power to exploit and subjugate. We, on the contrary, struggle because desire has no limit and (since the desire to exist and the desire to produce are one and the same thing) because life can be continuously, freely, and equally enjoyed and reproduced.

Some might object that the productive biopolitical universe still requires some form of command over it, and that realistically we should aim not at destroying big government but at putting our hands on its controls. We have to put an end to such illusions that have plagued the socialist and communist traditions for so long! On the contrary, from the standpoint of the multitude and its quest for autonomous self-government, we have to put an end to the continuous repetition of the same that Marx lamented 150 years ago when he said that all revolutions have only perfected the state instead of destroying it. That repetition has only become clearer in our century, when the great compromise (in its liberal, socialist, and fascist forms) among big government, big business, and big labor has forced the state to produce horrible new fruits: concentration camps, gulags, ghettos, and the like.

You are just a bunch of anarchists, the new Plato on the block will finally yell at us. That is not true. We would be anarchists if we were not to speak (as did Thrasymacus and Callicles, Plato's immortal interlocutors) from the standpoint of a materiality constituted in the networks of productive cooperation, in other words, from the perspective of a humanity that is constructed productively, that is constituted through the "common name" of freedom. No, we are not anarchists but communists who have seen how much repression and destruction of humanity have been wrought by liberal and socialist big governments. We have seen how all this is being re-created in imperial government, just when the circuits of productive cooperation have made labor power as a whole capable of constituting itself in government.

PART 4

THE DECLINE AND FALL OF EMPIRE

4.1

VIRTUALITIES

The people no longer exist, or not yet . . . *the people are missing.*
Gilles Deleuze

In the course of our argument we have generally dealt with Empire in terms of a critique of what is and what exists, and thus in ontological terms. At times, however, in order to reinforce the argumentation, we have addressed the problematic of Empire with an ethico-political discourse, calculating the mechanics of passions and interests—for example, when early in our argument we judged Empire as less bad or better than the previous paradigm of power from the standpoint of the multitude. English political theory in the period from Hobbes to Hume presents perhaps the paradigmatic example of such an ethico-political discourse, which began from a pessimistic description of presocial human nature and attempted through reliance on a transcendental notion of power to establish the legitimacy of the state. The (more or less liberal) Leviathan is less bad with respect to the war of all against all, better because it establishes and preserves peace.[1] This style of political theorizing, however, is no longer very useful. It pretends that the subject can be understood presocially and outside the community, and then imposes a kind of transcendental socialization on it. In Empire, no subjectivity is outside, and all places have been subsumed in a general "non-place." The transcendental fiction of politics can no longer stand up and has no argumentative utility because we all exist entirely within the realm of the social and the political. When we recognize this radical determination of postmodernity, political philosophy forces us to enter the terrain of ontology.

Outside Measure (The Immeasurable)

When we say that political theory must deal with ontology, we mean first of all that politics cannot be constructed from the outside. Politics is given immediately; it is a field of pure immanence. Empire forms on this superficial horizon where our bodies and minds are embedded. It is purely positive. There is no external logical machine that constitutes it. The most natural thing in the world is that the world appears to be politically united, that the market is global, and that power is organized throughout this universality. Imperial politics articulates being in its global extension—a great sea that only the winds and current move. The neutralization of the transcendental imagination is thus the first sense in which the political in the imperial domain is ontological.[2]

The political must also be understood as ontological owing to the fact that all the transcendental determinations of value and measure that used to order the deployments of power (or really determine its prices, subdivisions, and hierarchies) have lost their coherence. From the sacred myths of power that historical anthropologists such as Rudolf Otto and Georges Dumezil employed to the rules of the new political science that the authors of *The Federalist* described; from the Rights of Man to the norms of international public law—all of this fades away with the passage to Empire. Empire dictates its laws and maintains the peace according to a model of postmodern right and postmodern law, through mobile, fluid, and localized procedures.[3] Empire constitutes the ontological fabric in which all the relations of power are woven together—political and economic relations as well as social and personal relations. Across this hybrid domain the biopolitical structure of being is where the internal structure of imperial constitution is revealed, because in the globality of biopower every fixed measure of value tends to be dissolved, and the imperial horizon of power is revealed finally to be a horizon outside measure. Not only the political transcendental but also the transcendental as such has ceased to determine measure.

The great Western metaphysical tradition has always abhorred the immeasurable. From Aristotle's theory of virtue as measure[4] to Hegel's theory of measure as the key to the passage from existence to essence,[5] the question of measure has been strictly linked to that of transcendent order. Even Marx's theory of value pays its dues to this metaphysical tradition: his theory of value is really a theory of the measure of value.[6] Only on the ontological horizon of Empire, however, is the world finally outside measure, and here we can see clearly the deep hatred that metaphysics has for the immeasurable. It derives from the ideological necessity to given a transcendent ontological foundation to order. Just as God is necessary for the classical transcendence of power, so too measure is necessary for the transcendent foundation of the values of the modern state. If there is no measure, the metaphysicians say, there is no cosmos; and if there is no cosmos, there is no state. In this framework one cannot think the immeasurable, or rather, one *must not* think it. Throughout modernity, the immeasurable was the object of an absolute ban, an epistemological prohibition. This metaphysical illusion disappears today, however, because in the context of biopolitical ontology and its becomings, the transcendent is what is unthinkable. When political transcendence is still claimed today, it descends immediately into tyranny and barbarism.

When we say immeasurable, we mean that the political developments of imperial being are outside of every preconstituted measure. We mean that the relationships among the modes of being and the segments of power are always constructed anew and that they vary infinitely. The indexes of command (like those of economic value) are defined on the basis of always contingent and purely conventional elements. Certainly there are apexes and summits of imperial power which guarantee that contingency does not become subversive, that it is not united with the storms that arise on the seas of being—apexes such as the monopoly of nuclear arms, the control of money, and the colonization of ether. These royal deployments of Empire guarantee that the contingency becomes a necessity and does not descend into disorder. These higher powers, however, do not represent a figure of order or a measure of the cosmos; on the contrary, their effectiveness is based on destruction (by the bomb), on judgment (by money), and on fear (by communication).

One might ask at this point whether this idea of immeasurability does not imply the absolute negation of the concept of justice. The history of the idea of justice has indeed generally referred to some notion of measure, be it a measure of equality or a measure of proportionality. Furthermore, as Aristotle says, taking up a line from Theognis, "in justice all virtue is summed up."[7] Are we thus simply making a nonsensical nihilist claim when we assert that in the ontology of Empire value is outside measure? Are we claiming that no value, no justice, and indeed no virtue can exist? No, in contrast to those who have long claimed that value can be affirmed only in the figure of measure and order, we argue that value and justice can live in and be nourished by an immeasurable world. Here we can see once again the importance of the revolution of Renaissance humanism. *Ni Dieu, ni maître, ni l'homme*—no transcendent power or measure will determine the values of our world. Value will be determined only by humanity's own continuous innovation and creation.

Beyond Measure (The Virtual)

Even if the political has become a realm outside measure, value nonetheless remains. Even if in postmodern capitalism there is no longer a fixed scale that measures value, value nonetheless is still powerful and ubiquitous. This fact is demonstrated first of all by the persistence of exploitation, and second by the fact that productive innovation and the creation of wealth continue tirelessly—in fact, they mobilize labor in every interstice of the world. In Empire, the construction of value takes place *beyond measure*. The contrast between the immeasurable excesses of imperial globalization and the productive activity that is beyond measure must be read from the standpoint of the subjective activity that creates and re-creates the world in its entirety.

What we need to highlight at this point, however, is something more substantial than the simple claim that labor remains the central constituent foundation of society as capital transforms to its postmodern stage. Whereas "outside measure" refers to the impossibility of power's calculating and ordering production at a global level, "beyond measure" refers to the vitality of the productive context, the expression of labor as desire, and its capacities to constitute the biopolitical fabric of Empire from below. Beyond measure refers to *the new place in the non-place,* the place defined by the productive activity that is autonomous from any external regime of measure. Beyond measure refers to a *virtuality* that invests the entire biopolitical fabric of imperial globalization.

By the virtual we understand the set of powers to act (being, loving, transforming, creating) that reside in the multitude. We have already seen how the multitude's virtual set of powers is constructed by struggles and consolidated in desire. Now we have to investigate how the virtual can put pressure on the borders of the possible, and thus touch on the real. The passage from the virtual through the possible to the real is the fundamental act of creation.[8] Living labor is what constructs the passageway from the virtual to the real; it is the vehicle of possibility. Labor that has broken open the cages of economic, social, and political discipline and surpassed every regulative dimension of modern capitalism along with its state-form now appears as general social activity.[9] Labor is productive excess with respect to the existing order and the rules of its reproduction. This productive excess is at once the result of a collective force of emancipation and the substance of the new social virtuality of labor's productive and liberatory capacities.

In the passage to postmodernity, one of the primary conditions of labor is that it functions outside measure. The temporal regimentation of labor and all the other economic and/or political measures that have been imposed on it are blown apart. Today labor is immediately a social force animated by the powers of knowledge, affect, science, and language. Indeed, labor is the productive activity of a general intellect and a general body outside measure. Labor appears simply as the *power to act,* which is at once singular and universal: singular insofar as labor has become the exclusive domain of the brain and body of the multitude; and universal insofar as the desire that the multitude expresses in the movement from the virtual to the possible is constantly constituted as a *common thing.* Only when what is common is formed can production take place and can general productivity rise. Anything that blocks this power to act is merely an obstacle to overcome—an obstacle that is eventually outflanked, weakened, and smashed by the critical powers of labor and the everyday passional wisdom of the affects. The power to act is constituted by labor, intelligence, passion, and affect in one common place.

This notion of labor as the common power to act stands in a contemporaneous, coextensive, and dynamic relationship to the construction of community. This relationship is reciprocal such that on the one hand the singular powers of labor continuously create new common constructions, and, on the other hand, what is common becomes singularized.[10] We can thus define the virtual power of labor as a power of self-valorization that exceeds itself, flows over onto the other, and, through this investment, constitutes an expansive commonality. The common actions of labor, intelligence, passion, and affect configure a *constituent power.*

The process we are describing is not merely formal; it is material, and it is realized on the biopolitical terrain. The virtuality of action and the transformation of material conditions, which at times are appropriated by and enrich this power to act, are constituted in ontological mechanisms or apparatuses beyond measure. This ontological apparatus beyond measure is an *expansive power,* a power of freedom, ontological construction, and omnilateral dissemination.

This last definition could be considered redundant. If the power to act constructs value from below, if it transforms value according to the rhythm of what is common, and if it appropriates constitutively the material conditions of its own realization, then it is obvious that in it resides an expansive force beyond measure. This definition is not redundant, however, but rather adds a new dimension to the concept insofar as it demonstrates the positive character of the non-place and the irrepressibility of common action beyond measure. This expansive definition plays an anti-dialectical role, demonstrating the creativity of what is beyond measure. With reference to the history of philosophy, we could add, in order to define the sense of this expansive power, that whereas the definitions of the power to act in terms of the singular and the common are Spinozist, this last definition is really a Nietzschean conception. The omnilateral expansiveness of the power to act demonstrates the ontological basis of transvaluation, that is, its capacity not only to destroy the values that descend from the transcendental realm of measure but also to create new values.[11]

The ontological terrain of Empire, completely plowed and irrigated by a powerful, self-valorizing, and constituent labor, is thus planted with a virtuality that seeks to be real. The keys of possibility, or really of the modalities of being that transform the virtual into reality, reside in this realm beyond measure.

Parasite

One might object at this point that, despite the powers of the multitude, this Empire still exists and commands. We ourselves have amply described its functioning and highlighted its extreme violence. With respect to the virtuality of the multitude, however, imperial government appears as an empty shell or a parasite.[12] Does this mean that the investments of power that Empire continuously makes in order to maintain imperial order and the powerlessness of the multitude really are ineffective? If this were the case, then the argumentation we have been developing up to this point about the extrinsic character of imperial government with respect to the ontological developments of the multitude would be contradictory. The gap between virtuality and possibility that we think can be bridged from the standpoint of the action of the multitude is effectively held open by imperial domination. The two forces seem to stand in contradiction.

We do not, however, think that this is really a contradiction. Only in formal logic is contradiction static; contradiction is never static, however, in material logic (that is, political, historical, and ontological logic), which poses it on the terrain of the possible and thus on the terrain of power. Indeed, the relationship that imperial government imposes on the virtuality of the multitude is simply a static relationship of oppression. The investments of imperial government are essentially negative, deployed through procedures intended to order coercively the actions and events that risk descending into disorder. In all cases the effectiveness of imperial government is regulatory and not constituent, not even when its effects are long-lasting. The redundancies of imperial command configure at most the chronicle that records political life, or really the most feeble and repetitive image of the determinations of being.

The royal prerogatives of imperial government, its monopoly over the bomb, money, and the communicative ether, are merely destructive capacities and thus powers of negation. The action of imperial government intervenes in the multitude's project to suture together virtuality and possibility only by disrupting it and slowing it down. In this respect Empire does touch on the course of historical movement, but it cannot for that reason be defined as a positive capacity—on the contrary, the legitimacy of its command is only increasingly undermined by these movements.

When the action of Empire is effective, this is due not to its own force but to the fact that it is driven by the rebound from the resistance of the multitude against imperial power. One might say in this sense that resistance is actually prior to power.[13] When imperial government intervenes, it selects the liberatory impulses of the multitude in order to destroy them, and in return it is driven forward by resistance. The royal investments of Empire and all its political initiatives are constructed according to the rhythm of the acts of resistance that constitute the being of the multitude. In other words, the effectiveness of Empire's regulatory and repressive procedures must finally be traced back to the virtual, constitutive action of the multitude. Empire itself is not a positive reality. In the very moment it rises up, it falls. Each imperial action is a rebound of the resistance of the multitude that poses a new obstacle for the multitude to overcome.[14]

Imperial command produces nothing vital and nothing ontological. From the ontological perspective, imperial command is purely negative and passive. Certainly power is everywhere, but it is everywhere because everywhere is in play the nexus between virtuality and possibility, a nexus that is the sole province of the multitude. Imperial power is the negative residue, the fallback of the operation of the multitude; it is a parasite that draws its vitality from the multitude's capacity to create ever new sources of energy and value. A parasite that saps the strength of its host, however, can endanger its own existence. The functioning of imperial power is ineluctably linked to its decline.

Nomadism and Miscegenation

The ontological fabric of Empire is constructed by the activity beyond measure of the multitude and its virtual powers. These virtual, constituent powers conflict endlessly with the constituted power of Empire. They are completely positive since their "being-against" is a "being-for," in other words, a resistance that becomes love and community. We are situated precisely at that hinge of infinite finitude that links together the virtual and the possible, engaged in the passage from desire to a coming future.[15]

This ontological relation operates first of all on space. The virtuality of world space constitutes the first determination of the movements of the multitude—a virtuality that must be made real. Space that merely can be traversed must be transformed into a space of life; circulation must become freedom. In other words, the mobile multitude must achieve a global citizenship. The multitude's resistance to bondage—the struggle against the slavery of belonging to a nation, an identity, and a people, and thus the desertion from sovereignty and the limits it places on subjectivity—is entirely positive. Nomadism and miscegenation appear here as figures of virtue, as the first ethical practices on the terrain of Empire. From this perspective the objective space of capitalist globalization breaks down. Only a space that is animated by subjective circulation and only a space that is defined by the irrepressible movements (legal or clandestine) of individuals and groups can be real. Today's celebrations of the local can be regressive and even fascistic when they oppose circulations and mixture, and thus reinforce the walls of nation, ethnicity, race, people, and the like. The concept of the local, however, need not be defined by isolation and purity. In fact, if one breaks down the walls that surround the local (and thereby separate the concept from race, religion, ethnicity, nation, and people), one can link it directly to the universal. The concrete universal is what allows the multitude to pass from place to place and make its place its own. This is the common place of nomadism and miscegenation. Through circulation the common human species is composed, a multicolored Orpheus of infinite power; through circulation the human community is constituted. Outside every Enlightenment cloud or Kantian reverie, the desire of the multitude is not the cosmopolitical state but a common species.[16] As in a secular Pentecost, the bodies are mixed and the nomads speak a common tongue.

In this context, ontology is not an abstract science. It involves the conceptual recognition of the production and reproduction of being and thus the recognition that political reality is constituted by the movement of desire and the practical realization of labor as value. The spatial dimension of ontology today is demonstrated through the multitude's concrete processes of the globalization, or really the making common, of the desire for human community.

One important example of the functioning of this spatial dimension is demonstrated by the processes that brought an end to the Third World, along with all the glory and disgrace of its past struggles, the power of desires that ran throughout its processes of liberation, and the poverty of results that crowned its success. The real heroes of the liberation of the Third World today may really have been the emigrants and the flows of population that have destroyed old and new boundaries. Indeed, the postcolonial hero is the one who continually transgresses territorial and racial boundaries, who destroys particularisms and points toward a common civilization. Imperial command, by contrast, isolates populations in poverty and allows them to act only in the straitjackets of subordinated postcolonial nations. The exodus from localism, the transgression of customs and boundaries, and the desertion from sovereignty were the operative forces in the liberation of the Third World. Here more than ever we can recognize clearly the difference Marx defined between *emancipation* and *liberation.*[17] Emancipation is the entry of new nations and peoples into the imperial society of control, with its new hierarchies and segmentations; liberation, in contrast, means the destruction of boundaries and patterns of forced migration, the reappropriation of space, and the power of the multitude to determine the global circulation and mixture of individuals and populations. The Third World, which was constructed by the colonialism and imperialism of nation-states and trapped in the cold war, is destroyed when the old rules of the political discipline of the modern state (and its attendant mechanisms of geographical and ethnic regulation of populations) are smashed. It is destroyed when throughout the ontological terrain of globalization the most wretched of the earth becomes the most powerful being, because its new nomad singularity is the most creative force and the omnilateral movement of its desire is itself the coming liberation.

The power to circulate is a primary determination of the virtuality of the multitude, and circulating is the first ethical act of a counterimperial ontology. This ontological aspect of biopolitical circulation and mixture is highlighted even more when it is contrasted with other meanings attributed to postmodern circulation, such as market exchanges or the velocity of communication. Those aspects of speed and circulation belong, rather, to the violence of imperial command.[18] Exchanges and communication dominated by capital are integrated into its logic, and only a radical act of resistance can recapture the productive sense of the new mobility and hybridity of subjects and realize their liberation. This rupture, and only this rupture, brings us to the ontological terrain of the multitude and to the terrain on which circulation and hybridization are biopolitical. Biopolitical circulation focuses on and celebrates the substantial determinations of the activities of production, self-valorization, and freedom. Circulation is a global exodus, or really nomadism; and it is a corporeal exodus, or really miscegenation.

General Intellect and Biopower

We insisted earlier on the importance and limitations of Marx's notion of "general intellect" (Section 1.2). At a certain point in capitalist development, which Marx only glimpsed as the future, the powers of labor are infused by the powers of science, communication, and language. General intellect is a collective, social intelligence created by accumulated knowledges, techniques, and know-how. The value of labor is thus realized by a new universal and concrete labor force through the appropriation and free usage of the new productive forces. What Marx saw as the future is our era. This radical transformation of labor power and the incorporation of science, communication, and language into productive force have redefined the entire phenomenology of labor and the entire world horizon of production.

The danger of the discourse of general intellect is that it risks remaining entirely on the plane of thought, as if the new powers of labor were only intellectual and not also corporeal (Section 3.4). As we saw earlier, new forces and new positions of affective labor characterize labor power as much as intellectual labor does. Biopower names these productive capacities of life that are equally intellectual and corporeal. The powers of production are in fact today entirely biopolitical; in other words, they run throughout and constitute directly not only production but also the entire realm of reproduction. Biopower becomes an agent of production when the entire context of reproduction is subsumed under capitalist rule, that is, when reproduction and the vital relationships that constitute it themselves become directly productive. Biopower is another name for the real subsumption of society under capital, and both are synonymous with the globalized productive order. Production fills the surfaces of Empire; it is a machine that is full of life, an intelligent life that by expressing itself in production and reproduction as well as in circulation (of labor, affects, and languages) stamps society with a new collective meaning and recognizes virtue and civilization in cooperation.

The powers of science, knowledge, affect, and communication are the principal powers that constitute our anthropological virtuality and are deployed on the surfaces of Empire. This deployment extends across the general linguistic territories that characterize the intersections between production and life. Labor becomes increasingly immaterial and realizes its value through a singular and continuous process of innovation in production; it is increasingly capable of consuming or using the services of social reproduction in an ever more refined and interactive way. Intelligence and affect (or really the brain coextensive with the body), just when they become the primary productive powers, make production and life coincide across the terrain on which they operate, because life is nothing other than the production and reproduction of the set of bodies and brains.

The relationship between production and life has thus been altered such that it is now completely inverted with respect to how the discipline of political economy understands it. Life is no longer produced in the cycles of reproduction that are subordinated to the working day; on the contrary, life is what infuses and dominates all production. In fact, the value of labor and production is determined deep in the viscera of life. Industry produces no surplus except what is generated by social activity—and this is why, buried in the great whale of life, value is beyond measure. There would be no surplus if production were not animated throughout by social intelligence, by the general intellect and at the same time by the affective expressions that define social relations and rule over the articulations of social being. The excess of value is determined today in the affects, in the bodies crisscrossed by knowledge, in the intelligence of the mind, and in the sheer power to act. The production of commodities tends to be accomplished entirely through language, where by language we mean machines of intelligence that are continuously renovated by the affects and subjective passions.[19]

It should be clear at this point what constitutes *social cooperation* here on the surfaces of imperial society: the synergies of life, or really the productive manifestations of *naked life*. Giorgio Agamben has used the term "naked life" to refer to the negative limit of humanity and to expose behind the political abysses that modern totalitarianism has constructed the (more or less heroic) conditions of human passivity.[20] We would say, on the contrary, that through their monstrosities of reducing human beings to a minimal naked life, fascism and Nazism tried in vain to destroy the enormous power that naked life could become and to expunge the form in which the new powers of productive cooperation of the multitude are accumulated. One might say in line with this idea that the reactionary deliriums of fascism and Nazism were unleashed when capital discovered that social cooperation was no longer the result of the investment of capital but rather an autonomous power, the a priori of every act of production. When human power appears immediately as an autonomous cooperating collective force, capitalist prehistory comes to an end. In other words, capitalist prehistory comes to an end when social and subjective cooperation is no longer a product but a presupposition, when naked life is raised up to the dignity of productive power, or really when it appears as the wealth of virtuality.

The scientific, affective, and linguistic forces of the multitude aggressively transform the conditions of social production. The field on which productive forces are reappropriated by the multitude is a field of radical metamorphoses—the scene of a demiurgic operation. This consists above all in a complete revision of the production of cooperative subjectivity; it consists in an act, that is, of merging and hybridizing with the machines that the multitude has reappropriated and reinvented; it consists, therefore, in an exodus that is not only spatial but also mechanical in the sense that the subject is transformed into (and finds the cooperation that constitutes it multiplied in) the machine. This is a new form of exodus, an exodus toward (or with) the machine—a machinic exodus.[21] The history of the modern worker and of the subject of modern sovereignty already contains a long catalogue of machinic metamorphoses, but the hybridization of humans and machines is no longer defined by the linear path it followed throughout the modern period. We have reached the moment when the relationship of power that had dominated the hybridizations and machinic metamorphoses can now be overturned. Marx recognized that the conflict between workers and machines was a false conflict: "It took both time and experience before the workers learnt to distinguish between machinery and its employment by capital, and therefore to transfer their attacks from the material instruments of production to the form of society which utilizes these instruments."[22] Now the new virtualities, the naked life of the present, have the capacity to take control of the processes of machinic metamorphosis. In Empire the political struggle over the definition of machinic virtuality, or really over the different alternatives of the passage between the virtual and the real, is a central terrain of struggle. This new terrain of production and life opens for labor a future of metamorphoses that subjective cooperation can and must control ethically, politically, and productively.

Res Gestae/Machinae

In recent years there has been much talk of the end of history, and there have also been made many justified objections to the reactionary celebrations of an end of history that would see the present state of rule as eternal. It is certainly true, nonetheless, that in modernity the power of capital and its institutions of sovereignty had a solid hold on history and exerted their rule over the historical process. The virtual powers of the multitude in postmodernity signal the end of that rule and those institutions. *That* history has ended. Capitalist rule is revealed as a transitory period. And yet, if the transcendent teleology that capitalist modernity constructed is coming to an end, how can the multitude define instead a materialist telos?[23]

We will be able to respond to this question only after conducting a phenomenological and historical analysis of the relationship between virtuality and possibility, that is, after responding to the question if, how, and when the virtuality of the multitude passes through possibility and becomes reality. The ontology of the possible is in this sense the central terrain of analysis. This problematic has been posed by authors from Lukács to Benjamin, from Adorno to the later Wittgenstein, from Foucault to Deleuze, and indeed by nearly all those who have recognized the twilight of modernity. In all of these cases the question was posed against such tremendous metaphysical obstacles! And we can now see how pallid their responses were with respect to the enormity of the question. What is certain today is that the problematic does not risk repeating the old models of the metaphysical tradition, even the most powerful ones. In fact, every metaphysical tradition is now completely worn out. If there is to be a solution to the problem, it cannot help being material and explosive. Whereas our attention was first drawn to the intensity of the elements of virtuality that constituted the multitude, now it must focus on the hypothesis that those virtualities accumulate and reach a threshold of realization adequate to their power. This is the sense in which we speak of general intellect and its articulations in knowledge, affect, and cooperation; and similarly the sense in which we speak of the various forms of the collective exodus of those nomadic movements of the multitude that appropriate spaces and renew them.

Here we are dealing with two passages. The first consists in the fact that virtuality totalizes the field of the *res gestae*. Virtuality steps forward and demonstrates that the capacity of the *historia rerum gestarum* to dominate the active virtual singularities has definitively expired. This is the *historia* that comes to an end when the new virtualities emerge as powerful and liberate themselves from a being that is invested hegemonically by capital and its institutions. Today only the *res gestae* are charged with historical capacities, or rather, today there is no history, only historicity. The second passage consists in the fact that these singular virtualities as they gain their autonomy also become self-valorizing. They express themselves as machines of innovation. They not only refuse to be dominated by the old systems of value and exploitation, but actually create their own irreducible possibilities as well. Here is where a materialist telos is defined, founded on the action of singularities, a teleology that is a resultant of the *res gestae* and a figure of the machinic logic of the multitude.

The *res gestae,* the singular virtualities that operate the connection between the possible and the real, are in the first passage outside measure and in the second beyond measure. Singular virtualities, which are the hinge between possible and real, play both these cards: being outside measure as a destructive weapon (deconstructive in theory and subversive in practice); and being beyond measure as constituent power. The virtual and the possible are wedded as irreducible innovation and as a revolutionary machine.

4.2

GENERATION AND CORRUPTION

> You can not spill a drop of American blood without spilling the blood of the whole world . . . [O]ur blood is as the flood of the Amazon, made up of a thousand noble currents all pouring into one. We are not a nation, so much as a world; for unless we may claim all the world for our sire, like Melchisedec, we are without mother or father . . . Our ancestry is lost in the universal paternity . . . We are the heirs of all time, and with all nations we divide our inheritance.
>
> Herman Melville

> Fate has willed it that America is from now on to be at the center of Western civilization rather than on the periphery.
>
> Walter Lippmann

> There is no escaping American business.
>
> Louis-Ferdinand Céline

The theory of the constitution of Empire is also a theory of its decline, as European theorists of Empire have recognized for the last several thousand years. Already in Greco-Roman antiquity, Thucydides, Tacitus, and Polybius all recounted the sequence of rise and fall, as did later the Fathers of the Church and the theorists of early Christianity. In none of these cases when speaking of Empire was it simply a matter for them of repeating the classical theory of the alternation between "positive" and "negative" forms of government, because Empire by definition goes beyond this alternation. The internal crisis of the concept of Empire, however, became completely clear only in the Enlightenment period and the period of the construction of European modernity, when authors such as Montesquieu and Gibbon made the problem of the decadence of the Roman Empire one of the central topoi of the analysis of the political forms of the modern sovereign state.[1]

Rise and Fall (Machiavelli)

In classical antiquity the concept of Empire already presupposed crisis. Empire was conceived in the framework of a naturalist theory of the forms of government; and, even though it breaks the cyclical alternation of good and bad forms, it is not exempt from the destiny of the corruption of the city and civilization as a whole. History is dominated by Thyche (Fortune or Destiny), which at times inevitably ruins the perfection that Empire achieves. From Thucydides to Tacitus and from Athens to Rome, the necessary equilibrium between the forms of common life and command was situated in this linear destiny. Polybius' analyses of the Roman Empire broke with this conception of the cyclical character of historical development whereby the human construction of the political constantly shifts from the good to the bad forms of the city and power: from monarchy to tyranny, from aristocracy to oligarchy, and from democracy to anarchy, and then eventually begins a new cycle. Polybius claimed that the Roman Empire broke with this cycle by creating a synthesis of the good forms of power (see Section 3.5). Empire is thus understood not so much as rule over universal space and time, but rather as a movement that gathers together the spaces and the temporalities through the powers of the social forces that seek to liberate themselves from the natural cyclical character of the time of history. Surpassing the line of destiny, however, is aleatory. The synthesis of the good forms of government, the government of civic virtue, can defy destiny but cannot replace it. Crisis and decline are determinations that every day must be overcome.

During the European Enlightenment, authors such as Montesquieu and Gibbon rejected the naturalist conception of this process. The decline of Empire was explained in social scientific terms as a result of the impossibility of making last the historical and social constructions of the multitude and the virtue of its heroes. The corruption and decline of Empire were thus not a natural presupposition, determined by the cyclical destiny of history, but rather a product of the human impossibility (or at least the extreme difficulty) of governing an unlimited space and time. The limitlessness of Empire undermined the capacity to make the good institutions function and last. Nonetheless, Empire was an end toward which the desire and the civic virtue of the multitude and its human capacities to make history all tended. It was a precarious situation that could not support unbounded space and time, but instead ineluctably limited the universal aims of government to finite political and social dimensions. The Enlightenment authors told us that the government that approximates perfection will be constructed with moderation across limited space and time. Between Empire and the reality of command, therefore, there was a contradiction in principle that would inevitably spawn crises.

Machiavelli, looking back at the conception of the ancients and anticipating that of the moderns, is really the one who offers us the most adequate illustration of the paradox of Empire.[2] He clarified the problematic by separating it from both the naturalizing terrain of the ancients and the sociological terrain of the moderns, presenting it, rather, on the field of immanence and pure politics. In Machiavelli, expansive government is pushed forward by the dialectic of the social and political forces of the Republic. Only where the social classes and their political expressions are posed in an open and continuous play of counterpower are freedom and expansion linked together, and hence only there does Empire become possible. There is no concept of Empire, Machiavelli says, that is not a decisively expansive concept of freedom. Precisely in this dialectic of freedom, then, is where the elements of corruption and destruction reside. When Machiavelli discusses the fall of the Roman Empire, he focuses first and foremost on the crisis of civil religion, or really on the decline of the social relation that had unified the different ideological social forces and allowed them to participate together in the open interaction of counterpowers.

Christian religion is what destroyed the Roman Empire by destroying the civic passion that pagan society had sustained, the conflictual but loyal participation of the citizens in the continuous perfecting of the constitution and the process of freedom.

The ancient notion of the necessary and natural corruption of the good forms of government is thus radically displaced because they can be evaluated only in relation to the social and political relationship that organized the constitution. The Enlightenment and modern notion of the crisis of unbounded and uncontrollable space and time is similarly displaced because it too was led back to the realm of civic power: on this and no other basis can space and time be evaluated. The alternative is thus not between government and corruption, or between Empire and decline, but between on the one hand socially rooted and expansive government, that is, "civic" and "democratic" government, and on the other every practice of government that grounds its own power on transcendence and repression. We should be clear here that when we speak of the "city" or "democracy" in quotation marks as the basis for the expansive activity of the Republic, and as the only possibility for a lasting Empire, we are introducing a concept of participation that is linked to the vitality of a population and to its capacity to generate a dialectic of counterpowers—a concept, therefore, that has little to do with the classical or the modern concept of democracy. Even the reigns of Genghis Khan and Tamerlane were from this perspective somewhat "democratic," as were Caesar's legions, Napoleon's armies, and the armies of Stalin and Eisenhower, since each of them enabled the participation of a population that supported its expansive action. What is central in all of these cases, and in the general concept of Empire, is that a terrain of immanence be affirmed. Immanence is defined as the absence of every external limit from the trajectories of the action of the multitude, and immanence is tied only, in its affirmations and destructions, to regimes of possibility that constitute its formation and development.

Here we find ourselves back at the center of the paradox by which every theory of Empire conceives the possibility of its own decline—but now we can begin to explain it. If Empire is always an absolute positivity, the realization of a government of the multitude, and an absolutely immanent apparatus, then it is exposed to crisis precisely on the terrain of this definition, and not for any other necessity or transcendence opposed to it. Crisis is the sign of an alternative possibility on the plane of immanence—a crisis that is not necessary but always possible. Machiavelli helps us understand this immanent, constitutive, and ontological sense of crisis. Only in the present situation, however, does this coexistence of crisis and the field of immanence become completely clear. Since the spatial and temporal dimensions of political action are no longer the limits but the constructive mechanisms of imperial government, the coexistence of the positive and the negative on the terrain of immanence is now configured as an open alternative. Today the same movements and tendencies constitute both the rise and the decline of Empire.

Finis Europae (Wittgenstein)

The coexistence of the imperial spirit with signs of crisis and decline has appeared in many different guises in European discourse over the past two centuries, often as a reflection either on the end of European hegemony or on the crisis of democracy and the triumph of mass society. We have insisted at length throughout this book that the modern governments of Europe developed not *imperial* but *imperialist* forms. The concept of Empire nonetheless survived in Europe, and its lack of reality was continually mourned. The European debates about Empire and decline interest us for two primary reasons: first, because the crisis of the ideal of imperial Europe is at the center of these debates, and second, because this crisis strikes precisely in that secret place of the definition of Empire where the concept of democracy resides. Another element that we have to keep in mind here is the standpoint from which the debates were conducted: a standpoint that adopts the historical drama of the decline of Empire in terms of collective lived experience. The theme of *the crisis of Europe* was translated into a discourse on the decline of Empire and linked to the crisis of democracy, along with the forms of consciousness and resistance that this crisis implies.

Alexis de Tocqueville was perhaps the first to present the problem in these terms. His analysis of mass democracy in the United States, with its spirit of initiative and expansion, led him to the bitter and prophetic recognition of the impossibility for European élites to continue to maintain a position of command over world civilization.[3] Hegel had already perceived something very similar: "America is . . . the country of the future, and its world-historical importance has yet to be revealed in the ages which lie ahead . . . It is a land of desire for all those who are weary of the historical arsenal of old Europe."[4] Tocqueville, however, understood this passage in a much more profound way. The reason for the crisis of European civilization and its imperial practices consists in the fact that European virtue—or really its aristocratic morality organized in the institutions of modern sovereignty—cannot manage to keep pace with the vital powers of mass democracy.

The death of God that many Europeans began to perceive was really a sign of the expiration of their own planetary centrality, which they could understand only in terms of a modern mysticism. From Nietzsche to Burkhardt, from Thomas Mann to Max Weber, from Spengler to Heidegger and Ortega y Gasset, and numerous other authors who straddled the nineteenth and twentieth centuries, this intuition became a constant refrain that was sung with such bitterness![5] The appearance of the masses on the social and political scene, the exhaustion of the cultural and productive models of modernity, the waning of the European imperialist projects, and the conflicts among nations on questions of scarcity, poverty, and class struggle: all these emerged as irreversible signs of decline. Nihilism dominated the era because the times were without hope. Nietzsche gave the definitive diagnosis: "Europe is sick."[6] The two World Wars that would ravage its territories, the triumph of fascism, and now, after the collapse of Stalinism, the reappearance of the most terrible specters of nationalism and intolerance all stand as proof to confirm that these intuitions were in fact correct.

From our standpoint, however, the fact that against the old powers of Europe a new Empire has formed is only good news. Who wants to see any more of that pallid and parasitic European ruling class that led directly from the ancien régime to nationalism, from populism to fascism, and now pushes for a generalized neoliberalism? Who wants to see more of those ideologies and those bureaucratic apparatuses that have nourished and abetted the rotting European élites? And who can still stand those systems of labor organization and those corporations that have stripped away every vital spirit?

Our task here is not to lament the crisis of Europe, but rather to recognize in its analyses the elements that, while confirming its tendency, still indicate possible resistances, the margins of positive reaction, and the alternatives of destiny. These elements have often appeared almost against the will of the theorists of the crisis of their own times: it is a resistance that leaps to a future time—a real and proper future past, a kind of future perfect tense. In this sense, through the painful analyses of its causes, the crisis of European ideology can reveal the definition of new, open resources. This is why it is important to follow the developments of the crisis of Europe, because not only in authors such as Nietzsche and Weber but also in the public opinion of the times, the denunciation of the crisis revealed an extremely powerful positive side, which contained the fundamental characteristics of the new world Empire we are entering today. The agents of the crisis of the old imperial world became foundations of the new. The undifferentiated mass that by its simple presence was able to destroy the modern tradition and its transcendent power appears now as a powerful productive force and an uncontainable source of valorization. A new vitality, almost like the barbaric forces that buried Rome, reanimates the field of immanence that the death of the European God left us as our horizon. Every theory of the crisis of European Man and of the decline of the idea of European Empire is in some way a symptom of the new vital force of the masses, or as we prefer, of the desire of the multitude. Nietzsche declared this from the mountaintops: "I have absorbed in myself the spirit of Europe—now I want to strike back!"[7] Going beyond modernity means going beyond the barriers and transcendences of Eurocentrism and leads toward the definitive adoption of the field of immanence as the exclusive terrain of the theory and practice of politics.

In the years after the explosion of the First World War, those who had participated in the great massacre tried desperately to understand and control the crisis. Consider the testimonies of Franz Rosenzweig and Walter Benjamin. For both of them a kind of secular eschatology was the mechanism by which the experience of the crisis could be set free.[8] After the historical experience of war and misery, and also perhaps with an intuition of the holocaust to come, they tried to discover a hope and a light of redemption. This attempt, however, did not succeed in escaping the powerful undertow of the dialectic. Certainly the dialectic, that cursed dialectic that had held together and anointed European values, had been emptied out from within and was now defined in completely negative terms. The apocalyptic scene on which this mysticism searched for liberation and redemption, however, was still too implicated in the crisis. Benjamin recognized this bitterly: "The past carries with it a temporal index by which it is referred to redemption. There is a secret agreement between past generations and the present. Our coming was expected on earth. Like every generation that preceded us, we have been endowed with a *weak* Messianic power, a power to which the past has a claim."[9]

This theoretical experience arose precisely where the crisis of modernity appeared with the most intensity. On this same terrain other authors sought to break with the remnants of the dialectic and its powers of subsumption. It seems to us, however, that even the strongest thinkers of the day were not able to break with the dialectic and the crisis. In Max Weber the crisis of sovereignty and legitimacy can be resolved only through recourse to the irrational figures of charisma. In Carl Schmitt the horizon of sovereign practices can be cleared only by recourse to the "decision." An irrational dialectic, however, cannot resolve or even attenuate the crisis of reality.[10] And the powerful shadow of an aestheticized dialectic slips even into Heidegger's notion of a pastoral function over a scattered and fractured being.

For the real clarification of this scene, we are most indebted to the series of French philosophers who reread Nietzsche several decades later, in the 1960s.[11] Their rereading involved a reorientation of the standpoint of the critique, which came about when they began to recognize the end of the functioning of the dialectic and when this recognition was confirmed in the new practical, political experiences that centered on the production of subjectivity. This was a production of subjectivity as power, as the constitution of an autonomy that could not be reduced to any abstract or transcendent synthesis.[12] Not the dialectic but refusal, resistance, violence, and the positive affirmation of being now marked the relationship between the location of the crisis in reality and the adequate response. What in the midst of the crisis in the 1920s appeared as transcendence against history, redemption against corruption, and messianism against nihilism now was constructed as an ontologically definite position outside and against, and thus beyond every possible residue of the dialectic. This was a new materialism which negated every transcendent element and constituted a radical reorientation of spirit.

In order to understand the profundity of this passage, one would do well to focus on the awareness and anticipation of it in the thought of Ludwig Wittgenstein. Wittgenstein's early writings gave a new life to the dominant themes of early twentieth-century European thought: the condition of dwelling in the desert of sense and searching for meaning, the coexistence of a mysticism of the totality and the ontological tendency toward the production of subjectivity. Contemporary history and its drama, which had been stripped away from any dialectic, were then removed by Wittgenstein from any contingency. History and experience became the scene of a materialist and tautological refoundation of the subject in a desperate attempt to find coherence in the crisis. In the midst of World War I Wittgenstein wrote: “How things stand, is God. God is, how things stand. Only from the consciousness of the *uniqueness of my life* arises religion—science—and art.” And further: “This consciousness is life itself. Can it be an ethics even if there is no living being outside myself? Can there be any ethics if there is no living being but myself? If ethics is supposed to be something fundamental, there can. If I am right, then it is not sufficient for the ethical judgment that a world be given. Then the world in itself is neither good nor evil . . . Good and evil only enter through the *subject*. And the subject is not part of the world, but a boundary of the world.” Wittgenstein denounces the God of war and the desert of things in which good and evil are now indistinguishable by situating the world on the limit of tautological subjectivity: “Here one can see that solipsism coincides with pure realism, if it is strictly thought out.”[13] This limit, however, is creative. The alternative is completely given when, and only when, subjectivity is posed outside the world: “My propositions serve as elucidations in the following way: anyone who understands me eventually recognizes them as nonsensical, when he has used them—as steps—to climb up beyond them. (He must, so to speak, throw away the ladder after he has climbed up it.) He must transcend these propositions, and then he will see the world aright.”[14] Wittgenstein recognizes the end of every possible dialectic and any meaning that resides in the logic of the world and not in its marginal, subjective surpassing.

The tragic trajectory of this philosophical experience allows us to grasp those elements that made the perception of the crisis of modernity and the decline of the idea of Europe a (negative but necessary) condition of the definition of the coming Empire. These authors were voices crying out in the desert. Part of this generation would be interned in extermination camps. Others would perpetuate the crisis through an illusory faith in Soviet modernization. Others still, a significant group of these authors, would flee to America. They were indeed voices crying out in the desert, but their rare and singular anticipations of life in the desert give us the means to reflect on the possibilities of the multitude in the new reality of postmodern Empire. Those authors were the first to define the condition of the complete deterritorialization of the coming Empire, and they were situated in it just as the multitudes are situated in it today. The negativity, the refusal to participate, the discovery of an emptiness that invests everything: this means situating oneself peremptorily in an imperial reality that is itself defined by crisis. Empire is the desert and crisis is at this point indistinguishable from the tendency of history. Whereas in the ancient world the imperial crisis was conceived as the product of a natural cyclical history, and whereas in the modern world crisis was defined by a series of aporias of time and space, now figures of crisis and practices of Empire have become indistinguishable. The twentieth-century theorists of crisis teach us, however, that in this deterritorialized and untimely space where the new Empire is constructed and in this desert of meaning, the testimony of the crisis can pass toward the realization of a singular and collective subject, toward the powers of the multitude. The multitude has internalized the lack of place and fixed time; it is mobile and flexible, and it conceives the future only as a totality of possibilities that branch out in every direction. The coming imperial universe, blind to meaning, is filled by the multifarious totality of the production of subjectivity. The decline is no longer a future destiny but the present reality of Empire.

America, America

The flight of European intellectuals to the United States was an attempt to rediscover a lost place. Was not American democracy in fact founded on the democracy of exodus, on affirmative and nondialectical values, and on pluralism and freedom? Did not these values, along with the notion of new frontiers, perpetually re-create the expansion of its democratic basis, beyond every abstract obstacle of the nation, ethnicity, and religion? This music was played at times in a high form in the project of the "Pax Americana" proclaimed by the liberal leadership, and at times in a low form, represented by the American dream of social mobility and equal opportunity for wealth and freedom for every honest person—in short, "the American way of life." The New Deal's project to surmount the world crisis of the 1930s, which was so different from and so much more liberal than the European political and cultural projects to respond to the crisis, supported this conception of the American ideal. When Hannah Arendt claimed the American Revolution to be superior to the French because the American was an unlimited search for political freedom and the French a limited struggle over scarcity and inequality, she not only celebrated an ideal of freedom that Europeans no longer knew but also reterritorialized it in the United States.[15] In a certain sense, then, it seemed as if the continuity that had existed between U.S. history and the history of Europe was broken and that the United States had embarked on a different course, but really the United States represented for these Europeans the resurrection of an idea of freedom that Europe had lost.

From the standpoint of a Europe in crisis, the United States, Jefferson's "Empire of liberty," represented the renewal of the imperial idea. The great nineteenth-century American writers had sung the epic dimensions of the freedom of the new continent. In Whitman naturalism became affirmative and in Melville realism became desiring. An American place was territorialized in the name of a constitution of freedom and at the same time continually deterritorialized through the opening of frontiers and exodus. The great American philosophers, from Emerson to Whitehead and Pierce, opened up Hegelianism (or really the apologia of imperialist Europe) to the spiritual currents of a process that was new and immense, determinate and unlimited.[16]

The Europeans in crisis were enchanted by these siren songs of a new Empire. European Americanism and anti-Americanism in the twentieth century are both manifestations of the difficult relationship between Europeans in crisis and the U.S. imperial project. The American utopia was received in many different ways, but it functioned everywhere in twentieth-century Europe as a central reference point. The continuous preoccupation was manifest both in the spleen of the crisis and in the spirit of the avant-gardes, in other words, through the self-destruction of modernity and the indeterminate but uncontainable will to innovation that drove the last wave of great European cultural movements, from expressionism and futurism to cubism and abstractionism.

The military history of the double rescue of Europe by the U.S. armies in the two World Wars was paralleled by a rescue in political and cultural terms. American hegemony over Europe, which was founded on financial, economic, and military structures, was made to seem natural through a series of cultural and ideological operations. Consider, for example, how in the years surrounding the end of World War II the locus of artistic production and the idea of modern art shifted from Paris to New York. Serge Guilbaut recounts the fascinating story of how, when the Paris art scene had been thrown into disarray by war and Nazi occupation, and in the midst of an ideological campaign to promote the leading role of the United States in the postwar world, the abstract expressionism of New York artists such as Jackson Pollock and Robert Motherwell was established as the natural continuation and heir of European and specifically Parisian modernism. New York stole the idea of modern art:

> American art was thus described as the logical culmination of a long-standing and inexorable tendency toward abstraction. Once American culture was raised to the status of an international model, the significance of what was specifically American had to change: what had been characteristically American now became representative of "Western culture" as a whole. In this way American art was transformed from regional to international art and then to universal art . . . In this respect, postwar American culture was placed on the same footing as American economic and military strength: it was made responsible for the survival of democratic liberties in the "free" world.[17]

This passage in the history of artistic production and, more important, art criticism is simply one aspect of the multifaceted ideological operation that cast the U.S. global hegemony as the natural and ineluctable consequence of the crisis of Europe.

Paradoxically, even the ferocious European nationalisms, which had led to such violent conflicts over the first half of the century, were eventually displaced by a competition over who could better express a strong Americanism. Lenin's Soviet Union in fact may have heard the siren song of Americanism most clearly. The challenge was to replicate the results of the capitalism that had achieved its pinnacle in the United States. The Soviets argued against the means the United States employed and claimed instead that socialism could attain the same results more efficiently through hard labor and the sacrifice of freedom. This terrible ambiguity also runs throughout Gramsci's writings on Americanism and Fordism, one of the fundamental texts for understanding the American problem from the European point of view.[18] Gramsci saw the United States, with its combination of new Taylorist forms of the organization of labor and its powerful capitalist will to dominate, as the inevitable reference point for the future: it was the only path for development. For Gramsci, it was then a matter of understanding whether that revolution would be active (like that of Soviet Russia) or passive (as in Fascist Italy). The consonance between Americanism and state socialism should be obvious, with their parallel paths of development on the two sides of the Atlantic throughout the cold war, which led finally to dangerous competitions over space exploration and nuclear weapons. These parallel paths simply highlight the fact that a certain Americanism had penetrated into the heart of even its strongest adversary. The twentieth-century developments of Russia were to a certain extent a microcosm for those of Europe.

The refusal of European consciousness to recognize its decline often took the form of projecting its crisis onto the American utopia. That projection continued for a long time, as long as lasted the necessity and urgency to rediscover a site of freedom that could continue the teleological vision of which Hegelian historicism is perhaps the highest expression. The paradoxes of this projection multiplied, to the point where European consciousness, faced with its undeniable and irreversible decline, reacted by going to the other extreme: the primary site of competition, which had affirmed and repeated the formal power of the U.S. utopia, now represented its complete overturning. Solzhenitsyn's Russia became the absolute negative of the most caricatural and apologetic images of the U.S. utopia in the guise of Arnold Toynbee. It should come as no surprise that the ideologies of the end of history, which are as evolutionary as they are postmodern, should appear to complete this ideological mess. The American Empire will bring an end to History.

We know, however, that this idea of American Empire as the redemption of utopia is completely illusory. First of all, the coming Empire is not American and the United States is not its center. The fundamental principle of Empire as we have described it throughout this book is that its power has no actual and localizable terrain or center. Imperial power is distributed in networks, through mobile and articulated mechanisms of control. This is not to say that the U.S. government and the U.S. territory are no different from any other: the United States certainly occupies a privileged position in the global segmentations and hierarchies of Empire. As the powers and boundaries of nation-states decline, however, differences between national territories become increasingly relative. They are now not differences of nature (as were, for example, the differences between the territory of the metropole and that of the colony) but differences of degree.

Furthermore, the United States cannot rectify or redeem the crisis and decline of Empire. The United States is not the place where the European or even the modern subject can flee to resolve its uneasiness and unhappiness; there was no such place. The means to get beyond the crisis is the ontological displacement of the subject. The most important change therefore takes place inside humanity, since with the end of modernity also ends the hope of finding something that can identify the self outside the community, outside cooperation, and outside the critical and contradictory relationships that each person finds in a non-place, that is, in the world and the multitude. This is where the idea of Empire reappears, not as a territory, not in the determinate dimensions of its time and space, and not from the standpoint of a people and its history, but rather simply as the fabric of an ontological human dimension that tends to become universal.

Crisis

Postmodernization and the passage to Empire involve a real convergence of the realms that used to be designated as base and superstructure. Empire takes form when language and communication, or really when immaterial labor and cooperation, become the dominant productive force (see Section 3.4). The superstructure is put to work, and the universe we live in is a universe of productive linguistic networks. The lines of production and those of representation cross and mix in the same linguistic and productive realm. In this context the distinctions that define the central categories of political economy tend to blur. Production becomes indistinguishable from reproduction; productive forces merge with relations of production; constant capital tends to be constituted and represented within variable capital, in the brains, bodies, and cooperation of productive subjects. Social subjects are at the same time producers and products of this unitary machine. In this new historical formation it is thus no longer possible to identify a sign, a subject, a value, or a practice that is "outside."

The formation of this totality, however, does not eliminate exploitation. It rather redefines it, primarily in relation to communication and cooperation. Exploitation is the expropriation of cooperation and the nullification of the meanings of linguistic production. Consequently, resistances to command continually emerge within Empire. Antagonisms to exploitation are articulated across the global networks of production and determine crises on each and every node. Crisis is coextensive with the postmodern totality of capitalist production; it is proper to imperial control. In this respect, the decline and fall of Empire is defined not as a diachronic movement but as a synchronic reality. Crisis runs through every moment of the development and recomposition of the totality.

With the real subsumption of society under capital, social antagonisms can erupt as conflict in every moment and on every term of communicative production and exchange. Capital has become a world. Use value and all the other references to values and processes of valorization that were conceived to be outside the capitalist mode of production have progressively vanished. Subjectivity is entirely immersed in exchange and language, but that does not mean it is now pacific. Technological development based on the generalization of the communicative relationships of production is a motor of crisis, and productive general intellect is a nest of antagonisms. Crisis and decline refer not to something external to Empire but to what is most internal. They pertain to the production of subjectivity itself, and thus they are at once proper and contrary to the processes of the reproduction of Empire. Crisis and decline are not a hidden foundation nor an ominous future but a clear and obvious actuality, an always expected event, a latency that is always present.

It is midnight in a night of specters. Both the new reign of Empire and the new immaterial and cooperative creativity of the multitude move in shadows, and nothing manages to illuminate our destiny ahead. Nonetheless, we have acquired a new point of reference (and tomorrow perhaps a new consciousness), which consists in the fact that Empire is defined by crisis, that its decline has always already begun, and that consequently every line of antagonism leads toward the event and singularity. What does it mean, practically, that crisis is immanent to and indistinguishable from Empire? Is it possible in this dark night to theorize positively and define a practice of the event?

Generation

Two central impediments prevent us from responding to these questions immediately. The first is presented by the overbearing power of bourgeois metaphysics and specifically the widely propagated illusion that the capitalist market and the capitalist regime of production are eternal and insuperable. The bizarre naturalness of capitalism is a pure and simple mystification, and we have to disabuse ourselves of it right away. The second impediment is represented by the numerous theoretical positions that see no alternative to the present form of rule except a blind anarchic other and that thus partake in a mysticism of the limit. From this ideological perspective, the suffering of existence cannot manage to be articulated, become conscious, and establish a standpoint of revolt. This theoretical position leads merely to a cynical attitude and quietistic practices. The illusion of the naturalness of capitalism and the radicality of the limit actually stand in a relationship of complementarity. Their complicity is expressed in an exhausting powerlessness. The fact is that neither of these positions, neither the apologetic one nor the mystical one, manages to grasp the primary aspect of biopolitical order: its productivity. They cannot interpret the virtual powers of the multitude that tend constantly toward becoming possible and real. In other words, they have lost track of the fundamental productivity of being.

We can answer the question of how to get out of the crisis only by lowering ourselves down into biopolitical virtuality, enriched by the singular and creative processes of the production of subjectivity. How are rupture and innovation possible, however, in the absolute horizon in which we are immersed, in a world in which values seem to have been negated in a vacuum of meaning and a lack of any measure? Here we do not need to go back again to a description of desire and its ontological excess, nor insist again on the dimension of the "beyond." It is sufficient to point to the generative determination of desire and thus its productivity. In effect, the complete commingling of the political, the social, and the economic in the constitution of the present reveals a biopolitical space that—much better than Hannah Arendt's nostalgic utopia of political space—explains the ability of desire to confront the crisis.[19] The entire conceptual horizon is thus completely redefined. The biopolitical, seen from the standpoint of desire, is nothing other than concrete production, human collectivity in action. Desire appears here as productive space, as the actuality of human cooperation in the construction of history. This production is purely and simply human reproduction, the power of generation. Desiring production is generation, or rather the excess of labor and the accumulation of a power incorporated into the collective movement of singular essences, both its cause and its completion.

When our analysis is firmly situated in the biopolitical world where social, economic, and political production and reproduction coincide, the ontological perspective and the anthropological perspective tend to overlap. Empire pretends to be the master of that world because it can destroy it. What a horrible illusion! In reality we are masters of the world because our desire and labor regenerate it continuously. The biopolitical world is an inexhaustible weaving together of generative actions, of which the collective (as meeting point of singularities) is the motor. No metaphysics, except a delirious one, can pretend to define humanity as isolated and powerless. No ontology, except a transcendent one, can relegate humanity to individuality. No anthropology, except a pathological one, can define humanity as a negative power. Generation, that first fact of metaphysics, ontology, and anthropology, is a collective mechanism or apparatus of desire. Biopolitical becoming celebrates this "first" dimension in absolute terms.

Political theory is forced by this new reality to redefine itself radically. In biopolitical society, for example, fear cannot be employed, as Thomas Hobbes proposed, as the exclusive motor of the contractual constitution of politics, thus negating the love of the multitude. Or rather, in biopolitical society the decision of the sovereign can never negate the desire of the multitude. If those founding modern strategies of sovereignty were employed today with the oppositions they determine, the world would come to a halt because generation would no longer be possible. For generation to take place, the political has to yield to love and desire, and that is to the fundamental forces of biopolitical production. The political is not what we are taught it is today by the cynical Machiavellianism of politicians; it is rather, as the democratic Machiavelli tells us, the power of generation, desire, and love. Political theory has to reorient itself along these lines and assume the language of generation.

Generation is the *primum* of the biopolitical world of Empire. Biopower—a horizon of the hybridization of the natural and the artificial, needs and machines, desire and the collective organization of the economic and the social—must continually regenerate itself in order to exist. Generation is there, before all else, as basis and motor of production and reproduction. The generative connection gives meaning to communication, and any model of (everyday, philosophical, or political) communication that does not respond to this primacy is false. The social and political relationships of Empire register this phase of the development of production and interpret the generative and productive biosphere. We have thus reached a limit of the virtuality of the real subsumption of productive society under capital—but precisely on this limit the possibility of generation and the collective force of desire are revealed in all their power.

Corruption

Opposed to generation stands corruption. Far from being the necessary complement of generation, as the various Platonic currents of philosophy would like, corruption is merely its simple negation.[20] Corruption breaks the chain of desire and interrupts its extension across the biopolitical horizon of production. It constructs black holes and ontological vacuums in the life of the multitude that not even the most perverse political science manages to camouflage. Corruption, contrary to desire, is not an ontological motor but simply the lack of ontological foundation of the biopolitical practices of being.

In Empire corruption is everywhere. It is the cornerstone and keystone of domination. It resides in different forms in the supreme government of Empire and its vassal administrations, the most refined and the most rotten administrative police forces, the lobbies of the ruling classes, the mafias of rising social groups, the churches and sects, the perpetrators and persecutors of scandal, the great financial conglomerates, and everyday economic transactions. Through corruption, imperial power extends a smoke screen across the world, and command over the multitude is exercised in this putrid cloud, in the absence of light and truth.

It is no mystery how we recognize corruption and how we identify the powerful emptiness of the mist of indifference that imperial power extends across the world. In fact, the ability to recognize corruption is, to use a phrase of Descartes's, "la faculté la mieux partagée du monde," the most widely shared faculty in the world. Corruption is easily perceived because it appears immediately as a form of violence, as an insult. And indeed it is an insult: corruption is in fact the sign of the impossibility of linking power to value, and its denunciation is thus a direct intuition of the lack of being. Corruption is what separates a body and a mind from what they can do. Since knowledge and existence in the biopolitical world always consist in a production of value, this lack of being appears as a wound, a death wish of the socius, a stripping away of being from the world.

The forms in which corruption appears are so numerous that trying to list them is like pouring the sea into a teacup. Let us try nonetheless to give a few examples, even though they can in no way serve to represent the whole. In the first place, there is corruption as individual choice that is opposed to and violates the fundamental community and solidarity defined by biopolitical production. This small, everyday violence of power is a mafia-style corruption. In the second place, there is corruption of the productive order, or really exploitation. This includes the fact that the values that derive from the collective cooperation of labor are expropriated, and what was in the biopolitical *ab origine* public is privatized. Capitalism is completely implicated in this corruption of privatization. As Saint Augustine says, the great reigns are only the enlarged projections of little thieves. Augustine of Hippo, however, so realistic in this pessimistic conception of power, would be struck dumb by today's little thieves of monetary and financial power. Really, when capitalism loses its relationship to value (both as the measure of individual exploitation and as a norm of collective progress), it appears immediately as corruption. The increasingly abstract sequence of its functioning (from the accumulation of surplus value to monetary and financial speculation) is shown to be a powerful march toward generalized corruption. If capitalism is by definition a system of corruption, held together nonetheless as in Mandeville's fable by its cooperative cleverness and redeemed according to all its ideologies on right and left by its progressive function, then when measure is dissolved and the progressive telos breaks down, nothing essential remains of capitalism but corruption. In the third place, corruption appears in the functioning of ideology, or rather in the perversion of the senses of linguistic communication. Here corruption touches on the biopolitical realm, attacking its productive nodes and obstructing its generative processes. This attack is demonstrated, in the fourth place, when in the practices of imperial government the threat of terror becomes a weapon to resolve limited or regional conflicts and an apparatus for imperial development. Imperial command, in this case, is disguised and can alternately appear as corruption or destruction, almost as if to reveal the profound call that the former makes for the latter and the latter for the former. The two dance together over the abyss, over the imperial lack of being.

Such examples of corruption could be multiplied ad infinitum, but at the base of all these forms of corruption there is an operation of ontological nullification that is defined and exercised as the destruction of the singular essence of the multitude. The multitude must be unified or segmented into different unities: this is how the multitude has to be corrupted. This is why the ancient and modern concepts of corruption cannot be translated directly into the postmodern concept. Whereas in ancient and modern times corruption was defined in relation to the schemas and/or relations of value and demonstrated as a falsification of them in such a way that it could at times play a role in the change among the forms of government and the restoration of values, today, in contrast, corruption cannot play a role in any transformation of the forms of government because corruption itself is the substance and totality of Empire. Corruption is the pure exercise of command, without any proportionate or adequate reference to the world of life. It is command directed toward the destruction of the singularity of the multitude through its coercive unification and/or cruel segmentation. This is why Empire necessarily declines in the very moment of its rise.

This negative figure of command over productive biopower is even more paradoxical when viewed from the perspective of corporeality. Biopolitical generation directly transforms the bodies of the multitude. These are, as we have seen, bodies enriched with intellectual and cooperative power, and bodies that are already hybrid. What generation offers us in postmodernity are thus bodies "beyond measure." In this context corruption appears simply as disease, frustration, and mutilation. This is how power has always acted against enriched bodies. Corruption also appears as psychosis, opiates, anguish, and boredom, but this too has always happened throughout modernity and disciplinary societies. The specificity of corruption today is instead the rupture of the community of singular bodies and the impediment to its action—a rupture of the productive biopolitical community and an impediment to its life. Here we are thus faced with a paradox. Empire recognizes and profits from the fact that in cooperation bodies produce more and in community bodies enjoy more, but it has to obstruct and control this cooperative autonomy so as not to be destroyed by it. Corruption operates to impede this going "beyond measure" of the bodies through community, this singular universalization of the new power of bodies, which threaten the very existence of Empire. The paradox is irresolvable: the more the world becomes rich, the more Empire, which is based on this wealth, must negate the conditions of the production of wealth. Our task is to investigate how ultimately corruption can be forced to cede its control to generation.

4.3

THE MULTITUDE AGAINST EMPIRE

> The great masses need a *material religion of the senses* [*eine sinnliche Religion*]. Not only the great masses but also the philosopher needs it. Monotheism of reason and the heart, polytheism of the imagination and art, this is what we need . . . [W]e must have a new mythology, but this mythology must be at the service of ideas. It must be a mythology of *reason*.
>
> *Das älteste Systemprogramm des deutschen Idealismus,*
> by Hegel, Hölderlin, or Schelling

> We do not lack communication, on the contrary we have too much of it. We lack creation. *We lack resistance to the present.*
>
> Gilles Deleuze and Félix Guattari

Imperial power can no longer resolve the conflict of social forces through mediatory schemata that displace the terms of conflict. The social conflicts that constitute the political confront one another directly, without mediations of any sort. This is the essential novelty of the imperial situation. Empire creates a greater potential for revolution than did the modern regimes of power because it presents us, alongside the machine of command, with an alternative: the set of all the exploited and the subjugated, a multitude that is directly opposed to Empire, with no mediation between them. At this point, then, as Augustine says, our task is to discuss, to the best of our powers, "the rise, the development and the destined ends of the two cities . . . which we find . . . interwoven . . . and mingled with one another."[1] Now that we have dealt extensively with Empire, we should focus directly on the multitude and its potential political power.

The Two Cities

We need to investigate specifically how the multitude can become a *political subject* in the context of Empire. We can certainly recognize the existence of the multitude from the standpoint of the constitution of Empire, but from that perspective the multitude might appear to be generated and sustained by imperial command. In the new postmodern Empire there is no Emperor Caracalla who grants citizenship to all his subjects and thereby forms the multitude as a political subject. The formation of the multitude of exploited and subjugated producers can be read more clearly in the history of twentieth-century revolutions. Between the communist revolutions of 1917 and 1949, the great anti-fascist struggles of the 1930s and 1940s, and the numerous liberation struggles of the 1960s up to those of 1989, the conditions of the citizenship of the multitude were born, spread, and consolidated. Far from being defeated, the revolutions of the twentieth century have each pushed forward and transformed the terms of class conflict, posing the conditions of a new political subjectivity, an insurgent multitude against imperial power. The rhythm that the revolutionary movements have established is the beat of a new *aetas,* a new maturity and metamorphosis of the times.

The constitution of Empire is not the cause but the consequence of the rise of these new powers. It should be no surprise, then, that Empire, despite its efforts, finds it impossible to construct a system of right adequate to the new reality of the globalization of social and economic relations. This impossibility (which served as the point of departure for our argument in Section 1.1) is not due to the wide extension of the field of regulation; nor is it simply the result of the difficult passage from the old system of international public law to the new imperial system. This impossibility is explained instead by the revolutionary nature of the multitude, whose struggles have produced Empire as an inversion of its own image and who now represents on this new scene an uncontainable force and an excess of value with respect to every form of right and law.

To confirm this hypothesis, it is sufficient to look at the contemporary development of the multitude and dwell on the vitality of its present expressions. When the multitude works, it produces autonomously and reproduces the entire world of life. Producing and reproducing autonomously mean constructing a new ontological reality. In effect, by working, the multitude produces itself as singularity. It is a singularity that establishes a new place in the non-place of Empire, a singularity that is a reality produced by cooperation, represented by the linguistic community, and developed by the movements of hybridization. The multitude affirms its singularity by inverting the ideological illusion that all humans on the global surfaces of the world market are interchangeable. Standing the ideology of the market on its feet, the multitude promotes through its labor the biopolitical singularizations of groups and sets of humanity, across each and every node of global interchange.

Class struggles and revolutionary processes of the past undermined the political powers of nations and peoples. The revolutionary preamble that has been written from the nineteenth to the twentieth centuries has prepared the new subjective configuration of labor that comes to be realized today. Cooperation and communication throughout the spheres of biopolitical production define a new productive singularity. The multitude is not formed simply by throwing together and mixing nations and peoples indifferently; it is the singular power of a *new city*.

One might object at this point, with good reason, that all this is still not enough to establish the multitude as a properly political subject, nor even less as a subject with the potential to control its own destiny. This objection, however, does not present an insuperable obstacle, because the revolutionary past, and the contemporary cooperative productive capacities through which the anthropological characteristics of the multitude are continually transcribed and reformulated, cannot help revealing a telos, a material affirmation of liberation. In the ancient world Plotinus faced something like this situation:

> "Let us flee then to the beloved Fatherland": this is the soundest counsel . . . The Fatherland to us is There whence we have

> come, and There is the Father. What then is our course, what the manner of our flight? This is not a journey for the feet; the feet bring us only from land to land; nor need you think of a coach or ship to carry you away; all this order of things you must set aside and refuse to see: you must close the eyes and call instead upon another vision which is to be waked within you, a vision, the birth-right of all, which few turn to use.[2]

This is how ancient mysticism expressed the new telos. The multitude today, however, resides on the imperial surfaces where there is no God the Father and no transcendence. Instead there is our immanent labor. The teleology of the multitude is theurgical; it consists in the possibility of directing technologies and production toward its own joy and its own increase of power. The multitude has no reason to look outside its own history and its own present productive power for the means necessary to lead toward its constitution as a political subject.

A material mythology of reason thus begins to be formed, and it is constructed in the languages, technologies, and all the means that constitute the world of life. It is a material religion of the senses that separates the multitude from every residue of sovereign power and from every "long arm" of Empire. The mythology of reason is the symbolic and imaginative articulation that allows the ontology of the multitude to express itself as activity and consciousness. The mythology of languages of the multitude interprets the telos of an *earthly city,* torn away by the power of its own destiny from any belonging or subjection to a *city of God,* which has lost all honor and legitimacy. To the metaphysical and transcendent mediations, to the violence and corruption are thus opposed the absolute constitution of labor and cooperation, the earthly city of the multitude.

Endless Paths (The Right to Global Citizenship)

The constitution of the multitude appears first as a spatial movement that constitutes the multitude in limitless place. The mobility of commodities, and thus of that special commodity that is labor-power, has been presented by capitalism ever since its birth as the fundamental condition of accumulation. The kinds of movement of individuals, groups, and populations that we find today in Empire, however, cannot be completely subjugated to the laws of capitalist accumulation—at every moment they overflow and shatter the bounds of measure. The movements of the multitude designate new spaces, and its journeys establish new residences. Autonomous movement is what defines the place proper to the multitude. Increasingly less will passports or legal documents be able to regulate our movements across borders. A new geography is established by the multitude as the productive flows of bodies define new rivers and ports. The cities of the earth will become at once great deposits of cooperating humanity and locomotives for circulation, temporary residences and networks of the mass distribution of living humanity.

Through circulation the multitude reappropriates space and constitutes itself as an active subject. When we look closer at how this constitutive process of subjectivity operates, we can see that the new spaces are described by unusual topologies, by subterranean and uncontainable rhizomes—by geographical mythologies that mark the new paths of destiny. These movements often cost terrible suffering, but there is also in them a desire of liberation that is not satiated except by reappropriating new spaces, around which are constructed new freedoms. Everywhere these movements arrive, and all along their paths they determine new forms of life and cooperation—everywhere they create that wealth that parasitic postmodern capitalism would otherwise not know how to suck out of the blood of the proletariat, because increasingly today production takes place in movement and cooperation, in exodus and community. Is it possible to imagine U.S. agriculture and service industries without Mexican migrant labor, or Arab oil without Palestinians and Pakistanis? Moreover, where would the great innovative sectors of immaterial production, from design to fashion, and from electronics to science in Europe, the United States, and Asia, be without the "illegal labor" of the great masses, mobilized toward the radiant horizons of capitalist wealth and freedom? Mass migrations have become necessary for production. Every path is forged, mapped, and traveled. It seems that the more intensely each is traveled and the more suffering is deposited there, the more each path becomes productive. These paths are what brings the "earthly city" out of the cloud and confusion that Empire casts over it. This is how the multitude gains the power to affirm its autonomy, traveling and expressing itself through an apparatus of widespread, transversal territorial reappropriation.

Recognizing the potential autonomy of the mobile multitude, however, only points toward the real question. What we need to grasp is how the multitude is organized and redefined as a positive, political power. Up to this point we have been able to describe the potential existence of this political power in merely formal terms. It would be a mistake to stop here, without going on to investigate the mature forms of the consciousness and political organization of the multitude, without recognizing how much is already powerful in these territorial movements of the labor power of Empire. How can we recognize (and reveal) a constituent political tendency within and beyond the spontaneity of the multitude's movements?

This question can be approached initially from the other side by considering the policies of Empire that repress these movements. Empire does not really know how to control these paths and can only try to criminalize those who travel them, even when the movements are required for capitalist production itself. The migration lines of biblical proportions that go from South to North America are obstinately called by the new drug czars "the cocaine trail"; or rather, the articulations of exodus from North Africa and sub-Saharan Africa are treated by European leaders as "paths of terrorism"; or rather still, the populations forced to flee across the Indian Ocean are reduced to slavery in "Arabia félix"; and the list goes on. And yet the flows of population continue. Empire must restrict and isolate the spatial movements of the multitude to stop them from gaining political legitimacy. It is extremely important from this point of view that Empire use its powers to manage and orchestrate the various forces of nationalism and fundamentalism (see Sections 2.2 and 2.4). It is no less important, too, that Empire deploy its military and police powers to bring the unruly and rebellious to order.[3] These imperial practices in themselves, however, still do not touch on the political tension that runs throughout the spontaneous movements of the multitude. *All these repressive actions remain essentially external to the multitude and its movements.* Empire can only isolate, divide, and segregate. Imperial capital does indeed attack the movements of the multitude with a tireless determination: it patrols the seas and the borders; within each country it divides and segregates; and in the world of labor it reinforces the cleavages and borderlines of race, gender, language, culture, and so forth. Even then, however, it must be careful not to restrict the productivity of the multitude too much because Empire too depends on this power. The movements of the multitude have to be allowed to extend always wider across the world scene, and the attempts at repressing the multitude are really paradoxical, inverted manifestations of its strength.

This leads us back to our fundamental questions: How can the actions of the multitude become political? How can the multitude organize and concentrate its energies against the repression and incessant territorial segmentations of Empire? The only response that we can give to these questions is that the action of the multitude becomes political primarily when it begins to confront directly and with an adequate consciousness the central repressive operations of Empire. It is a matter of recognizing and engaging the imperial initiatives and not allowing them continually to reestablish order; it is a matter of crossing and breaking down the limits and segmentations that are imposed on the new collective labor power; it is a matter of gathering together these experiences of resistance and wielding them in concert against the nerve centers of imperial command.

This task for the multitude, however, although it is clear at a conceptual level, remains rather abstract. What specific and concrete practices will animate this political project? We cannot say at this point. What we can see nonetheless is a first element of a political program for the global multitude, a first political demand: *global citizenship*. During the 1996 demonstrations for the *sans papiers,* the undocumented aliens residing in France, the banners demanded "Papiers pour tous!" Residency papers for everyone means in the first place that all should have the full rights of citizenship in the country where they live and work. This is not a utopian or unrealistic political demand. The demand is simply that the juridical status of the population be reformed in step with the real economic transformations of recent years. Capital itself has demanded the increased mobility of labor power and continuous migrations across national boundaries. Capitalist production in the more dominant regions (in Europe, the United States, and Japan, but also in Singapore, Saudi Arabia, and elsewhere) is utterly dependent on the influx of workers from the subordinate regions of the world. Hence the political demand is that the existent fact of capitalist production be recognized juridically and that all workers be given the full rights of citizenship. In effect this political demand insists in postmodernity on the fundamental modern constitutional principle that links right and labor, and thus rewards with citizenship the worker who creates capital.

This demand can also be configured in a more general and more radical way with respect to the postmodern conditions of Empire. If in a first moment the multitude demands that each state recognize juridically the migrations that are necessary to capital, in a second moment it must demand control over the movements themselves. The multitude must be able to decide if, when, and where it moves. It must have the right also to stay still and enjoy one place rather than being forced constantly to be on the move. *The general right to control its own movement is the multitude's ultimate demand for global citizenship.* This demand is radical insofar as it challenges the fundamental apparatus of imperial control over the production and life of the multitude. Global citizenship is the multitude's power to reappropriate control over space and thus to design the new cartography.

Time and Body (The Right to a Social Wage)

Many elements arise on the endless paths of the mobile multitude in addition to the spatial dimensions we have considered thus far. In particular, the multitude takes hold of time and constructs new temporalities, which we can recognize by focusing on the transformations of labor. Understanding this construction of new temporalities will help us see how the multitude has the potential to make its action coherent as a real political tendency.

The new temporalities of biopolitical production cannot be understood in the frameworks of the traditional conceptions of time. In the *Physics,* Aristotle defines time by the measure of the movement between a before and an after. Aristotle's definition has the enormous merit of separating the definition of time from individual experience and spiritualism. Time is a collective experience that embodies and lives in the movements of the multitude. Aristotle, however, proceeds to reduce this collective time determined by the experience of the multitude to a transcendent standard of measure. Throughout Western metaphysics, from Aristotle to Kant and Heidegger, time has continuously been located in this transcendent dwelling place. In modernity, reality was not conceivable except as measure, and measure in turn was not conceivable except as a (real or formal) a priori that corralled being within a transcendent order. Only in postmodernity has there been a real break with this tradition—a break not with the first element of Aristotle's definition of time as a collective constitution but with the second transcendent configuration. In postmodernity, instead, time is no longer determined by any transcendent measure, any a priori: time pertains directly to existence. Here is where the Aristotelian tradition of measure is broken. In fact, from our perspective the transcendentalism of temporality is destroyed most decisively by the fact that it is now impossible to measure labor, either by convention or by calculation. Time comes back entirely under collective existence and thus resides within the cooperation of the multitude.

Through the cooperation, the collective existence, and the communicative networks that are formed and reformed within the multitude, time is reappropriated on the plane of immanence. It is not given a priori, but rather bears the stamp of collective action. The new phenomenology of the labor of the multitude reveals labor as the fundamental creative activity that through cooperation goes beyond any obstacle imposed on it and constantly re-creates the world. The activity of the multitude constitutes time beyond measure. Time might thus be defined as the immeasurability of the movement between a before and an after, an immanent process of constitution.[4] The processes of ontological constitution unfold through the collective movements of cooperation, across the new fabrics woven by the production of subjectivity. This site of ontological constitution is where the new proletariat appears as a constituent power.

This is a *new proletariat* and not a *new industrial working class.* The distinction is fundamental. As we explained earlier, "proletariat" is the general concept that defines all those whose labor is exploited by capital, the entire cooperating multitude (Section 1.3). The industrial working class represented only a *partial* moment in the history of the proletariat and its revolutions, in the period when capital was able to reduce value to measure. In that period it seemed as if only the labor of waged workers was productive, and therefore all the other segments of labor appeared as merely reproductive or even unproductive. In the biopolitical context of Empire, however, the production of capital converges ever more with the production and reproduction of social life itself; it thus becomes ever more difficult to maintain distinctions among productive, reproductive, and unproductive labor. Labor—material or immaterial, intellectual or corporeal—produces and reproduces social life, and in the process is exploited by capital. This wide landscape of biopolitical production allows us finally to recognize the full generality of the concept of proletariat. The progressive indistinction between production and reproduction in the biopolitical context also highlights once again the immeasurability of time and value. As labor moves outside the factory walls, it is increasingly difficult to maintain the fiction of any measure of the working day and thus separate the time of production from the time of reproduction, or work time from leisure time. There are no time clocks to punch on the terrain of biopolitical production; the proletariat produces in all its generality everywhere all day long.

This generality of biopolitical production makes clear a second programmatic political demand of the multitude: *a social wage and a guaranteed income for all.* The social wage stands opposed first of all to the family wage, that fundamental weapon of the sexual division of labor by which the wage paid for the productive labor of the male worker is conceived also to pay for the unwaged reproductive labor of the worker's wife and dependents at home. The family wage keeps family control firmly in the hands of the male wage earner and perpetuates a false conception of what labor is productive and what is not. As the distinction between production and reproductive labor fades, so too fades the legitimation of the family wage. The social wage extends well beyond the family to the entire multitude, even those who are unemployed, because the entire multitude produces, and its production is necessary from the standpoint of total social capital. In the passage to postmodernity and biopolitical production, labor power has become increasingly collective and social. It is not even possible to support the old slogan "equal pay for equal work" when labor cannot be individualized and measured. The demand for a social wage extends to the entire population the demand that all activity necessary for the production of capital be recognized with an equal compensation such that a social wage is really a guaranteed income. Once citizenship is extended to all, we could call this guaranteed income a citizenship income, due each as a member of society.

Telos (The Right to Reappropriation)

Since in the imperial realm of biopower production and life tend to coincide, class struggle has the potential to erupt across all the fields of life. The problem we have to confront now is how concrete instances of class struggle can actually arise, and moreover how they can form a coherent program of struggle, a constituent power adequate to the destruction of the enemy and the construction of a new society. The question is really how the body of the multitude can configure itself as a telos.

The first aspect of the telos of the multitude has to do with the senses of language and communication. If communication has increasingly become the fabric of production, and if linguistic cooperation has increasingly become the structure of productive corporeality, then the control over linguistic sense and meaning and the networks of communication becomes an ever more central issue for political struggle. Jürgen Habermas seems to have understood this fact, but he grants the liberated functions of language and communication only to individual and isolated segments of society.[5] The passage to postmodernity and Empire prohibits any such compartmentalization of the life world and immediately presents communication, production, and life as one complex whole, an open site of conflict. The theorists and practitioners of science have long engaged these sites of controversy, but today all of labor power (be it material or immaterial, intellectual or manual) is engaged in struggles over the senses of language and against capital's colonization of communicative sociality. All the elements of corruption and exploitation are imposed on us by the linguistic and communicative regimes of production: destroying them in words is as urgent as doing so in deeds. This is not really a matter of ideology critique if by ideology we still understand a realm of ideas and language that is superstructural, external to production. Or rather, in the imperial regime ideology, critique becomes directly the critique of both political economy and lived experience. How can sense and meaning be oriented differently or organized in alternative, coherent communicative apparatuses? How can we discover and direct the performative lines of linguistic sets and communicative networks that create the fabric of life and production? Knowledge has to become linguistic action and philosophy has to become a real *reappropriation of knowledge*.[6] In other words, knowledge and communication have to constitute life through struggle. A first aspect of the telos is posed when the apparatuses that link communication to modes of life are developed through the struggle of the multitude.

To every language and communicative network corresponds a system of machines, and the question of machines and their use allows us to recognize a second aspect of the telos of the multitude, which integrates the first and carries it further. We know well that machines and technologies are not neutral and independent entities. They are biopolitical tools deployed in specific regimes of production, which facilitate certain practices and prohibit others. The processes of construction of the new proletariat that we have been following go beyond a fundamental threshold here when the multitude recognizes itself as machinic, when it conceives of the possibility of a new use of machines and technology in which the proletariat is not subsumed as "variable capital," as an internal part of the production of capital, but is rather an autonomous agent of production. In the passage from the struggle over the sense of language to the construction of a new system of machines, the telos gains a greater consistency. This second aspect of the telos serves to make what has been constructed in language become a lasting, corporeal progression of desire in freedom. The hybridization of human and machine is no longer a process that takes place only on the margins of society; rather, it is a fundamental episode at the center of the constitution of the multitude and its power.

Since great collective means must be mobilized for this mutation, the telos must be configured as a collective telos. It has to become real as a site of encounter among subjects and a mechanism of the constitution of the multitude.[7] This is the third aspect of the series of passages through which the material teleology of the new proletariat is formed. Here consciousness and will, language and machine are called on to sustain the collective making of history. The demonstration of this becoming cannot consist in anything but the experience and experimentation of the multitude. Therefore the power of the dialectic, which imagines the collective formed through mediation rather than through constitution, has been definitively dissolved. The making of history is in this sense the construction of the life of the multitude.

The fourth aspect deals with biopolitics. The subjectivity of living labor reveals, simply and directly in the struggle over the senses of language and technology, that when one speaks of a collective means of the constitution of a new world, one is speaking of the connection between the power of life and its political organization. The political, the social, the economic, and the vital here all dwell together. They are entirely interrelated and completely interchangeable. The practices of the multitude invest this complex and unitary horizon—a horizon that is at once ontological and historical. Here is where the biopolitical fabric opens to the constitutive, constituent power.

The fifth and final aspect thus deals directly with the constituent power of the multitude—or really with the product of the creative imagination of the multitude that configures its own constitution. This constituent power makes possible the continuous opening to a process of radical and progressive transformation. It makes conceivable equality and solidarity, those fragile demands that were fundamental but remained abstract throughout the history of modern constitutions. It should come as no surprise that the postmodern multitude takes away from the U.S. Constitution what allowed it to become, above and against all other constitutions, an imperial constitution: its notion of a boundless frontier of freedom and its definition of an open spatiality and temporality celebrated in a constituent power. This new range of possibilities in no way guarantees what is to come. And yet, despite such reservations, there is something real that foreshadows a coming future: the telos that we can feel pulsing, the multitude that we construct within desire.

Now we can formulate a third political demand of the multitude: *the right to reappropriation.* The right to reappropriation is first of all the right to the reappropriation of the means of production. Socialists and communists have long demanded that the proletariat have free access to and control over the machines and materials it uses to produce. In the context of immaterial and biopolitical production, however, this traditional demand takes on a new guise. The multitude not only uses machines to produce, but also becomes increasingly machinic itself, as the means of production are increasingly integrated into the minds and bodies of the multitude. In this context reappropriation means having free access to and control over knowledge, information, communication, and affects—because these are some of the primary means of biopolitical production. Just because these productive machines have been integrated into the multitude does not mean that the multitude has control over them. Rather, it makes more vicious and injurious their alienation. The right to reappropriation is really the multitude's right to self-control and autonomous self-production.

Posse

The telos of the multitude must live and organize its political space against Empire and yet within the "maturity of the times" and the ontological conditions that Empire presents. We have seen how the multitude moves on endless paths and takes corporeal form by reappropriating time and hybridizing new machinic systems. We have also seen how the power of the multitude materializes within the vacuum that remains necessarily at the heart of Empire. Now it is a matter of posing within these dimensions the problem of the becoming-subject of the multitude. In other words, the virtual conditions must now become real in a concrete figure. Against the divine city, the earthly city must demonstrate its power as an apparatus of the mythology of reason that organizes the biopolitical reality of the multitude.

The name that we want to use to refer to the multitude in its political autonomy and its productive activity is the Latin term *posse*—power as a verb, as activity. In Renaissance humanism the triad *esse–nosse–posse* (being–knowing–having power) represented the metaphysical heart of that constitutive philosophical paradigm that was to go into crisis as modernity progressively took form. Modern European philosophy, in its origins and in its creative components that were not subjugated to transcendentalism, continually tended to pose posse at the center of the ontological dynamic: posse is the machine that weaves together knowledge and being in an expansive, constitutive process. When the Renaissance matured and reached the point of conflict with the forces of counterrevolution, the humanistic posse became a force and symbol of resistance, in Bacon's notion of *inventio* or experimentation, Campanella's conception of love, and Spinoza's usage of *potentia.* Posse is what a body and what a mind can do. Precisely because it continued to live in resistance, the metaphysical term became a political term. Posse refers to the power of the multitude and its telos, an embodied power of knowledge and being, always open to the possible.

Contemporary U.S. rap groups have rediscovered the term "posse" as a noun to mark the force that musically and literarily defines the group, the singular difference of the postmodern multitude. Of course, the proximate reference for the rappers is probably the *posse comitatus* of Wild West lore, the rough group of armed men who were constantly prepared to be authorized by the sheriff to hunt down outlaws. This American fantasy of vigilantes and outlaws, however, does not interest us very much. It is more interesting to trace back a deeper, hidden etymology of the term. It seems to us that perhaps a strange destiny has renewed the Renaissance notion and has, with a grain of madness, made the term once again deserving of its high political tradition.

From this perspective we want to speak of posse and not of "res-publica," because the public and the activity of singularities that compose it go beyond any object (*res*) and are constitutionally incapable of being corralled there. On the contrary, the singularities are producers. Like the Renaissance "posse," which was traversed by knowledge and resided at the metaphysical root of being, they too will be at the origin of the new reality of the political that the multitude is defining in the vacuum of imperial ontology. Posse is the standpoint that best allows us to grasp the multitude as singular subjectivity: posse constitutes its mode of production and its being.

As in all innovative processes, the mode of production that arises is posed against the conditions from which it has to be liberated. The mode of production of the multitude is posed against exploitation in the name of labor, against property in the name of cooperation, and against corruption in the name of freedom. It self-valorizes bodies in labor, reappropriates productive intelligence through cooperation, and transforms existence in freedom. The history of class composition and the history of labor militancy demonstrate the matrix of these ever new and yet determinate reconfigurations of self-valorization, cooperation, and political self-organization as an effective social project.

The first phase of properly capitalist worker militancy, that is, the phase of industrial production that preceded the full deployment of Fordist and Taylorist regimes, was defined by the figure of the *professional worker,* the highly skilled worker organized hierarchically in industrial production. This militancy involved primarily transforming the specific power of the valorization of the worker's own labor and productive cooperation into a weapon to be used in a project of *reappropriation,* a project in which the singular figure of the worker's own productive power would be exalted. A republic of worker councils was its slogan; a soviet of producers was its telos; and autonomy in the articulation of modernization was its program. The birth of the modern trade union and the construction of the party as vanguard both date from this period of worker struggles and effectively overdetermine it.

The second phase of capitalist worker militancy, which corresponded to the deployment of Fordist and Taylorist regimes, was defined by the figure of the *mass worker.* The militancy of the mass worker combined its own self-valorization as a refusal of factory work and the extension of its power over all mechanisms of social reproduction. Its program was to create a real *alternative* to the system of capitalist power. The organization of mass trade unions, the construction of the welfare state, and social-democratic reformism were all results of the relations of force that the mass worker defined and the overdetermination it imposed on capitalist development. The communist alternative acted in this phase as a counter-power within the processes of capitalist development.

Today, in the phase of worker militancy that corresponds to the post-Fordist, informational regimes of production, there arises the figure of the *social worker.* In the figure of the social worker the various threads of immaterial labor-power are being woven together. A constituent power that connects mass intellectuality and self-valorization in all the arenas of the flexible and nomadic productive social cooperation is the order of the day. In other words, the program of the social worker is a project of *constitution.* In today's productive matrix, the constituent power of labor can be expressed as self-valorization of the human (the equal right of citizenship for all over the entire sphere of the world market); as cooperation (the right to communicate, construct languages, and control communications networks); and as political power, or really as the constitution of a society in which the basis of power is defined by the expression of the needs of all. This is the organization of the social worker and immaterial labor, an organization of productive and political power as a biopolitical unity managed by the multitude, organized by the multitude, directed by the multitude—absolute democracy in action.

The posse produces the chromosomes of its future organization. Bodies are on the front lines in this battle, bodies that consolidate in an irreversible way the results of past struggles and incorporate a power that has been gained ontologically. Exploitation must be not only negated from the perspective of practice but also annulled in its premises, at its basis, stripped from the genesis of reality. Exploitation must be excluded from the bodies of immaterial labor-power just as it must be from the social knowledges and affects of reproduction (generation, love, the continuity of kinship and community relationships, and so forth) that bring value and affect together in the same power. The constitution of new bodies, outside of exploitation, is a fundamental basis of the new mode of production.

The mode of production of the multitude reappropriates wealth from capital and also constructs a new wealth, articulated with the powers of science and social knowledge through cooperation. Cooperation annuls the title of property. In modernity, private property was often legitimated by labor, but this equation, if it ever really made sense, today tends to be completely destroyed. Private property of the means of production today, in the era of the hegemony of cooperative and immaterial labor, is only a putrid and tyrannical obsolescence. The tools of production tend to be recomposed in collective subjectivity and in the collective intelligence and affect of the workers; entrepreneurship tends to be organized by the cooperation of subjects in general intellect. The organization of the multitude as political subject, as posse, thus begins to appear on the world scene. The multitude is biopolitical self-organization.

Certainly, there must be a moment when reappropriation and self-organization reach a threshold and configure a real event. This is when the political is really affirmed—when the genesis is complete and self-valorization, the cooperative convergence of subjects, and the proletarian management of production become a constituent power. This is the point when the modern republic ceases to exist and the postmodern posse arises. This is the founding moment of an earthly city that is strong and distinct from any divine city. The capacity to construct places, temporalities, migrations, and new bodies already affirms its hegemony through the actions of the multitude against Empire. Imperial corruption is already undermined by the productivity of bodies, by cooperation, and by the multitude's designs of productivity. The only event that we are still awaiting is the construction, or rather the insurgence, of a powerful organization. The genetic chain is formed and established in ontology, the scaffolding is continuously constructed and renewed by the new cooperative productivity, and thus we await only the maturation of the political development of the posse. We do not have any models to offer for this event. Only the multitude through its practical experimentation will offer the models and determine when and how the possible becomes real.

Militant

In the postmodern era, as the figure of the people dissolves, the militant is the one who best expresses the life of the multitude: the agent of biopolitical production and resistance against Empire. When we speak of the militant, we are not thinking of anything like the sad, ascetic agent of the Third International whose soul was deeply permeated by Soviet state reason, the same way the will of the pope was embedded in the hearts of the knights of the Society of Jesus. We are thinking of nothing like that and of no one who acts on the basis of duty and discipline, who pretends his or her actions are deduced from an ideal plan. We are referring, on the contrary, to something more like the communist and liberatory combatants of the twentieth-century revolutions, the intellectuals who were persecuted and exiled in the course of anti-fascist struggles, the republicans of the Spanish civil war and the European resistance movements, and the freedom fighters of all the anticolonial and anti-imperialist wars. A prototypical example of this revolutionary figure is the militant agitator of the Industrial Workers of the World. The Wobbly constructed associations among working people from below, through continuous agitation, and while organizing them gave rise to utopian thought and revolutionary knowledge. The militant was the fundamental actor of the "long march" of the emancipation of labor from the nineteenth to the twentieth centuries, the creative singularity of that gigantic collective movement that was working-class struggle.

Across this long period, the activity of the militant consisted, first of all, in practices of resistance in the factory and in society against capitalist exploitation. It consisted also, through and beyond resistance, in the collective construction and exercise of a counterpower capable of destructuring the power of capitalism and opposing it with an alternative program of government. In opposition to the cynicism of the bourgeoisie, to monetary alienation, to the expropriation of life, to the exploitation of labor, to the colonization of the affects, and so on, the militant organized the struggle. Insurrection was the proud emblem of the militant. This militant was repeatedly martyred in the tragic history of communist struggles. Sometimes, but not often, the normal structures of the rights state were sufficient for the repressive tasks required to destroy the counterpower. When they were not sufficient, however, the fascists and the white guards of state terror, or rather the black mafias in the service of "democratic" capitalisms, were invited to lend a hand to reinforce the legal repressive structures.

Today, after so many capitalist victories, after socialist hopes have withered in disillusionment, and after capitalist violence against labor has been solidified under the name of ultra-liberalism, why is it that instances of militancy still arise, why have resistances deepened, and why does struggle continually reemerge with new vigor? We should say right away that this new militancy does not simply repeat the organizational formulas of the old revolutionary working class. Today the militant cannot even pretend to be a representative, *even of the fundamental human needs of the exploited. Revolutionary political militancy today, on the contrary, must rediscover what has always been its proper form:* not representational but constituent activity. *Militancy today is a positive, constructive, and innovative activity. This is the form in which we and all those who revolt against the rule of capital recognize ourselves as militants today. Militants resist imperial command in a creative way. In other words, resistance is linked immediately with a constitutive investment in the biopolitical realm and to the formation of cooperative apparatuses of production and community. Here is the strong novelty of militancy today: it repeats the virtues of insurrectional action of two hundred years of subversive experience, but at the same time it is linked to a new world, a world that knows no outside. It knows only an inside, a vital and ineluctable participation in the set of social structures, with no possibility of transcending them. This inside is the productive cooperation of mass intellectuality and affective networks, the productivity of postmodern biopolitics. This militancy makes resistance into counterpower and makes rebellion into a project of love.*

There is an ancient legend that might serve to illuminate the future life of communist militancy: that of Saint Francis of Assisi. Consider his work. To denounce the poverty of the multitude he adopted that common condition and discovered there the ontological power of a new society. The communist militant does the same, identifying in the common condition of the multitude its enormous wealth. Francis in opposition to nascent capitalism refused every instrumental discipline, and in opposition to the mortification of the flesh (in poverty and in the constituted order) he posed a joyous life, including all of being and nature, the animals, sister moon, brother sun, the birds of the field, the poor and exploited humans, together against the will of power and corruption. Once again in postmodernity we find ourselves in Francis's situation, posing against the misery of power the joy of being. This is a revolution that no power will control—because biopower and communism, cooperation and revolution remain together, in love, simplicity, and also innocence. This is the irrepressible lightness and joy of being communist.

NOTES

PREFACE

1. On the declining sovereignty of nation-states and the transformation of sovereignty in the contemporary global system, see Saskia Sassen, *Losing Control? Sovereignty in an Age of Globalization* (New York: Columbia University Press, 1996).
2. On the concept of Empire, see Maurice Duverger, "Le concept d'empire," in Maurice Duverger, ed., *Le concept d'empire* (Paris: PUF, 1980), pp. 5–23. Duverger divides the historical examples into two primary models, with the Roman Empire on one side and the Chinese, Arab, Mesoamerican, and other Empires on the other. Our analyses pertain primarily to the Roman side because this is the model that has animated the Euro-American tradition that has led to the contemporary world order.
3. "Modernity is not a phenomenon of Europe as an *independent* system, but of Europe as center." Enrique Dussel, "Beyond Eurocentrism: The World System and the Limits of Modernity," in Fredric Jameson and Masao Miyoshi, eds., *The Cultures of Globalization* (Durham: Duke University Press, 1998), pp. 3–31; quotation p. 4.
4. Two interdisciplinary texts served as models for us throughout the writing of this book: Marx's *Capital* and Deleuze and Guattari's *A Thousand Plateaus*.
5. Ours is certainly not the only work that prepares the terrain for the analysis and critique of Empire. Although they do not use the term "Empire," we see the work of numerous authors oriented in this direction; they include Fredric Jameson, David Harvey, Arjun Appadurai, Gayatri Spivak, Edward Said, Giovanni Arrighi, and Arif Dirlik, to name only some of the best known.

1.1 WORLD ORDER

1. Already in 1974 Franz Schurmann highlighted the tendency toward a global order in *The Logic of World Power: An Inquiry into the Origins, Currents, and Contradictions of World Politics* (New York: Pantheon, 1974).

2. On the permutations of European pacts for international peace, see Leo Gross, "The Peace of Westphalia, 1648–1948," *American Journal of International Law,* 42, no. 1 (1948), 20–41.
3. Danilo Zolo, *Cosmopolis: Prospects for World Government,* trans. David McKie (Cambridge: Polity Press, 1997), is the one who expresses most clearly the hypothesis that the paradigm of the project of the new world order should be located back in the Peace of Vienna. We follow his analysis in many respects. See also Richard Falk, "The Interplay of Westphalia and Charter Conception of International Legal Order," in C. A. Blach and Richard Falk, eds., *The Future of International Legal Order* (Princeton: Princeton University Press, 1969), 1:32–70.
4. Hans Kelsen, *Das Problem des Souveränität und die Theorie des Völkerrechts: Beitrag zu einer Reinen Rechtslehre* (Tübingen: Mohr, 1920), p. 205. See also *Principles of International Law,* (New York: Rinehart, 1952), p. 586.
5. Kelsen, *Das Problem des Souveränität,* p. 319.
6. See Hans Kelsen, *The Law of the United Nations* (New York: Praeger, 1950).
7. On the legal history of the United Nations, see Alf Ross, *United Nations: Peace and Progress* (Totowa, N.J.: Bedminster Press, 1966); Benedetto Conforti, *The Law and Practice of the United Nations* (Boston: Kluwer Law International, 1996); Richard Falk, Samuel S. Kim, and Saul H. Mendlovitz, eds., *The United Nations and a Just World Order* (Boulder: Westview Press, 1991).
8. On the concept of "domestic analogy" both from the genealogical point of view and from that of international juridical politics, see Hedley Bull, *The Anarchical Society* (London: Macmillan, 1977); and above all Hidemi Suganami, *The Domestic Analogy and World Order Proposals* (Cambridge: Cambridge University Press, 1989). For a critical and realistic perspective against conceptions of a "domestic analogy," see James N. Rosenau, *Turbulence in World Politics: A Theory of Change and Continuity* (Princeton: Princeton University Press, 1990).
9. See Norberto Bobbio, *Il problema della guerra e le vie della pace* (Bologna: Il Mulino, 1984).
10. For Norberto Bobbio's position on these arguments, see primarily *Il terzo assente* (Turin: Edizioni Sonda, 1989). In general, however, on recent lines of internationalist thought and on the alternative between statist and cosmopolitan approaches, see Zolo, *Cosmopolis.*
11. See the work of Richard Falk, primarily *A Study of Future Worlds* (New York: Free Press, 1975); *The Promise of World Order* (Philadelphia: Temple University Press, 1987); and *Explorations at the Edge of Time* (Philadelphia:

Temple University Press, 1992). The origin of Falk's discourse and its idealist reformist line might well be traced back to the famous initial propositions posed by Grenville Clark and Louis B. Sohn, *World Peace through World Law* (Cambridge, Mass.: Harvard University Press, 1958).

12. In Section 2.4 we will discuss briefly the work of authors who challenge the traditional field of international relations from a postmodernist perspective.
13. "Capitalism was from the beginning an affair of the world-economy . . . It is a misreading of the situation to claim that it is only in the twentieth century that capitalism has become 'world-wide.'" Immanuel Wallerstein, *The Capitalist World-Economy* (Cambridge: Cambridge University Press, 1979), p. 19. The most complete reference on this point is Immanuel Wallerstein, *The Modern World System,* 3 vols. (New York: Academic Press, 1974–1988). See also Giovanni Arrighi, *The Long Twentieth Century* (London: Verso, 1995).
14. See, for example, Samir Amin, *Empire of Chaos* (New York: Monthly Review Press, 1992).
15. For our analyses of the Roman Empire we have relied on some of the classic texts, such as Gaetano de Sanctis, *Storia dei Romani,* 4 vols. (Turin: Bocca, 1907–1923); Hermann Dessau, *Geschichte der römanischen Keiserzeit,* 2 vols. (Berlin: Weidmann, 1924–1930); Michael Rostovzeff, *Social and Economic History of the Roman Empire,* 2 vols. (Oxford: Clarendon Press, 1926); Pietro de Francisci, *Genesi e struttura del principato augusteo* (Rome: Sampaolesi, 1940); and Santo Mazzarino, *Fra Oriente ed Occidente* (Florence: La Nuova Italia, 1947).
16. See Johannes Adam Hartung, *Die Lehre von der Weltherrschaft im Mittelalter* (Halle, 1909); Heinrich Dannenbauer, ed., *Das Reich: Idee und Gestalt* (Stuttgart: Cotta, 1940); Georges de Lagarde, "La conception médiéval de l'ordre en face de l'umanisme, de la Renaissance et de la Reforme," in Congresso internazionale di studi umanistici, *Umanesimo e scienza politica* (Milan: Marzorati, 1951); and Santo Mazzarino, *The End of the Ancient World,* trans. George Holmes (New York: Knopf, 1966).
17. See Michael Walzer, *Just and Unjust Wars,* 2nd ed. (New York: Basic Books, 1992). The renewal of just war theory in the 1990s is demonstrated by the essays in Jean Bethke Elshtain, ed., *Just War Theory* (Oxford: Basil Blackwell, 1992).
18. One should distinguish here between *jus ad bellum* (the right to make war) and *jus in bello* (law in war), or really the rules of the correct conduct of war. See Walzer, *Just and Unjust Wars,* pp. 61–63 and 90.
19. On the Gulf War and justice, see Norberto Bobbio, *Una guerra giusta? Sul conflitto del Golfo* (Venice: Marsilio, 1991); Ramsey Clark, *The Fire*

This Time: U.S. War Crimes in the Gulf (New York: Thunder's Mouth Press, 1992); Jürgen Habermas, *The Past as Future,* trans. Max Pensky (Lincoln: University of Nebraska Press, 1994); and Jean Bethke Elshtain, ed., *But Was It Just? Reflections on the Morality of the Persian Gulf War* (New York: Doubleday, 1992).

20. For the influence of Niklas Luhmann's systematism on international juridical theory, see the essays by Gunther Teubner in Gunther Teubner and Alberto Febbrajo, eds., *State, Law, and Economy as Autopoietic Systems* (Milan: Giuffrè, 1992). An adaptation of John Rawls's ethico-juridical theories was attempted by Charles R. Beitz in *Political Theory and International Relations* (Princeton: Princeton University Press, 1979).
21. This concept was introduced and articulated in James Rosenau, "Governance, Order, and Change in World Politics," in James Rosenau and Ernst-Otto Czempiel, *Governance without Government* (Cambridge: Cambridge University Press, 1992).
22. At one extreme, see the set of essays assembled in V. Rittenberger, ed., *Beyond Anarchy: International Cooperation and Regimes* (Oxford: Oxford University Press, 1994).
23. See Hans Kelsen, *Peace through Law* (Chapel Hill: University of North Carolina Press, 1944).
24. On Machiavelli's reading of the Roman Empire, see Antonio Negri, *Il potere costituente* (Milan: Sugarco, 1992), pp. 75–96; in English, *Insurgencies: Constituent Power and the Modern State,* trans. Maurizia Boscagli (Minneapolis: University of Minnesota Press, 1999).
25. For a reading of the juridical passage from modernity to postmodernity, see Michael Hardt and Antonio Negri, *Labor of Dionysus: A Critique of the State-Form* (Minneapolis: University of Minnesota Press, 1994), chaps. 6 and 7.
26. It is strange how in this internationalist debate almost the only work of Carl Schmitt that is taken up is *Der Nomos der Erde im Völkerrecht des Jus Publicum Europaeum* (Cologne: Greven, 1950), when really precisely in this context his more important work is *Verfassungslehre,* 8th ed. (Berlin: Duncker & Humblot, 1993), and his positions developed around the definition of the concept of the political and the production of right.
27. In order to get a good idea of this process it may be enough to read together the disciplinary classics of international law and international economics, linking their observations and prescriptions, which emerge from different disciplinary formations but share a certain neorealism, or really a realism in the Hobbesian sense. See, for example, Kenneth Neal Waltz, *Theory of International Politics* (New York: Random House, 1979);

and Robert Gilpin, *The Political Economy of International Relations* (Princeton: Princeton University Press, 1987).

28. In order to get an initial idea of the vast and often confused literature on this topic, see Gene Lyons and Michael Mastanduno, eds., *Beyond Westphalia? State Sovereignty and International Intervention* (Baltimore: Johns Hopkins University Press, 1995); Arnold Kanter and Linton Brooks, eds., *U.S. Intervention Policy for the Post–Cold War World* (New York: Norton, 1994); Mario Bettati, *Le droit d'ingérence* (Paris: Odile Jacob, 1995); and Maurice Bernard, *La fin de l'ordre militaire* (Paris: Presses de Sciences Politiques, 1995).
29. On the ethics of international relations, in addition to the propositions of Michael Walzer and Charles Beitz already cited, see also Stanley Hoffmann, *Duties beyond Borders* (Syracuse: Syracuse University Press, 1981); and Terry Nardin and David R. Mapel, eds., *Traditions of International Ethics* (Cambridge: Cambridge University Press, 1992).
30. We are refering here to the two classic texts: Montesquieu, *Considerations on the Causes of the Greatness of the Romans and Their Decline,* trans. David Lowenthal (New York: Free Press, 1965); and Edward Gibbon, *The History of the Decline and Fall of the Roman Empire,* 3 vols. (London: Penguin, 1994).
31. As Jean Ehrard has amply shown, the thesis that the decline of Rome began with Caesar was continually reproposed throughout the historiography of the age of Enlightenment. See Jean Ehrard, *La politique de Montesquieu* (Paris: A. Colin, 1965).
32. The principle of the corruption of political regimes was already implicit in the theory of the forms of government as it was formulated in the Sophistic period, which was later codified by Plato and Aristotle. The principle of "political" corruption was later translated into a principle of historical development through theories that grasped the ethical schemes of the forms of government as cyclical temporal developments. Of all the proponents of different theoretical tendencies who have embarked on this endeavor (and the Stoics are certainly fundamental in this regard), Polybius is the one who really described the model in its definitive form, celebrating the creative function of corruption.

1.2 BIOPOLITICAL PRODUCTION

1. The passage from disciplinary society to the society of control is not articulated explicitly by Foucault but remains implicit in his work. We follow the excellent commentaries of Gilles Deleuze in this interpretation. See Gilles Deleuze, *Foucault* (Paris: Minuit, 1986); and "Post-scriptum

sur les sociétés de contrôle," in *Pourparlers* (Paris: Minuit, 1990). See also Michael Hardt, "The Withering of Civil Society," *Social Text,* no. 45 (Winter 1995), 27–44.

2. See primarily Michel Foucault, *The History of Sexuality,* trans. Robert Hurley (New York: Vintage, 1978), 1:135–145. For other treatments of the concept of biopolitics in Foucualt's opus, see "The Politics of Health in the Eighteenth Century," in *Power/Knowledge,* ed. Colin Gordon (New York: Pantheon, 1980), pp. 166–182; "La naissance de la médecine sociale," in *Dits et écrits* (Paris: Gallimard, 1994), 3:207–228, particularly p. 210; and "Naissance de la biopolitique," in *Dits et écrits,* 3:818–825. For examples of work by other authors following Foucault's notion of biopolitics, see Hubert Dreyfus and Paul Rabinow, eds., *Michel Foucault: Beyond Structuralism and Hermeneutics* (Chicago: University of Chicago Press, 1992), pp. 133–142; and Jacques Donzelot, *The Policing of Families,* trans. Robert Hurley (New York: Pantheon, 1979).
3. Michel Foucault, "Les mailles du pouvoir," in *Dits et écrits* (Paris: Gallimard, 1994), 4:182–201; quotation p. 194.
4. Many thinkers have followed Foucault along these lines and successfully problematized the welfare state. See primarily Jacques Donzelot, *L'invention du social* (Paris: Fayard, 1984); and François Ewald, *L'état providence* (Paris: Seuil, 1986).
5. See Karl Marx, "Results of the Immediate Process of Production," trans. Rodney Livingstone, published as the appendix to *Capital,* trans. Ben Fowkes (New York: Vintage, 1976), 1:948–1084. See also Antonio Negri, *Marx beyond Marx,* trans. Harry Cleaver, Michael Ryan, and Maurizio Viano (New York: Autonomedia, 1991).
6. See Max Horkheimer and Theodor Adorno, *The Dialectic of Enlightenment,* trans. John Cumming (New York: Herder and Herder, 1972).
7. See Gilles Deleuze and Félix Guattari, *A Thousand Plateaus,* trans. Brian Massumi (Minneapolis: University of Minnesota Press, 1987).
8. See, for example, Peter Dews, *Logics of Disintegration: Poststructuralist Thought and the Claims of Critical Theory* (London: Verso, 1987), chaps. 6 and 7. When one adopts this definition of power and the crises that traverse it, Foucault's discourse (and even more so that of Deleuze and Guattari) presents a powerful theoretical framework for critiquing the welfare state. For analyses that are more or less in line with this discourse, see Claus Offe, *Disorganized Capitalism: Contemporary Transformations of Work and Politics* (Cambridge, Mass.: MIT Press, 1985); Antonio Negri, *Revolution Retrieved: Selected Writings* (London: Red Notes, 1988); and the essays by Antonio Negri included in Michael Hardt and Antonio

Negri, *Labor of Dionysus* (Minneapolis: University of Minnesota Press, 1994), pp. 23–213.

9. The notions of "totalitarianism" that were constructed during the period of the cold war proved to be useful instruments for propaganda but completely inadequate analytical tools, leading most often to pernicious inquisitional methods and damaging moral arguments. The numerous shelves of our libraries that are filled with analyses of totalitarianism should today be regarded only with shame and could be thrown away with no hesitation. For a brief sample of the literature on totalitarianism from the most coherent to the most absurd, see Hannah Arendt, *The Origins of Totalitarianism* (New York: Harcourt, Brace, 1951); and Jeanne Kirkpatrick, *Dictatorships and Double Standards* (New York: Simon and Schuster, 1982). We will return to the concept of totalitarianism in more detail in Section 2.2.
10. We are referring here to the thematics of *Mobilmachtung* that were developed in the Germanic world primarily in the 1920s and 1930s, more or less from Ernst Jünger to Carl Schmitt. In French culture, too, such positions emerged in the 1930s, and the polemics around them have still not died down. The figure of Georges Bataille is at the center of this discussion. Along different lines, on "general mobilization" as a paradigm of the constitution of collective labor power in Fordist capitalism, see Jean Paul de Gaudemar, *La mobilisation générale* (Paris: Maspero, 1978).
11. One could trace a very interesting line of discussions that effectively develop the Foucauldian interpretation of biopower from Jacques Derrida's reading of Walter Benjamin's "Critique of Violence" ("Force of Law," in Drucilla Cornell, Michel Rosenfeld, and David Gray Carlson, eds., *Deconstruction and the Possibility of Justice* [New York: Routledge, 1992], pp. 3–67) to Giorgio Agamben's more recent and more stimulating contribution, *Homo sacer: il potere sovrano e la nuda vita* (Turin: Einaudi, 1995). It seems fundamental to us, however, that all of these discussions be brought back to the question of the productive dimensions of "bios," identifying in other words the materialist dimension of the concept beyond any conception that is purely naturalistic (life as "zoè") or simply anthropological (as Agamben in particular has a tendency to do, making the concept in effect indifferent).
12. Michel Foucault, "La naissance de la médecine sociale," in *Dits et écrits* (Paris: Gallimard, 1994), 3:210.
13. See Henri Lefebvre, *L'ideologie structuraliste* (Paris: Anthropos, 1971); Gilles Deleuze, "A quoi reconnait-on le structuralisme?" in François Châtelet, ed., *Histoire de la philosophie,* vol. 8 (Paris: Hachette, 1972), pp. 299–335;

and Fredric Jameson, *The Prison-House of Language* (Princeton: Princeton University Press, 1972).

14. When Deleuze formulates his methodological differences with Foucault in a private letter written in 1977, the primary point of disagreement comes down precisely to just such a question of production. Deleuze prefers the term "desire" to Foucault's "pleasure," he explains, because desire grasps the real and active dynamic of the production of social reality whereas pleasure is merely inert and reactive: "Pleasure interrupts the positivity of desire and the constitution of its plane of immanence." See Gilles Deleuze, "Désir et plaisir," *Magazine Littéraire,* no. 325 (October 1994), 59–65; quotation p. 64.
15. Félix Guattari has perhaps developed the extreme consequences of this type of social critique, while carefully avoiding falling into the anti–"grand narrative" style of postmodernist argument, in his *Chaosmosis,* trans. Paul Bains and Julian Pefanis (Sydney: Power Publications, 1995). From a metaphysical point of view, among the followers of Nietzsche, we find roughly analogous positions expressed in Massimo Cacciari, *DRAN: méridiens de la décision dans la pensée contemporaine* (Paris: L'Éclat, 1991).
16. In English, see primarily the essays in Paolo Virno and Michael Hardt, eds., *Radical Thought in Italy* (Minneapolis: University of Minnesota Press, 1996). See also Christian Marazzi, *Il posto dei calzini: la svolta linguistica dell'economia e i suoi effetti nella politica* (Bellinzona: Edizioni Casagrande); and numerous issues of the French journal *Futur antérieur,* particularly nos. 10 (1992) and 35–36 (1996). For an analysis that appropriates central elements of this project but ultimately fails to capture its power, see André Gorz, *Misère du présent, richesse du possible* (Paris: Galilée, 1997).
17. The framework on which this line of inquiry is built is both its great wealth and its real limitation. The analysis must in effect be carried beyond the constraints of the "workerist" (*operaista*) analysis of capitalist development and the state-form. One of its limitations, for example, is highlighted by Gayatri Spivak, *In Other Worlds: Essays in Cultural Politics* (New York: Routledge, 1988), p. 162, who insists on the fact that the conception of value in this line of Marxist analysis may function in the dominant countries (including in the context of certain streams of feminist theory) but completely misses the mark in the context of the subordinated regions of the globe. Spivak's questioning is certainly extremely important for the problematic we are developing in this study. In fact, from a methodological point of view, we would say that the most profound and solid problematic complex that has yet been elaborated for the critique of biopolitics is found in feminist theory, particularly Marxist and socialist

feminist theories that focus on women's work, affective labor, and the production of biopower. This presents the framework perhaps best suited to renew the methodology of the European "workerist" schools.

18. The theories of the "turbulence" of the international order, and even more of the new world order, which we cited earlier (see primarily the work of J. G. Ruggie), generally avoid in their explanation of the causes of this turbulence any reference to the contradictory character of capitalist relations. Social turbulence is considered merely a consequence of the international dynamics among state actors in such a way that turbulence can be normalized within the strict disciplinary limits of international relations. Social and class struggles are effectively hidden by the method of analysis itself. From this perspective, then, the "productive bios" cannot really be understood. The same is more or less the case for the authors of the world-systems perspective, who focus primarily on the cycles of the system and systemic crises (see the works of Wallerstein and Arrighi cited earlier). Theirs is in effect a world (and a history) without subjectivity. What they miss is the function of the productive bios, or really the fact that capital is not a thing but a social relationship, an antagonistic relationship, one side of which is animated by the productive life of the multitude.
19. Giovanni Arrighi, *The Long Twentieth Century* (London: Verso, 1995), for example, claims such a continuity in the role of capitalist corporations. For an excellent contrasting view in terms of periodization and methodological approach, see Luciano Ferrari Bravo, "Introduzione: vecchie e nuove questioni nella teoria dell'imperialismo," in Luciano Ferrari Bravo, ed., *Imperialismo e classe operaia multinazionale* (Milan: Feltrinelli, 1975), pp. 7–70.
20. See, from the perspective of political analysis, Paul Kennedy, *Preparing for the Twenty-first Century* (New York: Random House, 1993); and from the perspective of economic topography and socialist critique, David Harvey, *The Condition of Postmodernity* (Oxford: Blackwell, 1989).
21. Marx, *Capital,* 1:742.
22. On this point the bibliography we could cite is seemingly endless. In effect, theories of advertising and consumption have been integrated (just in time) into the theories of production, to the point where we now have ideologies of "attention" posed as economic value! In any case, for a selection of the numerous works that touch on this field, one would do well to see Susan Strasser, *Satisfaction Guaranteed: The Making of the American Mass Market* (New York: Pantheon, 1989); Gary Cross, *Time and Money: The Making of Consumer Culture* (New York: Routledge,

1993); and, for a more interesting analysis from another perspective, The Project on Disney, *Inside the Mouse* (Durham: Duke University Press, 1995). The production of the producer, however, is not only the production of the consumer. It also involves the production of hierarchies, mechanisms of inclusion and exclusion, and so forth. It involves finally the production of crises. From this point of view, see Jeremy Rifkin, *The End of Work: The Decline of Global Labor Force and the Dawn of the Post-market Era* (New York: Putnam, 1995); and Stanley Aronowitz and William DiFazio, *The Jobless Future* (Minneapolis: University of Minnesota Press, 1994).

23. We are indebted to Deleuze and Guattari and their *A Thousand Plateaus* for the most fully elaborated phenomenological description of this industrial-monetary-world-nature, which constitutes the first level of the world order.
24. See Edward Comor, ed., *The Global Political Economy of Communication* (London: Macmillan, 1994).
25. See Stephen Bradley, ed., *Globalization, Technologies, and Competition: The Fusion of Computers and Telecommunications in the 90s* (Cambridge, Mass.: Harvard Business School Press, 1993); and Simon Serfaty, *The Media and Foreign Policy* (London: Macmillan, 1990).
26. See Jürgen Habermas, *Theory of Communicative Action,* trans. Thomas McCarthy (Boston: Beacon Press, 1984). We discuss this relationship between communication and production in more detail in Section 3.4.
27. See Hardt and Negri, *Labor of Dionysus,* chaps. 6 and 7.
28. Despite the extremism of the authors presented in Martin Albrow and Elizabeth King, eds., *Globalization, Knowledge, and Society* (London: Sage, 1990), and the relative moderation of Bryan S. Turner, *Theories of Modernity and Postmodernity* (London: Sage, 1990), and Mike Featherstone, ed., *Global Culture, Nationalism, Globalization, and Modernity* (London: Sage, 1991), the differences among their various positions are really relatively minor. We should always keep in mind that the image of a "global civil society" is born not only in the minds of certain postmodernist philosophers and among certain followers of Habermas (such as Jean Cohen and Andrew Arato), but also and more importantly in the Lockean tradition of international relations. This latter group includes such important theorists as Richard Falk, David Held, Anthony Giddens, and (in certain respects) Danilo Zolo. On the concept of civil society in the global context, see Michael Walzer, ed., *Toward a Global Civil Society* (Providence: Berghahn Books, 1995).
29. With the iconoclastic irony of Jean Baudrillard's more recent writings such as *The Gulf War Did Not Take Place,* trans. Paul Patton (Bloomington:

Indiana University Press, 1995), a certain vein of French postmodernism has gone back to a properly surrealist framework.

30. There is an uninterrupted continuity from the late cold war notions of "democracy enforcing" and "democratic transition" to the imperial theories of "peace enforcing." We have already highlighted the fact that many moral philosophers supported the Gulf War as a just cause, whereas juridical theorists, following the important lead of Richard Falk, were generally opposed. See, for example, Richard Falk, "Twisting the U.N. Charter to U.S. Ends," in Hamid Mowlana, George Gerbner, and Herbert Schiller, eds., *Triumph of the Image: The Media's War in the Persian Gulf* (Boulder: Westview Press, 1992), pp. 175–190. See also the discussion of the Gulf War in Danilo Zolo, *Cosmopolis: Prospects for World Government,* trans. David McKie (Cambridge: Polity Press, 1997).

31. For a representative example, see Richard Falk, *Positive Prescriptions for the Future,* World Order Studies Program occasional paper no. 20 (Princeton: Center for International Studies, 1991). To see how NGOs are integrated into this more or less Lockean framework of "global constitutionalism," one should refer to the public declarations of Antonio Cassese, president of the United Nations Criminal Court in Amsterdam, in addition to his books, *International Law in a Divided World* (Oxford: Clarendon Press, 1986), and *Human Rights in a Changing World* (Philadelphia: Temple University Press, 1990).

32. Even the proposals to reform the United Nations proceed more or less along these lines. For a good bibliography of such works, see Joseph Preston Baratta, *Strengthening the United Nations: A Bibliography on U.N. Reform and World Federalism* (New York: Greenwood, 1987).

33. This is the line that is promoted in some of the strategic documents published by the U.S. military agencies. According to the present Pentagon doctrine, the project of the enlargement of market democracy should be supported by both adequate microstrategies that are based on (both pragmatic and systemic) zones of application and the continual identification of critical points and fissures in the antagonistic strong cultural blocs that would lead toward their dissolution. In this regard, see the work of Maurice Rounai of the Strategic Institute in Paris. See also the works on U.S. interventionism cited in Section 1.1, note 28.

34. One should refer, once again, to the work of Richard Falk and Antonio Cassese. We should emphasize, in particular, how a "weak" conception of the exercise of judicial functions by the U.N. Court of Justice has gradually, often under the influence of Left political forces, been transformed into a "strong" conception. In other words, there is a passage

from the demand that the Court of Justice be invested with the functions of judicial sanction that come under the authority of the U.N. structure to the demand that the court play a direct and active role in the decisions of the U.N. and its organs regarding norms of parity and material justice among states, to the point of carrying out direct intervention in the name of human rights.

35. See Max Weber, *Economy and Society,* trans. Guenther Roth and Claus Wittich (Berkeley: University of California Press, 1968), vol. 1, chap. 3, sec. 2, "The Three Pure Types of Authority," pp. 215–216.

1.3 ALTERNATIVES WITHIN EMPIRE

1. We mean to "flirt with Hegel" here the way Marx described in the famous postscript to volume 1 of *Capital* (trans. Ben Fowkes [New York: Vintage, 1976]) of January 24, 1873 (pp. 102–103). As they did to Marx, Hegel's terms seem useful to us to frame the argument, but quickly we will run up against the real limit of their utility.
2. This presentation is admittedly simplified, and many studies present much more sophisticated discussions of place. It seems to us, however, that these political analyses always come back to a notion of "defending" or "preserving" the bounded local identity or territory. Doreen Massey argues explicitly for a politics of place in which place is conceived not as bounded but as open and porous to flows beyond, in *Space, Place, and Gender* (Minneapolis: University of Minnesota Press, 1994), in particular p. 5. We would contend, however, that a notion of place that has no boundaries empties the concept completely of its content. For an excellent review of the literature and an alternative conception of place, see Arif Dirlik, "Place-based Imagination: Globalism and the Politics of Place," unpublished manuscript.
3. We will return to the concept of the nation at greater length in Section 2.2.
4. "I view location as a fundamental material attribute of human activity but recognize that location is socially produced." David Harvey, *The Limits of Capital* (Chicago: University of Chicago Press, 1984), p. 374. Arjun Appadurai also discusses "the production of locality" in a way consistent with Harvey and with our argument in *Modernity at Large: Cultural Dimensions of Globalization* (Minneapolis: University of Minnesota Press, 1996), pp. 178–199.
5. Erich Auerbach, *Mimesis: The Representation of Reality in Western Literature,* trans. Willard Trask (Princeton: Princeton University Press, 1953).
6. This methodological connection between critique and construction that rests firmly on the basis of a collective subject was articulated well in

Marx's own historical writings and developed by various traditions of heterodox Marxist historiography in the twentieth century, such as the work of E. P. Thompson, the Italian workerist writers, and the South Asian subaltern historians.

7. See, for example, Guy Debord's *Society of the Spectacle,* trans. Donald Nicholson-Smith (New York: Zone Books, 1994), which is perhaps the best articulation, in its own delirious way, of the contemporary consciousness of the triumph of capital.
8. For a good example of this deconstructionist method that demonstrates its virtues and its limitations, see the work of Gayatri Spivak, in particular her introduction to Ranajit Guha and Gayatri Spivak, eds., *Selected Subaltern Studies* (New York: Oxford University Press, 1988), pp. 3–32.
9. See Arif Dirlik, "Mao Zedong and 'Chinese Marxism,'" in Saree Makdisi, Cesare Casarino, and Rebecca Karl, eds., *Marxism beyond Marxism* (New York: Routledge, 1996), pp. 119–148. See also Arif Dirlik, "Modernism and Antimodernism in Mao Zedong's Marxism," in Arif Dirlik, Paul Healy, and Nick Knight, eds., *Critical Perspectives on Mao Zedong's Thought* (Atlantic Heights, N.J.: Humanities Press, 1997), pp. 59–83.
10. On the tactical ambiguities of the "national politics" of the socialist and communist parties, see primarily the work of the Austro-Marxists, such as Otto Bauer's *Die Nationalitätenfrage und die Sozialdomocratie* (Vienna: Wiener Volksbuchhandlung, 1924); and Stalin's influential "Marxism and the National Question," in *Marxism and the National and Colonial Question* (New York: International Publishers, 1935), pp. 3–61. We will return to these authors in Section 2.2. For a special and particularly interesting case, see Enzo Traverso, *Les marxistes et la question juive* (Paris: La Brèche, 1990).
11. On the cycle of anti-imperialist struggles in the late nineteenth and early twentieth centuries (seen from the Chinese perspective), see Rebecca Karl, *Staging the World: China and the Non-West at the Turn of the Twentieth Century* (Durham: Duke University Press, forthcoming).
12. On the hypothesis that struggles precede and prefigure capitalist development and restructuring, see Antonio Negri, *Revolution Retrieved* (London: Red Notes, 1988).
13. This notion of the proletariat might thus be understood in Marx's own terms as the personification of a strictly economic category, that is, the subject of labor under capital. As we redefine the very concept of labor and extend the range of activities understood under it (as we have done elsewhere and will continue to do in this book), the traditional distinction

between the economic and the cultural breaks down. Even in Marx's most economistic formulations, however, proletariat must be understood really as a properly *political* category. See Michael Hardt and Antonio Negri, *Labor of Dionysus* (Minneapolis: University of Minnesota Press, 1994), pp. 3–21; and Antonio Negri, "Twenty Theses of Marx," in Saree Makdisi, Cesare Casarino, and Rebecca Karl, eds., *Marxism beyond Marxism* (New York: Routledge, 1996), pp. 149–180.

14. See Michael Hardt, "Los Angeles Novos," *Futur antérieur,* no. 12/13 (1991), 12–26.
15. See Luis Gomez, ed., *Mexique: du Chiapas à la crise financière,* Supplement, *Futur antérieur* (1996).
16. See primarily *Futur antérieur,* no. 33/34, *Tous ensemble! Réflections sur les luttes de novembre-décembre* (1996). See also Raghu Krishnan, "December 1995: The First Revolt against Globalization," *Monthly Review,* 48, no. 1 (May 1996), 1–22.
17. Karl Marx, *The Eighteenth Brumaire of Louis Bonaparte* (New York: International Publishers, 1963), p. 121.
18. See Gilles Deleuze, "Postscript on Control Societies," in *Negatiations,* trans. Martin Joughin (New York: Columbia University Press, 1995), pp. 177–182.
19. In opposition to the theories of the "weakest link," which not only were the heart of the tactics of the Third International but also were largely adopted by the anti-imperialist tradition as a whole, the Italian *operaismo* movement of the 1960s and 1970s proposed a theory of the "strongest link." For the fundamental theoretical thesis, see Mario Tronti, *Operai e capitale* (Turin: Einaudi, 1966), esp. pp. 89–95.
20. One can find ample and continuous documentation of these techniques of disinformation and silencing in publications ranging from *Le Monde Diplomatique* to *Z Magazine* and the *Covert Action Bulletin.* Noam Chomsky has tirelessly worked to unveil and counter such disinformation in his numerous books and lectures. See, for example, Edward Herman and Noam Chomsky, *Manufacturing Consent: The Political Economy of Mass Media* (New York: Pantheon, 1988). The Gulf War presented an excellent example of the imperial management of communication. See W. Lance Bennett and David L. Paletz, eds., *Taken by Storm: The Media, Public Opinion, and U.S. Foreign Policy in the Gulf War* (Chicago: University of Chicago Press, 1994); and Douglas Kellner, *The Persian Gulf TV War* (Boulder: Westview Press, 1992).
21. This operation of flattening the struggles in the form of an inverted homology with the system is adequately represented by the (in other

respects quite impressive and important) work of Immanuel Wallerstein and the world systems school. See, for example, Giovanni Arrighi, Terence Hopkins, and Immanuel Wallerstein, *Antisystemic Movements* (London: Verso, 1989).

22. Keeping in mind the limitations we mentioned earlier, one should refer here to the work of Félix Guattari, particularly the writings of his final period such as *Chaosmosis,* trans. Paul Bains and Julian Pefanis (Sydney: Power Publications, 1995).

POLITICAL MANIFESTO

1. Louis Althusser, "Machiavel et nous," in *Écrits philosophiques et politiques,* vol. 2, ed. François Matheron (Paris: Stock/IMEC, 1995), pp. 39–168; subsequently cited in text.
2. See Baruch Spinoza, *Theologico-Political Treatise,* vol. 1 of *Chief Works,* trans. R. H. M. Elwes (New York: Dover, 1951).

2.1 TWO EUROPES, TWO MODERNITIES

1. Robert Musil, *The Man without Qualities,* trans. Sophie Wilkins (New York: Knopf, 1995), 2:1106.
2. Johannes Duns Scotus, *Opus Oxoniense,* Book IV, Distinctio XIII, Quaestio I, in *Opera Omnia,* vol. 8 (Hildesheim: Georg Olms Verlagsbuchhandlung, 1969), p. 807.
3. Dante Alighieri, *De Monarchia,* ed. Louis Bertalot (Frankfurt: Friedrichsdorf, 1918), Book I, chap. 4, p. 14.
4. Nicholas of Cusa, "Complementum theologicum," in *Opera,* vol. 2 (Frankfurt: Minerva, 1962), chap. 2, fol. 93b (facsimile reproduction of edition edited by Jacques Le Fevre [Paris: 1514]).
5. Giovanni Pico della Mirandola, *Of Being and Unity,* trans. Victor Hamm (Milwaukee: Marquette Univesity Press, 1943), pp. 21–22.
6. Carolus Bovillus (Charles de Bovelles), *Il libro del sapiente,* ed. Eugenio Garin (Turin: Einaudi, 1987), chap. 22, p. 73.
7. Francis Bacon, *Works,* ed. James Spalding, Robert Ellis, and Donald Heath (London: Longman and Co., 1857), 1:129–130.
8. Galileo Galilei, *Opere* (Florence: G. Berbèra Editore, 1965), 7:128–129.
9. William of Ockham, *A Short Discourse on the Tyrannical Government,* trans. John Kilcullen (Cambridge: Cambridge University Press, 1992), Book III, chap. 16, p. 104. The translator renders the phrase "multitudo fidelium" as "congregation of the faithful."
10. See Marsilius of Padua, *Defensor Pacis* (Cambridge: Cambridge University Press, 1928).

11. This revolutionary aspect of the origins of modernity can be read in its clearest and most synthetic form in the work of Spinoza. See Antonio Negri, *The Savage Anomaly,* trans. Michael Hardt (Minneapolis: University of Minnesota Press, 1991).
12. The various nineteenth- and twentieth-century philosophical frameworks of negative thought, from Nietzsche to Heidegger and Adorno, are fundamentally right to foresee the end of modern metaphysics and to link modernity and crisis. What these authors generally do not recognize, however, is that there are two modernities at play here and that the crisis is a direct result of their conflict. For this reason they are unable to see the alternatives within modernity that extend beyond the limits of modern metaphysics. On negative thought and crisis, see Massimo Cacciari, *Krisis: saggio sulla crisis del pensiero negativo da Nietzsche a Wittgenstein* (Milan: Feltrinelli, 1976).
13. On these passages in European modernity, see Ernst Bloch, *The Principle of Hope,* 3 vols., trans. Neville Plaice, Stephen Plaice, and Paul Knight (Cambridge, Mass.: MIT Press, 1986); and (in a completely different intellectual and hermeneutic context) Reinhart Koselleck, *Critique and Crisis: Enlightenment and the Pathogenesis of Modern Society* (Cambridge, Mass.: MIT Press, 1988).
14. Samir Amin, *Eurocentrism,* trans. Russell Moore (New York: Monthly Review Press, 1989), pp. 72–73.
15. Baruch Spinoza, *Ethics,* in *The Collected Works of Spinoza,* ed. Edwin Curley, vol. 1 (Princeton: Princeton University Press, 1985), Part IV, Proposition 67, p. 584.
16. Ibid., Part V, Proposition 37, p. 613.
17. Our discussion draws on the work of Ernst Cassirer, *The Philosophy of the Enlightenment,* trans. Fritz C. A. Koelln and James P. Pettegrove (Princeton: Princeton University Press, 1951); Max Horkheimer and Theodor Adorno, *Dialectic of Enlightenment,* trans. John Cumming (New York: Continuum, 1972); and Michel Foucault, "What Is Enlightenment?" in *Ethics: Subjectivity and Truth,* vol. 1 of *The Essential Works of Foucault 1954–1984,* ed. Paul Rabinow (New York: New Press, 1997), pp. 303–319.
18. See Jacques Chevalier, *Pascal* (Paris: Plon, 1922), p. 265.
19. René Descartes, "Letter to Mersenne (15 April 1630)," in *Philosophical Letters,* ed. Anthony Kenny (Oxford: Blackwell, 1970), p. 11. For the original French version, see *Oeuvres complètes,* ed. Charles Adam and Paul Tannery (Paris: Vrin, 1969), 1:145.
20. See Antonio Negri, *Descartes politico o della ragionevole ideologia* (Milan: Feltrinelli, 1970).

21. For a more recent example that continues along this transcendental line of European complacency, see Massimo Cacciari, *Geo-filosofia dell'Europa* (Milan: Adelphi, 1994).
22. See Arthur Schopenhauer, *The World as Will and Representation,* trans. E. F. J. Payne, 2 vols. (New York: Dover, 1966).
23. Ibid., "Preface to the Second Edition," p. xxi.
24. G. W. F. Hegel, *Elements of the Philosophy of Right,* trans. H. B. Nisbet, ed. Allen Wood (Cambridge: Cambridge University Press, 1991), §258 Addition, p. 279 (translation modified).
25. Thomas Hobbes, *The Elements of Law* (Cambridge: Cambridge University Press, 1928), Part II, Book 10, paragraph 8, p. 150.
26. Jean Bodin, *On Sovereignty: Four Chapters from the Six Books of the Commonwealth,* ed. and trans. Julian Franklin (Cambridge: Cambridge University Press, 1992), p. 23 (from Book I, chap. 8).
27. Jean-Jacques Rousseau, *On the Social Contract,* in *The Collected Writings of Rousseau,* vol. 4, ed. Roger Master and Christopher Kelly (Hanover, N.H.: University Press of New England, 1994), Book I, chap. 6, p. 138.
28. See Bodin, *On Sovereignty.*
29. C. B. Macpherson, *The Political Theory of Possessive Individualism* (Oxford: Oxford University Press, 1962).
30. See Arif Dirlik, *The Postcolonial Aura* (Boulder: Westview Press, 1997).
31. Adam Smith, *The Nature and Causes of the Wealth of Nations* (Oxford: Clarendon Press, 1976), Book IV, chap. ii, paragraph 9, p. 456.
32. Ibid., Book IV, Chapter ix, paragraph 51, p. 687.
33. Hegel, *Elements of the Philosophy of Right,* §261, p. 283.
34. See Michel Foucault, "La 'gouvernementalité,'" in *Dits et écrits* (Paris: Gallimard, 1994), 3:635–657.
35. See our discussion of Foucault's notion of biopower in Section 1.2.
36. See primarily Max Weber, *Economy and Society,* 2 vols., trans. Guenther Roth and Claus Wittich (Berkeley: University of California Press, 1968).
37. Friedrich Nietzsche, *Thus Spake Zarathustra,* trans. Thomas Common (New York: Modern Library, 1967), chap. 35, "The Sublime Ones," p. 111.

2.2 SOVEREIGNTY OF THE NATION-STATE

1. For an extensive analysis of both the common form and the variants throughout Europe, see Perry Anderson, *Lineages of the Absolutist State* (London: New Left Books, 1974).
2. See Ernst Kantorowicz, *The King's Two Bodies: A Study in Medieval Political Theology* (Princeton: Princeton University Press, 1957); and his essay

"Christus-Fiscus," in *Synopsis: Festgabe für Alfred Weber* (Heidelberg: Verlag Lambert Schneider, 1948), pp. 223–235. See also Marc Leopold Bloch, *The Royal Touch: Sacred Monarchy and Scrofula in England and France,* trans. J. E. Anderson (London: Routledge and Kegan Paul, 1972).

3. For an analysis that links the economic transition from feudalism to capitalism to the development of modern European philosophy, see Franz Borkenau, *Der Übergang vom feudalen zum bürgerlichen Weltbild: Studien zur Geschichte der Philosophie der Manufakturperiode* (Paris: Félix Alcan, 1934). For an excellent discussion of the philosophical literature on this problematic, see Alessandro Pandolfi, *Genéalogie et dialectique de la raison mercantiliste* (Paris: L'Harmattan, 1996).
4. See Pierangelo Schiera, *Dall'arte de governo alle scienze dello stato* (Milan, 1968).
5. See Benedict Anderson, *Imagined Communities: Reflections on the Origin and Spread of Nationalism* (London: Verso, 1983).
6. See Étienne Balibar, "The Nation Form: History and Ideology," in Étienne Balibar and Immanuel Wallerstein, *Race, Nation, Class* (London: Verso, 1991), pp. 86–106. See also Slavoj Žižek, "Le rêve du nationalisme expliqué par le rêve du mal radical," *Futur antérieur,* no. 14 (1992), pp. 59–82.
7. The relevant essays by Luxemburg are collected in Rosa Luxemburg, *The National Question,* ed. Horace Davis (New York: Monthly Review Press, 1976). For a careful summary of Luxemburg's positions, see Joan Cocks, "From Politics to Paralysis: Critical Intellectuals Answer the National Question," *Political Theory,* 24, no. 3 (August 1996), 518–537. Lenin was highly critical of Luxemburg's position primarily because she failed to recognize the "progressive" character of the nationalism (even the bourgeois nationalism) of subordinated countries. Lenin thus affirms the right to national self-determination, which is really the right to secession for all. See V. I. Lenin, *The Right of Nations to Self-Determination* (Westport, Conn.: Greenwood Press, 1951), pp. 9–64.
8. Jean Bodin, *Six Books of the Commonwealth,* trans. M. J. Tooley (Oxford: Blackwell, 1955), Book VI, chap. 6, p. 212 (translation modified).
9. For excellent interpretations of Bodin's work that situate it solidly in the dynamics of sixteenth-century Europe, see Julian H. Franklin, *Jean Bodin and the Rise of Absolutist Theory* (Cambridge: Cambridge University Press, 1973); and Gérard Mairet, *Dieu mortel: essai de non-philosophie de l'État* (Paris: PUF, 1987). For a more general view that traces the development of the notion of sovereignty in the long history of European political thought, see Gérard Mairet, *Le principe de souveraineté* (Paris: Gallimard, 1997).

10. See Friedrich Meinecke, *Die Idee der Staatsräson in der neueren Geschichte* (Munich: Oldenbourg, 1924). See also the articles gathered by Wilhelm Dilthey in *Weltanschauung und Analyse des Menschen seit Renaissance und Reformation,* vol. 2 of *Gesammelte Schriften* (Leipzig: Teubner, 1914).
11. With the notable exception of the work by Otto von Gierke, *The Development of Political Theory,* trans. Bernard Freyd (New York: Norton, 1939).
12. See Friedrich Meinecke, *Historicism: The Rise of a New Historical Outlook,* trans. J. E. Anderson (London: Routledge and Kegan Paul, 1972).
13. To recognize the seeds of Hegel's idealism in Vico, see Benedetto Croce, *The Philosophy of Giambattista Vico,* trans. R. G. Collingwood (New York: Russell and Russell, 1964); along with Hayden White, "What Is Living and What Is Dead in Croce's Criticism of Vico," in Giorgio Tagliacozzo, ed., *Giambattista Vico: An International Symposium* (Baltimore, Johns Hopkins University Press, 1969), pp. 379–389. White emphasizes how Croce translated Vico's work into idealist terms, making Vico's philsophy of history into a philosophy of spirit.
14. See Giambattista Vico, *De Universi Juris principio et fine uno,* in *Opere giuridiche* (Florence: Sansoni, 1974), pp. 17–343; and Johann Gottfried Herder, *Reflections on the Philosophy of the History of Mankind,* trans. Frank Manuel (Chicago: University of Chicago Press, 1968).
15. Emmanuel-Joseph Sieyès, in a rather different context, declares the absolute priority of the nation explicitly: "The nation exists prior to everything, it is the origin of everything." See *Qu'est-ce que le Tiers État?* (Geneva: Droz, 1970), p. 180.
16. On the work of Sieyès and the developments of the French Revolution, see Antonio Negri, *Il potere costituente: saggio sulle alternative del moderno* (Milan: Sugarco, 1992), chap. 5, pp. 223–286.
17. For an excellent analysis of the distinction between the multitude and the people, see Paolo Virno, "Virtuosity and Revolution: The Political Theory of Exodus," in Paolo Virno and Michael Hardt, eds., *Radical Thought in Italy* (Minneapolis: University of Minnesota Press, 1996), pp. 189–210.
18. Thomas Hobbes, *De Cive* (New York: Appleton Century-Crofts, 1949), Chapter XII, section 8, p. 135.
19. See Étienne Balibar, "Racism and Nationalism," in Étienne Balibar and Immanuel Wallerstein, *Race, Nation, Class* (London: Verso, 1991), pp. 37–67. We will return to the question of the nation in the colonial context in the next chapter.
20. See, for example, Robert Young, *Colonial Desire: Hybridity in Theory, Culture, and Race* (London: Routledge, 1995).

21. See Sieyès, *Qu'est-ce que le Tiers État.*
22. See Roberto Zapperi's Introduction, ibid., pp. 7–117.
23. Well over one hundred years later Antonio Gramsci's notion of the national-popular was conceived as part of an effort to recuperate precisely this hegemonic class operation in the service of the proletariat. For Gramsci, national-popular is the rubric under which intellectuals would be united with the people, and thus it is a powerful resource for the construction of a popular hegemony. See Antonio Gramsci, *Quaderni del carcere* (Turin: Einaudi, 1977), 3:2113–20. For an excellent critique of Gramsci's notion of the national-popular, see Alberto Asor Rosa, *Scrittori e popolo,* 7th ed. (Rome: Savelli, 1976).
24. Johann Gottlieb Fichte, *Addresses to the German Nation,* trans. R. F. Jones and G. H. Turnbull (Westport Conn.: Greenwood Press, 1979).
25. We should note that the various liberal interpretations of Hegel, from Rudolf Haym to Franz Rosenzweig, only succeeded in recuperating his political thought by focusing on its national aspects. See Rudolf Haym, *Hegel und sein Zeit* (Berlin, 1857); Franz Rosenzweig, *Hegel und der Staat* (Munich, 1920); and Eric Weil, *Hegel et l'État* (Paris: Vrin, 1950). Rosenzweig is the one who best understands the tragedy of the unavoidable connection between the nation and ethicality in Hegel's thought. See Franz Rosenzweig, *The Star of Redemption,* trans. Willaim Hallo (New York: Holt, Rinehart and Winston, 1971); and the excellent interpretation of it, Stéphane Moses, *Système et révélation: la philosophie de Franz Rosenzweig* (Paris: Seuil, 1982).
26. "[Socialists] must therefore unequivocally demand that the Social-Democrats of the *oppressing* countries (of the so-called "great" nations in particular) should recognize and defend the right of the *oppressed* nations to self-determination in the political sense of the word, i.e., the right to political separation." Lenin, *The Right of Nations to Self-Determination,* p. 65.
27. See Malcolm X, "The Ballot or the Bullet," in *Malcolm X Speaks* (New York: Pathfinder, 1989), pp. 23–44. For a discussion of Malcolm X's nationalism, particularly in his efforts to found the Organization of Afro-American Unity during the last year of his life, see William Sales, Jr., *From Civil Rights to Black Liberation: Malcolm X and the Organization of Afro-American Unity* (Boston: South End Press, 1994).
28. Wahneema Lubiano, "Black Nationalism and Black Common Sense: Policing Ourselves and Others," in Wahneema Lubiano, ed., *The House That Race Built* (New York: Vintage, 1997), pp. 232–252; quotation p. 236. See also Wahneema Lubiano, "Standing in for the State: Black

Nationalism and 'Writing' the Black Subject," *Alphabet City,* no. 3 (October 1993), pp. 20–23.

29. The question of "black sovereignty" is precisely the issue at stake in Cedric Robinson's critique of W. E. B. Du Bois's support for Liberia in the 1920s and 1930s. Robinson believes that Du Bois had uncritically supported the forces of modern sovereignty. See Cedric Robinson, "W. E. B. Du Bois and Black Sovereignty," in Sidney Lemelle and Robin Kelley, eds., *Imagining Home: Culture, Class, and Nationalism in the African Diaspora* (London: Verso, 1994), pp. 145–157.
30. Jean Genet, "Interview avec Wischenbart," in *Oeuvres complètes,* vol. 6 (Paris: Gallimard, 1991), p. 282. In general, on Genet's experience with the Black Panthers and the Palestinians, see his final novel, *Prisoner of Love,* trans. Barbara Bray (Hanover, N.H.: Wesleyan University Press, 1992).
31. Benedict Anderson maintains that philosophers have unjustly disdained the concept of nation and that we should view it in a more neutral light. "Part of the difficulty is that one tends unconsciously to hypostatize the existence of Nationalism-with-a-big-N (rather as one might Age-with-a-capital-A) and then classify 'it' as *an* ideology. (Note that if everyone has an age, Age is merely an analytical expression.) It would, I think, make things easier if one treated it as if it belonged with 'kinship' and 'religion,' rather than with 'liberalism' or 'fascism.'" Anderson, *Imagined Communities,* p. 5. Everyone belongs to a nation, as everyone belongs to (or has) an age, a race, a gender, and so forth. The danger here is that Anderson *naturalizes* the nation and our belonging to it. We must on the contrary denaturalize the nation and recognize its historical construction and political effects.
32. On the relationship between class struggle and the two World Wars, see Ernst Nolte, *Der Europäische Bürgerkrieg, 1917–1945* (Frankfurt: Propyläen Verlag, 1987).
33. The primary text to be conidered in the context of Austrian social-democratic theorists is Otto Bauer, *Die Nationalitätenfrage und die Sozialdemokratie* (Vienna: Wiener Volksbuchhandlung, 1924). English translations of exerpts from this book are included in *Austro-Marxism,* trans. Tom Bottomore and Patrick Goode (Oxford: Clarendon Press, 1978).
34. See Joseph Stalin, "Marxism and the National Question," in *Marxism and the National and Colonial Question* (New York: International Publishers, 1935), pp. 3–61.
35. We adopt this term from, but do not follow in the political perspective of, J. L. Talmon, *The Origins of Totalitarian Democracy* (London: Secker and Warburg, 1952).

36. Cited in Roberto Zapperi's Introduction to Sieyès, *Qu'est-ce que le Tiers État,* pp. 7–117; quotation p. 77.

2.3 THE DIALECTICS OF COLONIAL SOVEREIGNTY

1. "The darker side of the Renaissance underlines . . . the rebirth of the classical tradition as a justification of colonial expansion." Walter Mignolo, *The Darker Side of the Renaissance: Literacy, Territoriality, and Colonization* (Ann Arbor: University of Michigan Press, 1995), p. vi.
2. Bartolomé de Las Casas, *In Defense of the Indians,* ed. Stafford Poole (De Kalb: Northern Illinois University Press, 1974), p. 271. See also Lewis Hanke, *All Mankind Is One: A Study of the Disputation between Bartolomé de Las Casas and Juan Gines de Sepulveda in 1550 on the Intellectual and Religious Capacity of the American Indians* (De Kalb: Northern Illinois University Press, 1974).
3. Quoted in C. L. R. James, *The Black Jacobins,* 2nd ed. (New York: Random House, 1963), p. 196.
4. Aimé Césaire, *Toussaint Louverture: la révolution française et le problème colonial* (Paris: Présence Africaine, 1961), p. 309.
5. See Eugene Genovese, *From Rebellion to Revolution: Afro-American Slave Revolts in the Making of the Modern World* (Baton Rouge: Louisiana State University Press, 1979), p. 88.
6. Karl Marx, *Capital,* trans. Ben Fowkes (New York: Vintage, 1976), 1:925.
7. Karl Marx, "The British Rule in India," in *Surveys from Exile,* vol. 2 of *Political Writings* (London: Penguin, 1973), p. 306.
8. Karl Marx, "The Native States," in *Letters on India* (Lahore: Contemporary India Publication, 1937), p. 51.
9. Marx, "The British Rule in India," p. 307.
10. Karl Marx, "The Future Results of British Rule in India" in *Surveys from Exile,* vol. 2 of *Political Writings* (London: Penguin, 1973), p. 320.
11. Aijaz Ahmad points out that Marx's description of Indian history seems to be taken directly from Hegel. See Aijaz Ahmad, *In Theory: Classes, Nations, Literatures* (London: Verso, 1992), pp. 231 and 241.
12. Marx, "The Future Results of British Rule in India," p. 320.
13. Robin Blackburn, *The Overthrow of Colonial Slavery, 1776–1848* (London: Verso, 1988), pp. 3 and 11.
14. See Elizabeth Fox Genovese and Eugene Genovese, *Fruits of Merchant Capital: Slavery and Bourgeois Property in the Rise and Expansion of Capitalism* (Oxford: Oxford University Press, 1983), p. vii.
15. Blackburn, *The Overthrow of Colonial Slavery,* p. 8.
16. The relationship between wage labor and slavery in capitalist development is one of the central problematics elaborated in Yann Moulier Boutang,

De l'esclavage au salariat: économie historique du salariat bridé (Paris: Presses universitaries de France, 1998).

17. This is one of the central arguments of Robin Blackburn's *Overthrow of Colonial Slavery*. See, in particular, p. 520.
18. Moulier Boutang, *De l'esclavage au salariat,* p. 5.
19. Franz Fanon, *The Wretched of the Earth,* trans. Constance Farrington (New York: Grove Press, 1963), p. 38. On the Manichaean divisions of the colonial world, see Abdul JanMohamed, "The Economy of Manichean Allegory: The Function of Racial Difference in Colonialist Literature," *Critical Inquiry,* 12, no. 1 (Autumn 1985), 57–87.
20. Fanon, *The Wretched of the Earth,* p. 42.
21. Edward Said, *Orientalism* (New York: Vintage, 1978), pp. 4–5 and 104.
22. Cultural anthropology has conducted a radical self-criticism in the past few decades, highlighting how many of the strongest early veins of the discipline participated in and supported colonialist projects. The early classic texts of this critique are Gérard Leclerc, *Anthropologie et colonialisme: essai sur l'histoire de l'africanisme* (Paris: Fayard, 1972); and Talal Asad, ed., *Anthropology and the Colonial Encounter* (London: Ithaca Press, 1973). Among the numerous more recent works, we found particularly useful Nicholaus Thomas, *Colonialism's Culture: Anthropology, Travel, and Government* (Princeton: Princeton University Press, 1994).
23. This argument is developed clearly in Valentin Mudimbe, *The Invention of Africa: Gnosis, Philosophy, and the Order of Knowledge* (Bloomington: Indiana University Press, 1988), see esp. pp. 64, 81, and 108.
24. Ranajit Guha, *An Indian Historiography of India: A Nineteenth-Century Agenda and Its Implications* (Calcutta: Centre for Studies in Social Sciences, 1988), p. 12.
25. *An Inquiry into the causes of the insurrection of negroes in the island of St. Domingo* London and Philadelphia: Crukshank, 1792), p. 5.
26. See Paul Gilroy, *The Black Atlantic* (Cambridge, Mass.: Harvard University Press, 1993), pp. 1–40.
27. See Franz Fanon, *Black Skin, White Masks,* trans. Charles Lam Markmann (New York: Grove Press, 1967), pp. 216–222.
28. Jean-Paul Sartre, "Black Orpheus," in *"What Is Literature?" and Other Essays* (Cambridge, Mass.: Harvard University Press, 1988), p. 296.
29. Jean-Paul Sartre, "Preface," in Fanon, *The Wretched of the Earth,* p. 20.
30. "In fact, negritude appears like the upbeat [*le temps faible*] of a dialectical progression: the theoretical and practical affirmation of white supremacy is the thesis; the position of negritude as an antithetical value is the moment of negativity. But this negative moment is not sufficient in itself,

and these black men who use it know this perfectly well; they know that it aims at preparing the synthesis or realization of the human being in a raceless society. Thus, negritude is *for* destroying itself; it is a "crossing to" and not an "arrival at," a means and not an end." Sartre, "Black Orpheus," p. 327.

31. Fanon, *The Wretched of the Earth,* p. 52.
32. Ibid., pp. 58–65.
33. See Malcolm X, "The Ballot or the Bullet," in *Malcolm X Speaks* (New York: Pathfinder, 1989), pp. 23–44.
34. We should remember that within the sphere of communist and socialist movements, the discourse of nationalism not only legitimated the struggle for liberation from colonial powers but also served as a means of insisting on the autonomy and differences of local revolutionary experiences from the models of dominant socialist powers. For example, Chinese nationalism was the banner under which Chinese revolutionaries could resist Soviet control and Soviet models, translating Marxism into the language of the Chinese peasantry (that is, into Mao Zedong thought). Similarly, in the subsequent period, revolutionaries from Vietnam to Cuba and Nicaragua insisted on the national nature of struggles in order to assert their autonomy from Moscow and Beijing.
35. Charter of the United Nations, Article 2.1, in Leland Goodrich and Edvard Hambro, *Charter of the United Nations* (Boston: World Peace Foundation, 1946), p. 339.
36. Partha Chatterjee, *Nationalist Thought and the Colonial World: A Derivative Discourse?* (London: Zed Books, 1986), p. 168.

CONTAGION

1. Louis-Ferdinand Céline, *Journey to the End of the Night,* trans. Ralph Manheim (New York: New Directions, 1983), p. 145 (translation modified); subsequently cited in text.
2. See Cindy Patton, *Global AIDS / Local Context,* forthcoming; and John O'Neill, "AIDS as a Globalizing Panic," in Mike Featherstone, ed., *Global Culture: Nationalism, Globalization, and Modernity* (London: Sage, 1990), pp. 329–342.

2.4 SYMPTOMS OF PASSAGE

1. Arif Dirlik, *The Postcolonial Aura: Third World Criticism in the Age of Global Capitalism* (Boulder: Westview Press, 1997), pp. 52–83; quotation p. 77.
2. See, for example, Jane Flax, *Thinking Fragments* (Berkeley: University of California Press, 1990), p. 29.

3. For an explanation of how many postmodernist theorists conflate the varieties of modernist thought under the single rubric of "the Enlightenment," see Kathi Weeks, *Constituting Feminist Subjects* (Ithaca: Cornell University Press, 1998), chap. 2.
4. bell hooks, *Yearning: Race, Gender, and Cultural Politics* (Boston: South End Press, 1990), p. 25.
5. Jane Flax, *Disputed Subjects* (London: Routledge, 1993), p. 91.
6. What is necessary for a postmodernist critique is first to identify what "modernist" means in the field and then to pose a successor paradigm that is in some way consistent with some form of postmodernist thinking. Consider, for example, a field that might at first sight seem an unlikely candidate for such an operation: public administration, that is, the study of bureaucracies. The modernist paradigm of research that dominates the field is defined by a "prescription of neutral public administration ascribed to Wilson (separation of politics from administration), Taylor (scientific management), and Weber (hierarchical command)." Charles Fox and Hugh Miller, *Postmodern Public Administration: Toward Discourse* (Thousand Oaks, Calif.: Sage, 1995), p. 3. Scholars who are convinced that this paradigm is outdated and leads to undemocratic governmental practice can use postmodernist thinking as a weapon to transform the field. In this case, they propose "non-foundational discourse theory" as a postmodernist model that will create more active public interactions and thus democratize bureaucracy (p. 75).
7. See James Der Derian and Michael Shapiro, eds., *International/Intertextual Relations: Postmodern Readings of World Politics* (Lexington, Mass.: Lexington Books, 1989); Jim George, *Discourses of Global Politics: A Critical (Re)Introduction to International Relations* (Boulder: Lynne Rienner Publications, 1994); and Michael Shapiro and Hayward Alker, Jr., eds., *Territorial Identities and Global Flows* (Minneapolis: University of Minnesota Press, 1996).
8. Homi Bhabha, *The Location of Culture* (London: Routledge, 1994), p. 18.
9. Gyan Prakash, "Postcolonial Criticism and Indian Historiography," *Social Text,* no. 31/32 (1992), 8.
10. See Edward Said, *Culture and Imperialism* (New York: Vintage, 1993), pp. 282–303.
11. Edward Said, "Arabesque," *New Statesman and Society,* 7 (September 1990), 32.
12. Anders Stephanson gives an excellent account of the conceptions of the United States as a "new Jerusalem" in *Manifest Destiny: American Expansionism and the Empire of Right* (New York: Hill and Wang, 1995).
13. "Like most visions of a 'golden age,' the 'traditional family' . . . evaporates on close examination. It is an ahistorical amalgam of structures,

values, and behaviors that never co-existed in the same time and place." Stephanie Coontz, *The Way We Never Were: American Families and the Nostalgia Trap* (New York: Basic Books, 1992), p. 9.

14. Fazlur Rahman, *Islam and Modernity: Transformation of an Intellectual Tradition* (Chicago: University of Chicago Press, 1984), p. 142.
15. "The fundamentalism of the humiliated Islamic world is not a tradition of the past but a postmodern phenomenon: the inevitable ideological reaction to the failure of Western modernization." Robert Kurz, "Die Krise, die aus dem Osten Kam," translated into Italian in *L'onore perduto del lavoro,* trans. Anselm Jappe and Maria Teresa Ricci (Rome: Manifestolibri, 1994), p. 16. More generally, on contemporary fallacies around notions of tradition and group identity, see Arjun Appadurai, "Life after Primordialism," in *Modernity at Large* (Minneapolis: University of Minnesota Press, 1996), pp. 139–157.
16. Akbar Ahmed, *Postmodernism and Islam* (New York: Routledge, 1992), p. 32.
17. Rahman, *Islam and Modernity,* p. 136.
18. Robert Reich, *The Work of Nations* (New York: Random House, 1992), pp. 8 and 3.
19. See Arjun Appadurai, "Disjuncture and Difference in the Global Cultural Economy," in *Modernity at Large* (Minneapolis: University of Minnesota Press, 1996), pp. 27–47.
20. See, for example, Jean Baudrillard, *Selected Writings,* ed. Mark Poster (Oxford: Blackwell, 1988); and Umberto Eco, *Travels in Hyper-reality,* trans. William Weaver (London: Picador, 1986), pp. 3–58.
21. Stephen Brown, *Postmodern Marketing* (London: Routledge, 1995), p. 157. Whereas marketing practice is postmodernist, Brown points out, marketing theory remains stubbornly "modernist" (which here means positivistic). Elizabeth Hirschman and Morris Holbrook also bemoan the resistance of marketing theory and consumer research to postmodernist thinking in *Postmodern Consumer Research: The Study of Consumption as Text* (Newbury Park, Calif.: Sage, 1992).
22. See George Yudice, "Civil Society, Consumption, and Governmentality in an Age of Global Restructuring: An Introduction," *Social Text,* no. 45 (Winter 1995), 1–25.
23. William Bergquist, *The Postmodern Organization: Mastering the Art of Irreversible Change* (San Francisco: Jossey-Bass, 1993), p. xiii. See also the essays in David Boje, Robert Gephart, Jr., and Tojo Joseph Thatchenkery, eds., *Postmodern Management and Organizational Theory* (Thousand Oaks, Calif.: Sage, 1996).
24. See Avery Gordon, "The Work of Corporate Culture: Diversity Management," *Social Text,* 44, vol. 13, no. 3 (Fall/Winter 1995), 3–30.

25. See Chris Newfield, "Corporate Pleasures for a Corporate Planet," *Social Text,* 44, vol. 13, no. 3 (Fall/Winter 1995), 31–44.
26. See Fredric Jameson, *Postmodernism, Or, The Cultural Logic of Late Capitalism* (Durham: Duke University Press, 1991); and David Harvey, *The Condition of Postmodernity* (Oxford: Blackwell, 1989).

2.5 NETWORK POWER: U.S. SOVEREIGNTY AND THE NEW EMPIRE

1. Alexander Hamilton, James Madison, and John Jay, *The Federalist,* ed. Max Beldt (Oxford: Blackwell, 1948), p. 37. This passage is from Federalist no. 9, written by Hamilton.
2. See J. G. A. Pocock, *The Machiavellian Moment: Florentine Political Thought and the Atlantic Republican Tradition* (Princeton: Princeton University Press, 1975); and J. C. D. Clark, *The Language of Liberty, 1660–1832* (Cambridge: Cambridge University Press, 1994).
3. On the Atlantic passage of the republican tradition from the English Revolution to the American Revolution, see Antonio Negri, *Il potere costituente* (Milan: Sugarco, 1992), chaps. 3 and 4, pp. 117–222; and David Cressy, *Coming Over: Migration and Communication between England and New England in the Seventeenth Century* (Cambridge: Cambridge University Press, 1987).
4. Again, see Negri, *Il potere costituente.* See also J. G. A. Pocock, "States, Republics, and Empires: The American Founding in Early Modern Perspective," in Terence Ball and J. G. A. Pocock, eds., *Conceptual Change and the Constitution* (Lawrence: University Press of Kansas, 1988), pp. 55–77.
5. See Polybius, *The Rise of the Roman Empire,* trans. Ian Scott-Kilvert (Harmondsworth: Penguin, 1979), Book VI, pp. 302–352.
6. See Alexis de Tocqueville, *Democracy in America,* 2 vols. (New York: Knopf, 1994), in particular the Author's Introduction, 1:3–16.
7. See Hannah Arendt, *On Revolution* (New York: Viking, 1963).
8. We are refering directly here to Max Weber, *The Protestant Ethic and the Spirit of Capitalism,* trans. Talcott Parsons (New York: Scribner's, 1950); but see also Michael Walzer, *Exodus and Revolution* (New York: Basic Books, 1985).
9. For detailed analyses of the conflicts within the Constitution, see primarily Michael Kammen, *A Machine That Would Go of Itself* (New York: Knopf, 1986).
10. Throughout his reading of Polybius in the *Discourses,* Machiavelli insists on the necessity that the Republic expand so as not to fall into corruption. See Negri, *Il potere costituente,* pp. 75–97.
11. The combination of reformism and expansionism in the "Empire of Right" is presented wonderfully by Anders Stephanson, *Manifest Destiny:*

American Expansion and the Empire of Right (New York: Hill and Wang, 1995).

12. Virgil, Ecologue IV, in *Opera,* ed. R. A. B. Mynors (Oxford: Clarendon Press, 1969), verses 4–5, p. 10. The original reads, "Ultima Cumaei uenit iam carminis aetas; / magnus ab integro saeclorum nascitur ordo."
13. Bruce Ackerman proposes a periodization of the first three regimes or phases of U.S. constitutional history. See *We The People: Foundations* (Cambridge, Mass.: Harvard University Press, 1991), in particular pp. 58–80.
14. "What one shared above all was a sense of an entirely new kind of country, uniquely marked by social, economic, and spatial *openness.*" Stephanson, *Manifest Destiny,* p. 28.
15. Marx explained the economic origins of the United States when analyzing the American economist Henry Charles Carey. The United States is "a country where bourgeois society did not develop on the foundation of the feudal system, but developed rather from itself." Karl Marx, *Grundrisse,* trans. Martin Nicolaus (New York: Vintage, 1973), p. 884. Marx also discusses the difference of capitalist development in the United States (along with the other settler colonies, such as Australia), in *Capital,* trans. Ben Fowkes (New York: Vintage, 1976), 1:931–940. For Tocqueville's analysis of the socioeconomic roots of the United States, see *Democracy in America,* vol. 1, chaps. 2 and 3, pp. 26–54.
16. Thomas Jefferson "saw expansion as the indispensable concomitant of a stable, secure, and prosperous Empire of Liberty." Robert Tucker and David Hendrickson, *Empire of Liberty: The Statecraft of Thomas Jefferson* (Oxford: Oxford University Press, 1990), p. 162.
17. U.S. Constitution, Article I, section 2. On the three-fifths rule, see John Chester Miller, *The Wolf by the Ears: Thomas Jefferson and Slavery* (New York: Free Press, 1977), pp. 221–225.
18. For a brief history of the crises in the Constitution precipated by black slavery from the Constitutional Convention to the Civil War, see Kammen, *A Machine That Would Go of Itself,* pp. 96–105.
19. On the emergence of the U.S. industrial working class as a powerful force in the late nineteenth and early twentieth centuries, see David Brody, *Workers in Industrial America: Essays on Twentieth-Century Struggles* (Oxford: Oxford University Press, 1980), pp. 3–47; Stanley Aronowitz, *False Promises: The Shaping of American Working-Class Consciousness* (New York: McGraw-Hill, 1973), pp. 137–166; and Bruno Ramirez, *When Workers Fight: The Politics of Industrial Relations in the Progressive Era, 1898–1916* (Westport, Conn.: Greenwood Press, 1978).

20. For a good analysis of the relationship between U.S. expansionism and European imperialism in terms of foreign policy, see Akira Iriye, *From Nationalism to Internationalism: U.S. Foreign Policy to 1914* (London: Routledge and Kegan Paul, 1977).
21. Cited in Frank Ninkovich, "Theodore Roosevelt: Civilization as Ideology," *Diplomatic History,* 20, no. 3 (Summer 1986), 221–245; quotation pp. 232–233. Ninkovich demonstrates clearly how Roosevelt's imperialism was solidly grounded in the ideology of the "spread of civilization."
22. On Woodrow Wilson and the fortunes of progressive internationalism, see Thomas Knock, *To End All Wars: Woodrow Wilson and the Quest for a New World Order* (Oxford: Oxford University Press, 1992).
23. See Antonio Negri, "Keynes and the Capitalist Theory of the State," in Michael Hardt and Antonio Negri, *Labor of Dionysus* (Minneapolis: University of Minnesota Press, 1994), pp. 23–51.
24. The effects of Monroe's original declaration were ambiguous at best, and Ernst May has argued that the doctrine was born as much from domestic political pressures as international issues; see *The Making of the Monroe Doctrine* (Cambridge, Mass.: Harvard University Press, 1975). The doctrine only really became an effective foreign policy with Theodore Roosevelt's imperialist campaigns, and particularly with the project to build the Panama Canal.
25. For the long history of U.S. military interventions in Latin America and particularly in Central America, see Ivan Musicant, *The Banana Wars: A History of United States Military Intervention in Latin America* (New York: Macmillan, 1990); Noam Chomsky, *Turning the Tide: U.S. Intervention in Central America and the Struggle for Peace* (Boston: South End Press, 1985); Saul Landau, *The Dangerous Doctrine: National Security and U.S. Foreign Policy* (Boulder: Westview Press, 1988).
26. William Chafe poses 1968 as a shift of regime in the United States from the perspective of a social historian: "Any historian who uses the word 'watershed' to describe a given moment runs the risk of oversimplifying the complexity of the historical process. However, if the word is employed to signify a turning point that marks the end to domination by one constellation of forces and the beginning of domination by another, it seems appropriate as a description of what took place in America in 1968." William Chafe, *The Unfinished Journey: America since World War II* (Oxford: Oxford University Press, 1986), p. 378. Chafe captures precisely what we mean by a shift in the constitutional regime, that is, the end of domination by one constellation of forces and the beginning of domination by another. For Chafe's analysis of the republican spirit of the movements, see pp. 302–342.

2.6 IMPERIAL SOVEREIGNTY

1. Immanuel Kant, "An Answer to the Question: 'What Is Enlightenment?' " in *Political Writings,* ed. Hans Reiss, 2nd ed. (Cambridge: Cambridge University Press, 1991), pp. 54–60.
2. Michel Foucault, "What Is Enlightenment," in *Ethics: Subjectivity and Truth,* vol. 1 of *The Essential Works of Foucault 1954–1984,* ed. Paul Rabinow (New York: New Press, 1997), pp. 303–319.
3. Ibid., p. 315.
4. On the relationship between modern metaphysics and political theory, see Antonio Negri, *The Savage Anomaly,* trans. Michael Hardt (Minneapolis: University of Minnesota Press, 1991).
5. We find versions of this spatial configuration of inside and outside among many of the contemporary philosophers we most admire—even writers such as Foucault and Blanchot who move away from the dialectic, and even Derrida, who dwells on that margin between inside and outside that is the most ambiguous and most murky point of modern thought. For Foucault and Blanchot, see Foucault's essay "Maurice Blanchot: The Thought from Outside," trans. Brian Massumi, in *Foucault/Blanchot* (New York: Zone Books, 1987). For Derrida, see *Margins of Philosophy,* trans. Alan Bass (Chicago: University of Chicago Press, 1982).
6. Fredric Jameson, *Postmodernism, Or, The Cultural Logic of Late Capitalism* (Durham: Duke University Press, 1991), p. ix.
7. We are thinking here primarily of Hannah Arendt's notion of the political articulated in *The Human Condition* (Chicago: University of Chicago Press, 1958).
8. For Los Angeles, see Mike Davis, *City of Quartz* (London: Verso, 1990), pp. 221–263. For São Paulo, see Teresa Caldeira, "Fortified Enclaves: The New Urban Segregation," *Public Culture,* no. 8 (1996); 303–328.
9. See Guy Debord, *Society of the Spectacle,* trans. Donald Nicholson-Smith (New York: Zone Books, 1994).
10. Francis Fukuyama, *The End of History and the Last Man* (New York: Free Press, 1992).
11. "We have watched the war machine . . . set its sights on a new type of enemy, no longer another State, or even another regime, but 'l'ennemi quelconque' [the whatever enemy]." Gilles Deleuze and Félix Guattari, *A Thousand Plateaus,* trans. Brian Massumi (Minneapolis: University of Minnesota Press, 1987), p. 422.
12. There are undoubtedly zones of deprivation within the world market where the flow of capital and goods is reduced to a minimum. In some cases this deprivation is determined by an explicit political decision (as in the trade sanctions against Iraq), and in other cases it follows from the

implicit logics of global capital (as in the cycles of poverty and starvation in sub-Saharan Africa). In all cases, however, these zones do not constitute an outside to the capitalist market; rather they function within the world market as the most subordinated rungs of the global economic hierarchy.

13. For an excellent explanation of Foucault's concept of the diagram, see Gilles Deleuze, *Foucault,* trans. Seán Hand (Minneapolis: University of Minnesota Press, 1988), pp. 34–37.
14. See Étienne Balibar, "Is There a 'Neo-Racism'?" in Étienne Balibar and Immanuel Wallerstein, *Race, Nation, Class* (London: Verso, 1991), pp. 17–28; quotation p. 21. Avery Gordon and Christopher Newfield identify something very similar as liberal racism, which is characterized primarily by "an antiracist attitude that coexists with support for racist outcomes," in "White Mythologies," *Critical Inquiry,* 20, no. 4 (Summer 1994), 737–757, quotation p. 737.
15. Balibar, "Is There a 'Neo-Racism'?" pp. 21–22.
16. See Walter Benn Michaels, *Our America: Nativism, Modernism, and Pluralism* (Durham: Duke University Press, 1995); and "Race into Culture: A Critical Genealogy of Cultural Identity," *Critical Inquiry,* 18, no. 4 (Summer 1992), 655–685. Benn Michaels critiques the kind of racism that appears in cultural pluralism, but does so in a way that seems to support a new liberal racism. See Gordon and Newfield's excellent critique of his work in "White Mythologies."
17. Deleuze and Guattari, *A Thousand Plateaus,* p. 178.
18. Ibid., p. 209.
19. See Lauren Berlant, *The Queen of America Goes to Washington City: Essays on Sex and Citizenship* (Durham: Duke University Press, 1997). On her formulation of the reactionary reversal of the slogan "The personal is the political," see pp. 175–180. For her excellent analysis of the "intimate public sphere," see pp. 2–24.
20. The liberal order of Empire achieves the kind of "overlapping consensus" proposed by John Rawls in which all are required to set aside their "comprehensive doctrines" in the interests of tolerance. See John Rawls, *Political Liberalism* (New York: Columbia University Press, 1993). For a critical review of his book, see Michael Hardt, "On Political Liberalism," *Qui Parle,* 7, no. 1 (Fall/Winter 1993), 140–149.
21. On the (re)creation of ethnic identities in China, for example, see Ralph Litzinger, "Memory Work: Reconstituting the Ethnic in Post-Mao China," *Cultural Anthropology,* 13, no. 2 (1998), pp. 224–255.
22. Gilles Deleuze, "Postscript on Control Societies," in *Negotiations,* trans. Martin Joughin (New York: Columbia University Press, 1995), pp. 177–182; quotation p. 179.

23. See Phillipe Bourgois, *Ethnicity at Work: Divided Labor on a Central American Banana Plantation* (Baltimore: Johns Hopkins University Press, 1989).
24. See Aristotle, *De generatione et corruptione,* trans. C. J. F. Williams (Oxford: Oxford University Press, 1982). In general, on the philosophical conceptions of generation and corruption, see Reiner Schürmann, *Des hégémonies brisées* (Mouvezin: T.E.R., 1996).

REFUSAL

1. See in particular Gilles Deleuze, "Bartleby, ou la formule," in *Critique et clinique* (Paris: Minuit, 1993), pp. 89–114; and Giorgio Agamben, "Bartleby o della contingenza," in *Bartleby: la formula della creazione* (Macerata: Quodlibet, 1993), pp. 47–92.
2. J. M. Coetzee, *The Life and Times of Michael K* (Harmondsworth: Penguin, 1983), p. 151.
3. Étienne de La Boétie, *The Politics of Obedience: The Discourse of Voluntary Servitude,* trans. Harry Kurz (New York: Free Life Editions, 1975), pp. 52–53. In French, *Discours de la servitude volontaire,* in *Oeuvres complètes* (Geneva: Slatkine, 1967), pp. 1–57; quotation p. 14.

INTERMEZZO: COUNTER-EMPIRE

1. Gilles Deleuze and Félix Guattari, *Anti-Oedipus,* trans. Robert Hurley, Mark Lane, and Helen Lane (Minneapolis: University of Minnesota Press, 1983), p. 239.
2. One of the best historical accounts of the IWW is contained in John Dos Passos's enormous novel *USA* (New York: Library of America, 1996). See also Joyce Kornbluh, ed., *Rebel Voices: an I.W.W. Anthology* (Ann Arbor: University of Michigan Press, 1964).
3. "It would be possible to write a whole history of the inventions made since 1830 for the sole purpose of providing capital with weapons against working-class revolt." Karl Marx, *Capital,* trans. Ben Fowkes (New York: Vintage, 1976), 1:563.
4. On the changing relation between labor and value, see Antonio Negri, "Twenty Theses on Marx," in Saree Makdisi, Cesare Casarino, and Rebecca Karl, eds., *Marxism Beyond Marxism* (New York: Routledge, 1996), pp. 149–180; and Antonio Negri, "Value and Affect," *boundary2,* 26, no. 2 (Summer 1999).
5. Deleuze and Guattari, *Anti-Oedipus,* p. 29 (translation modified).
6. One of the most important novels of the Italian Resistance is Elio Vittorini's *Uomini e no* (Men and not men) in which being human means being against. Nanni Balestrini's tales about class struggle in Italy in the 1960s and 1970s take up this positive determination of being-against. See

in particular *Vogliamo tutto* (Milan: Feltrinelli, 1971); and *The Unseen,* trans. Liz Heron (London: Verso, 1989).

7. Yann Moulier Boutang argues that the Marxian concept of the "industrial reserve army" has proven to be a particularly strong obstacle to our understanding the power of this mobility. In this framework the divisions and stratifications of the labor force in general are understood as predetermined and fixed by the quantitative logic of development, that is, by the productive rationalities of capitalist rule. This rigid and univocal command is seen as having such power that all forms of labor power are considered as being purely and exclusively determined by capital. Even unemployed populations and migrating populations are seen as springing from and determined by capital as a "reserve army." Labor power is deprived of subjectivity and difference since it is considered completely subject to the iron laws of capital. See Yann Moulier Boutang, *De l'esclavage au salariat* (Paris: Presses universitaires de France, 1998).
8. Friedrich Nietzsche, *The Will to Power,* trans. Walter Kaufman and R. J. Hollingdale (New York: Vintage, 1968), p. 465 (no. 868, November 1887–March 1888).
9. We describe exodus as one of the motors of the collapse of Real Socialism in our *Labor of Dionysus* (Minneapolis: University of Minnesota Press, 1994), pp. 263–269.
10. The first passage is from Walter Benjamin, "Erfahrung und Armut," in *Gesammelte Schriften,* ed. Rolf Tiedemann and Hermann Schweppenhäussen (Frankfurt: Suhrkamp, 1972), vol. 2, pt. 1, pp. 213–219; quotation p. 215. The second passage is from "The Destructive Character," in *Reflections,* ed. Peter Demetz (New York: Schocken Books, 1978), pp. 302–303.
11. On the migrations of sexuality and sexual perversion, see François Peraldi, ed., *Polysexuality* (New York: Semiotext(e), 1981); and Sylvère Lotringer, *Overexposed: Treating Sexual Perversion in America* (New York: Pantheon, 1988). Arthur and Marilouise Kroker also emphasize the subversiveness of bodies and sexualities that refuse purity and normalization in essays such as "The Last Sex: Feminism and Outlaw Bodies," in Arthur and Marilouise Kroker, eds., *The Last Sex: Feminism and Outlaw Bodies* (New York: St. Martin's Press, 1993). Finally, the best source for experiments of corporeal and sexual transformations may be the novels of Kathy Acker; see, for example, *Empire of the Senseless* (New York: Grove Press, 1988).
12. On posthuman permutations of the body, see Judith Halberstam and Ira Livingston, "Introduction: Posthuman Bodies," in Judith Halberstam and Ira Livingston, eds., *Posthuman Bodies* (Bloomington: Indiana University

Press, 1995), pp. 1–19; and Steve Shaviro, *The Cinematic Body* (Minneapolis: University of Minnesota Press, 1993). For another interesting exploration of the potential permutations of the human body, see Alphonso Lingis, *Foreign Bodies* (New York: Routledge, 1994). See also the performance art of Stelarc, such as Stelarc, *Obsolete Body: Suspensions* (Davis, Calif.: J. P. Publications, 1984).

13. The primary texts that serve as the basis for a whole range of work that has been done across the boundaries of humans, animals, and machines are Donna Haraway, *Simians, Cyborgs, and Women: The Reinvention of Nature* (New York: Routledge, 1991); and Deleuze and Guattari, *Anti-Oedipus,* esp. pp. 1–8. Numerous studies have been published in the 1990s, particularly in the United States, on the political potential of corporeal nomadism and transformation. For three of the more interesting feminist examples from very different perspectives, see Rosi Braidotti, *Nomadic Subjects: Embodiment and Sexual Difference in Contemporary Feminist Theory* (New York: Columbia University Press, 1994); Camilla Griggers, *Becoming-Woman in Postmodernity* (Minneapolis: University of Minnesota Press, 1996); and Anna Camaiti Hostert, *Passing* (Rome: Castelvecchi, 1997).
14. Control and mutation are perhaps the defining themes of cyberpunk fiction. It is sufficient to see the seminal text, William Gibson, *Neuromancer* (New York: Ace, 1984). The most fascinating explorations of these themes, however, are probably found in the novels of William Burroughs and the films of David Cronenberg. On Burroughs and Cronenberg, see Steve Shaviro, *Doom Patrols: A Theoretical Fiction about Postmodernism* (London: Serpent's Tail, 1997), pp. 101–121.
15. This counsel against normalized bodies and normalized lives was perhaps the central principle of Félix Guattari's therapeutic practice.
16. "The proletariat . . . appears as the heir to the nomad in the Western world. Not only did many anarchists invoke nomadic themes originating in the East, but the bourgeoisie above all were quick to equate proletarians and nomads, comparing Paris to a city haunted by nomads." Gilles Deleuze and Félix Guattari, *A Thousand Plateaus,* trans. Brian Massumi (Minneapolis: University of Minnesota Press, 1987), p. 558, note 61.
17. See Antonio Negri's essay on Jacques Derrida's *Specters of Marx,* "The Specter's Smile," in Michael Spinker, ed., *Ghostly Demarcations* (London: Verso, 1999) pp. 5–16.

3.1 THE LIMITS OF IMPERIALISM

1. For sources on the imperialism debate from Kautsky to Lenin, see the excellent bibliography provided in Hans-Ulrich Wehler, ed., *Imperialismus*

(Cologne: Kiepenheuer and Witsch, 1970), pp. 443–459. For the debates over imperialism that developed between the two World Wars and continued up to the 1960s, see the bibliography in Dieter Senghaas, ed., *Imperialismus und strukturelle Gewalt* (Frankfurt: Suhrkamp, 1972), pp. 379–403. For a useful English-language summary of the debates, see Anthony Brewer, *Marxist Theories of Imperialism: A Critical Survey* (London: Routledge and Kegan Paul, 1980).

2. Karl Marx, *Grundrisse,* trans. Martin Nicolaus (New York: Vintage, 1973), p. 408; subsequently cited in text. For Marx's discussion of the internal "barriers" of capitalist production, see also *Capital,* vol. 3, trans. David Fernbach (London: Penguin, 1981), pp. 349–375.
3. The following argument raises the specter of *underconsumptionist* theories, which argue that the inability to consume all the commodities produced is capitalism's fatal flaw and will necessarily lead to collapse. Many Marxist and non-Marxist economists have convincingly argued against any idea that the capitalist tendency to produce too much or consume too little will be catastrophic. For an evaluation of underconsumptionist arguments in Marx and Luxemburg, see Michael Bleaney, *Under-consumption Theories* (New York: International Publishers, 1976), pp. 102–119 and 186–201; and Ernest Mandel, Introduction to Karl Marx, *Capital,* vol. 2, trans. David Fernbach (Harmondsworth: Penguin, 1977), pp. 69–77. See also Nikolai Bukharin's influential critique of Rosa Luxemburg in *Imperialism and the Accumulation of Capital,* ed. Kenneth Tarbuck, trans. Rudolf Wichmann (London: Allen Lane, 1972), pp. 151–270, We should point out that economic necessity based on quantitative calculations is sometimes the form but never the substance of Marx's or Luxemburg's arguments. Any necessity is really historical and social. What Marx and Luxemburg identified was an economic barrier that helps explain how capital has historically been driven or induced to expand, to move outside itself and incorporate new markets within its realm.
4. For Marx's analysis of the abstinence theory of capitalist consumption, see *Capital,* vol. 1, trans. Ben Fowkes (New York: Vintage, 1976), pp. 738–746, and *Capital,* 3:366.
5. "The total mass of commodities, the total product, must be sold, both that portion which replaces constant and variable capital and that which represents surplus-value. If this does not happen, or happens only partly, or only at prices that are less than the price of production, then although the worker is certainly exploited, his exploitation is not realized as such for the capitalist and may even not involve any realization of the surplus value extracted." Marx, *Capital,* 3:352.

6. Ibid., 3:353.
7. On the expansion of production and markets, see Marx, *Grundrisse,* p. 419; *Capital,* 1:910–911; 2:470–471; 3:349–355.
8. "The *true barrier* to capitalist production is *capital itself.*" Marx, *Capital,* 3:358.
9. Rosa Luxemburg, *The Accumulation of Capital,* trans. Agnes Schwarzchild (New York: Monthly Review Press, 1968), pp. 365–366 and 467. Luxemburg's analysis of capitalist accumulation, her critiques of Marx, and her theory of the collapse of capitalism have all been highly contested ever since her book first appeared. For good summaries of the issues at stake, see Mandel's Introduction to *Capital,* 2:11–79, especially pp. 62–69; Joan Robinson, Introduction to Luxemburg, *The Accumulation of Capital,* pp. 13–28; and Paul Sweezy, *The Theory of Capitalist Development* (New York: Oxford University Press, 1942), pp. 202–207.
10. Fernand Braudel, *Capitalism and Material Life, 1400–1800,* trans. Miriam Kochan (New York: Harper and Row, 1973), p. 308.
11. Luxemburg, *The Accumulation of Capital,* p. 358.
12. Ibid., p. 372.
13. Rudolf Hilferding, *Finance Capital: A Study of the Latest Phase of Capitalist Development,* ed. Tom Bottomore (London: Routledge and Kegan Paul, 1981), p. 314.
14. Marx and Engels, *Manifesto of the Communist Party* (London: Verso, 1998), p. 40.
15. On uneven development and the geographical differences of capitalist expansion, see David Harvey, *The Limits to Capital* (Chicago: University of Chicago Press, 1984); and Neil Smith, *Uneven Development: Nature, Capital, and the Production of Space* (Oxford: Blackwell, 1984).
16. Luxemburg, *The Accumulation of Capital,* p. 446.
17. "Like the power of which it is the most global expression, imperialism is not a notion that can form the object of any explicit definition that orginates from economic concepts. Imperialism can only be grasped on the basis of a fully developed theory of the state." Michel Aglietta, *A Theory of Capitalist Regulation,* trans. David Fernbach (London: New Left Books, 1979), p. 30.
18. See primarily V. I. Lenin, *Imperialism: The Highest Stage of Capitalism* (New York: International Publishers, 1939), and *Notebooks on Imperialism,* vol. 39 of *Collected Works* (Moscow: Progress Publishers, 1977).
19. See Hilferding, *Finance Capital,* in particular pp. 183–235. Hilferding's analysis relies heavily on Marx's theory of the equalization of the general rate of profit through competition; see *Capital,* 3:273–301.

20. Karl Kautsky, "Zwei Schriften zum Umlernen," *Die Neue Zeit,* April 30, 1915, p. 144. Excerpts from Kautsky's writings on imperialism are included in *Karl Kautsky: Selected Political Writings,* ed. and trans. Patrick Goode (London: Macmillan, 1983), pp. 74–96.
21. V. I. Lenin, "Preface to N. Bukharin's Pamphlet, Imperialism and the World Economy," in *Collected Works* (Moscow: Progress Publishers, 1964), 22:103–107; quotation p. 106. See also Lenin, *Imperialism,* pp. 111–122. We should note here that although Lenin is certainly correct in claiming that Kautsky's position is a deviation from Marx's method when he ignores the potential conflicts and practical opportunities of the present situation, Kautsky's reading of the tendency toward a unified world market does indeed find resonance in Marx's work, particularly in his articles on colonialism in India, where he posed a linear tendency of imperialist development toward the formation of a world market. See in particular Karl Marx, "The Future Results of British Rule in India," in *Surveys from Exile,* vol. 2 of *Political Writings* (London: Penguin, 1973), pp. 319–325.
22. Lenin, "Preface to N. Bukharin's Pamphlet, Imperialism and the World Economy," p. 107.
23. See Antonio Negri, *La fabbrica della strategia: 33 lezioni su Lenin* (Padua: CLEUP, 1976).
24. On Lenin's debt to Hobson, see Giovanni Arrighi, *The Geometry of Imperialism: The Limits of Hobson's Paradigm,* trans. Patrick Camiller (London: Verso, 1978), pp. 23–27.
25. Cecil Rhodes, cited in Lenin, *Imperialism,* p. 79.
26. It is particularly important to give credit where credit is due today, when we seem to be confronted with numerous versions of historical revisionism. Poor Gramsci, communist and militant before all else, tortured and killed by fascism and ultimately by the bosses who financed fascism—poor Gramsci was given the gift of being considered the founder of a strange notion of hegemony that leaves no place for a Marxian politics. (See, for example, Ernesto Laclau and Chantal Mouffe, *Hegemony and Socialist Strategy: Towards a Radical Democratic Politics* [London: Verso, 1985], especially pp. 65–71.) We have to defend ourselves against such generous gifts!
27. See Roman Rosdolsky, *The Making of Marx's "Capital,"* trans. Peter Burgess (London: Pluto Press, 1977).
28. On the missing volume on the wage, see Antonio Negri, *Marx Beyond Marx,* trans. Harry Cleaver, Michael Ryan, and Maurizio Viano (New York: Autonomedia, 1991), pp. 127–150; and Michael Lebowitz, *Beyond*

Capital: Marx's Political Economy of the Working Class (London: Macmillan, 1992). On the question of the existence of a Marxist theory of the state, see the debate between Norberto Bobbio and Antonio Negri in Norberto Bobbio, *Which Socialism?* (Cambridge: Polity Press, 1987).

29. Marx, *Grundrisse,* p. 408.
30. Fernand Braudel, *Afterthoughts on Material Civilization and Capitalism,* trans. Patricia Ranum (Baltimore: Johns Hopkins University Press, 1977), p. 64.

CYCLES

1. "I occasionally get just as tired of the slogan 'postmodern' as anyone else, but when I am tempted to regret my complicity with it, to deplore its misuses and its notoriety, and to conclude with some reluctance that it raises more problems than it solves, I find myself pausing to wonder whether any other concept can dramatize the issues in quite so effective and economical a fashion." Fredric Jameson, *Postmodernism, or, The Cultural Logic of Late Capitalism* (Durham: Duke University Press, 1991), p. 418.
2. Giovanni Arrighi, *The Long Twentieth Century: Money, Power, and the Origins of Our Times* (London: Verso, 1994).
3. Ibid., p. 332.

3.2 DISCIPLINARY GOVERNABILITY

1. See James Devine, "Underconsumption, Over-investment, and the Origins of the Great Depression," *Review of Radical Political Economics,* 15, no. 2 (Summer 1983), 1–27. On the economic crisis of 1929, see also the classic analysis of John Kenneth Galbraith, *The Great Crash, 1929* (Boston: Houghton Mifflin, 1954), which focuses on speculation as the cause of the crisis; and, more recently, Gérard Duménil and D. Lévy, *La dynamique du capital: un siècle d'économie americaine* (Paris: PUF, 1996). More generally, on the theoretical problems that the 1929 crisis bequeathed to twentieth-century political economy, see Michel Aglietta, *A Theory of Capitalist Regulation,* trans. David Fernbach (London: New Left Books, 1979); and Robert Boyer and Jacques Mistral, *Accumulation, inflation, crises* (Paris: PUF, 1978).
2. John Maynard Keynes was perhaps the person with the clearest foresight at the Versailles Conference. Already at the conference and then later in his essay "The Economic Consequences of Peace," he denounced the political egotism of the victors which would become one of the contributing factors to the economic crisis of the 1920s.
3. This type of interpretation of the economic and political crisis of 1929 should be contrasted very strongly to "revisionist" historiographical con-

ceptions in the style of François Furet, Ernst Nolte, and Renzo De Felice. It demonstrates the great importance of the *economic* element in the definition of the political choices of the twentieth century. The revisionist histories, on the contrary, read the developments of the century as a linear progression of ideas that are often posed in dialectical opposition, with fascism and communism occupying the defining poles. See, for example, François Furet, *Le passé d'une illusion: essai sur l'idée communiste au XXe siècle* (Paris: Robert Laffont, 1995), especially the chapter in which he discusses the relationship between communism and fascism (pp. 189–248).

4. See Jon Halliday, *A Political History of Japanese Capitalism* (New York: Pantheon, 1975), pp. 82–133.
5. It is above all the "liberal" historiography of authors such as Arthur Meier Schlesinger that has insisted on the synthetic characteristics of American progressivism. See his *Political and Social Growth of the American People, 1865–1940,* 3rd ed. (New York: Macmillan, 1941). See also Arthur Ekirch, Jr., *Progressivism in America: A Study of the Era from Theodore Roosevelt to Woodrow Wilson* (New York: New Viewpoints, 1974).
6. This is the central development traced by Michel Aglietta in *A Theory of Capitalist Regulation,* and by Benjamin Coriat in *L'atelier et le chronomètre* (Paris: Christian Bourgois, 1979). See also Antonio Negri, "Keynes and the Capitalist Theory of the State," in Michael Hardt and Antonio Negri, *Labor of Dionysus* (Minneapolis: University of Minnesota Press, 1994), pp. 23–51; and "Crisis of the Planner-State: Communism and Revolutionary Organisation," in *Revolution Retrieved* (London: Red Notes, 1988), pp. 91–148. A good analysis of the New Deal and Keynesianism is also provided by Suzanne de Brunhoff, *The State, Capital, and Economic Policy,* trans. Mike Sonenscher (London: Pluto Press, 1978), pp. 61–80.
7. The notion of discipline developed by Michel Foucault certainly has a different focus from the one we employ here, but we are refering to the same practices and the same globality of application. Foucault's primary theoretical concerns are that discipline is deployed through institutional architectures, that the power of discipline is located not in some central source but in the capillary formations at its point of exercise, and that the subjectivities are produced by internalizing discipline and enacting its practices. This is all equally valid for our consideration here. Our primary focus, however, is on how the practices and relationships of disciplinarity that originated in the factory regime came to invest the entire social terrain as a mechanism of both production and government, that is, as a regime of social production.

8. The fundamental text that describes this development and anticipates its results is Max Horkheimer and Theodor Adorno, *Dialectic of Enlightenment,* trans. John Cumming (New York: Herder and Herder, 1972), which was written in the mid-1940s. Numerous other works followed in the description of disciplinary society and its implacable development as a "biopolitical society," works coming out of different cultural and intellectual traditions but completely coherent in defining the tendency. For the two strongest and most intelligent poles of this range of studies, see Herbert Marcuse, *One-Dimensional Man* (Boston: Beacon Press, 1964), for what we might call the Anglo-German pole; and Michel Foucault, *Discipline and Punish,* trans. Alan Sheridan (New York: Pantheon, 1977), for the Latin pole.
9. Freda Kirchwey, "Program of Action," *Nation,* March 11, 1944, pp. 300–305; cited in Serge Guilbaut, *How New York Stole the Idea of Modern Art: Abstract Expressionism, Freedom, and the Cold War,* trans. Arthur Goldhammer (Chicago: University of Chicago Press, 1983), p. 103.
10. On the spread of the New Deal model to the other dominant countries after the Second World War, see Paul Kennedy, *The Rise and Fall of the Great Powers: Economic Change and Military Conflict from 1500 to 2000* (New York: Random House, 1987), pp. 347–437; and Franz Schurmann, *The Logic of World Power: An Inquiry into the Origins, Currents, and Contradictions of World Politics* (New York: Pantheon, 1974).
11. On the history of the decolonization process in general, see Marc Ferro, *Histoire des colonisations: des conquêtes aux indépendences, XIIIe–XXe siècle* (Paris: Seuil, 1994); Frank Ansprenger, *The Dissolution of the Colonial Empires* (London: Routledge, 1989); and R. F. Holland, *European Decolonization, 1918–1981* (London: Macmillan, 1985).
12. On the effect of U.S. hegemony on decolonization struggles, see Giovanni Arrighi, *The Long Twentieth Century* (London: Verso, 1994), pp. 69–75; and François Chesnais, *La mondialisation du capital,* rev. ed. (Paris: Syros, 1997).
13. Harry S. Truman, *Public Papers* (Washington, D.C.: United States Government Printing Office, 1947), p. 176; cited in Richard Freeland, *The Truman Doctrine and the Origins of McCarthyism* (New York: Schocken, 1971), p. 85. On the rigid bipolar ideological divisions imposed by the cold war, see again Kennedy, *The Rise and Fall of the Great Powers,* pp. 373–395; and Schurmann, *The Logic of World Power.*
14. On the decentering of manufacturing and service production (coupled with the centralization of command), see two books by Saskia Sassen, *The Mobility of Labor and Capital: A Study in International Investment and*

Labor Flow (Cambridge: Cambridge University Press, 1988), especially pp. 127–133; and *The Global City: New York, London, Tokyo* (Princeton: Princeton University Press, 1991), pp. 22–34. More generally, on the mobility of capital and the countervailing or limiting factors, see David Harvey, *The Limits to Capital* (Chicago: University of Chicago Press, 1984), pp. 417–422.

15. See Wladimir Andreff, *Les multinationales globales* (Paris: La Découverte, 1995); and Kenichi Ohmae, *The End of the Nation-State: The Rise of Regional Economies* (New York: Free Press, 1995).
16. On the resistances of peasants to capitalist discipline, see James Scott, *Weapons of the Weak: Everyday Forms of Peasant Resistance* (New Haven: Yale University Press, 1985), p. 235 and passim.
17. On the economic projects of modernization in Mao's China, see Maurice Meisner, *Mao's China and After,* 2nd ed. (New York: Free Press, 1986), pp. 113–139.
18. Robert Sutcliffe, for example, writes, "No major country has yet become rich without having become industrialized . . . Greater wealth and better living standards under any political system are closely connected with industrialization." Robert Sutcliffe, *Industry and Underdevelopment* (Reading, Mass.: Addison-Wesley, 1971).
19. On global and peripheral Fordism, see primarily Alain Lipietz, *Mirages and Miracles: The Crises of Global Fordism,* trans. David Marcey (London: Verso, 1987); and "Towards a Global Fordism?" *New Left Review,* no. 132 (1982), 33–47. On the reception of Lipietz's work among Anglo-American economists, see David Ruccio, "Fordism on a World Scale: International Dimensions of Regulation," *Review of Radical Political Economics,* 21, no. 4 (Winter 1989), 33–53; and Bob Jessop, "Fordism and Post-Fordism: A Critical Reformulation," in Michael Storper and Allen Scott, eds., *Pathways to Industrialization and Regional Development* (London: Routledge, 1992), pp. 46–69.
20. See, for example, Giovanni Arrighi and John Saul, "Socialism and Economic Development in Tropical Africa," in *Essays on the Political Economy of Africa* (New York: Monthly Review Press, 1973), pp. 11–43; John Saul, "Planning for Socialism in Tanzania," in Uchumi Editorial Board, ed., *Towards Socialist Planning* (Dar Es Salaam: Tanzania Publishing House, 1972), pp. 1–29; and Terence Hopkins, "On Economic Planning in Tropical Africa," *Co-existence,* 1, no. 1 (May 1964), 77–88. For two appraisals of the failure of economic development strategies and planning in Africa (but which both still imagine the possibility of an "alternative" socialist development), see Samir Amin, *Maldevelopment: Anatomy of a*

Global Failure (London: Zed Books, 1990), especially pp. 7–74; and Claude Ake, *Democracy and Development in Africa* (Washington, D.C.: The Brookings Institution, 1996).

21. For an interesting personal account of the Bandung Conference and its significance, see Richard Wright, *The Color Curtain: A Report on the Bandung Conference* (New York: World, 1956). The major speeches delivered at the conference are included in George McTurnan Kahin, *The Asian-African Conference* (Ithaca: Cornell University Press, 1956). On the nonalignment movement, see Leo Mates, *Nonalignment: Theory and Current Policy* (Belgrade: Institute for International Politics and Economics, 1972); and M. S. Rajan, *Nonalignment and Nonalignment Movement* (New Delhi: Vikas Publishing, 1990).
22. On nomadism and the constitution of subjectivities, see Gilles Deleuze and Félix Guattari, *A Thousand Plateaus,* trans. Brian Massumi (Minneapolis: University of Minnesota Press, 1987), especially pp. 351–423.
23. On the formal and real subsumption in Marx, see primarily Karl Marx, *Capital,* vol. 1, trans. Ben Fowkes (New York: Vintage, 1976), pp. 1019–38.

PRIMITIVE ACCUMULATIONS

1. Karl Marx, *Capital,* vol. 1, trans. Ben Fowkes (New York: Vintage, 1976), p. 918.
2. See primarily Samir Amin, *Accumulation on a World Scale,* trans. Brian Pearce (New York: Monthly Review Press, 1974); and Andre Gunder Frank, *Capitalism and Underdevelopment in Latin America* (New York: Monthly Review Press, 1967).

3.3 RESISTANCE, CRISIS, TRANSFORMATION

1. On crisis and the restructuring of capitalist production in the 1960s and 1970s, see Michael Piore and Charles Sabel, *The Second Industrial Divide* (New York: Basic Books, 1984). On the financial and economic crisis, see Robert Boyer and Jacques Mistral, *Accumulation, inflation, crises* (Paris: PUF, 1978).
2. See Antonio Negri, "Marx on Cycle and Crisis," in *Revolution Retrieved* (London: Red Notes, 1988), pp. 43–90.
3. See the historical essays "Do You Remember Revolution?" written collectively and "Do You Remember Counter-revolution?" by Paolo Virno in Paolo Virno and Michael Hardt, eds., *Radical Thought in Italy* (Minneapolis: University of Minnesota Press, 1996), pp. 225–259. See also Paolo Carpignano, "Note su classe operaia e capitale in America negli anni

sessanta," in Sergio Bologna, Paolo Carpignano, and Antonio Negri, *Crisi e organizzazione operaia* (Milan: Feltrinelli, 1976), pp. 73–97.

4. On the "welfare explosion of the 1960s," see Frances Fox Piven and Richard Cloward, *Regulating the Poor: The Functions of Public Welfare* (New York: Pantheon, 1971), in particular pp. 183–199. See also Piven and Cloward, *The New Class War: Reagan's Attack on the Welfare State and Its Consequences* (New York: Pantheon, 1982).
5. See Luciano Ferrari Bravo, "Introduzione: vecchie e nuove questioni nella teoria dell'imperialismo," in Luciano Ferrari Bravo, ed., *Imperialismo e classe operaia multinazionale* (Milan: Feltrinelli, 1975), pp. 7–70.
6. Claude Ake goes so far as to characterize the entire world capitalist system as a conflict between "bourgeois countries" and "proletarian countries" in *Revolutionary Pressures in Africa* (London: Zed Books, 1978), p. 11.
7. This Third Worldist perspective is implicit in much of the writing of Immanuel Wallerstein, Andre Gunder Frank, and Samir Amin.
8. For a thorough historical account of the events and the protagonists at the Bretton Woods Conference, see Armand Van Dormael, *Bretton Woods: Birth of a Monetary System* (London: Macmillan, 1978). For a historical account that gives a broader view of the comprehensive U.S. preparation for hegemony in the postwar period by posing the economic planning at Bretton Woods together with the political planning at Dumbarton Oaks, see George Schild, *Bretton Woods and Dumbarton Oaks: American Economic and Political Postwar Planning in the Summer of 1944* (New York: St. Martin's Press, 1995).
9. Giovanni Arrighi, *The Long Twentieth Century* (London: Verso, 1994), p. 278–279.
10. On the international financial crisis that began in the 1970s with the collapse of the Bretton Woods mechanisms, see Peter Coffey, *The World Monetary Crisis* (New York: St. Martin's Press, 1974); and Arrighi, *The Long Twentieth Century,* pp. 300–324.
11. On Eurodollar finance as an element of the crisis, see Jeffry Frieden, *Banking on the World: The Politics of American International Finance* (New York: Harper and Row, 1987), pp. 79–122.
12. On the convertibility of the dollar and the Nixon maneuver in 1971, see David Calleo and Benjamin Rowland, *America and the World Political Economy: Atlantic Dreams and National Realities* (Bloomington: Indiana University Press, 1973), pp. 87–117; and Coffey, *The World Monetary Crisis,* pp. 25–42.
13. On the limits of Fordism and the need for capital to find a post-Fordist schema of production and accumulaton, see Benjamin Coriat, *L'atelier et*

le robot: essai sur le fordisme et la production de masse à l'âge de l'électronique (Paris: Christian Bourgois, 1990).

14. Fredric Jameson argues that the social struggles of the 1960s in the First World, particularly in the United States and France, follow in the line of (and even derive from) the powerful decolonization and liberation movements in the Third World during the 1950s and 1960s. See Fredric Jameson, "Periodizing the 60s," in *Ideologies of Theory: Essays, 1971–1986* (Minneapolis: University of Minnesota Press, 1988), 2:178–208, especially pp. 180–186.
15. See Giovanni Arrighi, "Marxist Century, American Century: The Making and Remaking of the World Labor Movement," in Samir Amin, Giovanni Arrighi, Andre Gunder Frank, and Immanuel Wallerstein, *Transforming the Revolution: Social Movements and the World System* (New York: Monthly Review Press, 1990), 54–95.
16. Robin Kelley provides an exemplary account of the dynamics of proletarian refusal and the creation of alternative forms of life in his wonderful U.S. black working-class history, *Race Rebels: Culture, Politics, and the Black Working Class* (New York: Free Press, 1994).
17. In ecological thought, too, at least in its most productive paradigms, we can see clearly that the "nature" in question is equally human and nonhuman; ecology involves not just the preservation of things, but the production of relationships and the production of subjectivity as well. See Félix Guattari, *Les trois écologies* (Paris: Galilée, 1989); and Verena Andermatt Conley, *Ecopolitics: The Environment in Poststructuralist Thought* (London: Routledge, 1997). Franco Piperno continues this "ecological" line of thought, albeit in a different register, in *Elogio dello spirito pubblico meridionale* (Rome: Manifestolibri, 1997).
18. In her effort to think the importance and real limits of the "outside," Rosa Luxemburg may have been the first great ecological thinker of the twentieth century. The best examples of Marxist ecological thought in authors such as André Gorz and James O'Connor adopt a form of argument similar to Luxemburg's anti-imperialist position (although their work does not derive directly from hers): capitalist production necessarily implies an expansion into and destruction of nature, which not only has tragic consequences for life on the planet but also undermines the future viability of capitalism itself. For André Gorz, see *Ecology as Politics,* trans. Patsy Vigderman and Jonathan Cloud (Boston: South End Press, 1980); for James O'Connor, see "Capitalism, Nature, Socialism: A Theoretical Introduction," *Capitalism, Nature, Socialism,* 1, no. 1 (1989), 11–38.
19. "Late capitalism thus appears as the period in which all branches of the economy are fully industrialized for the first time; to which one could

further add . . . the increasing mechanization of the superstructure." Ernest Mandel, *Late Capitalism,* trans. Joris De Bres (London: Verso, 1978), pp. 190–191.

20. "This purer capitalism of our own time thus eliminated the enclaves of precapitalist organization it had hitherto tolerated and exploited in a tributary way." Fredric Jameson, *Postmodernism, or, The Cultural Logic of Late Capitalism* (Durham: Duke University Press, 1990), p. 36.
21. We do not mean to suggest that capital can perpetually through technological advances reconcile its destructive relationship with its (human and nonhuman) environment. What technological advance can do is shift the terrain of conflict and defer the crisis, but limits and antagonisms remain.
22. Stanley Aronowitz offers a useful reassessment of the panoply of U.S. social movements in the 1960s in *The Death and Rebirth of American Radicalism* (London: Routledge, 1996), pp. 57–90.
23. Again see Kelley, *Race Rebels,* especially pp. 17–100 on the hidden histories of resistance.
24. On the history of the refusals posed by U.S. feminist movements in the 1960s and 1970s, see Alice Echols, *Daring to Be Bad: Radical Feminism in America, 1967–1975* (Minneapolis: University of Minnesota Press, 1989).
25. See, for example, Judith Butler, "Merely Cultural," *New Left Review,* no. 227 (January–February 1998), 33–44. The most influential text for the political interpretation of "new social movements" along these lines is Ernesto Laclau and Chantal Mouffe, *Hegemony and Socialist Strategy: Towards a Radical Democratic Politics* (London: Verso, 1985).
26. See Antonio Negri, *The Politics of Subversion: A Manifesto for the Twenty-first Century,* trans. James Newell (Oxford: Polity Press, 1989).
27. Fredric Jameson, for example, argues that the collapse of the Soviet Union was "due, not to its failure, but to its success, at least as far as modernization is concerned." See his "Actually Existing Marxism," in Saree Makdisi, Cesare Casarino, and Rebecca Karl, eds., *Marxism Beyond Marxism* (London: Routledge, 1996), pp. 14–54; quotation p. 43. More generally on how cold war propaganda (from both sides) blinded us to the real movements of social history within the Soviet regime, see Moshe Lewin, *The Making of the Soviet System* (New York: Pantheon, 1985).
28. See Leon Trotsky, *The Revolution Betrayed,* trans. Max Eastman (Garden City, N.Y.: Doubleday, 1937); and Cornelius Castoriadis, *Devant la guerre* (Paris: Fayard, 1981). See also a series of article by Denis Berger on the collapse of the Soviet Union, "Perestroïka: la révolution réellement existante?" *Futur antérieur,* no. 1 (1990), 53–62; "Que reste-t-il de la perestroïka?" *Futur antérieur,* no. 6 (1991), 15–20; and "L'Unione Soviétique à l'heure du vide," *Futur antérieur,* no. 8 (1991), 5–12.

29. It seems to us that one could make a parallel argument about the changing social practices of the Chinese proletariat in the post-Mao era leading up to the "Cultural Fever" movement in the 1980s. See Xudong Zhang, *Chinese Modernism in the Era of Reforms* (Durham: Duke University Press, 1997). Zhang makes clear the fabulous creativity released during this period.

3.4 POSTMODERNIZATION

1. The texts that set the terms for an enormous literature that debates the periodization of the phases of modern production are Daniel Bell, *Coming of Post-industrial Society* (New York: Basic Books, 1973); and Alain Touraine, *Post-industrial Society,* trans. Leonard Mayhew (New York: Random House, 1971).
2. See Manuel Castells and Yuko Aoyama, "Paths towards the Informational Society: Employment Structure in G-7 Countries, 1920–90," *International Labour Review,* 133, no. 1 (1994), 5–33; quotation p. 13.
3. On the false historical analogies that contributed to the debt crisis of Third World countries, see Cheryl Payer, *Lent and Lost: Foreign Credit and Third World Development* (London: Zed Books, 1991).
4. The classic presentations of the theories of underdevelopment and dependency are Andre Gunder Frank, *Capitalism and Underdevelopment in Latin America* (New York: Monthly Review Press, 1967); and Fernando Enrique Cardoso and Enzo Faletto, *Dependency and Development in Latin America,* trans. Marjory Mattingly Urquidi (Berkeley: University of California Press, 1979). For a very concise critique of stages of development arguments, see Immanuel Wallerstein, *The Capitalist World-Economy* (Cambridge: Cambridge University Press, 1979), pp. 3–5.
5. The discourse of development was an illusion, but it was a real and effective illusion that established its own structures and institutions of power throughout the "developing" world. On the institutionalization of development, see Arturo Escobar, *Encountering Development: The Making and Unmaking of the Third World* (Princeton: Princeton University Press, 1995), pp. 73–101.
6. For a critique of the developmentalist ideology of dependency theories, see ibid., pp. 80–81.
7. See, for example, Claude Ake, *A Political Economy of Africa* (Harlow, Essex: Longman, 1981), p. 136. This is also the general framework presented in the work of Andre Gunder Frank and Samir Amin.
8. Robert Musil, *The Man without Qualities,* trans. Sophie Wilkins (New York: Knopf, 1995), 2:367.

9. François Bar, "Information Infrastructure and the Transformation of Manufacturing," in William Drake, ed., *The New Information Infrastructure: Strategies for U.S. Policy* (New York: Twentieth Century Fund Press, 1995), pp. 55–74; quotation p. 56.
10. See Robert Chase and David Garvin, "The Service Factory," in Gary Pisano and Robert Hayes, eds., *Manufacturing Renaissance* (Boston: Harvard Business School Press, 1995), pp. 35–45.
11. See Castells and Aoyama, "Paths towards the Informational Society," pp. 19–28.
12. Manuel Castells describes the most subordinated regions of the global economy as a "Fourth World." See his essay "The Informational Economy and the New International Division of Labor," in Martin Carnoy, Manuel Castells, Stephen Cohen, and Fernando Enrique Cardoso, *The New Global Economy in the Information Age* (University Park: Pennsylvania State University Press, 1993), pp. 15–43.
13. Castells and Aoyama, "Paths towards the Informational Society," p. 27.
14. Pierre Levy, *Collective Intelligence: Mankind's Emerging World in Cyberspace* (New York: Plenum Press, 1997).
15. On the comparison between the Fordist and Toyotist models, see Benjamin Coriat, *Penser à l'envers: travail et organisation dans l'entreprise japonaise* (Paris: Christian Bourgois, 1994). For a brief history of the early developments of Toyota production methods, see Kazuo Wada, "The Emergence of the 'Flow Production' Method in Japan," in Haruhito Shiomi and Kazuo Wada, eds., *Fordism Transformed: The Development of Production Methods in the Automobile Industry* (Oxford: Oxford University Press, 1995), pp. 11–27.
16. We are thinking primarily of Jürgen Habermas's conceptual division between communicative and instrumental action in works such as *The Theory of Communicative Action,* trans. Thomas McCarthy (Boston: Beacon Press, 1984). For an excellent critique of this Habermasian division, see Christian Marazzi, *Il posto dei calzini: la svolta linguistica dell'economia e i suoi effetti nella politica* (Bellinzona, Switzerland: Casagrande, 1995), pp. 29–34.
17. For a definition and analysis of immaterial labor, see Maurizio Lazzarato, "Immaterial Labor," in Paolo Virno and Michael Hardt, eds., *Radical Thought in Italy* (Minneapolis: University of Minnesota Press, 1996), pp. 133–147. See also the glossary entry on immaterial labor at the end of the same collection, p. 262.
18. Peter Drucker understands the passage toward immaterial production in extreme terms. "The basic economic resource—'the means of production,' to use the economist's term—is no longer capital, nor natural

resources (the economist's 'land'), nor 'labor.' *It is and will be knowledge.*" Peter Drucker, *Post-capitalist Society* (New York: Harper, 1993), p. 8. What Drucker does not understand is that knowledge is not given but produced and that its production involves new kinds of means of production and labor.

19. Robert Reich, *The Work of Nations: Preparing Ourselves for 21st-Century Capitalism* (New York: Knopf, 1991), p. 177. What is most important to Reich is in fact that advantage—and finally national dominance—will be won in the global economy along the lines of these new divisions, through the geographical distribution of these high- and low-value tasks.
20. See Karl Marx, *Capital,* vol. 1, trans. Ben Fowkes (New York: Vintage, 1976), pp. 131–137.
21. See Dorothy Smith, *The Everyday World as Problematic: A Feminist Sociology* (Boston: Northeastern University Press, 1987), especially pp. 78–88.
22. Marx in his time conceived cooperation as the result of the actions of the capitalist, who functioned like an orchestra conductor or a field general, deploying and coordinating productive forces in a common effort. See *Capital,* 1:439–454. For an analysis of the contemporary dynamics of social and productive cooperation, see Antonio Negri, *The Politics of Subversion: A Manifesto for the Twenty-first Century,* trans. James Newell (Oxford: Polity Press, 1989).
23. See Saskia Sassen, *The Global City: New York, London, Tokyo* (Princeton: Princeton University Press, 1991).
24. On the network enterprise, see Manuel Castells, *The Rise of the Network Society* (Oxford: Blackwell, 1996), pp. 151–200.
25. Bill Gates, *The Road Ahead* (New York: Viking, 1995), p. 158.
26. A number of Italian scholars read the decentralization of network production in the small and medium-sized enterprises of northern Italy as an opportunity to create new circuits of *autonomous labor.* See Sergio Bologna and Andrea Fumagalli, eds., *Il lavoro autonomo di seconda generazione: scenari del postfordismo in Italia* (Milan: Feltrinelli, 1997).
27. On the growth of "producer services" in concentrated centers of control, see Sassen, *The Global City,* pp. 90–125.
28. Peter Cowhey, "Building the Global Information Highway: Toll Booths, Construction Contracts, and Rules of the Road," in William Drake, ed., *The New Information Infrastructure* (New York: Twentieth Century Fund Press, 1995), pp. 175–204; quotation p. 175.
29. On rhizomatic and arborescent structures, see Gilles Deleuze and Félix Guattari, *A Thousand Plateaus,* trans. Brian Massumi (Minneapolis: University of Minnesota Press, 1987), pp. 3–25.

30. On the false egalitarian promises of the "information superhighway" in the United States, see Herbert Schiller, *Information Inequality: The Deepening Social Crisis in America* (New York: Routledge, 1996), especially pp. 75–89. For a more global analysis of the unequal distribution of information and technology, see William Wresch, *Disconnected: Haves and Have-Nots in the Information Age* (New Brunswick, N.J.: Rutgers University Press, 1996).

3.5 MIXED CONSTITUTION

1. For an analysis of the passages of Marx's and Engel's work that deal with the theory of the state, see Antonio Negri, "Communist State Theory," in Michael Hardt and Antonio Negri, *Labor of Dionysus* (Minneapolis: University of Minnesota Press, 1994), pp. 139–176.
2. See M. C. Ricklefs, *A History of Modern Indonesia,* 2nd ed. (London: Macmillan, 1993). The complex relationship among the Dutch administration, traditional Javanese authorities, and economic powers at the beginning of the twentieth century is described beautifully in Pramoedya Ananta Toer's great four-volume historical novel, *The Buru Quartet,* trans. Max Lane (London: Penguin Books, 1982–1992).
3. See Brian Gardner, *The East India Company* (London: Rupert Hart-Davis, 1971); and Geoffrey Wheatcroft, *The Randlords* (New York: Atheneum, 1986).
4. Marx argued that the greater concentration and centralization of capital acted against the forces of competition and was thus a destructive process for capital. See Karl Marx, *Capital,* vol. 3, trans. David Fernbach (London: Penguin, 1981), pp. 566–573. Lenin took up this same argument in his analysis of the monopoly phase of capital: monopolies destroy competition, which is the foundation of capitalist development. See V. I. Lenin, *Imperialism: The Highest Stage of Capitalism* (New York: International Publishers, 1939), pp. 16–30.
5. See, for example, Richard Barnet and John Cavanagh, *Global Dreams: Imperial Corporations and the New World Order* (New York: Simon and Schuster, 1994).
6. The concept of the "autonomy of the political," which belongs to the tradition of political theology, was given its first great definition by the political theologian Thomas Hobbes. The concept was raised to even greater heights by Carl Schmitt; see principally *The Concept of the Political,* trans. George Schwab (New Brunswick, N.J.: Rutgers University Press, 1976); and *Verfassungslehre,* 8th ed. (Berlin: Duncker & Humblot, 1993). The political is understood here as the foundation of every social relation-

ship and the originary evaluation or "decision" that constructs the sphere of power and thus guarantees the space of life. It is interesting to note that Schmitt's conception of the political is ineluctably tied to the juridical definition of the nation-state and inconceivable outside of its realm. Schmitt himself seems to recognize this fact after having witnessed the catastrophe of the German nation-state. See Carl Schmitt, *Der Nomos der Erde im Völkerrecht des jus publicum europaeum* (Cologne: Greven Verlag, 1950). The most extensive consideration of Schmitt's conception of the political that we know is contained in Carlo Galli, *Genealogia della politica: C. Schmitt e la crisi del pensiero politico moderno* (Bologna: Il Mulino, 1996). This critique of Scmitt's concept of the "autonomy of the political" should also be applied to the various positions that in some way derive from his thought. At two extremes we can cite Leo Strauss, who tried to appropriate Schmitt's concept under his own liberal conception of natural right, and Mario Tronti, who sought to find in the autonomy of the political a terrain that could support a compromise with liberal political forces in a period when the Western European communist parties were in deep crisis. For Strauss's interpretation of Schmitt's text and their ambiguous relationship, see Heinrich Meier, *Carl Schmitt and Leo Strauss: The Hidden Dialogue,* trans. J. Harvey Lomax (Chicago: University of Chicago Press, 1995). For Tronti, see *L'autonomia del politico* (Milan: Feltrinelli, 1977).

7. There are numerous excellent critiques of the media and their purported objectivity. For two good examples, see Edward Said, *Covering Islam: How the Media and the Experts Determine How We See the Rest of the World* (New York: Pantheon, 1981); and Edward Herman and Noam Chomsky, *Manufacturing Consent: The Political Economy of Mass Media* (New York: Pantheon, 1988).
8. See, for example, Elise Boulding, "IGOs, the UN, and International NGOs: The Evolving Ecology of the International System," in Richard Falk, Robert Johansen, and Samuel Kim, eds., *The Constitutional Foundations of World Peace* (Albany: SUNY Press, 1993), pp. 167–188; quotation p. 179.
9. For characterizations of the activities of various kinds of NGOs, see John Clark, *Democratizing Development: The Role of Voluntary Organizations* (West Hartford, Conn.: Kumarian Press, 1990); Lowell Livezey, *Nongovernmental Organizations and the Ideas of Human Rights* (Princeton: The Center of International Studies, 1988); and Andrew Natsios, "NGOs and the UN System in Complex Humanitarian Emergencies: Conflict or Cooperation?" in Peter Diehl, ed., *The Politics of Global Governance: International Organizations in an Independent World* (Boulder: Lynne Reiner, 1997), pp. 287–303.

10. James Petras, "Imperialism and NGOs in Latin America," *Monthly Review,* 49 (December 1997), 10–27.
11. See Polybius, *The Rise of the Roman Empire,* trans. Ian Scott-Kilvert (Harmondsworth: Penguin, 1979), Book VI, pp. 302–352.
12. See G. A. Pocock, *The Machiavellian Moment: Florentine Political Thought and the Atlantic Republican Tradition* (Princeton: Princeton University Press, 1975).
13. On the transformation from a model of bodies to a functional model in the U.S. Constitution, see Antonio Negri, *Il potere costituente: saggio sulle alternative del moderno* (Milan: Sugarco, 1992), chap. 4, pp. 165–222.
14. It is interesting to note here that, at least since the constitutionalism of the Weimar Republic, the continental European tradition of constitutional thought has also adopted these principles, which were presumed to belong only to the Anglo-Saxon world. The fundamental texts for the German tradition in this regard are Max Weber, *Parlament und Regierung im neugeordneten Deutschland* (Munich: Duncker & Humblot, 1918); Hugo Preuss, *Staat, Recht und Freiheit* (Tübingen: Mohr, 1926); and Hermann Heller, *Die Souveranität* (Berlin: W. de Gruyter, 1927).
15. Generally the analyses that come from the Left are the ones that insist most strongly that the genesis of Empire activates the "bad" forms of government. See, for example, Étienne Balibar, *La crainte des masses* (Paris: Galilée, 1997), a book which in other regards is extremely open to the analysis of the new processes of the (mass) production of subjectivity.
16. For an analysis of these processes and a good discussion of the relevant bibliography, see Yann Moulier Boutang, "La revanche des externalités: globalisation des économies, externalités, mobilité, transformation de l'économie et de l'intervention publique," *Futur antérieur,* no. 39–40 (Fall 1997), pp. 85–115.
17. It should be clear from what we have said thus far that the theoretical condition underlying our hypotheses has to involve a radically revised analysis of reproduction. In other words, any theoretical conception that regards reproduction as simply part of the circulation of capital (as classical economics, Marxian theory, and neoclassical theories have done) cannot deal critically with the conditions of our new situation, particularly those resulting from the political-economic relations of the world market in postmodernity. Our description of biopower in Section 1.2 is the beginning of such a revised analysis of reproduction. For the definition of some fundamental elements that relate to the integration of labor, affect, and biopower, see Antonio Negri, "Value and Affect" and Michael Hardt, "Affective Labor," *boundary2,* 26, no. 2 (Summer 1999).

18. We are refering once again to the work of Michel Foucault and to Gilles Deleuze's interpretation of it. See our discussion in Section 1.2.
19. This first variable and the analysis of the functioning of the network in constitutional terms relates in certain respects to the various autopoietic theories of networks. See, for example, the work of Humberto Maturana and Francisco Varela. For an excellent analysis of systems theory in the context of postmodern theories, see Cary Wolfe, *Critical Environments* (Minneapolis: University of Minnesota Press, 1998).
20. The various advances in systems theories contribute also to our understanding of this second variable. Niklas Luhmann's work has been the most influential for the analysis of autopoietic systems in terms of legal and social philosophy.
21. Jameson offers an excellent critique of "the conception of mass culture as sheer manipulation." He argues that although mass culture is "managed," it nonetheless contains utopian possibilities. See Fredric Jameson, "Reification and Utopia in Mass Culture," in *Signatures of the Visible* (New York: Routledge, 1992), pp. 9–34.
22. See Guy Debord, *Society of the Spectacle,* trans. Donald Nicholson-Smith (New York: Zone Books, 1994); and *Comments on the Society of the Spectacle* (London: Verso, 1990).
23. Fredric Jameson, "Totality as Conspiracy," in *The Geopolitial Aesthetic: Cinema and Space in the World System* (Bloomington: Indiana University Press, 1992), pp. 9–84.
24. Thomas Hobbes, *Leviathan,* ed. C. B. Macpherson (London: Penguin, 1968), p. 200.
25. See Brian Massumi, ed., *The Politics of Everyday Fear* (Minneapolis: University of Minnesota Press, 1993).

3.6 CAPITALIST SOVEREIGNTY

1. Gilles Deleuze and Félix Guattari, *Anti-Oedipus,* trans. Robert Hurley, Mark Lane, and Helen Lane (Minneapolis: University of Minnesota Press, 1983), p. 224.
2. On Deleuze and Guattari's conception of the axiomatic of capital, see Gilles Deleuze and Félix Guattari, *A Thousand Plateaus,* trans. Brian Massumi (Minneapolis: University of Minnesota Press, 1987), pp. 452–473.
3. Robert Blanché, *Axiomatics,* trans. G. B. Keene (New York: Free Press of Glencoe, 1962), pp. 30–31.
4. There is, of course, one element of transcendence and segmentation that is essential to the functioning of capital, and that is class exploitation. This is a boundary, however flexible or indiscernible it may be at times, that capital must maintain throughout society. Class divisions continue

to be centrally effective in the new segmentations that we investigate later in this section.

5. See Michel Foucault, "La 'gouvernementalité,'" in *Dits et écrits* (Paris: Gallimard, 1994), 3:635–657; and *Il faut defendre la société* (Paris: Seuil/ Gallimard, 1997).
6. See Michael Hardt and Antonio Negri, *Labor of Dionysus* (Minneapolis: University of Minnesota Press, 1994), pp. 257–259.
7. See Michael Hardt, "The Withering of Civil Society," *Social Text,* no. 45 (Winter 1995), 27–44.
8. For an excellent explanation of Foucault's conception of the diagram, see Gilles Deleuze, *Foucault,* trans. Seán Hand (Minneapolis: University of Minnesota Press, 1988), pp. 34–37.
9. On the relation between identity and belonging and on the constitution of a "whatever" subjectivity, see Giorgio Agamben, *The Coming Community,* trans. Michael Hardt (Minneapolis: University of Minnesota Press, 1993).
10. Rosa Luxemburg, *The Accumulation of Capital,* trans. Agnes Schwarzchild (New York: Monthly Review Press, 1968), p. 446.
11. The classic work in this regard is Samir Amin's *Accumulation on a World Scale,* trans. Brian Pearce (New York: Monthly Review Press, 1974).
12. See Mike Davis, *City of Quartz: Excavating the Future in Los Angeles* (London: Verso, 1990), pp. 221–263.
13. Michel Aglietta has demonstrated clearly in structural terms the violent and dictatorial powers of monetary regimes. See his *La violence de la monnaie* (Paris: PUF, 1982). See also the essays in Werner Bonefeld and John Holloway, eds., *Global Capital, National State, and the Politics of Money* (London: Macmillan, 1995).

4.1 VIRTUALITIES

1. On this style of political theorizing, see C. B. Macpherson, *The Political Theory of Possessive Individualism: Hobbes to Locke* (New York: Oxford University Press, 1962); and Albert O. Hirschman, *The Passions and the Interests: Political Arguments for Capitalism before Its Triumph* (Princeton: Princeton University Press, 1977).
2. On the immanent relation between politics and ontology, see Antonio Negri, *The Savage Anomaly,* trans. Michael Hardt (Minneapolis: University of Minnesota Press, 1991); and Baruch Spinoza, *Theologico-Political Treatise,* in *The Chief Works of Spinoza,* vol. 1, trans. R. H. M. Elwes (New York: Dover Press, 1951), pp. 1–278.
3. On postmodern right and postmodern law, see Michael Hardt and Antonio Negri, *Labor of Dionysus* (Minneapolis: University of Minnesota Press, 1994), chap. 6, pp. 217–261.

4. See Rémi Brague, *Du temps chez Platon et Aristote* (Paris: PUF, 1982).
5. G. W. F. Hegel, *Science of Logic,* trans. A. V. Miller (Atlantic Highlands, N.J.: Humanities Press International, 1989), pp. 327–385.
6. The measure of value means its orderly exploitation, the norm of its social division, and its capitalist reproduction. Certainly Marx goes beyond Marx, and one should never pretend that his discussions of labor and value are only a discourse on measure: beyond value, labor is always the living power of being. See Antonio Negri, "Twenty Theses on Marx," in Saree Makdisi, Cesare Casarino, and Rebecca Karl, eds., *Marxism Beyond Marxism* (New York: Routledge, 1996), pp. 149–180.
7. Aristotle, *Nicomachean Ethics,* trans. Terence Irwin (Indianapolis: Hackett, 1985), p. 119 (1129b30).
8. On the virtual, see Gilles Deleuze and Félix Guattari, *What Is Philosophy?,* trans. Hugh Tomlinson and Graham Burchell (New York: Columbia University Press, 1994); and Gilles Deleuze, *Bergsonism,* trans. Hugh Tomlinson and Barbara Habberjam (New York: Zone, 1988), pp. 94–103. Our conception of virtuality and its relationship to reality is somewhat different from the one that Deleuze derives from Bergson, which distinguishes between the passage from the virtual to the actual and that from the possible to the real. Bergson's primary concern in this distinction and in his affirmation of the virtual-actual couple over the possible-real is to emphasize the creative force of being and highlight that being is not merely the reduction of numerous possible worlds to a single real world based on resemblance, but rather that being is always an act of creation and unforeseeable novelty. See Henri Bergson, "The Possible and the Real," in *The Creative Mind,* trans. Mabelle Andison (New York: Philosophical Library, 1946), pp. 91–106. We certainly do recognize the need to insist on the creative powers of virtuality, but this Bergsonian discourse is insufficient for us insofar as we also need to insist on the reality of the being created, its ontological weight, and the institutions that structure the world, creating necessity out of contingency. On the passage from the virtual to the real, see Gilbert Simondon, *L'individu et sa genèse physico-biologique* (Paris: PUF, 1964); and Brian Massumi, "The Autonomy of Affect," *Cultural Critique,* no. 31 (Fall 1995), 83–109.
9. Marx's discussions of abstraction have a double relation to this discourse of virtuality and possibility. One might do well in fact to distinguish between two Marxian notions of abstraction. On the one hand, and on the side of capital, abstraction means separation from our powers to act, and thus it is a negation of the virtual. On the other hand, however, and on the side of labor, the abstract is the general set of our powers to act,

the virtual itself. See Antonio Negri, *Marx Beyond Marx,* trans. Harry Cleaver, Michael Ryan, and Maurizio Viano (New York: Autonomedia, 1991); and Karl Marx, *Grundrisse,* trans. Martin Nicolaus (New York: Vintage, 1973), pp. 83–111.

10. On the relation between the singular and the common, see Giorgio Agamben, *The Coming Community,* trans. Michael Hardt (Minneapolis: University of Minnesota Press, 1993).
11. See primarily Friedrich Nietzsche, *On the Genealogy of Morals,* trans. Walter Kaufman and R. J. Hollingdale (New York: Vintage, 1967).
12. See Bernard Aspe and Muriel Combes, "Du vampire au parasite," *Futur antérieur,* no. 35–36 (1996), 207–219.
13. On the priority of resistance to power, see Gilles Deleuze, *Foucault,* trans. Seán Hand (Minneapolis: University of Minnesota Press, 1988), p. 89: "The final word on power is that *resistance comes first.*"
14. This dialectic of obstacle and limit, with respect to the power of the mind on the one hand and political power on the other, was well understood by that current of the phenomenology of subjectivity that (in contrast to the Heideggerian current) recognized Nazism and thus the capitalist state as the true limit of historical progress. From Husserl to Sartre we find the central effort to transform limit into threshold, and in many ways Foucault takes up this same line. See Edmund Husserl, *Crisis of European Sciences and Transcendental Phenomenology,* trans. David Carr (Evanston, Ill.: Northwestern University Press, 1970); Jean-Paul Sartre, *Critique of Dialectical Reason,* trans. Quentin Hoare (London: Verso, 1990); and Deleuze, *Foucault.*
15. See Jacques Rancière, *La mesentante: politique et philosophie* (Paris: Galilée, 1995).
16. One example of such a Kantian reverie is Lucien Goldmann, *Mensch, Gemeinschaft und Welt in der Philosophie Immanuel Kants* (Zurich: Europa Verlag, 1945).
17. See Karl Marx, "On the Jewish Question," in *Early Writings,* trans. Rodney Livingstone and Gregor Benton (London: Penguin, 1975), pp. 211–241.
18. See Paul Virilio, *L'insecurité du territoire* (Paris: Stock, 1976).
19. On the importance of the linguistic in the contemporary economy, see Christian Marazzi, *Il posto dei calzini: la svolta linguistica dell'economia e i suoi effetti nella politica* (Bellinzona: Casagrande, 1995).
20. See Giorgio Agamben, *Homo sacer: il potere sovrano e la nuda vita* (Turin: Einaudi, 1995).
21. On this conception of the machinic, see Félix Guattari, *L'inconscient machinique: essais de schizo-analyse* (Fontenay-sous-Bois: Encres/Recherches,

1979); and Gilles Deleuze and Félix Guattari, *Anti-Oedipus,* trans. Robert Hurley, Mark Lane, and Helen Lane (Minneapolis: University of Minnesota Press, 1983).

22. Karl Marx, *Capital,* vol. 1, trans. Ben Fowkes (New York: Vintage, 1976), pp. 554–555.
23. Obviously when we speak about a materialist telos we are speaking about a telos that is constructed by subjects, constituted by the multitude in action. This involves a materialist reading of history which recognizes that the institutions of society are formed through the encounter and conflict of social forces themselves. The telos in this case in not predetermined but constructed in the process. Materialist historians such as Thucydides and Machiavelli, like the great materialist philosophers such as Epicurus, Lucretius, and Spinoza, have never negated a telos constructed by human actions. As Marx wrote in the introduction to the *Grundrisse,* it is not the anatomy of the ape that explains that of humans but, vice versa, the anatomy of humans that explains that of the ape (p. 105). The telos appears only afterwards, as a result of the actions of history.

4.2 GENERATION AND CORRUPTION

1. See Charles de Secondat Montesquieu, *Considerations of the Causes of the Greatness of the Romans and Their Decline,* trans. David Lowenthal (New York: Free Press, 1965); and Edward Gibbon, *Decline and Fall of the Roman Empire,* 3 vols. (New York: Knopf, 1993).
2. See Machiavelli, *Discourses,* trans. Leslie Walker (New Haven: Yale University Press, 1950); and Antonio Negri, *Il potere costituente* (Milan: Sugarco, 1992), pp. 75–96.
3. Alexis de Tocqueville, *Democracy in America,* trans. George Lawrence (New York: Harper and Row, 1966).
4. G. W. F. Hegel, *Lectures on the Philosophy of World History,* trans. H. B. Nisbet (Cambridge: Cambridge University Press, 1975), p. 170.
5. Massimo Cacciari provides a stimulating analysis of the fortunes and decline of the idea of Europe with his usual erudition in *Geo-filosofia dell'Europa* (Milan: Adelphi, 1994).
6. Friedrich Nietzsche, *The Gay Science,* trans. Walter Kaufman (New York: Random House, 1974), p. 99 (sec. 24).
7. Friedrich Nietzsche, *Werke,* ed. Giorgio Colli and Mazzino Montinari (Berlin: de Gruyter, 1967), vol. 8, pt. 1, p. 77; cited in Cacciari, *Geo-filosofia dell'Europa,* p. 9. The original passage reads, "Ich habe den Geist Europas in mich genommen—nun will ich den Gegenschlag thun!"
8. See Franz Rosenzweig, *The Star of Redemption,* trans. William Hallo (New York: Holt, Rinehart and Winston, 1971).

9. Walter Benjamin, "Theses of the Philosophy of History," in *Illuminations,* trans. Harry Zohn (New York: Schocken, 1968), pp. 253–264; quotation p. 254 (Thesis 2).
10. On the fortunes of European irrationalism, see Georg Lukács, *The Destruction of Reason,* trans. Peter Palmer (London: Merlin, 1980).
11. We are referring primarily to Gilles Deleuze, Michel Foucault, and Jacques Derrida.
12. See Hans Jürgen Krahl, *Konstitution und Klassenkampf* (Frankfurt: Neue Kritik, 1971).
13. Ludwig Wittgenstein, *Notebooks, 1914–16,* ed. G. H. von Wright and G. E. M. Anscombe, 2nd ed. (Chicago: University of Chicago Press, 1979), pp. 79–80 (August 1 and 2 and September 2, 1916).
14. Ludwig Wittgenstein, *Tractatus Logico-Philosophicus,* trans. D. F. Pears and B. F. McGuinness (London: Routledge, 1961), p. 74.
15. Hannah Arendt, *On Revolution* (New York: Viking, 1963).
16. Gilles Deleuze often sings the praises of American literature for its nomadism and deterritorializing powers. It seems that for Deleuze, America represents a liberation from the closed confines of European consciousness. See, for example, "Whitman" and "Bartleby, ou la formule," in *Critique et clinique* (Paris: Minuit, 1993), pp. 75–80 and 89–114.
17. Serge Guilbaut, *How New York Stole the Idea of Modern Art: Abstract Expressionism, Freedom, and the Cold War,* trans. Arthur Goldhammer (Chicago: University of Chicago Press, 1983).
18. See Antonio Gramsci, "Americanism and Fordism," in *Selections from the Prison Notebooks,* trans. Quintin Hoare and Geoffrey Nowell Smith (New York: International Publishers, 1971), pp. 279–318.
19. Hannah Arendt has become a favorite author for political theorists in the United States and Europe who want to reconceive politics. See, for example, the essays in Bonnie Honig, ed., *Feminist Interpretations of Hannah Arendt* (University Park: Pennsylvania State University Press, 1995); and Craig Calhoun and John McGowan, eds., *Hannah Arendt and the Meaning of Politics* (Minneapolis: University of Minnesota Press, 1997).
20. On the philosophical conceptions of generation and corruption, see Reiner Schürmann, *Des hégémonies brisées* (Mouvezin: T.E.R., 1996).

4.3 THE MULTITUDE AGAINST EMPIRE

1. Saint Augustine, *The City of God,* trans. Henry Bettenson (Harmondsworth: Penguin, 1972), p. 430 (Book XI, Chapter 1).
2. Plotinus, *Enneads,* trans. Stephen MacKenna (London: Faber and Faber, 1956), p. 63 (1.6.8).

3. On the military powers of Empire, see Manuel De Landa, *War in the Age of Intelligent Machines* (New York: Zone, 1991).
4. On the constitution of time, see Antonio Negri, *La costituzione del tempo* (Rome: Castelvecchi, 1997); and Michael Hardt, "Prison Time," *Genet: In the Language of the Enemy, Yale French Studies,* no. 91 (1997), 64–79. See also Eric Alliez, *Capital Times,* trans. Georges Van Den Abeel (Minneapolis: University of Minnesota Press, 1996).
5. See Jürgen Habermas, *Theory of Communicative Action,* trans. Thomas McCarthy (Boston: Beacon Press, 1984). André Gorz similarly recognizes only a fraction of the proletariat as relating to the new communicative lines of production in *Farewell to the Working Class,* trans. Michael Sonenscher (Boston: South End Press, 1982).
6. Here we are following the intriguing etymology that Barbara Cassin gives for the term "philosophy."
7. On the constitutive notion of the encounter, see Louis Althuser's late works written after his confinement in the 1980s, in particular "Le courant souterrain du matérialisme de la rencontre," in *Écrits philosophiques et politiques,* vol. 1 (Paris: STOCK/IMEC, 1994), pp. 539–579.

INDEX